A TREE
FIRMLY PLANTED

JONATHAN M. BELL

INTRODUCTION

PSALM 1:3

He shall be like a tree

Planted by the rivers of water,

That brings forth its fruit in its season,

Whose leaf also shall not wither;

I wrote this devotion to help Christians succeed in their daily walks. This success comes with the stability of a tree with a large root system being constantly fed with rivers of water that is able to withstand all the pressures that may come its way looking to bring it down.

A successful Christian walk also comes with fruitfulness or productivity where the life of God is being manifested in them and through them. This fruit is a pleasure to the Christian and also will bring others to enjoy an incredible personal relationship with God.

In addition to stability and fruitfulness, a successful Christian will be alive and thriving with energetic passion and not withered like a leaf with no life. This leaf, like an healthy Christian life, will be attractive with the beautiful color of God's love adorning it.

Finally, the successful life of a Christian will prosper because God is bringing about His perfect will which is what true success really is. The prospering Christian will be all that God has intended it to be and a source of God's love and life here on planet earth that will transcend into all of eternity.

The book is designed as a daily devotional that goes alongside The One Year Bible. At the top of each page is a daily scripture reading that will take one through the entire Bible in a year in a systematic fashion. The devotion is taken directly from the daily reading to help the reader to focus and meditate throughout the day on a specific lesson. I know without a shadow of doubt that a Christian who takes time to regularly read God's Word, then meditate on it and do it will be like A Tree Firmly Planted.

IN THE BEGINNING GOD

//

GENESIS 1:1

"In the beginning God."

This verse sets the tone for the rest of the whole Bible. In it we find the information needed to answer most of life's questions. Knowing the foundation for life, we can then know how we should live. Isn't that the most important question we have? How should one live their life? In order to live life right we must understand its origin.

Here is what this very first verse of the bible teaches us:

1. ALL MATERIAL MATTER HAS A BEGINNING

This verse answers the question of beginning. It tells us that there was a point and time that nothing became something. It tells us that the world as we know it, and all that is in it, didn't exist at one time and then at the hand of a designer it came into being.

2. THERE IS A BEING, OR SOURCE, OF ALL THAT IS CREATED

It tells us that there was a cause of all; that there was a designer, a creator.

3. THAT BEING IS CALLED GOD

We are told that the source of all creation is called God, or Elohim, in the Hebrew language.

4. GOD HAS NO BEGINNING

We then know that all that is created comes from a creator named God who was not created but is eternal.

5. HE CREATED ALL FROM NOTHING

The word in the Hebrew for "created" is "Bara" which means created out if nothing. It means that at one time nothing material existed and then the creator brought it into being.

6. NOTHING EXISTS WITHOUT GOD

We have a designer and not the result of random occurrences. How else can one explain how things got here without a creator/designer? There is no other explanation. Even evolutionist can't explain how the stuff got here to evolve. Only a preexistent creator/designer can explain that.

7. GOD IS ONE BUT THREE

We have more information given about the supreme almighty being called God who is the creator/designer of all that exists. The word for God here is "Elohim" in the Hebrew language, which means that there is one God, in plural. "E" would be singular, "el" would be two and Elohim would be more than two. This is the teaching of the Bible called the Trinity meaning there is one God in three persons; The Father, The Son and the Holy Spirit.

8. GOD IS SYSTEMATIC AND ORDERLY

Looking at creation one can tell that there is order to it versus randomness. The sun comes up and the sun goes down. The seasons come and the seasons go. The earth rotates around the sun and also rotates on its axis. Babies grow into toddlers, toddlers to children, children to teenagers, teenagers to adults and adults to elderly.

9. ALL CREATION NATURALLY IS SUBSERVIENT TO THE CREATOR

The creator is supreme to the creation and therefore the creation follows the creator and not the other way around.

10. GOD HAS A PLAN

As God brought all into being, He did it according to His plan therefore has a plan and purpose for mankind.

11. GOD IS OUTSIDE OF TIME

In order for there to be a creator that begins something that didn't exist, that creator must be outside of time.

• • •

THE LESSON here is that the only reasonable explanation for the biggest questions of life can be found in the explanation given by the only one who was there and the only one who did it. Starting with God and working from God first, you are on your way to living your live in harmony with your purpose and with the proper arrangement of the details of life.

FOLLOWING GOD BY FOLLOWING HIS WORD

///

GENESIS 3:1

> *Now the serpent was more cunning than any beast of the field which the Lord God had made. And he said to the woman, "Has God indeed said, 'You shall not eat of every tree of the garden'?"*

"Has God indeed said" is a challenge we face from the enemy constantly. Eve knew what God said and even repeated back what God said. What God said was simple and direct, easy to understand and for the benefit of Eve and her family. It was to protect her and bless her. It was to give her peace and joy. It was to protect her quality of life and preserve her family. It was to bring good and maintain intimacy with God.

The challenge was really a threat by Satan to destroy. When Satan challenges us to doubt Gods Word it is a threat to all that God wants to do and be in our lives. Only death and destruction can come of it. Satan will use cunning, or in other words he is good at tricking us to fall into his traps of deception and lies. He will make them sound right, and even loving and good. Remember, it is God who gives life and tells us how to walk in the light of life. Satan is dark and can only bring us into darkness.

· · ·

THE LESSON here is to follow God by following His Word. His Word is truth; it is a lamp unto your feet and a light unto your path. It is freeing not restrictive. It is perfect and true. It is the way and leads us to "the Way," Jesus Himself. Ultimately, that is what really matters. Watch the threats that challenge Gods Word by saying, "Has God really said that?" "Does He really mean that?" "Does He really care?" "Is it that big of a deal?" "Isn't it just a small thing?"

Don't be deceived, God's Word is life! He loves you so much He has given you His Word.

FAITH ALWAYS WINS

MATTHEW 4:4

> *But He answered and said, "It is written, 'Man shall not live by bread alone, but by every word that proceeds from the mouth of God.'"*

Jesus was tempted to do what was easy, convenient and helpful to His own self. He was hungry from fasting for forty days and the devil took this opportunity to tempt Jesus. Satan is an opportunist and likes to take advantage of us when we are at our weakest and in the areas where we are weak. The answer to victory is always faith.

Faith will carry us though our vulnerable and weak moments and strengthen these vulnerabilities and weaknesses at the same time. Jesus would have no problem turning the stones into bread, but the bigger issue was not the fulfillment of His need but obedience to His Father. So Jesus chose the more difficult, inconvenient, and denial of His self to trust His Father and live according to His Fathers plan. The result was that God had the victory. This is living by faith.

Living by faith is trusting God and what He says. Even when, or especially when, it is hard, inconvenient and painful. We will discover that through our faith, God actually strengthens our weakness and removes our vulnerabilities. Living by faith brings us closer to God and shows us how He loves to take care of us and provide for us.

In the end, our faith is very valuable. So valuable that God allows it to be tested in order for it to grow and be strengthened.

. . .

THE LESSON is that faith will always win. This is why Satan attacks it so heavily. Living by faith is living by what God says and when what God says is in conflict with what anybody or anything else says (even our fleshly cravings and desires) choose faith and you will be choosing great things, better things, God's things.

FOLLOW ME

//

MATTHEW 4:19

"Then He said to them follow me and I will make you fishers of men"

Following Jesus is going in the direction He is going. It requires us, as in the case of Peter and Andrew , to trust that Jesus is the Way, the Truth and the Life. Peter and Andrew didn't know where they were going but they knew that following Jesus would get them to the right place. We won't always know where we're going, but as long as were following Jesus we know that will end up in the right place.

The key then, is to follow. Following Jesus will mean that he will lead us to people, especially people, that need to know Jesus. He told Peter and Andrew that if they followed him, He would make them fishers of men and this is where following Jesus will always take us. To the broken, the needy, the lost, the hurting – those are who Jesus would go after. As children of God and followers of Jesus we will be fishers of men. Jesus will bring us those opportunities divinely and supernaturally, leading us to those who need to know Jesus. He says that the fields are white and ready for the harvest.

. . .

THE LESSON is that if you are following Jesus you will be finding men and women and sharing the gospel with them, just as Jesus did. Jesus came to save that which was lost and now he's given you the great commission to do the same. You have been called, anointed, empowered and given everything that needed to go into all the world and make disciples. That's what following Jesus will lead you to.

BLESSED ARE THE PERSECUTED

MATTHEW 5:11-12

> *"Blessed are you when they revile and persecute you, and say all kinds of evil against you falsely for My sake. Rejoice and be exceedingly glad, for great is your reward in heaven, for so they persecuted the prophets who were before you."*

It may seem odd to equate persecution with blessed. How can persecution be a blessing. Here in the Sermon on the Mount, Jesus teaches a different perspective than those without God can see. Those without God can only see what is best for self, best as it pertains to how something will affect "me, myself and I." Persecution then is seen as bad because it means suffering and affliction which those without God can't see as beneficial. However, Jesus presents a view from a different perspective; a deeper perspective, a heavenly perspective and an eternal perspective.

You see, with God, the earthly world is not the goal, is not heaven and is not supreme. The earthly world as we now know it is seen as fallen, marred, controlled by Satan (with limitations) and heading to a merciful end. To God, the world is a place to begin a relationship with Him and live for Him. How we live here in this world will translate into eternity.

This world, then, can be seen as a place of testing to see what we really want. A place where we decide our eternal destiny. Therefore this world will involve struggle and as our text states, "persecution." Persecution that is being spoken of here is the opposition that comes from the forces of this world that oppose God. The same forces that hated and killed a perfect, sinless, loving, caring man who was actually God Himself on a rescue mission to save man.

. . .

THE LESSON here then is that when you live for God you will be persecuted. The blessing is that these persecutions contribute to your eternal existence. The blessing is that you will identify with Christ. The blessing is closeness and intimacy with Christ. The blessing is God's strength and power made available to carry you through. The blessing is that you will see the world for what is, unmasked. Most importantly, the blessing is Jesus Himself becoming the most important possession in the world to you. As the song says "you can have all this world, just give me Jesus."

LOVE YOUR ENEMIES

MATTHEW 5:44

> *"But I say to you, love your enemies, bless those who curse you, do good to those who hate you, and pray for those who spitefully use you and persecute you,"*

Love your enemies! This direct command is easy to understand but may be one of the hardest things to do. Why is loving an enemy hard? Enemies are those who are against us, who have hurt us or pose a threat to us. How can one do this?

The answer is to first know who your true enemy is. For a believer in Jesus Christ, our enemy is not any person, it is Satan and his demons. That is why we are told in Ephesians 6 that our battle is not flesh and blood. Satan may use people but in the end he is the enemy. Knowing this allows us to love our "enemies," or those who come against us on earth, because this is how we defeat our real enemy, Satan.

Satan wants us to fight, to hate and to lash out at others. When we do this we are not defeating the real enemy but instead falling in his trap. Instead, when we love our enemies we strike Satan with harmful blows. As the Bible says, love never fails. We defeat Satan with love.

This doesn't necessarily mean that we don't need to set proper boundaries with some, but it does mean we always see behind the person to the true enemy. As believers, this is how God is revealed in us. Everyone loves those that are good to them and do what they want them to do, but a true believer shows his stripes by doing something that is supernatural—loving our enemies. It is amazing what this will do to an enemy.

Jesus exemplified this with Judas. Knowing all along that Judas would betray him, Jesus loved him so well that none of the other disciples could tell that Judas was any different than they. When Jesus was eating with His disciples and said that one there with them would betray Him, all the disciples looked around wondering who it was. This is how to love our enemies.

. . .

THE LESSON is clear, your job is to love, even those who are against you. God has given you the grace and power to do it, are we willing?

ISAAC OR ISHMAEL?

GENESIS 16:2

> *"So Sarai said to Abram, "See now, the LORD has restrained me from bearing children. Please, go in to my maid; perhaps I shall obtain children by her." And Abram heeded the voice of Sarai."*

Abraham had been given a promise that he would have descendants as numerous as the sand in sea. With his wife, Sarah, past childbearing age, it didn't seem like God could or would do it. These are critical times for God's people. When we can't see how God will fulfill His plan in our lives. We may feel neglected or forgotten. We may even feel, as in the case of Abraham and Sarai, that the Lord is against us, restraining us from full potential and blessing. How we respond in these times is so crucial.

When it seems hopeless, it's not. It is just God presenting an opportunity to something really big. You see, in order for there to be the supernatural, the natural must be exhausted. When we can't fix the situation, when we can't change it, when we think we are just stuck, then get ready. Persevering faith will bring forth the supernatural. Keep forging on, don't grow weary, don't lose heart because desperate times are God's specialty. Stay faithful, obedient and most importantly don't take matters in your own hands. That's what Abraham and Sarai did. They tried to help God by having the promise come from Hagar's womb and not Sarai's. Their thinking may have been "we have the promise but not the promise manufacturer," so we will have to manufacture our own promise. In essence, we will help God out.

The child, Ishmael, was not the promised son. Abraham and Sarai may have looked at Ishmael and said "look what we have done" in the same way we can manufacture pseudo spiritual happenings and producers and say " wow, look what we have done, isn't God good?" When in reality it is just a work of the flesh. When God is at work, it is obvious and better than man can produce.

. . .

THE LESSON is when it looks the worst, God is at His best. Trust Him to be faithful to complete what He has started in your life (Philippians 1:6) He wants to show you His power and His might. In the end Abraham and Sarai did have their own son together, the promised son, just as God had said. This son, Isaac, was a fulfillment of Gods promise that was above and beyond the natural. If you want to see God work in your life this way, where there is no doubt as to who brought about the miracle and the promise, then let God do His thing, let Him work and let Him give you your Isaac, not your Ishmael.

WORRY

///

MATTHEW 6:25

> *"Therefore I say to you, do not worry about your life, what you will eat or what you will drink; nor about your body, what you will put on. Is not life more than food and the body more than clothing?*

Life, we are told, is not something to worry about. I think we all would love to put this in practice but it really seems impossible. Worry is a feeling or emotion that comes when we are afraid of what may come or happen. It really stems from fear. It also comes from a feeling of losing control of an outcome we desire. Knowing where worry comes from will help us to not worry.

We have some great insight about worry in our text and how to deal with it. The teaching is to look past the things, which so often occupy our focus. Life, Jesus says, is "more than" what we eat or wear. Life is more, deeper, bigger than our human desires and needs. Jesus is encouraging us to look at life beyond what we see on the surface, where we only see fragments of the whole. Jesus says that what we worry about has much more about it than the seen.

Maybe you are seeing something that scares you and not the big picture that God is in control. He is the One who calms the storms, holds the world in His hands and has subdued all things, putting them under His control. Whatever your worry, look deeper, look beyond with the eye of faith and when you see Jesus you will see everything, including your fears, swallowed up by the God who cares.

· · ·

THE LESSON here is, you can trust Jesus to take care of you. When it seems that there is something to fear it's because you are not looking at the bigger picture. Maybe you have "cropped" Jesus out of the picture. Imagine a picture of a lion about to devour a young child, to the horror of the observer. Then as you look deeper you see that lion chained to a steel cage bar. The child is safe just outside the reach of the lion.

TESTING

//

GENESIS 22:12

> *"And He said, 'Do not lay your hand on the lad, or do anything to him; for now I know that you fear God, since you have not withheld your son, your only son, from Me.'"*

Abraham had been given a promise that He would be the father of a nation with many descendants and much land. He was asked to get up and go from his homeland to a destination unknown. He showed great faith to do that. Yet with Abraham, we find that God has to prepare the man for the promise before the man can receive the promise, and the bigger the promise, the bigger the preparation.

So it was, Abraham went on to be tested and he failed at these tests. Twice he asked his wife Sarah to pretend she wasn't his wife so that he wouldn't be harmed. Failed tests are not the end of us, but rather they can be used to grow us if we learn from them and grow in our faith. We see how Abraham's tests prepared him for the granddaddy of all tests; the offering of his son, the son of promise, the son who represented the fulfillment of all his other promises. Without Isaac how would there be more descendants than the stars in the sky?

We see this great faith, which started Abraham's journey, now develop into a faith ready to be tested at its very core. Would Abraham withhold anything from God? Would he hide what was most precious to him from testing? Would his faith trust God with what was most dear to him? No doubt, God had prepared him for this. He would not have been ready any earlier but through the perfectly guided hand of the Almighty, whom forged an unwavering faith through time and directed pressure, Abraham was ready.

So it is, that as Abraham was willing to give all to God in obedience, we see a great lesson of faith and an encouragement of good.

. . .

THE LESSON is that good comes through testing, not bad. Know that God is preparing you, the vessel, to receive the promise. When you can trust God, you can let go and not need to withhold anything from Him. You can give yourself completely to Him. Take heart in times of testing, God loves you enough to show you His greatness and fulfill His promises.

TRUSTING THE LORD

PROVERBS 3:5

> *"Trust in the LORD with all your heart,*
> *And lean not on your own understanding;*
> *In all your ways acknowledge Him,*
> *And He shall direct your paths."*

One theme running through the entire Bible is God saying, "Trust Me." Every possible example and every possible way that God can show us that we can trust Him is given between the covers of our leather binding. All of human history screams that God has said what He means and means what He says. It screams that God is in control and has a plan for the world and for our lives as we place ourselves in His hands. The question, then, is do we trust Him and does our trust have limits?

This verse not only says to "trust The Lord" but to do it with "all our heart." This means without reservation. With everything we have embracing His will and plan with unguarded acceptance. The only way we can do this is to know Him. To know Him is to know His love, His grace, His mercy, His care, His concern, His kindness, and His peace. To know Him is to know He will never fail us. He will never abandon us. He will never forsake us. He will never tire of us. He will never quit on us. To know Him is to know He is faithful to us.

To know Him is to know that it is easy to trust one who is so trustworthy. God delights in showing us that we can trust Him and breaks down the walls and barriers that can often build up from life's hurts and accumulated losses. God even allows us to go through trials so that we turn to Him in times of desperation. We learn in these times that to trust God in all of life's seasons is the most free a human being can be.

· · ·

THE LESSON is to simply "trust in the God of the Bible." This not only makes sense, but it also will lead you in the right direction in life ("He shall direct our paths"). He will never lead you down the wrong path and will fulfill all His promises to you. You will never regret a simple childlike faith in the One who knows the end from the beginning and promises to "work all things together for good (Romans 8:28)" Have you taken Him up on that promise? Have you put your trust in Him?

MASTERING YOUR FEARS

MATTHEW 8:23

> *"Now when He got into a boat, His disciples followed Him. And suddenly a great tempest arose on the sea, so that the boat was covered with the waves. But He was asleep. Then His disciples came to Him and awoke Him, saying, 'Lord, save us! We are perishing!'"*

Fear had gripped the disciples as the storm screamed "death." Every thud of the crashing waves was a terrifying reminder of their vulnerability to the greater forces of Mother Nature that they found themselves in. Their cry revealed the cause of their fear, "we are perishing" they yelled. Desperate, they looked to the "storm tamer," Jesus.

The "Storm Tamer" was asleep, unfazed by the threat. The disciples knew Jesus could do supernatural things but as the next verse revealed, they didn't know the extent of His power and His willingness to use it. That may be our struggle. We know Jesus is powerful, but "can He and will He help in my storm?" Really, all they needed to know, and all we need to know, that with Jesus, everything is going to be ok. When they woke Jesus and He calmed the storm, they were surprised that the wind and waves obeyed Jesus.

Jesus rebuked the disciples because fear replaced faith. In this we find the simple answer to fear, faith. Looking past the threat to the one that is in control of the threat. Knowing that God is not alarmed at anything that may come our way gives us confidence that, with our lives in His hands, we need not be alarmed either.

. . .

THE LESSON here is that you too can rest, having peace, even in the storms, because there is nothing Jesus can't handle. In fact, nothing is even hard for Him. What may look like a sudden storm is really an opportunity to show that you know God is in control. Storms are faith opportunities in disguise. Nothing is too big for the "Storm Tamer," not any one of what you are going through. Let faith master you, then your fears will be mastered.

Genesis 26:17 27:46, Matthew 9:1 17,
Psalm 10:16 18, Proverbs 3:9 10

MERCY

//

MATTHEW 9:13

> *"But go and learn what this means: 'I desire mercy and not sacrifice.' For I
> did not come to call the righteous, but sinners, to repentance."*

When asked why Jesus ate with tax collectors and sinners Jesus said, "those who
are well have no need of a Physician but those who are sick." Then He made this
statement in Matthew 9:13 suggesting that they needed to learn mercy if they
were going to understand why He was eating with the "sin" crowd. This also suggests that the "Pharisees" or religious rule crowd were lacking in mercy in their
religious practices. That these "Pharisees" had the religious rules down pat and
yet they missed the whole point how religion should properly affect our hearts
toward others.

Mercy is the key. Mercy draws us near to others and draws them near to us. Mercy identifies with others and wants the best for them. Mercy is understanding
and desirous of helping. This mercy comes first of an understanding of our own
need of mercy. Understanding that we, as much as anyone else, need mercy and
that no matter how good we are, we fall hopelessly short of the righteousness
required by God to be accepted by Him. Our own need for mercy forces us to
cry out to God, asking for help. This is the heart of Christianity and the rebuke
to self righteousness that falls so short of any goodness compared to God's goodness. God Himself considers our best morality as a used menstrual rag. (Sorry
for the visual but that's what the Bible says, giving us a graphic picture of our
own righteousness compared to His perfect righteousness).

· · ·

THE LESSON here is to remember to add mercy to all you do, just as Christ is
merciful to you. Remember that no amount of good works or morality will erase
that fact, that you are a sinner. That's why Jesus came, so that He could be your
righteousness, fulfilling the requirements of the law, which demands perfect
sinlessness. Jesus was completely sinless, taking your place in judgment on the
cross so that now, by faith in Him, you can be righteous. And this righteousness
that comes by faith gives you the same heart Jesus had for the sinner, a heart of
mercy. As the Apostle Paul said, "I am the chief of sinners" (1 Timothy 1:15).

Genesis 28:1 29:35, Matthew 9:18 38,
Psalm 11:1 7, Proverbs 3:11 12

THE HARVEST IS READY

MATTHEW 9:37

> *"Then He said to His disciples, 'The harvest truly is plentiful, but the laborers are few. Therefore pray the Lord of the harvest to send out laborers into His harvest.'"*

Jesus asks the disciples to pray about a condition He is observing that truly needs divine intervention. He is looking at the multitudes of people that were lost, confused, misguided and disoriented. This applies to the human condition without a true Shepherd, Jesus. Shepherds would lead the sheep, care for them, feed them, nurse them and protect them. Sheep would do well as long as the followed the Shepherd. Following was what sheep were good at. However, without a good shepherd to follow, the sheep would be totally lost and their behavior would reflect their pain of insecurity.

Jesus sees this and has compassion. He sees us the same way. No matter how we disguise it or pretend it's not there, humans, like sheep, feel lost and insecure without a relationship with the Good Shepherd Jesus Christ. A Christian has a secure, well lead disposition as they keep their eyes on and follow the Shepherd. These sheep, like their Shepherd, will have compassion on the lost sheep as well. They will desire those lost sheep to connect with the Shepherd.

The prayer then is that Jesus is recognizing that there are more of these lost sheep than there are found sheep that can show the lost sheep the way.

Jesus compares this situation to a harvest that is ready to be picked but there aren't enough people to pick it. The prayer is interesting in that Jesus didn't say pray for the lost sheep here, like we so often do, but for the people to go and "pick" them. Now of course there is nothing wrong with praying for lost sheep, but the emphasis here is to pray for people to go out because there are many who are lost that are ready to receive the gospel. What a great promise. Dont say "four months and then comes the harvest" as to wait for something more to happen. Look around and you will see the harvest or time is now. There is ripe fruit in our lives right now, all around us, ready to be picked. There are many waiting for someone to tell them the good news and introduce them to the Good Shepherd.

. . .

THE LESSON here is to see that the world is full of those ready to receive salvation in Jesus Christ. They just need someone to tell them. Pray that people will tell them, and maybe you also should pray for yourself, that you would tell them. Pray that you would be a laborer that is intentional about sharing the gospel. They are out there waiting, they are all around you, will you tell them?

THE PURE WORD

PSALM 12:6

> *The words of the LORD are pure words, Like silver tried in a furnace of earth, Purified seven times.*

God's words come without any hint of impurity. When He speaks there is nothing on the communication that is not right. There is nothing that is not true. There is no deceit and no false manipulative motives. Whatever He says is and whatever is He says. His words are the standard by which all else is measured and has proven over time it's purity and rightness.

Over thousands of years God has spoken and moved men by the Holy Spirit to record those words. The Holy Bible is Gods word to man. The greatest privilege of man is that God has been mindful of him to make sure we received His communication. Critics and skeptics have come and gone but God's Word still stands as revelation of God, never to fail and always to complete what it says.

God's Word contains internal proof that it is from God and not man, one of which is the foretelling of events long before they happen and basing the credibility of God's Word on the requirement of 100% accuracy. It has been put to the test in every way and by all different types of tests and yet it stands. Like silver put through the process of removing the dross by heating in a clay crucible so the impurities rise to the top to be removed, God's Word stands the test of time. In fact, just as God said, heaven and earth will pass away but His Word will endure forever.

Jesus is the word made flesh. He is the pure word, without sin, spot or blemish. He is the manifested Word tempted in every way, understanding what we go through and the struggle of life.

· · ·

THE LESSON here is that your response to God's Word will determine your life, not only here but also in eternity. Are you building your life on the foundation that will stand forever? You have a guarantee, a promise that you will never regret basing your life upon God's Word, which will never fail.

LIFE

///

MATTHEW 10:39

"He who finds his life will lose it, and he who loses his life for My sake will find it."

One of the most important lessons we can lean about life, but also one of the most difficult, is that "life is not all about me." Generally, we are obsessed with ourselves. Me, myself and I takes center ring in the circus of life it's easy to view ourselves as the sun in which all the world revolves around. This is human nature. We are narcissists at birth and very good at it.

The words of Jesus give us a different perspective. These words come from the One who came to give us life, and that life in abundance. Jesus' words give us a totally different way to live and complete freedom from self-intoxication.

He says "he who finds his life will lose it." In other words, those who live for themselves will lose out on life. How ironic is that? Naturally we think that is the way to live, but the Creator and Sustainer of life says that is not how to live. Why is that? The reason is that life comes from God and not man. Man, when disconnected from God is disconnected from life, while connecting to God can only come by disconnecting from self. So to really live is to release ourselves into Gods hands by letting God be the center and not us.

. . .

THE LESSON here is that the secret of life is to live it for God. To do this you must have a bigger view than yourself. A view that expands until it sees the true meaning of life where you realize "it's not about me." When you lose your life to God you get back everything in return. His will, His way, His plan is perfect. God never makes you less, He only make you more. Lose your life into Gods almighty arms and you will find everything you really want. It is all found in Christ.

REST

MATTHEW 11:28-30

"Come to Me, all you who labor and are heavy laden, and I will give you rest. Take My yoke upon you and learn from Me, for I am gentle and lowly in heart, and you will find rest for your souls. For My yoke is easy and My burden is light."

How do you see God? When you pray how do you see God? Here we have a description of Jesus that helps us see Him the way we should. He is gentle, lowly, and easy. He is inviting and welcoming. It is so important we see God this way. Some may see Him as One to fear, One who is hard, rough and authoritatively dictatorial. Maybe as One who looks to strike us down and is mad at us. We feel like hiding from Him instead of coming to Him.

These words of our Lord are for the tired, weighted down, hurt and burdened. The wonderful words of The Lord "come to Me." These are three of the most revealing and helpful words of the human language. These words tell us if the burden we are carrying is too heavy, the wrong person is carrying the burden.

· · ·

THE LESSON here is to rest by surrendering control of whatever it is you are struggling with or burdened by that. Remember that as a human you are limited and fragile. You will feel the effects of your weakness when you, in an effort to be self sufficient and independent, take life in your own hands. Jesus says to us" come to Me'" He is able. He can handle it. He will give you rest. Will you take Him up on his offer? Will pride get in your way? Or will you learn to say, in whatever we are wrestling with to finally say "Lord, it's Your problem." "I'm tired Lord, I'm stressed, I'm worried, I'm coming to You, I'm attaching myself to You, carry me Lord." You will know if you have really "come to Him" if you feel the burden lift, the peace come, and your soul at rest.

JANUARY 17

Genesis 35:1 36:43, Matthew 12:1 21,
Psalm 15:1 5, Proverbs 3:21 26

WHAT DOES GOD DESIRE?

///

MATTHEW 12:7-8

> *"But if you had known what this means, 'I desire mercy and not sacrifice,'*
> *you would not have condemned the guiltless. For the Son of Man is Lord*
> *even of the Sabbath."*

Jesus, responding to the criticism of the Pharisees in regards to the disciples pluck-ing and eating grain on the Sabbath, teaches a very important lesson. Reaching back to the Old Testament, He points out that even David knew the proper place of the law. Jesus points out a misunderstanding the most "religious" of the time had, which can be a misunderstanding we can have. The misunderstanding was this, that keeping rules is more important than keeping compassion.

The correction to their misunderstanding is stated as "I desire mercy and not sacrifice." In other words, what Jesus wants is that which comes from His own heart for humanity. That if we understand theology correctly we will see people, not rules, and our ability to follow them is what religion is all about. That we would never let a rule interfere with love. That we would treat others in the same tender hearted way as Jesus did. That when God is working in our lives and we are walking with Him, the way we see others will be as He saw them, as the Bible says "for God so love the world." Mercy being the extension of love is at the heart of God's heart.

. . .

THE LESSON here is to let mercy be the measure of our religion, not rule obey-ing. It's not how many times you go to church, how many chapters of your Bible you read, not how much you give, not how much you serve in church, but how you love. Those activities are important, but only to the point to where they done in love and lead to love. They are not the end in themselves, they are vehicles to love and know and grow in God's love. That is where it all starts. God's love for us, received, enjoyed and shared. This is what God desires, "mercy not sacrifice."

WHEN LIFE IS THE PITTS

GENESIS 37:24

> *"Then they took him and cast him into a pit. And the pit was empty; there was no water in it."*

On the journey of God fulfilling the dreams He has placed in our hearts, we may unexpectedly find ourselves in a pit. God gave Joseph a dream; it was God's plan for His life. It was God's purpose for him and Joseph's heart was full of the burden to have God fulfill it. The dream was big, unforeseeable and unimaginable. It was bigger than Joseph could have dreamed on his own, yet on the way, he found himself in a pit.

God has a dream for all of us who are His children. We may not know the specifics but we have things in our heart that feel like a burden, an unfulfilled feeling of God hasn't brought all this feeling in my heart together quite yet. We may feel like we do when we have an unfinished project lingering, or as if there is still much more than we can see at the moment. We may feel stagnant, dry and empty like Joseph in the empty dry pit. What we may not realize is that pits are part of the process of fulfillment.

Pits aren't graves but places of preparation and positioning. You see, as in the case of Joseph, the pit not only was a place to learn humility and trust, but also a place that would position Joseph to be taken to the next place which would ultimately lead to the place of fulfillment. Without the pit there would be no selling of Joseph to the Midianite traders who took Joseph to Egypt, where he needed to be for the dream to be fulfilled. The pit was just one of a series of supernatural, God ordained circumstances that all led up to where Joseph was to be all along.

• • •

THE LESSON here is to trust in God's plan even when it looks bleak. God has a plan that He is working out in your life and your job is to to trust that plan, even when you are in the pits. God is not finished; He is just positioning you and preparing you. Life is like a motion picture, not a snapshot. One frame doesn't make a movie and one picture captured in a moment of time doesn't tell the whole story. Let God work it all out as He "will be faithful to complete what He has started in you. (Philippians 1:6)"

HEAVEN

//

PSALM 17:15

"As for me, I will see Your face in righteousness; I shall be satisfied when I awake in Your likeness."

The struggle of life never escapes our awareness. With every movement of time comes the friction of earthly existence. From the womb we are immersed into the fight for survival. We struggle for breath, for food, for oxygen. We fight against disease and infection. Gravity pushes down on us without mercy. Then as David, there are those around us we have to be careful of, those who look to harm our families and us. Such is life in the big city of brokenness. Even our own flesh betrays us, pulling us way from God and into sin and wickedness.

David's thoughts in our scripture, take him home so to speak. He is not overcome with earths realities but heavens glories. The hope of heaven is the believers delight. Earthly existence is swallowed up by the glories of eternity. David's confidence was riveted on seeing Jesus, which is the glory of heaven. Seeing Jesus face to face would be without the veil of sin stained flesh, but with sinless glorified bodies of righteousness enabling a unhindered connection and one in which there would be no more fleshly opposition to our Godly desires.

The moment of heavenly entrance will be a closing of our eyes on earth and an opening of the eye in an eternal bliss, absent of all struggle, friction and resistance. What struggle is to earth, satisfaction is to heaven. Heaven won't be in us as it is now, but we will be in it. Love, joy, peace, beauty, excitement and awe won't be a possibility but a undiminished state of existence without levels or amounts but fixed in an eternal, immeasurable state of being. We will never tire and never have less than what the fullness of heaven is and will never not be.

· · ·

THE LESSON here is to view everything in light of Heaven. Remember, that no matter the struggle, you are going to heaven. As much as can be enjoyed here on earth in your relationship with God through Christ, it will not compare to the glories of heaven. As you keep your eyes on Jesus, the captain of your salvation, you will experience His presence here with great satisfaction. But as each tick of the clock takes you closer to home you know heaven is "much better by far" (Philippians 1:23). Knowing what awaits you will enable you to face whatever your struggle because this is only temporary, but heaven is forever. Keep your eyes on heaven and earth will serve you well. You will be its master instead of it mastering you.

FRUITFUL IN THE LAND OF AFFLICTION

//

GENESIS 41:51-52

> *"Joseph called the name of the firstborn Manasseh: 'For God has made me forget all my toil and all my father's house.' And the name of the second he called Ephraim: 'For God has caused me to be fruitful in the land of my affliction.'"*

Manasseh and Ephraim, two names of the sons of Joseph because they are descriptive of what God had done in Joseph's life. Two names that also describe what God will do in the lives of those who have placed themselves in God's hands. We too will have emblems of God's faithfulness, tokens of His goodness and trophies of His grace. In the end it will be all worth it, it will be all perfect and right. Just keep going in faith because God is not finished until our lives have brought forth His fruit.

In fact, John tells us in His gospel (John 15:16) that "You did not choose Me, but I chose you and appointed you that you should go and bear fruit, and that your fruit should remain." This, our purpose and plan God has mapped out for us. This plan is not something we can bring about ourselves but a plan God brings forth through us. Like a branch that comes off a vine, we will be fruitful through our connection to God. This is what the Bible calls "abiding" and is when a Christian lives by faith, that the Holy Spirit brings about spiritual fruit, like sap brings life from the vine to the branch. This is what we see God doing in the life of Joseph.

Through Joseph's faith, God was working His plan. All Joseph had to go on was a promise that came in a dream that God had given him. Times of betrayal, loneliness, injustice, abandonment, imprisonment and mistreatment could not altar what God had set in place. No man can stop God's will in our life. Our job is to continue to trust God knowing He is faithful.

· · ·

THE LESSON here is to know that God will not let you down so just keep going, by faith. In the end, you will never regret putting your life in God's hands. You will, as Joseph, "forget all our toil in our fathers house," meaning when God's plan comes to fruition, the hard days of struggle will seem as such a small price to pay compared to the greatness of God's plan. You will also see that in the affliction God caused fruitfulness. You will have a life well spent, eternally rewarded and abundantly fruitful. It will be through toil and affliction that God brings His best and most numerous fruit.

Genesis 42:18 43:34, Matthew 13:47 14:12,
Psalm 18:16 36, Proverbs 4:7 10

CHOICES

PSALMS 18:30

"As for God, His way is perfect; The word of the LORD is proven; He is a shield to all who trust in Him."

Life is filled with choices. There many options to choose from, so many roads to take, so many paths given. It is amazing how many choices we have to make in a day. What's even more amazing is how each little choice can make such a big difference leading us in certain directions in life. I think it could be said that our choices determine our lives.

Regardless of the consequences, we must look to honor God in our decisions. This is how we will know that we are making the right decisions. A good question to ask is "does this honor God?" In the end, that is all that really matters. We will make the wrong decisions when we think about how the decision will effect "ME" and what will be best for "ME." Just because we can do something doesn't mean we should do it.

Lot is a great example of choosing what was best for himself. When given the power of choice by his Uncle Abraham, he used his power to "choose for HIMSELF" instead of choosing for God. His choice was based on what the eye could see, the best land, the best place for self and the best thing for him according to what the eye could see. The decision predictably turned out to be a bad one as he and his family got sucked up into a vortex of sin and carnality by moving so close to Sodom and Gomorrah. His decision caused him to live with a tormented soul, we are told by Peter. Abraham, on the other hand let God choose, and the decision was right, perfect and blessed. God saw what Lot and Abraham could not. God's way turned out to be right, it turned out to be perfect, as it always will.

· · ·

THE LESSON here is clear, God's way is perfect. The text goes on to say His word is proven. God's perfect way is revealed in His proven Word. So in making decisions, choose to honor God or better yet, let Him choose by asking Him in all decisions "God, what do you want to do, what decision will honor You?" When you do this you will find yourself doing scripture, doing His will and doing life the way it's suppose to be done, His way. You will find that this is what a disciple does and this is a life lived for Christ by faith where His will is done through you. He will take imperfect people down a perfect path that leads to a perfect Savior and a perfected life. It's just the perfection of the Perfecter at work creating His perfect masterpiece, you!

GET OUT OF THE BOAT

///

MATTHEW 14:28

> *"And Peter answered Him and said, "Lord, if it is You, command me to come to You on the water."*

Have you ever asked God to do something "crazy" in your life? Something so beyond you, that only faith would be able to carry you through? Peter, here, did just that. Seeing Jesus walk on water he asked Jesus to command him to do the same thing. This is interesting because he didn't just do it, but asked God to command him to do it. He understood that if God says it, commands it, then it is. So his approach was to ask God to "command" him. Maybe you should pray about asking God to command you to do something "crazy."

Reading the Bible gives us this sense that God does extraordinary things through ordinary people. No doubt the serious student of the Bible at times wonders if they could be Peter, Paul, Moses, David etc. One has to wonder if God will do things in our lives as well. Things that can't be explained, things that point to God, things that scream "supernatural." Of course God can do them, but will He?

The answer is yes! God can and will do the extraordinary. Not for our glory but for His. Like Peter, it is faith to ask God to do it that is the key. I find it interesting that only Peter got out of the boat. Even after Peter walked on water and the others saw him, they still didn't ask Jesus to command them to do likewise. The boat was safer, more comfortable and more predictable. Walking on water required absolute dependence on God. Once on the water, Peter had nothing to help him but Jesus alone. This is why I believe that the great works of God happen through those who are willing to step out in faith, to places where faith is all there is. This is the place of head scratching miracles, the place of walking on water.

· · ·

THE LESSON here is that you too can have an unexplainable, supernatural life, where God is working that which can only be explained by pointing to God. You have to be willing to step out of the boat to live on faith alone. You have to be willing to ask God to do something crazy in your life. You have to want to be water walkers instead of boat sitters. Take a moment to pray, "Jesus, do something that I can't do, do something that gives you glory, and do something that will bring me closer to You. Lord, Command me."

DESIRE

PSALM 19:14

> *"Let the words of my mouth and the meditation of my heart Be acceptable in Your sight, O LORD, my strength and my Redeemer."*

The desire to please God is a new desire of a "new creation in Christ." When God enters ones life, He actually inhabits them and becomes one with them. In other words, where we once merely looked to please ourselves, the "new creation in Christ" has desires that go beyond oneself to God. The new creation craves for God, for God things and for relational intimacy with God. This is how we know we are a "new creation in Christ."

David, here, speaks as one who has these great desires. He wants his words to be acceptable to God. He desires that there would be no wrong in His words. That in itself is a great desire. Then, he desires that his inward man also be acceptable to God. It is possible to say with our mouth things we don't believe in our hearts. That is what acting is all about. God, however, wants sincerity and honesty before Him. He wants our true self, the self within, to be honoring Him. Just as a young child can recite Bible verses and sing Bible songs for their parents without experiencing the same reality within. We too can pay "lip service" to God. However, desiring to have our inward person, the secret person, the unseen us, be acceptable to God is truly the desire of a "new creation in Christ." This desire goes beyond the normal human desire that merely wants to be accepted by other men.

• • •

THE LESSON, here, is to follow after those Godly desires God placed in your heart. As a Christian you will crave God just like a baby craves milk. As God transforms you from inside out, it is your inward person that is most important, as that is what God sees. The good news is that God works in you, to want to do what He wants you to do (Philippians2:13). You desire it. God is your redeemer and strength, He has saved you and will strengthen you, giving you the desire to do God's will. The bottom line is, think about your inward self being right with God, and all else will fall in line.

GUARD YOUR HEART

//

PROVERBS 4:3

"Keep your heart with all diligence,
For out of it spring the issues of life."

Protecting our heart, or our "inner self," is easy to overlook. We can make the mistake of neglecting the "inner self" because we are behaving correctly outwardly. However, the real us, the "inside us," must be protected as the highest priority. Our "inner self" can be harmed, damaged and polluted by what is allowed to cross the protective walls of our will. We have the ability to say yes or no to what comes into our "inner self."

This warning in our Proverb is to first recognize this fact that, like a well filled with pure water, our "heart" when made clean by the blood of Jesus Christ is also pure. Jesus gives us a new heart, a pure heart, a heart that loves Godly things, good things and lovely things. Our new hearts can be affected by what we allow or tolerate to enter into it. So we have this all-important warning. A warning that will have an impact on our lives. In fact, it can be said, that what we allow into our inner person will have an impact on our enjoyment of God, our enjoyment of life, our influence in life and our consistency in our walks with God.

It is clear, there can be no doubt, that who we are can be influenced by what we look at, listen to, and think about. The question is, are we protecting ourselves? In a society that worships entertainment and pleasure, guarding our hearts can be confusing at times. Knowing what is harmful and toxic to our hearts when it is also funny and amusing, and understanding what may be wrong with something that everyone is doing, or that doesn't seem to be a "big deal."

Have we gotten used to that which is damaging to us but now we see it as normal? Have we gotten use to a sub-optimal enjoyment of God? Have we settled for a Christianity that is not Biblical, not spiritual and not thriving and growing in the wonderful love and grace of Jesus Christ? No doubt, God knows the importance of our inner person and the effects worldly, sinful and evil dark things will do to us. Could it be that we have underestimated the effects of sin, darkness and the power of Satan to influence us? Could it be that depression, untamed lust, hate, anger, frustration and all other sort of symptoms we may suffer from are merely tainted wells of our heart that have been polluted by that which is harmful to our souls? We must look at this exhortation in the Proverb, examine our tolerance of that which is not of the Lord and wonder if this may be the reason we don't seem to experience the greatness of our salvation and the inexplicable joys of the Lord. Could we be infected by spiritual fruit flies that are eating away at our spiritual fruit?

. . .

THE LESSON, here, is that when your inward self is right with God, all else will fall in line. Think about not merely outward obedience, but inner obedience. Purity of your thought life, purity of your affections and purity of what you bow down to or worship in our heart. Think about what you think about and what you cherish and what you adore. The inner sanctuary of our inner person is where true Godly interactions occurs, not merely in outward expression. You can express outwardly something different than what your worship inwardly, thus deceiving yourself and others. God desires truth in your inward parts, and love from your core. Be careful of this little trick of the enemy. Behavior is no substitute for worship. God wants your heart. Love Him with it!

TURNING EVIL INTO GOOD

GENESIS 50:20

> *"But as for you, you meant evil against me; but God meant it for good, in order to bring it about as it is this day, to save many people alive."*

God is so good in His work. He is a master in bringing forth good. He is not hindered by opposition and He is not deterred by evil. He will accomplish all that He has set out to do and will show His greatness by His plan. This is good news for His children because much of this plan involves us. When we entrust our lives into His hands He takes the responsibility to bring about good in us and through us. The encouragement we take from knowing this gives us great hope when facing adversity.

Joseph is a perfect example of this. Given a promise from God through a dream, he came against many threats to this dream. In the moment, it looked as if the dream had died. It looked as if evil had won and darkness was stronger than light. The twist to Joseph's life was that not only did God overcome the opposition to Joseph, He actually used the opposition to further His plan. God will do the same for us.

Joseph recognizes this incredible way God works as he says, "you (his brothers that threw him in a pit, then sold him into slavery) meant evil against me, but God meant it for good, in order to bring about as it is this day, to save many people alive." I believe this use of evil to bring about good is what being "more" than a conqueror means. It is one thing to directly defeat evil by overcoming evil with good, but then to use evil to bring about good is "more" than conquering. God uses Satan's own devices directly against him.

Jesus was attacked with evil. Satan looked to kill him and end his reign and crush the possibility for salvation for mankind. He used evil men to kill Jesus, who was an innocent man. It was that same evil that brought about the greatest good for mankind as Jesus not only died, paying the penalty for our sins, but He also rose again, conquering death and making the way for eternal life for all those who would believe. God turned evil to good.

. . .

THE LESSON here is that evil will be turned to good when met with faith. You can rest in Him, knowing that "no weapon formed against you shall prosper" (Isaiah 54:17). Whatever may come your way, God is bigger. He will always bring about good. You may be in a spot where you feel as if all is lost and there is no way out. You may feel as if there is no hope or that your life is ruined. Learn this great lesson, turn to God and let Him turn evil into good.

Exodus 2:11 3:22, Matthew 17:10 27,
Psalm 22:1 18, Proverbs 5:7 14

SIN

///////////////////////////////////////

EXODUS 3:7

> *"And the LORD said: 'I have surely seen the oppression of My people who are in Egypt, and have heard their cry because of their taskmasters, for I know their sorrows.'"*

Oppression is a word that speaks of misery, affliction and trouble. It speaks of being controlled by something. It speaks of one who is not in control of their own life but one who is being controlled by another or by something else. It speaks of slavery and ownership by another. Such was the terrible plight of the Children of Israel under the harsh control of the Egyptian King. This also is a picture of sin and it's rule over the human heart.

Egypt is a type of the world in the Bible. Jesus said that we "can't serve two masters because we will love one and hate the other" (Matthew 6:24). There isn't two ways about that. It's an either or thing. John the Apostle said not to love the world or the things in the world and that if we do, the love of the Father is not in us. James the Apostle said that to be a friend of the world is to be an enemy of God. The Apostle John also said that the world consists of "the lust of the flesh, the lust of the eye and the pride of life." The picture becomes clearer for us as we see that we, like the children of Israel, are slaves to the world that uses sin to control us and keep us oppressed and in bondage. It is, as in our text, a harsh taskmaster that takes away from us , hurts us and controls us.

This is why God heard the cry of the people of Israel and raised up a deliverer in Moses who would lead the people out of their slavery to sin. Moses pictures for us Jesus, who delivers us from the tyranny of our sin. Jesus came to set us free and break the control of the harsh taskmaster. Jesus has overcome and provided the way out, the only way. He is our deliverer.

. . .

THE LESSON here is to see sin for what it is. Sin wants to master and destroy you. Sin will ultimately take a person to hell unless Jesus frees them .

This is why the gospel is such good news. Jesus came to deliver sinners who couldn't deliver themselves. He came to do what you couldn't do. He came to set the captives free. Slaves no more, free in Jesus. Have you been set free? Cry out to Jesus, recognize you're a slave to sin, and in need of a deliverer, place your faith in Him and you will be free. If you already have, rejoice that your sins are forgiven.

UNLESS YOU ARE CONVERTED

MATTHEW 18:3

> *"Assuredly, I say to you, unless you are converted and become as little children, you will by no means enter the kingdom of heaven."*

Possibly one of the most important questions one can ask is "how can I get to heaven?" Life is more than what we see now and we are constantly confronted with our own mortality. We all die, so what happens next? The disciples were one step ahead of this question as they were wondering about what their life would be like when they die. They already knew Jesus was the Way, but now they wanted to be the greatest in heaven. This sets the stage for Jesus to answer the all-important question "how can one get to heaven?"

We all think about what's next, in one way or another, and we all have opinions about that. However, we cannot come to any worthwhile conclusions until we look to the One who really knows. You see, we all have innate instincts about Heaven. We all have eternal desires and as the Bible says, "He has set eternity in our hearts." What we do with those instincts will determine our eternity.

Jesus came to bring life and immortality to light through the gospel. This means that He has shown us the way, that there is life after death and how we may have life in heaven. Jesus tells the disciples that "conversion" is necessary. That means we have to be changed. That we can't go to heaven unless something happens. This is what Jesus came to do. His mission was to be a sacrifice for our sins and take our place in judgment. He came so that we could be converted.

He says there is no entrance into heaven without it. This conversion is also called "born again" because it is a spiritual birth. We are not born into this world "spiritual." We must have this birth which is an act of faith. The gospel is the seed and faith is what makes it come alive. So Jesus once again stresses the answer to one of the most important questions, "How can I go to Heaven?"

. . .

THE LESSON is that all humans are born sinners and are in desperate need of God's mercy and grace to be saved. Jesus opens the door to salvation and those who will humble themselves and come to Him, like a child coming to their parents for help, will be saved. The kingdom of heaven is for those who do.

THROUGH

PSALM 23:4

"Yea, though I walk through the valley of the shadow of death, I will fear no evil; For You are with me; Your rod and Your staff, they comfort me."

One of the most important and easily overlooked words in this most magnificent scripture is "through."

"Through" is also an easily overlooked application of the scripture in our own lives. The worth of this word is knowing how God works in our lives when we are in the valley. Knowing that He calls us to go "through" and not around and not back.

Knowing that "through" is God's path, we can expect our Good Shepherd Jesus Christ to be with us. He will not leave us alone as orphans, but as our comforter and protector He will make sure we arrive to our destination safely. His rod will protect us from being overcome by our enemies and from being overwhelmed by our fears. His staff will lead us on to goodness and kindness, to rest and peace, joy and strength. We will be comforted by our "Good Shepherd" all the way "through."

We are to keep walking by faith because these "valleys of the shadow of death" are not permanent but temporary. They lead us to our destination and are not our destination, in and of themselves, but merely a passageway that prepares us for our destination. We may have wounds, pain that we are going through, meant to develop us and add depth of character to our lives. It is faith that allows The Good Shepherd to heal our wounds. It is fear and retreat, or avoidance, that keeps the wound festering and open. When we go "through" we come out healed and the wound turns into a scar.

The scar, like the wounds in Jesus' hands, become emblems of grace and mercy that have developed us into the people God made us to be. The scars add character and are a part of who we are, only they are healed and stronger than before the wound. Scars are not bad, but are battle wounds of a battle tested warrior for Christ. They show our worth and are spiritual metals of honor.

. . .

THE LESSON here is that there is only one way to get to the other side of the valley and that is "through." When tempted to retreat or avoid, when tempted to fear of fall, remember that there is greatness on the other side. God is doing something great, have faith, and keep walking.

RICHES

///

MATTHEW 19:23-24

> *"Then Jesus said to His disciples, 'Assuredly, I say to you that it is hard for a rich man to enter the kingdom of heaven. And again I say to you, it is easier for a camel to go through the eye of a needle than for a rich man to enter the kingdom of God.'"*

Scripture doesn't encourage us to be ambitious about wealth. In fact, scripture has a low view of wealth as a way to live life. Now wealth in and of itself is not a bad thing, but it is our attitude towards it that counts. Wealth typically is a means for one to be worldly and not Godly. Wealth has a tendency to corrupt and foster arrogance. The worst effect of wealth is that it can cause a false sense of security that masks our true need for God.

It is true that money can't buy happiness. If I told you could have all the money you wanted but could not be happy, would you take it? If I told you that you could buy the biggest house in the best area with the best car and the best furniture and decorations to fill it with but you could not have peace, would you want it? You see, money is really not the issue, it's the effect we want money to have on our well being that we want. When we think money is the vehicle to bring us only what comes from God, then we have fallen into the money trap.

If we thought about money correctly we would see it like dynamite. We would see it as having great potential to cause great harm to us, if not put in its proper place and used correctly. Few do! We would see it as something that can take away our true riches like love, joy, peace and satisfaction. We would see it not as something to live for but something that can get in the way of what we are to live for. We would see it as that which can interfere with coming to salvation in Jesus Christ.

In our text we see just that. The picture drawn is one of absurdity, camel going through the eye of a needle is like a rich man going to heaven, and it's basically impossible. In context, it's when money has taken the place of God in our lives, which is very difficult to prevent. That's why the Bible says "the love of money is the root of all evil." It's our attitude toward money, which is very intoxicating, and very few use it well, without it becoming an idol.

. . .

THE LESSON, here, to understand money the way God does seeing money as a way to serve God and not self. May you work hard at whatever you do with your eye on Jesus and not money. May you do all as "unto The Lord" and may that be the greatest motivation for your effort. May you use your resources, recognizing where they truly come from, to build God's kingdom and bless others. May you trust God as your provider and may you be responsible stewards of all that is given to you. May you be the master over your money and not let our money be your master. May you find all you need in Jesus, the only place to truly find peace and happiness. May you be rich in God, where true riches are.

SERVANTS

MATTHEW 20:28

*"Just as the Son of Man did not come to be served, but to serve, and to give
His life a ransom for many."*

One of life's little secrets is found here in a statement made by Jesus. It is the secret of the blessing of serving. Typically we think being served is best. We want to be over others, served by others and catered to by others. We may see this as the superior position or the meaning of life. While being taken care of can be nice, true joy is not found in being served but in being a servant.

The mother of James and John asked if her sons could be high ranking in God's kingdom by sitting on the right and left hand of Jesus. As a good parent she thought that their high status was something that would be great for them. Jesus told her that those positions are for who God the Father chooses and prepares through suffering. In other words, selfish ambition will be an unfulfilling pursuit because God is the one who raises people up and puts people in positions for His purposes. Not that ambition is bad, it's selfish ambition that is bad. When we work hard to attain our own glory and merely our own benefit, we will find an empty pot of gold at the end of that rainbow. Jesus says that the motivation to be over people for our own gain is the mind set of those who don't know God and only think in worldly terms. However, when we do all that we do for The Lord, we are now servants of the Most High God and will find that this is where true joy is found.

As Christians, we are made to be serve. Our new spiritual DNA is wired that way. When we see ourselves as servants we don't concern ourselves with position, power or praises of men, but we are now able to just serve the Lord in whatever capacity He desires. No matter if He wants us to serve Him at the top or the bottom, with a lot or a little, in good times or bad times, it doesn't matter. What matters is that we are serving Him. We can now be free to serve and leave the details to Him. We can say, "I'm just a servant of God, serving Him however He wants."

. . .

THE LESSON here, is that Jesus Himself, the Lord of Lords and the King of Kings, came to serve and not be served. You too must remember that you are a servant. You are to serve Him by serving others and you are to give yourself completely to that endeavor. God will give you the grace to do it, even when you feel like you can't, because He wants to show you that His grace is sufficient for you and His strength is made perfect in your weakness. Blessed are the servants for it is then that they are like Jesus.

Exodus 12:14 13:16, Matthew 20:29 21:22,
Psalm 25:16 22, Proverbs 6:12 15

PRAYER

///

MATTHEW 21:13

> *"He said to them, 'The Scriptures declare, "My Temple will be called a house of prayer," but you have turned it into a den of thieves!"'*

Prayer is at the heart of worship and there is no substitute for it. Jesus brings forth this great truth, that when people gather together to worship God, praying should be a big part of it. He actually labels "His house" as a praying house. That is what His house is all about. What would your "house" be labeled?

Is your house a praying house? Whether that be our church body, our homes, our families and our own temple, ourselves? Jesus is conveying the centrality of Christian life as that of a prayer life. He sees prayer as the perfume and power. Jesus also sees that when prayer is neglected it creates a vacuum in which non-spiritual, ungodly and worldly activities will enter in. No doubt this is a strategy of the enemy Satan. We see this very thing take place prior to this verse, where people were being taken advantage of in the name of God. Jesus reacted by aggressively turning over the tables of the "money changers" and driving them out. This is the attitude we must have toward anything that takes the place of, or interferes with, prayer. We must drive it out.

• • •

THE LESSON here, is that "your house" should be a house of prayer. The driving force behind church gatherings, our homes, our families and our own lives should be that of prayer. So much so that your life would be labeled "a prayer." If need be, drive out anything that interferes. Let prayer be your passion, your delight and your joy. Let it be your default to every problem and every circumstance. In good times and bad times, let it be your first response. Let prayer be the label over all you do. Let your house be a house of prayer.

STAND STILL

EXODUS 14:13-14

> *"And Moses said to the people, 'Do not be afraid. Stand still, and see the salvation of the Lord, which He will accomplish for you today. For the Egyptians whom you see today, you shall see again no more forever. The Lord will fight for you, and you shall hold your peace.'"*

"Just stand still" was Moses' plan, when the Egyptian Army surrounded the Israelites. Have you ever had a plan like that? When surrounded by trouble on all sides, with nowhere to turn. What a plan! Seems too easy, maybe even irresponsible. Seems like we need to take the bull by the horns or make an opening where there is none.

Now, that doesn't mean that we don't take action. It means that we know Who gives the victory. It means we are trusting God and not ourselves. It means we are looking to Him for deliverance. It means we lean on Him for strength. It means we trust Him to bring about the victory.

When we allow God to be God in our battles, we don't have to be afraid because with God all things to work together for good. We don't have to be afraid because, "if God be for us who can be against us?" We don't have to be afraid because good always overcome evil. We don't have to be afraid because God has a plan.

When we stand still, we watch God work. We experience the thrill of seeing God do the impossible. We see the thrill of God working out what we cannot, the thrill of victory and overcoming power. This is part of the romance of being a Christian, watching God work.

When we "stand still," God will fight for us. He is undefeated and has no comparison. He is battle ready and battle tested. He is proven and unshaken. He is a warrior and wants to fight our battles. No weapon that comes against Him will prevail.

When we "stand still," we can be calm knowing God will act on our behalf. We can either keep fighting ourselves or say, "Lord, I am not going to take matters into my own hands but I am going to surrender control over to You."

· · ·

THE LESSON here is to see that, in the end it's not much of a choice but to "stand still, stay calm, don't be afraid," because The Lord Himself will fight for you."

THE WOOD

EXODUS 15:25

> *"So he cried out to the Lord, and the Lord showed him a tree. When he cast it into the waters, the waters were made sweet."*

With the children of Israel were thirsty and in need of water, God led them to a place called Marah, or bitter. The water was too bitter to drink so they complained against Moses. Moses then cries out to the Lord and the Lord tells him what to do to get water. All along God was going to give them water, but He also lets them experience what it's like without it.

In our lives, God will also let us experience pain, suffering and hardship, even though He is going to take care of us. In our reading, God didn't just give them water the moment right before they felt thirsty, but He really let them get thirsty. It's interesting that God does this. He will take care of us but will also let us taste that in which He will rescue us from. We are not promised exemption from pain, but provision in the pain.

What does God teach us before coming to rescue us? He teaches us to trust Him, to depend on Him and to always put the wood in. Just like He told Moses to do here. God showed Moses the wood and told him to throw it in the water, which made the water good. Just like Jesus, when He died on a wooden cross, when everything looked so wrong, He was making everything perfectly right. The wood makes the bitter in life, sweet. The wood makes everything good. The wood is where we become God's children and His responsibility. The wood is where Jesus showed how much He cares for us and loves us. The wood is the place of reconciliation and forgiveness.

· · ·

THE LESSON here, is that no matter how bitter life is, Jesus makes it sweet. Remember the wood, the wood that Jesus hung upon; and as you do, remember Jesus already died in place of you, He has already given you life, forgiveness, grace and mercy. If you've blown it you are covered. As you apply the wood you now have everything needed in Jesus. He is the adequacy for the inadequate, He is the strength for the weak, He is the life for the dead, He is the light for darkness, and He is the bread for the hungry. He makes the bitter, sweet. Just don't leave out the wood

FEBRUARY 3

Exodus 17:8 19:15, Matthew 22:34 23:12,
Psalm 27:7 14, Proverbs 6:27 35

HUMILITY AND PRIDE

MATTHEW 23:12

> *"And whoever exalts himself will be humbled, and he who humbles himself will be exalted."*

Jesus, speaking to the arrogant religious set, hits at what keeps them from true religion, which is a relationship with God. Like Satan himself, the beautiful angel who fell from heaven because of pride, these religious leaders didn't even know God was standing right in front them because of their pride.

Pride blinds us to spiritual realities. The Pharisees spent their whole lives in religious activities and yet, they knew more about rules and rituals then about the living God. Their self righteous attainments gave them a sense of superiority over the very ones they should have been leading to God. Instead, they kept people from God and even drove them away. Pride is a killer and will destroy. Pride says we are good enough on our own. Pride says we don't need forgiveness and we don't need help. Pride says we don't need God. When we are full of ourselves we can't be filled with God.

Humility however, is the place of restoration. It is when we discover that our need is far beyond our ability to meet it. It is where we ask for God's help instead of demanding He acquiesce to our demands. It's when we say His way is better than our way. It's when we know we are weak and He is strong. It's when we know we are nothing without Him. It's when we ask for mercy rather than showing our goodness. Humility is where God comes to the rescue and where a true relationship with Him begins.

· · ·

THE LESSON here is to know that you are in all desperate need of God's help. He will do what you can't. He will save, forgive, and redeem you. Humility is the place of the strong. Humility is the place of the exalted.

Exodus 19:16 21:21, Matthew 23:13 39,
Psalm 28:1 9, Proverbs 7:1 5

SATISFACTION

EXODUS 20:17

"You shall not covet."

Coveting is wanting what you don't have. This particular sin is often the root of many other sins. This sin is an attack on our vulnerability to not be satisfied. The Bible tells us that our flesh is never satisfied. So you see, we have quite the problem. An unsatisfied soul will crave for satisfaction and if not met with God then our restless hearts will look elsewhere.

Our vulnerability lies in the fact that we need satisfaction but think we can find it in unsatisfying things. A person or thing will never satisfy our souls. Sure, there may be short term temporary satisfaction, but that is all it is. We will soon look for the next experience, the next thrill, the next buzz, the next achievement, the next rush or the next new thing. Whatever it is, our souls will still long for satisfaction.

Our souls cannot be quieted with the material but only with the spiritual. Satan will come along and tempt us by bringing all sorts of appealing things into our lives and tell us that we will be happier and better off having it. Advertising uses this same technique to get us to feel like we need something that we never knew we did before. Anyone who has bought something impulsively knows that the feeling of satisfaction is short lived and the need for the next thing comes again to the unsatisfied soul.

. . .

THE LESSON here is that only God can truly satisfy. When He is your Shepherd you shall not want. He is the satisfaction of the soul. He is the everlasting well. He is the overflowing cup. He is the answer to an unsatisfied heart. When tempted remember that what you are really craving is Jesus and He will satisfy your deepest longings. He is your need. When you have Him you will be in need of nothing. In Him you have everything you need that pertains to life and Godliness. Remember that Jesus came to give you life, and that more abundantly. God withholds nothing from you that is good. Jesus satisfies.

DECEPTION AND TRUTH

//

MATTHEW 24:11

"Then many false prophets will rise up and deceive many."

Speaking to His disciples about the "last days" Jesus tells them that the last days will be characterized by deception. The word "deception" literally means to "wander or stray from the truth." The word speaks of trickery, seduction and error.

These deceptions will be carried out by "false prophets", who are religious phonies that speak false things disguised as truth, and sadly many will fall for it. In 2 Thessalonians 2:9, we read that the Anti-Christ will be in the world doing Satan's work through power, signs and lying wonders. That means there will be supernatural empowerment involved in the deception.

With such an aggressive agenda to deceive, it will be impossible for one to avoid the lies of Satan. We see great deception even now in our world and much of it comes in the name of so-called "good." Religious deception is at the core of the deceit and much attention will be given to "unity, tolerance and progressive or relative truth."

Knowing this, as Jesus has told us in advance, what can we do? It all has to do with the truth, and that truth is revealed in the Bible. 2 Thessalonians 2:10 says, "they did not receive the love of the truth," and that is why people will be deceived. The truth, then, is what sets us free and God's Word will keep us safely insulated from falsehood, lies and deceit. J. C. Ryle said, "the best safeguard against false doctrine is the Bible, regularly read, regularly prayed over, and regularly studied."

· · ·

THE LESSON here, is to make sure you are basing your life on the truth revealed in God's Word. Truth must be what you love, what you cherish, what you contend for and what you honor. Truth is what builds faith, brings freedom, and is the source of light. Truth is from God and God cannot lie. Rid yourself of falsehood, philosophies of the world, teachings of men not founded in the Bible. Measure everything against the Word of God and let it dictate your reality. Don't let feelings, or what you may think is right, be your truth for we are easily deceived. In the end, opinions really don't matter because they will come and go, but the truth will stand forever.

FEBRUARY 6

Exodus 23:14 25:40, Matthew 24:29 51,
Psalm 30:1 12, Proverbs 7:24 27

TURNING SORROW TO JOY

///

PSALM 30:5b

"Weeping may endure for a night, But joy comes in the morning."

Sorrow is an inevitable part of life. Just as "every rose has its thorn," so every life has it's sorrow. As humans, we are made to feel emotions and no matter how much we try to avoid it, we will sorrow. The good news is, for a Christian, sorrow does have a purpose and is beneficial when seen in the proper light and dealt with by faith. From our text we can learn four great lessons about sorrow.

First of all, sorrow heightens our experience of joy. Like a mountain climber scaling the largest mountain, the summit is made all the more sweet in the end. Great sorrow brings about great joy in the end. God knows this and will allow us to taste the bitter flavor of sorrow in order to satisfy us the sweetness of joy.

Secondly, we see here in the text that there is an end to sorrow. That it is not a permanent condition but a passageway to joy. As the saying goes, " this to shall pass;" so sorrow will pass as well. It is a temporary state that has a definite end. No matter how bad it may seem, it is only for a night and is leading to something better. You may not know when or how or even if it will be on this side of eternity, but it will definitely be worth it in the end.

Thirdly, sorrow is always shorter than joy. It may be that you are in the nighttime of weeping but that beautiful light of day is coming and will shine so brightly that your sorrow will seem faint in comparison. Sorrow is for a moment but joy is forever. As dark as your night is, the sun will shine the darkness away. Instead of counting the moments of your weeping, count it a privilege to suffer as Christ did. Soon your weeping will turn to rejoicing.

Finally, sorrow is followed by joy. As it is said about Jesus regarding the cross, "for the joy set before Him, He endured the cross." The Christian always has this assurance. He knows that good will come, that joy is the next stop. The Christian knows that no matter how bad it seems, he will not be overcome. He knows there is always hope and that God is always purposely in control bringing about His perfect good through our lives.

· · ·

THE LESSON here is knowing that now you may be weeping, but joy is coming. He will turn your mourning into dancing. He will lift your sorrow.

FAITHFUL SERVANTS

MATTHEW 25:20-21

> *"So he who had received five talents came and brought five other talents, saying, 'Lord, you delivered to me five talents; look, I have gained five more talents besides them.' His lord said to him, 'Well done, good and faithful servant; you were faithful over a few things, I will make you ruler over many things. Enter into the joy of your lord.'"*

God does not demand from us that which He hasn't put in us. He does not expect us to be "producers" of His kingdom fruit as those who have to manufacture something that is not there. God is gracious and kind, giving us that in which we are to simply use in order to bring forth spiritual productivity.

In our text we see a parable about God's kingdom, or His realm of operation. First of all, He gave "five talents" to one servant, "two talents" to another servant and "one talent" to another. A talent can be seen as a resource. God gives different amounts of resources to each of us and it is up to Him how much He gives. He does so according to His plan and it's not really our concern or issue what we are given. That is completely God's department.

What is important is "faithfulness." This is what we have the ability to control. This is "our part" or "our department." In other words, God gives and we use.

For the Christian, we know that all our faithfulness is rewarded. Whatever we do for the Lord out of our response to what we have is seen, blessed and reciprocated by God Himself. God will never be "out-given" or "outdone." He will never be a "debtor" to man. He is generous and will give more as we are faithful to what we have. This is one of the great secrets of the Kingdom of God, "give, and it shall be given unto you."

• • •

THE LESSON here is to keep you focus on being faithful and let God add the increase. . Take advantage of how you are made, what He has laid on your heart, where you spend your time, what people He has put in your life and what abilities you have. Even with your shortcomings, disabilities, failures and heartbreaks, can be used by God for His glory. Use everything to bless, to share, to bring people to Jesus. Don't worry about what others are doing unless you are celebrating with them, but rather, concern yourself with what is in front of you, and what you have, and simply be faithful and God will take care of the rest.

Exodus 28:1 43, Matthew 25:31 26:13,
Psalm 31:9 18, Proverbs 8:12 13

THE LEAST

///

MATTHEW 25:40

> *"And the King will answer and say to them, 'Assuredly, I say to you, inasmuch as you did it to one of the least of these My brethren, you did it to Me.'"*

Our relationship with the Lord should be seen in how we treat our fellow man. In other words, our vertical relationship should impact our horizontal relationships. That is, by the way, how the cross is formed, with a vertical beam connected to a horizontal beam. It is also what Jesus said in Matthew 22:37-40 that in essence, all the commandments are summed up by loving God (vertical) and loving others (horizontal). No doubt, it is our new relationship with Christ that comes by His work of atonement on the cross that enables us to do so.

In our text, Jesus is speaking about the true and false believers, and how they will be separated when He comes back at the end of the tribulation. The sheep, or true believers, will enter into the millennial kingdom and the goats, false or non-believers, will enter everlasting torment. The distinguishing characteristic will be how they treat others, especially the Jews, who will be hated and hunted down during the tribulation.

Now Jesus is not teaching that we can go to heaven by caring well for others, but that our care for others demonstrates our true relationship with God. Especially how we treat the Jews who are generally hated by the world, but should be loved by those who know God. So, a person's relationship with God will be revealed by their care, compassion and love for others; especially, but not limited to, the Jews.

We all struggle in this area but we all should see our hearts changing toward others as we grow in our relationship with Christ. We will see behind what others may present. We will see the need, the hurt and the cries for help beyond the face or beyond the words. We will see the soul and the need for a Savior. Especially in those who need it most, who the world sees as "the least." Those who can't help themselves, those who others have no time for, or those who aren't valued by their society or culture.

· · ·

THE LESSON here, is to be mindful of those around you and who need help. They are God's children and He loves them very much. He wants to help them, to love them and to bless them with His love. He wants them to know they are important and valued. He places them all around us, maybe as tests to see our willingness to love like He does. They may even be angels in disguise. Jesus gave His life for them, the question is, will we? "As you did it to the least of these My brethren, you did it to me." Go love people like Jesus did.

Exodus 29:1 30:10, Matthew 26:14 46,
Psalm 31:19 24, Proverbs 8:14 26

OUR SOUL

MATTHEW 26:15-16

> *"'What are you willing to give me if I deliver Him to you?' And they count-ed out to him thirty pieces of silver. So from that time he sought opportu-nity to betray Him."*

This statement is made by Judas Iscariot when he went to the Chief Priest to betray Jesus. This, after being with Jesus, watching Him perform miracles, lis-tening to His authoritative supernatural teaching and experiencing His love and kindness. Judas was a greatly privileged man to have this incredible experience with God Himself, and yet, it wasn't enough to save His soul. Judas shows us that it is not enough to be "around" Jesus, or to merely know "about" Him. It's not enough that others think you are on His side and that you even serve Him. Judas did all that and yet, was not saved.

The end did not turn out well for Judas. Immediately after betraying Jesus he died by hanging himself. Later, his body fell headfirst to the ground and his bowels came out. What was missing from Judas' life was that he never put his trust in Jesus as His Lord and Savior. There is a big difference between belief and trust. There is a big difference between doing spiritual activities and religious ex-ercises than actually trusting Jesus for salvation. The Bible tells us even demons believe. What they don't do is trust. That is the question we must ask ourselves, have we put our trust in Christ alone for the forgiveness of sins and am I trusting Him in my life today to be my light and my life?

What it came down to with Judas was that he desired the world over God. If we live for the world our hopes end here. If we live for Christ our hope is endless. God's hope is eternal and His promises are true. As the missionary Jim Elliot once said, "a man is not a fool who gives up what he can't keep, to gain what he can't lose." In Christ our hope is in heaven and our future is eternally glorious. For the Christian, the world is the worst it will ever get, but for the unbeliever, the world is the best it will ever be.

Finally, Judas was willing to sell Jesus out for 30 pieces of silver. He gave up eter-nity for that in which he never even used. He was like many who give up their eternity for that which won't last. I hope and pray you have not betrayed Jesus at the expense of your soul.

. . .

THE LESSON here is knowing that there is nothing more valuable than your own soul. Before making deals with it, make sure your soul belongs to Jesus. Then you will have the best deal that exists; redemption, forgiveness of your sins, eternity in heaven and peace with God. Give your soul to Jesus and you will have made the best decision one could ever make.

Exodus 30:11 31:18, Matthew 26:47 68,
Psalm 32:1 11, Proverbs 8:27 32

BETRAYAL

MATTHEW 26:48-50

> *"Now His betrayer had given them a sign, saying, 'Whomever I kiss, He is the One; seize Him.' Immediately he went up to Jesus and said, 'Greetings, Rabbi!' and kissed Him. But Jesus said to him, 'Friend, why have you come?'"*

This interaction between Jesus and Judas is very interesting. This is the moment of betrayal, which can be one of the most difficult pains to deal with. Betrayal is hard because it is a hurt from one you have trusted and is often unexpected. Betrayal can make one cynical toward the world and bring about "trust issues." Betrayal can leave the betrayed with unanswered questions and continuous insult to injury because there is often no resolution or repentance. It is a wound that can be opened up time and time again and is often dealt with by asking "why?" However, betrayal is not too big for God to heal.

In our text we see the heartless Judas actually betraying Jesus with a kiss. That is often how betrayal works. The one who betrays us is also pretending to care about us. Judas approaches Jesus and says, "Greetings, Rabbi" with enthusiasm and then his very kiss is the sign to take Jesus away.

Jesus shows us how we can deal with betrayal. He sees the whole plot in a bigger light. He sees it through the eyes of "sovereignty" or through the working out of God's plan. He doesn't see Himself as a victim of circumstances but as a selected member of God's grace and loving plan. He doesn't hate Judas, knowing that even the betrayal will work out for good and that no man can alter God's plan in our lives. He sees that his betrayal is not the end but is the unfolding of God's plan. He deals with the apparent injustice and unfairness by knowing God has allowed it. He sees Satan as the real enemy behind the scenes manipulating situations, but in reality Satan is actually falling into God's plan. This is how we must see betrayal.

. . .

THE LESSON, here that betrayal is not final because God is faithful. You have been selected to suffer in a certain way because God wants to bless you in a magnificent way. Remember that Jesus Himself was betrayed, and He understands exactly what you are going through. The way to overcome is to trust God, don't lean on your own understanding, turn to Him for healing and know that all will turn out for good. No need to be cynical, no need to have trust issues because when we trust in the Lord we are safe and free. In the end, God has bigger and better things ahead.

PARADISE IN GOD'S PRESENCE

EXODUS 33:14

"And He said, 'My Presence will go with you, and I will give you rest.'"

God's presence, and our conscious awareness of it, is the ideal condition of Mankind. It is paradise on earth. No person place or thing will bring us perfect peace like Jesus will. Maybe you are feeling weak, run down and tired like you are running in fumes. If you are, run to Jesus.

God's presence means that we are first of all at peace "with" God by the extermination of our sin through the sacrifice of Christ. Our faith in Him is what makes his sacrifice our own. We are now no longer enemies of God but friends with God. Jesus taking our place in judgment has satisfied his wrath. His presence now enters us. What a relief that is.

Secondly, we have the peace "of" God as we walk in fellowship with Him. This means that God is working in our lives, with a plan and a direction. Our cooperation with that plan and walking in the same direction as Him, brings about a unity of our will with God's will. This will require some sacrifice and surrender as our wills are often in conflict with God's will. When we insist on "having it our way," we will experience some friction in our fellowship with God. The answer is always obedience to His will and not our own. God will bless our obedience and we will experience His presence as a result.

. . .

THE LESSON here, is to make God's presence your highest priority. This is what makes life glorious no matter what your state or condition. It's not a place, an achievement, a condition of life or a certain state of being, but it is God's presence as we walk in His perfect will. This is paradise on earth and where you will find our rest. There is no utopia, paradise or Nirvana on earth, but there is God's presence, which is better by far.

FEBRUARY 12

Exodus 34:1 35:9, Matthew 27:15 31,
Psalm 33:12 22, Proverbs 9:1 6

CHOICES

///

MATTHEW 27:22

> *"Pilate said to them, 'What then shall I do with Jesus who is called Christ?' They all said to him, 'Let Him be crucified!'"*

Pilate was put in a position where he had to make a choice. This choice was thrust upon him as the blood-thirsty crowd wanted Jesus killed. Pilate knew Jesus was innocent and even his wife told him to avoid any wrongdoing on behalf of Jesus. On the one hand was the crowd, the repercussions from them and the threat to his position of power. On the other hand was his conscience, doing what was right and being on God's side.

There is no greater torment than the torment of violating one's own conscience. No temporary gain is worth the irritation to our soul that comes from doing what we know not to do. As hard as it may be to choose Jesus in making our choices, the pain of choosing against Him is far worse and with great consequences. To choose Jesus in all our choices takes faith, faith that Jesus is the Way, the Truth, and the life.

All decisions come down to, "what then shall I do with Jesus." When choosing a spouse, how will Jesus fit in to the marriage? When choosing a career path, a sin decision, a compromise, a grey area, our entertainment, how we use our time, etc., ask what role Jesus plays in the choice and how He will be involved if you make it. Ask if you will have to compromise your relationship with Him, if you will have to leave Him out or if He is fully embraced in it. Will you deny Him in your decisions or embrace Him? Making decisions based on "what's best for me" will always lead to making the wrong choice. No matter how hard it may be to make the right decision, we will never regret choosing Jesus, His will, His plan and His way. No matter how it ends up we will have a clear conscience, and there is no amount of pleasure that's worth the peace of a clear conscience, and if we have chosen poorly, we can repent and have our conscience restored to peace by confessing our sins to Jesus and asking for forgiveness.

. . .

THE LESSON here is that decisions become very simple when we choose Jesus. Looking at Him and His life and ministry on earth shows us that God's will is better than our will. All your decisions boil down to saying, "what then shall I do with Christ." Choose Christ and His way and you will always choose right.

FORSAKEN

MATTHEW 27:46

> *"And about the ninth hour Jesus cried out with a loud voice, saying, 'Eli, Eli, lama sabachthani?' that is, 'My God, My God, why have You forsaken Me?'"*

The darkest moment of all eternity is recorded right here when Jesus says "My God, My God, why have you forsaken me?" At this moment, God the Father turned away from God the Son and forsook Him. The first and second member of the Trinity, apart from each other, so we could be joined in. This was the moment when our sins were placed on Jesus, to the point to where He actually became sin. This was the moment where death, humiliation, pain, misery, darkness and wrath which were all ours became His. This was the moment the Father had to turn because He could have no part of sin. This was the moment that Jesus' darkest day became our brightest. More than the physical pain, it was the pain of separation that Jesus agonized over in the garden where His sweat turned to blood. His separation was our separation that He bore and tells us how amazing our connection with God is and how much God the Father and God the Son loves us, cares for us and is committed to us. God the Son was willing to be forsaken and God the Father was pleased to forsake, all on account of us. The only way we could unite with God, would be that God would take our place and be forsaken.

$$\cdot \ \cdot \ \cdot$$

THE LESSON from this unfathomable dark day is that God loves you deeper than you could ever know. You never have to doubt or question His love. God proved His love for you and put the cross in the place of the question mark. The cross answers the question once and for all that asks, "Does God really love me?" The cross says yes and the darkest moment of the cross says, "I'll go all the way for you."

> *There is now no more separation,*
> *No more condemnation,*
> *Brought into the vine*
> *Sharing the divine*
> *Jesus was forsaken so we could be taken,*
> *Together forever, Jesus and me, one for eternity.*

FEBRUARY 14

Exodus 37:1 38:31, Matthew 28:1 20,
Psalm 34:11 22, Proverbs 9:9 10

GO

//

MATTHEW 28:19

> *"Go therefore and make disciples of all the nations, baptizing them in the name of the Father and of the Son and of the Holy Spirit, teaching them to observe all things that I have commanded you; and lo, I am with you always, even to the end of the age. Amen."*

The resurrected Jesus gives instructions to His disciples in light of Jesus having all authority given to Him in heaven and earth. The basis for His instructions come from His position of authority, His power of resurrection and His purpose of making disciples. Within His instructions is the bestowal of His enabling, for when God directs He also enables.

The nearness of Jesus to His disciples, both physically and spiritually, makes the command even more impacting for they saw Jesus alive, watched Him perform miracles, heard Him preach truth, witnessed His death and now are speaking to Him alive again. They would be encouraged by Jesus, as He spoke to them, commanding them to do what He Himself did. The newly resurrected Jesus would now work through them, as well as us, with the same resurrection power to make disciples.

The command was to "go." That the reality of the risen Christ would not only be realized in them but also through them. That just as Jesus died and rose again for them, He also died and rose again for others. This truth wasn't meant to be quarantined like a virus, but spread like a cure. This is what the gospel is, the cure for all men infected with sin. The one and only cure that was now entrusted to the disciples and all believers everywhere. This was what their life's all consuming passion was to be, as it is with us.

The best part about it all is that Jesus said He would be with us. Whenever a great command would be given in the Old Testament to the Children of Israel, God would say He would be with them. No mountain too high, no enemy too great, no obstacle too difficult because God is with us.

· · ·

THE LESSON here is to go! Go in power, authority, strength and confidence because God is with you. Make it your aim to make disciples and invest in others. Christ will be with you and your life will mean something for all eternity. Go and bless, go and be blessed, for God is with you. If God be for you nothing can stop you. Just Go!

TESTING

MARK 1:12

"Immediately the Spirit drove Him into the wilderness."

The public ministry of Jesus began after His testing. Interesting to see that testing came before ministry. I have found this very thing to be true. That God uses a vessel that has been forged by fire in order to withstand the pressures it will encounter in the battles. Jesus was sent to the training grounds of a spiritual soldier to prepare for those battles.

The text explains that it was the Spirit that drove Jesus to the place of testing. This was all part of God's plan and not a random event without purpose and promise. Testing, then, is part of God's plan and necessary in order to bring about the spiritual qualities required for the soldier. This suggests that testing is the way of strength, and that strength is developed through testing. This means that if we want to be used and fruitful, strong and faithful, we must go through the testing. If Jesus did, then we will as well.

· · ·

THE LESSON here, is that God is deeply invested in "the vessel," which is you. He will allow testing and you can be encouraged to know that He will test you because it's needed and He cares about you. He wants to bring about the very best in you. When you are in a place of a testing, know God is building your life to the highest potential that you are capable of. If you desire to be used greatly, expect to be tested severely. Great tests produce great soldiers, equipped for the Masters use. Don't run away from Jesus, but run to Him. He's been there before Himself, and will see you through to the finish line.

FEBRUARY 16

Leviticus 1:1 3:17, Mark 1:29 2:12,
Psalm 35:17 28, Proverbs 9:13 18

FORGIVEN

MARK 2:7B

"Who can forgive sins but God alone?"

The nature of sin is such that it is beyond human capacity to deal with. The religious leaders (scribes) pointed this out in regards to what Jesus was saying and doing. He was claiming the He could forgive sin and then He performed miracles demonstrating that He has the power to do so. The Scribes, not believing Jesus was God, claimed Jesus was blaspheming. They would be correct if Jesus was not God, but Jesus proved that He was.

Sin is the one single problem that keeps man from God. Sin and sin alone. Once one understands that one sin, in thought or action, is enough to keep one from Heaven and the presence of God, we must then ask ourselves what can be done about our sin. Most people think they can try and be good enough. However, like a clean dog and a dirty dog, they are still dogs. We are still sinners no matter how good and how nice we are. So if all have sinned and all can do nothing to eradicate that sin and sin keeps us from heaven, then what can be done?

The answer lies beyond us and can only be found in God Himself. We need not to be good to go the heaven, we need to be forgiven. This is what Jesus is saying He can do. He can forgive because He is not infected with sin. One prisoner cannot tell another prisoner he is free to go. Someone who is not a prisoner and that has authority can exonerate a prisoner. Jesus is saying that He is the judge and He has the authority.

However, a judge also has to be fair. He couldn't just let prisoners out who have committed crimes. We would be upset because of our sense of justice. It wouldn't seem right. This is where grace and justice collide. How can there be both? This is the message of the gospel.

At the cross, the Judge who had committed no crime paid the penalty for the criminals that did. All mankind are the guilty and Jesus, the righteous judge, took our place in judgment. At the cross, the Perfect paid the price for the imperfect. Sinless Jesus paid the debt of sinful man. Justice was served as Jesus took the penalty and grace was given. He extends forgiveness to those who receive by faith. Grace then is forgiveness extended to the guilty who don't deserve to be forgiven. Grace then, from our standpoint is not fair, if it was it wouldn't be grace. Grace is getting what we don't deserve. Grace is free but cost Jesus everything.

. . .

THE LESSON here is that God alone can forgive sins. He waits with open arms to receive the sinner who asks for forgiveness. Don't let anything stop you from God's forgiveness and receive His free offer.

No more condemnation,
No more guilt,
Sin was taken and Jesus brought hope.
Forgiven at last by the Judge who stepped down,
Taking our place in judgment and securing our crown.

ALL YOU WANT

PSALM 36:8

> "They are abundantly satisfied with the fullness of Your house, and You give them drink from the river of Your pleasures."

God is not negative and restrictive, offering a lower quality of life, inferior to a life of sinful indulgence. This is the lie Satan wants people to believe. The depiction of the angel on one side and the devil on the other giving instructions, with the angel saying no and the devil saying yes, does not paint an accurate picture.

The devil wants us to indulge our sinful nature in order to hurt us. He tempts with a life of indulgence and pleasure, in a way that says, "this is living" or "this is the life" merely as attractive bait to hook us into his harmful lifestyle. This is a life of pain and destruction, not the other way around. Think about how a life would look if one did whatever they felt like doing and acted upon every thought that came to mind. It's not hard to imagine how that would end up.

God, however, is positive, open and welcoming. He offers abundance, satisfaction and fullness without repercussion. The difference is, God offers that of the spiritual realm where true satisfaction and life is found. He says drink of the rivers of pleasures that are found in Him. Come, receive, fill up, drink and enjoy to the fullest. It is God who gives and is generously bestowing all that we truly crave and desire.

. . .

THE LESSON here is that only God can truly satisfy. All else is an artificial replacement that never really satisfies. When we are in The Lord and living for His will, it's all green lights, it's all go, it's all yes and yes and amen. Stay on God's track and there are no brakes but only a gas pedal. So go for God, take all of Him you want and He will satisfy to the full. Dive into His River of life, soak it up and drink it in. Have a full and overflowing cup of His grace and mercy. He invites you in to His banquet table, which is all you can eat. God is more than enough let Him show you.

DELIGHT IN THE LORD

PSALM 37:4

"Delight yourself also in the LORD, and He shall give you the desires of your heart."

Our hearts have big desires. They crave for things and want things. To desire is to be human and alive. However, not all our desires are good. Many of our desires are evil and harmful. This verse then sets the condition for our desires. We see that God grants our desires based on our delighting in Him.

When we delight in Him, we are worshipfully enjoying His presence and acknowledging His goodness. We are basking in the glory of His Holiness. We are praising His control over life events and are surrendered to His love and faithfulness. We are so caught up in Him that we lose ourselves. This is when our desires are His desires. This is when God's greatness overwhelms our selfish and self-serving wants and we can say, "all I want is what You want Lord." This is where our will comes into alignment with His will. Our false cravings and desires absorb into God's highest cravings and desires when we put Him first. It's this place of selfless ecstasy and endless delight that we find God's higher purpose.

This delighting is a prerequisite for God's giving the desires of our hearts.

• • •

THE LESSON here is that when you delight in Him, everything else takes care of itself. It doesn't work any other way. God is not a servant to our sinful, selfish, self-serving and ultimately harmful desires. When you delight in Him, He will change your heart and you will want what He wants. Our desires will be bigger than ever because you will desire greater things than your own hearts and minds think of. You will be astonished at how much bigger God's plan for your life is than our own. you will not only want the biggest and best of all things but God also promises to give them to you. Your new desires will erupt like a volcano from our delighting souls. Make the Lord your delight and He will delight in giving you the desires of your heart.

BE YOU

//

PSALM 37:23

> *"The steps of a good man are ordered by the LORD, and He delights in his way."*

When life seems out of control this verse speaks us back to reality. Life for the Christian is never out of control. It may seem like it because we are looking at our own ability to control things. We may have pictured what "normal" is and our life may not fit that mold. We may think about what we want and how having what we want will fulfill our desires. God, however, is the divine orchestrator of our lives. He Who makes sure the earth is tilted just so perfectly, Who orders the sun to rise and set, Who orders the seasons, sets the stars and actively runs the universe down to the building blocks of molecules. This God is in control of our lives, ordering, or directing our steps.

As He directs we can rest knowing that our lives are not wasted but useful. We may not always see it and feel it, but God is delighting in us and in control of the events of our lives. He loves our lives and the events of it because He is directing. In His efficient and effective way, He is working everything together for good. We are not random beings, victims of circumstance but divinely created beings made perfectly in every way to fulfill our calling and purpose on earth. We look the way we do, talk the way we do, have the personalities we do, think the way we do and are wired the way we are for His perfect purpose. He gives and He takes away, blessed be the Lord.

· · ·

THE LESSON here is that you are perfectly you. Only you can be who you were made to be. When you try and be something other than yourself, you give up the perfection of which you were created. Better to be fully you, thankful for all you are and for every special way you have been designed. Be thankful for the events of your life, good and bad, because God is working out the perfection of His perfect plan in you. Embrace who you are, be you, and then you will be the best in the whole world at something, that is at being you. Nobody else can be you and fulfill the plan God has laid out specifically for you. God delights in you just the way you are. You are a magnificent creation. Be true to you, nothing more nothing less, God knows what He is doing, and has made you the best at being you.

WAITING

PSALM 37:34

> *"Wait on the LORD,*
> *And keep His way,*
> *And He shall exalt you to inherit the land;"*

Patience is not a favorite word of most. Patience is an affront to our desire for instant gratification. The flesh says now and yet the spirit is content when. This conflict is resolved by the way we wait. Biblical waiting is not like standing in line at the grocery store doing nothing while life stays on hold until we complete the mission. Biblical waiting is active and is the mission. It's not the end that is the goal it is the process of what God is doing at the moment that is the goal. Biblical waiting is continuous activity of God developing His plan in which the whole process is the goal.

Here in our text we see that waiting is accompanied by keeping His way. This means that we keep going in God's direction knowing that we are heading some-where and we don't take matters into our own hands or force the issue. Inactive waiting leads to fleshly uprisings. Active waiting enjoys the present experience with God and knows God is taking us somewhere. When all we care about is the end result, we will be tempted to go our way instead of keeping to God's way.

• • •

THE LESSON here is knowing that God is in the process of exalting you. This is His way. Deviating from His way is deviating from exalting. He is also giving you land, or in other words, He is giving you more of what has already been given to you yet through you active waiting, He is preparing and developing you to be able to take the territory. Take heart, enjoy God in the process of waiting and know God's best work takes time. In the end you will find that the greatest reward is always Himself and not what He will do. He Himself is alway your ex-ceedingly great reward, whether you are waiting, reaping or sowing. Find Him and you have found your reward. He is always worth the waiting.

TOUCHING JESUS

MARK 5:28

"For she said, 'If only I may touch His clothes, I shall be made well.'"

A desperate woman in a desperate situation came to Jesus wanting to touch Him. Exhausting all her material resources and still ailing from a physical ailment that caused unmitigated bleeding, probably a gynecological issue, she had no where else to turn but to the only one who could help.

What came out of her desperation was a desire to touch Jesus. Whatever condition we may be in, touching Jesus is always the answer. God may put us in positions to bring about the greatest desire of all. Whatever it takes, pray for an all consuming desire to touch Jesus for in this desire we find all we ever want.

Touching Jesus then comes first from a desire to do so. We have to want to. We have to be willing to be inconvenienced, willing to break from the norm, willing to put aside the busyness, willing to part with those menacing distractions and mindless preoccupations with things that really don't matter. Then it takes faith to come to Him, believing He is the answer and fulfillment of all our needs and desires. Finally it takes humility to say I can't do it myself and I need help.

. . .

THE LESSON here is to know that the result of touching Jesus is wellness. You are never well until you are "in touch" or connected with Him. It means to be made whole by the Great Physician of our souls. It means to be rightly oriented with the source of life. It means you are rightly aligned with the Lover of our Soul and Completer of your life. Touching Jesus is to be made well and you will never be well until you do.

BECOMING TOO FAMILIAR

MARK 6:4-6

> *"But Jesus said to them, 'A prophet is not without honor except in his own country, among his own relatives, and in his own house.' Now He could do no mighty work there, except that He laid His hands on a few sick people and healed them. And He marveled because of their unbelief."*

Jesus taught in the synagogue of His hometown, no doubt to reach those most familiar with Him. They were astonished at His teaching at first, wondering where He got such truth, wisdom, power and authority. However, their astonishment turned into being offended once they found out who was teaching them. Familiarity breeds contempt as they say. The crowds were simply too familiar with Jesus to take Him seriously. They had seen Him grow up and was one of them. They knew not that He was also the Creator and Sustainer of the world. As powerful as His teaching was, they couldn't get past who He was. They were too familiar with Jesus to believe.

Jesus could not do a mighty work there. This shows how even the greatest Pastors, the most powerful evangelists and the most dynamic ministries can have little impact without the belief of those hearing and receiving. Even acknowledging the power of the ministry and teaching is not enough without belief. The cause of this type of unbelief is familiarity.

We find an important warning here in that we too can become too familiar with our "church service" or with our "prayer time" or with our Bibles. We can be too familiar with the gospel message and the worship songs to the point of robotic responses that yield no connection with God. This tragic dilemma restricts the mighty working of a God to mechanical superficial ritualistic religion devoid of the life and power of God Himself.

• • •

THE LESSON here is that in all your acts of worship, make it about the One, Jesus Christ Himself. The activity you do is a means to an end, and the end is Jesus. It's not the activity in and of itself that brings the mighty work, but Jesus, through your faith working the supernatural in ordinary natural life. When you get to a place of familiarity, come back to the place of wonder and awe found in the life of the Lord of all. There is nothing common or boring about Him but an unending reservoir of new life, new revelation, wonder and awe.

Leviticus 14:1 57, Mark 6:30 56,
Psalm 40:1 10, Proverbs 10:11 12

COME ASIDE

MARK 6:31

> *"And He said to them, 'Come aside by yourselves to a deserted place and rest a while.' For there were many coming and going, and they did not even have time to eat."*

Life is hectic. We are over stimulated and under rested. We are pushed and pulled to exhaustion. While the world screams at us with unyielding demands, God says rest.

There is a price to pay for overcrowded lives that yield to the screams of the urgent while neglecting the refreshment of our Savior. The price comes at a great expense to our physical, emotional and spiritual well being. We suffer the loss of peace, joy and most importantly our enjoyment of God.

In the midst of a very active time for the disciples, Jesus speaks these all important and tender words, "rest awhile." This rest would require them to, "come aside to a deserted place." There is a good practical lesson here that there are times, probably more often than not, that we must get away to a quite place for a quite time with Jesus

. . .

THE LESSON here is to consider that maybe you need to get away with Jesus. Maybe you are getting burned out and thin on patience. Maybe your relationship with God has suffered and you no longer hear from Him or sense His presence. Maybe you are emotionally tired with nothing more to give. If you are, the answer is right here in Jesus' words. When we find our rest through a quite time with Him we will find that we are much more effective to meet life's challenges and to fulfill our calling with love, joy, strength, peace and Joy.

> *Rest in Jesus,*
> *come aside by yourself,*
> *life is hectic*
> *and will wear you out.*
> *Refreshment will come,*
> *filling up your heart,*
> *we can't do it with out Him,*
> *and it's never too late to start.*

WORSHIP

MARK 7:7

> *"And in vain they worship Me, teaching as doctrines the commandments of men."*

Worshiping God is what a Christian does. It means that we honor and exalt God in whatever we are doing. Jesus said that the way we are to worship is in Spirit and in truth. True worship then comes from the Spirit within us, which will be according to the truth revealed in God's Word. It's easy to mistake church attendance, Christian service and/or singing Christian songs, in and of themselves as worship. It's the heart behind what we do that is worship.

Our scripture tells us that there is false worship. That's what one may think is worship is really not worship at all, at least not true worship. It says that worshiping in any other way but in Spirit and is truth is to worship in vain. In other words, worshiping gods other than the God of the Bible is empty worship. In addition, worship using unbiblical and man-made traditions is meaningless. Specifically, here, Jesus was quoting from Isaiah speaking about those who worship by adding rules and regulations not in the Bible and/or making those rules and regulations more important than the truth in God's Word.

. . .

THE LESSON here, is that your highest privilege as a Christian is your status as a worshiper. Worship is the greatest thing you can do and you do it through your everyday actions and choices that demonstrate God is your King. you honor Him giving Him His due and ascribing Him His worth. you do that simply by the Spirit in truth.

It's not complicated because the Spirit will drive you from within. There may be times set aside to worship, and you may have different ways you worship in those special times, but in the end worship looks like obedience to God's Word in everyday life, bringing about supernatural power of the Holy Spirit, bringing truth to life which glorifies God.

Worship is a lifestyle,
exalting our King.
Giving God honor,
Praise in everything.

Leviticus 16:29 18:30, Mark 7:24 8:10,
Psalm 41:1 13, Proverbs 10:15 16

MINISTRY

MARK 8:8

"So they ate and were filled, and they took up seven large baskets of left-over fragments."

The question the disciples proposed to Jesus was, "how can the multitudes be satisfied in the wilderness?" How can anyone be satisfied in a dry and thirsty land? How can one who is thirsty find water where there is none or food where it's barren. There are Spiritual implications here as the human heart seeks spiritual fulfillment above all else yet cannot find spiritual food or drink in the wilderness of the world.

In answering the disciples question Jesus asks what resources they were able to give. Four thousand needed food and water yet all they had was seven loaves of bread and a few small fishes. However, God was there. Whenever we face insurmountable odds remember that God is there. Whenever we see great need, yet there is great inadequacy to meet the need, remember God is never inadequate, only we are.

The way God met the multitudes need is a great lesson about ministry. He took what they had. The first step in ministry is giving ourselves to God. It's not that we will meet the need with what we have, it's that God wants to meet the need through our surrender. He won't work through us until He has us. When He has us, He works.

Next Jesus broke the bread that was given to Him. In the same way, in order to use us to feed the multitudes in ministry, God will break us. He will break us of our selfish tendencies, of our pride, of our selfish ambition, our conceit and of our self reliance. It is then that Jesus will bless and supernaturally work through us to feed the starving souls who are desperate for spiritual food.

In the end, the people ate and were filled. They even had leftovers.

• • •

THE LESSON here is seeing what ministry actually is and how it works. It is God working through your surrendered vessel, broken and offered to the multitudes. There are starving souls, some outside of The Lord, who have never even eaten of the bread of life, Jesus Christ, and those who have eaten but are so spiritually starved for the lack of spiritual food that they are emaciated spiritually. Ministry is God's work through surrendered, broken vessels meeting the needs of those starving souls. You can do nothing on your own, but everything with God.

PURSUE

PSALM 42:1

"As the deer pants for the water brooks,
So pants my soul for You, O God."

Panting describes a deep desire that comes from a deep need. It describes one who longs for something or craves something deep down. The psalmist is feeling this deep longing that is coming from his soul. He says his soul is panting for God.

His longing is comparable to a thirsty deer who is desperate. This is what is in the heart of all true believers. This is what distinguishes a true believer from one who is not. You see, when we are born again we are new creations in Christ and have a new appetite for God. Our soul cries out "Abba Father" as a crying baby would cry for their mommy or daddy.

· · ·

THE LESSON here is to ask yourself the question, do you long for God, pant for Him and deeply desire Him? Is He your desire? Is He what you want? Maybe not? Or maybe at one time? Maybe there is something quenching your desire. The indulgence in worldly junk food quenching your appetite for God. The interesting thing is, when you pursue God like a deer pants for water, you will have a deeper longing for God and not the world. It's your pursuit that brings hunger and desire. The more you pursue the more you pant. Make Him your life's passion and when you do, you will hunger and be satisfied all at the same time. This is genius of God!!

DEALING WITH DEPRESSION

//

PSALM 43:5

> *"Why are you cast down, O my soul? And why are you disquieted within me? Hope in God; For I shall yet praise Him, The help of my countenance and my God."*

Depression is often the result of hopelessness. It's when we can't see any good coming our way and when we are overtaken by the darkness of the day. Even the Godly can struggle with depression as we see here in the Psalm. What can one do to get out of despair?

The Psalmist works though his "cast down" and "disquieted" soul by broadening his view of things to include God in His pain. Hope is restored when our hope is in an unchanging and everlasting God. We see here, as the Psalmist shifts his focus from himself to God, he finds relief.

Now he sees that which is bigger than what he is going through, instead of being overwhelmed by his own inability to deal with his problems. He sees hope because God not only can help but will help. God is an ever-present help in our time of need. He is always available with His eternally powerful yet caring arms to comfort guide and bring about good in our lives.

Turning to God brings hope that inspires praise. He sees a God that cares and is so thankful that now he is giving God the response of a faith that knows God is in control and on His side. He is trusting God and responding to God's power and position with a happy heart. He has gone from depression to praise by simply shifting his focus to God and trusting in Him.

He finishes with saying "my God" as he personalizes God as His own. He wasn't speaking of "a god" but "my God." His God was personal, relatable, and capable. His God was infallible.

. . .

THE LESSON here is that there is a spiritual help for depression:

1. Hope in God
2. Trust God
3. Praise God
4. Personalize God

GREATNESS

MARK 9:35

> *"And He sat down, called the twelve, and said to them, 'If anyone desires to be first, he shall be last of all and servant of all.'"*

The disciples were arguing about who would be the greatest. Jesus overheard and said, "if anyone desires to be first, he shall be last of all and servant of all." God sees things completely different, if not completely the opposite of what we oftentimes think. He explains that greatness in the eyes of the final judge, is humility and a servant's heart.

In every believer is a heart like Jesus, one that is most happy and content putting others first. The joy is in the act of serving and not necessarily in the results of it. Jesus sees success as the willingness to be lower so others could be higher. This is something every Christian should do from a sincere heart of love, helping others by serving them. This servant's heart is so different than the selfish, self-centered attitude of the opportunistic disciples who were arguing over their own greatness

The wary Jesus sees it, greatness is in proportion to our being a servant. What a great way to see our lives. God will energize us and bestow greatness as we serve. The question is, is that how we see ourselves? When we see ourselves as servants, we are free from self promotion and competitive impulses that may pit us against another brother or sister in the Lord. We are free from striving to get ahead of others and be in positions of power. We can simply let God lead and direct our lives and we can stay focused on serving where ever we are and whatever we are doing.

. . .

THE LESSON here is that to see yourself correctly you must see yourselves as a servant. Serve, serve, serve and let God fill, fill, fill. Be content with the honor of being a servant and don't worry about being better or greater than others. Just serve, taking the lower place, lifting up and honoring those around you. Then you will be great to God and that is what matters.

MARCH 1

Leviticus 24:1 25:46, Mark 10:13 31,
Psalm 44:9 26, Proverbs 10:20 21

WORDS

//

PROVERBS 10:20

"The tongue of the righteous is choice silver;"

Words carry power. Power to help and power to hurt. Power to build and power to tear down. Power to bring healing or power to injure. We have a great responsibility in our words. Have you thought about how you use them?

The Christian has words of eternity. A person of faith, having been made righteous by the blood of Christ, has the ability to speak the language of heaven with words that come from the Spirit within. These words, when spoken out of the inspiration of the Spirit, will feed others in a way that goes beyond mere mental pleasantries to the core of their being.

. . .

THE LESSON here is to use your words wisely. Be intentional in how you use words with the goal of edification. Use your words for God's purposes, especially when sharing the gospel, which is the most important words we have. There is nothing more heavenly than the words that connect people to heaven. Speak truth, speak love, speak life into others, and your words will resonate into eternity, outliving your own life.

HAPPINESS

PSALM 45:7

> *"You love righteousness and hate wickedness; therefore God, Your God, has anointed You with the oil of gladness more than Your companions."*

The happiest man that has ever walked the earth was none other than Jesus Himself. The first chapter of the book of Hebrews verse nine quotes this exact verse and says it is speaking about Jesus. One may not always see Jesus in this way as He was also a man of sorrows, yet Jesus knew the key to happiness and lived happy like no one else.

Happiness is perhaps the most sought after quality by mankind. Here we find very simply that it is an effect and not a cause. In other words, happiness cannot be a goal because it is a result of a goal.

So what is it that makes one happy? It can ONLY come from being in a right relationship with God.

We see it in our text that Jesus loved righteousness and hated wickedness and as a result He was anointed with happiness. This suggests that evil, sin and wickedness are joy robbers. Ironically, the world says just the opposite. What the world offers will never truly satisfy and give what it promises. In fact, there is no true happiness apart from God. It's all a trap to take our happiness away.

· · ·

THE LESSON here is that happiness is in direct proportion to your attitude toward sin and righteousness. In one sense, a Christian has been made righteous in Christ through faith in Jesus. This is the ultimate righteousness and the greatest joy. Then to walk in that righteousness, by living out your faith, practically will give you a hunger and thirst for righteousness. This very simple truth is the way to happiness. Love good and hate evil. It's that simple.

PRAYER

//

MARK 11:17

> *"Then He taught, saying to them, 'Is it not written, "My house shall be called a house of prayer for all nations."'"*

Prayer is the activity of the House of God. Not that it is the only activity, but every activity must be driven by it. Prayer is the instrument of power, which makes it God's work and not mans work. Prayer shows dependence and trust.

It's easy to minimize prayer, especially as ministry gets busy or things get up and running. A sure sign of fleshly ministry is one that can run without prayer. When organization charts, systems and procedures rather than prayer drive ministry, that ministry has put more faith in them than God. Not those those are bad, it's just bad when they take the place of prayer. A prayer-less church is a powerless church. It will not be effective in reaching a dark lost world, prayer will!

· · ·

THE LESSON here is that a praying church is a God driven church. Prayer must be at the heart of all Christian activity. Prayer depends on God to move or else fail. A praying church is a church that will see the miraculous and go beyond what man can do. Fervent, believing prayer will shake the foundations of Hell and disrupt the influence of darkness. Prayer is the power behind all Christian work and the power for your daily life.

CERTAINTY

PROVERBS 10:25

"When the whirlwind passes by, the wicked is no more, but the righteous has an everlasting foundation."

Certainty is hard to come by. What can we really be certain of? What guarantees are there? What can we count on? When you think about it, what are you counting on? What is your certainty in and how certain is it?

In our Proverb we see a contrast between two different types of people and the certainty they have. These two types are really the only two categories of people there are. It calls them the wicked and the righteous. We are either in one category or the other. We are either the wicked or the righteous. Each category comes with a type of certainty.

The wicked are those who never receive God's forgiving grace, who are never washed by the blood of Jesus Christ and who reject Him as their Lord and Savior. The result is that they are carried away by the wind of the world. They have no footing and will be taken by the empty philosophies of the world. They are conformed to the world and tragically are no more. Death is the passing into a Godless eternity where there is weeping and gnashing of teeth. It's where the worm dies not and the fire is never quenched. They live a life of uncertainty and are confronted with their eternal rejection of hope. The wicked have a certain end to an uncertain life.

The righteous, on the other hand, have an everlasting foundation, who have been made righteous because of God's grace. They have received forgiveness and have been made righteous by the blood of the Lamb. Their certainty is certain because it is the certainty of that which is unchanging and not subject to any varying circumstances. Their certainty is in the infallible Jesus Christ alone.

· · ·

THE LESSON here is that you have confidence to live life and to have a certain future. Doubt is removed and the ultimate question is answered as your life is built on that which stands forever. Be thankful, move forward, no more doubt, future secure. Life in Christ cannot be more certain, more secure or made more stable. We are on a solid rock, immovable and unshakable because Jesus is the everlasting foundation.

AVOIDING MISTAKES

//

MARK 12:24

> *"Jesus answered and said to them, 'Are you not therefore mistaken, because you do not know the Scriptures nor the power of God?'"*

Mistakes are common in life. As the saying goes "to err is human." If left to ourselves, to try and figure things out, we will be greatly mistaken in most things. That's why God has given us the answers in His word, the Bible. Without it we are lost and confused, like trying to find our way out of a dark forest without light or a compass.

A good question to ask yourself is, "where do I see that plainly in the Bible, where do I see that taught or practiced by Jesus, where do I see that taught or practiced by the disciples and/or where do I see that addressed in the Epistles or letters written in the Bible?" What has become an unbiblical practice or a man made tradition in my life?

Jesus points out the reason for the Sadducees mistaken understanding of eternity. He gives two reasons which are the same reasons we will error. It was because they did not know the scriptures and they did not know the power of God. The point Jesus is making is that we can't just make up our own stuff. We can't correctly draw conclusions based on our experiences nor can we base our conclusions merely on our limited observation. The reason is, as for the Sadducees, that we can't know everything. We are finite or limited in our understanding. We don't know it all, in fact we can't even come close. I wouldn't want to stake my eternity on my own understanding when I am limited and make mistakes over and over again.

The key then, as Jesus points out, is knowing the scriptures and following the Holy Spirit. This is where eternal truth lies. This is where God's power gives light. These two, the scriptures and the Holy Spirit, provide the two-fold witness to that which the human mind can't know and understand on its own.

. . .

THE LESSON here is to know what the scriptures say and let the Holy Spirit draw you into all truth. Base what is true on what God says and not your own understanding. Let God dictate truth to you and not the other way around. In the scriptures you will find life, eternal life, and how to have a relationship with God. Let the truth set you free and the power of God light your path. Everything comes into focus when we see through the eyes of God.

GIVING

MARK 12:44

> *"For they all put in out of their abundance, but she out of her poverty put in all that she had, her whole livelihood."*

Giving is a real test of our heart. It reveals what is important to us and what we value. Giving is what God is and what He exemplified when He was on earth. He gave all He had to make others rich. We are challenged with this in the text.

As people were giving, some gave a lot and one poor lady very little. On the surface it might see as if those who gave a lot were more spiritual and Godly because of the amount. However, the poor widow was recognized for what she gave because it really cost her something. She gave all she had, which in proportion to the rich givers was much more.

Be careful not to be manipulated by some religious profiteer who wants you to make them rich through manipulating you with this scripture. The point is not to make another man rich but an expression of our heart of trust and dependence on a God.

• • •

THE LESSON here is "it is more blessed to give than receive." Exemplified by our Lord, your giving is more about your heart than about the amount. God is not poor and is not needy of your donations. Giving is what you need. Remember that all you have is from God and giving will keep you humble and free from entanglement to the world. Giving will keep you dependent and trusting. Giving will show what you value and where your priorities are. Giving makes you more like Jesus. It's not just giving money, it is everything, your time, energy, talents and gifts. Give because He gave.

Numbers 8:1 9:23, Mark 13:14 37,
Psalm 50:1 23, Proverbs 10:29 30

WATCH

//

MARK 13:37

"And what I say to you, I say to all: Watch!"

Jesus' word here, "watch" is so relevant to us today. Basically Jesus is saying to pay attention, look at what's going on, be aware. Jesus, like a lifeguard, is saying there is danger, there are sharks and there are riptides. Do we know where they are and what they look like?

Danger is all around and if the Christian, who is hated by the world, isn't aware of their life it's easy to fall prey. One way we can fall prey is to get sucked in. The Bible says, "be not conformed to this world but be transformed." We are either being conformed or transformed. Conformity is being shaped into a mold from outside pressure. Transformed is being formed from inward pressure. So we either look more like the world or more like Christ. It all depends which pressure we submit to.

Jesus is specifically talking about being watchful of the events going on in the world that relate to His coming back. He speaks of certain signs and how knowing these signs will cause one to live as if Jesus can come at any moment. As the Christian is aware of what to look for, and then they see them occurring, they become hopeful and mindful of living for God.

· · ·

THE LESSON here is that as a Christian you are a watcher. Watch you life, watch for signs. Be sober minded and not drunk with the world's tonic. Watch the scriptures and watch your prayer life. Watch who needs help and who needs prayer. Watch who needs to hear the gospel and watch for hurting people. Watch by praying, serving and using your gift. Watch because you don't know the day or the hour but you know it's close. When you watch, you will see things more clearly. Watching is a Christian's best friend.

COMPLAINING

NUMBERS 11:1

"Now when the people complained, it displeased the LORD;"

Complaining is an attitude of the heart expressed through the mouth. It reveals unhappiness about something. Complaining is the opposite of being thankful, which is an attitude of gratitude. It shows that one's heart is happy and at peace with things. At any given moment we have things to be thankful for and things to complain about. How do we have a grateful heart and give thanks instead of complaining?

The Children of Israel were complaining because they were tired of eating mana. They had it everyday and wanted some variety. What they forgot was that God was doing something special. What they grew tired of was actually God teaching them the importance depending on Him, how He is the provider, how perfect the food was for the exact nutritional needs they had, and that God is faithful and will always be there for them. What was actually something special that God was doing was seen by them as something to complain about.

. . .

THE LESSON here is to see the difference between a thankful heart and a complaining heart? It all comes down to seeing God, trusting God and knowing that He is always working something that will be good in the end. Thankfulness is not just words but a belief that God is working all things together for good. This belief transcends circumstances and sees the orchestrator, God, conducting a masterpiece for your life. Through every note, every movement and every bar, God is piecing together your life that glorifies the Master. Give thanks, God is at work.

OVERCOMERS

NUMBERS 13:30

> *"Then Caleb quieted the people before Moses, and said, 'Let us go up at once and take possession, for we are well able to overcome it.'"*

God will put us in positions to be overcomers. An overcomer needs something to overcome, otherwise there will be nothing great about his faith. A faith that is never needed is dead, but a faith that clings to God in the face of adversity is alive and ready to overcome.

The Children of Israel were put in such a position. God said that He gave them the land yet there were great obstacles in the way. Those obstacles were bigger than they could handle and that's just the way God planned it. The Children of Israel were to live by faith so that God would be their strength and not themselves. They were put in a spot to either believe God or be controlled by fear. We will also be put in places where our options will be to trust or to fear. We choose.

Caleb saw the obstacles, but He also saw God. He was excited for God to work and demonstrate His power. He had no hesitation because he believed God, he knew God was bigger and He knew God would not let him down. Faith sees circumstances as opportunities for God to show His power and opportunities to be overcomers. Fear looks at the obstacle in comparison to our ability and says let's go home.

. . .

THE LESSON here is that you as a Christian are an overcomer. Your faith is the key to overcoming and obstacles, which in comparison to God, are nothing. In times of testing you have a God who is for you, which means nothing can be against you. He will not fail, He will not let you down. No enemy is too large for God, just an opportunity to overcome. The bigger the obstacle the greater the victory if you just have faith.

DENYING GOD

PSALM 53:1

> *"The fool has said in his heart,*
> *'There is no God.'"*

The original definition of the word "lunatic" is "a mind with out God." It takes a real effort to think that there is a creation without a creator. No one in their right mind would come to such conclusions. We wouldn't think that about anything else. However, when it comes to God, we can rationalize Him out of existence in the most absurd ways.

There is definitely a dark force behind disbelief. The Bible says that no one is without excuse because all can know God through all that is seen around in creation. Ultimately it comes down to not wanting to know God rather than not being able to know God. Any person who truly desires to know the truth can come to that knowledge simply by praying to God and asking Him to show them. A genuine seeker will never be denied.

. . .

THE LESSON here is to see that it is foolish to deny God's existence. It's better to wise up and look around. It's wise to ask God, to seek Him and to open your heart to Him. To live in denial of your creator is to live without the source of all there is, to miss your purpose and to reject eternity. Don't be foolish with the most important thing there is, your free will to acknowledge the obvious. God is the creator of all.

MARCH 11

Numbers 15:17 16:40, Mark 15:1 47,
Psalm 54:1 7, Proverbs 11:5 6

THE VEIL

//

MARK 15:38

"Then the veil of the temple was torn in two from top to bottom."

The veil meant separation. Separation that the Jews would feel from God was always before them. They would know that the holiness of God was so different than their own un-holiness. That veil would say to them restriction, barrier, prohibited, keep out and stay back. That veil was the veil that separated the Holy of Holies in the temple from the holy Place in the temple.

There are two different compartments with the Holy of Holies being the inner-most compartment or room in the sanctuary where the presence of God was. That special room was restricted to the high priest; and to him it was restricted to once a year, through very precise execution of holy procedures that had to be executed perfectly, in order for him to survive entering into the Holy of Holies.

This veil, at the death of Christ, was torn in two from top to bottom. The signif-icance of the veil was that the prohibited became an invitation. The restricted became the opening and the barrier became a welcoming. The veil was torn from the top to the bottom indicating that it was God who tore the veil and not man. It was all based on the sacrifice of Jesus, that now His holiness became our holiness and our scarlet sin became white as snow.

Jesus took our place and bore our sin so that we could have His place in righteousness. And now, the greatest privilege of man is open to all who would place their faith in Jesus Christ. He made the way, opened the door and let us in behind the veil into the presence of God for the purpose of fellowship, or in other words, relationship and even friendship. And now we can boldly come to the throne of grace in time of need with full access to Jesus Christ in a personal relationship with Him. There's no more barrier but only the open arms of the scarred Savior, Jesus our Lord.

. . .

THE LESSON of the veil is that there are no more barriers to living in the presence of God. You will have no greater joy than the joy of your communion with Him. Don't let anything keep you from the place of God's presence. Live there, breathe there and linger long there. Bask in His glory because it is wide open and the place where God's children belong.

The veil, a barrier no more.
Torn in two, by the cross Jesus bore.
Access granted, Come who will, Jesus awaits, your heart He will fill.

THE GOSPEL

MARK 16:15

> *"And He said to them, 'Go into all the world and preach the gospel to every creature.'"*

The gospel is the most powerful and important message in all the world. It is the greatest need of the human race and the greatest display of love God has shown mankind. The gospel is the power of God to salvation for those who believe. The gospel is the message of the church and the responsibility of every Christian.

Jesus here says to "go." The believer is on a mission to "go" and preach the gospel. This is the great calling of Christians as ambassadors of Jesus Christ and as those who have been given the "ministry of reconciliation." Jesus empowers us to go and empowers us to preach. We have been entrusted with the words of life and death. That's what it's all about.

Notice the responsibility is on the action of going and preaching and not in the results. Our job is to simply preach the gospel and the results are up to God. The reality of our command comes into focus when we understand the gospel and the power of it. That we have words that can change a persons entire eternal destiny. That without it a person will spend eternity in a place of torment and punishment without ever any chance to escape. The fact that nothing can ever be done to escape hell is the most frightening part of it all. Yet, we have the words of salvation and redemption through Jesus Christ.

· · ·

THE LESSON here is simply to go and preach the gospel. Preach Jesus, God who became man and lived a sinless life, who died for your sins. Preach Jesus who rose again from the dead and sits at the right hand of God the Father. Jesus said that "God so loved the world that He gave His only begotten Son, that whoever believes in Me will not perish but have eternal life." Go tell, go preach, go into all the world. The gospel, God's grace, the church's message, the world's hope.

GOD CARES

PSALM 56:8

> *"You number my wanderings;*
> *Put my tears into Your bottle;*
> *Are they not in Your book?"*

The sweetness of this scripture is to know how much God cares about us. He really, really cares. He cares how we feel, He cares about what we go through and He cares about what is going in our lives. He cares more than we know and more than we can ever imagine. Not only does He care but He also acts on His care. In other words, it's not as if He just watches from a bleacher in the sky as a spectator in our lives, but He is actively involved in bringing about good in our lives.

Satan comes along and whispers to us that we don't matter, that God doesn't care and that nothing really matters. His purpose is to sabotage our relationship with God, our relationships with others, our Ministries and the plan God has for our lives. He wants us to think that we aren't valued and that feelings don't really matter. We then forget the value God places in us, and how much we matter to Him. We can feel insignificant and ultimately we will want to give up, go into a shell and withdrawal from God and others. Here are 15 things to help us remember when we are struggling with our value and doubting how much God cares.

1. Valuing self comes from knowing and believing how much God values us. Ie. the cross, Romans 8:32, fearfully and wonderfully made, look at the sparrows.

2. Satan is a liar. The one who tells us we are worthless and that our feelings are unimportant. He is the father of lies.

3. It's a spiritual warfare issue and we win this through taking every thought captive to the obedience of Christ. Faith is the key. Rejecting Satan's lies and believing Gods truth.

4. People will let us down because they are people. They don't dictate the truth, God does. Be careful of how you let other people's opinions effect you.

5. It's possible you are letting the wrong people in your life. Nobody is perfect but you need to be around genuine people who genuinely love God and love you.

6. Our past experiences can leave us vulnerable in certain areas of our lives and Satan knows that and will attack us there. If faith is applied these weaknesses will become our strengths.

7. Your value is all wrapped up in Christ and you could not be more valuable than you already are.

8. Your weaknesses will give you a greater ability to minister to others with the same struggles.

9. When you find your value in Christ you are free from the response of others toward you.

10. Many Christians have the same struggles.

11. When God uses you, you will be a target.

12. Your struggle keeps you humble.

13. Your struggle keeps you dependent.

14. Maybe God is showing you areas where you have not trusted Him order to free you.

15. Even Jesus was not valued in His feelings and many other ways. Yet He found God's value, as will you, in God's plan working itself out in your life.

. . .

THE LESSON then is to remember that God cares about you. You matter to Him and are valued beyond measure.

THE CROSS

NUMBERS 21:8

> *"Then the LORD said to Moses, 'Make a fiery serpent, and set it on a pole; and it shall be that everyone who is bitten, when he looks at it, shall live.'"*

The Old Testament is a book of preview. The events recorded scream of redemption, sacrifice, blood, forgiveness, atonement and Messiah. These "shadows" don't make sense without the substance behind the shadow. We find the fulfillment of these shadows in the substance of Jesus Christ. Here we find one such shadow, pointing to the cross and forgiveness in Christ.

The Children of Israel were dealing with fiery serpents that were biting and killing them. The solution was to make a bronze serpent, put it up on a pole and look at it. It took the lifting up the very thing that was biting them to cure their poisonous affliction. Jesus, likewise became sin to cure us of our sin. The result would be life based on the cure provided. All they had to do was look.

What would keep someone from being cured? They would have to turn from their own way to God's way. They would have to believe they could be healed. They would have to humble themselves. You see, all the work was done, they just had to receive it by faith. There was nothing else they could have done to be cured and death would result from their infection. What a perfect picture of the cross.

. . .

THE LESSON here is to remember that at the cross the cure for your sin resides and the antidote for your infection lies. There is not one thing you can do to cure yourself, to make the sin go away. You are sin and sin is you. Sinful beings can't fix their sin anymore than cancer can kill cancer. You need an antidote that is sinless and that has power over sin and death. Jesus is that answer and the cross is where the solution took place. What would keep one from being saved, only the rejection of the savior. Look to Jesus and be saved.

GOSSIP

PROVERBS 11:13

> *"A talebearer reveals secrets,*
> *But he who is of a faithful spirit conceals a matter."*

Gossip is the devil's gold. He uses it to destroy people in the most acceptable manner. Gossip is a form of bonding that connects people by mutually lowering another, while elevating the gossipers. It makes the gossipers feel better about themselves and artificially mends their insecurities.

Our text proclaims that talebearers, a type of gossip, like to share details about others with information meant to be kept confidential. Trust was given in cases where secrets were told. That's the worst type of gossip. One who violates a confidence by exposing a secret not meant to be exposed.

Other secrets may be in the form of weakness, that we all have, that may only be known to a few. The talebearer loves to share the weaknesses of others and put them on display for all to see. Why would one do this? The heart behind it is evil, triggered by ones own insecurities, and the need to be bigger or more important than they are, or to hurt another that they don't like or have envy toward.

• • •

THE LESSON here is to be faithful to God by being faithful with the information you have. Speak that which is <u>helpful</u>, <u>needful</u> and <u>necessary</u> when speaking of others. Don't take too lightly how we make others look in our conversations. Speak edification, impart grace and do it with love. Give mercy and the benefit of the doubt. Ask why you are saying what you're going to say and when in doubt, saying nothing is always better than not. Stop gossip and you stop the work of the enemy.

OUR DEFENDER

///

PSALM 59:16

> *"But I will sing of Your power; Yes, I will sing aloud of Your mercy in the morning; For You have been my defense And refuge in the day of my trouble."*

When we place our life in God's hands, we give over the rights to ourselves. We become His responsibility. What a great place to put ourselves, right into the hands of a gracious and merciful God. It is His responsibility to defend us as well. To know God as your defender is to know no worry.

David, here in our text, is rejoicing at the acknowledgment of a God being his defender. He has history to look back upon and see all of God's divine protection and deliverance. He knows that same God will do the same in the future. He recognizes God doing what he could not do himself and the power God has over all that may come against him. How different things look when we rejoice in God instead of fearing our trouble and enemies.

. . .

THE LESSON here is to remember that you are God's problem and your problems are really His. Submitting to His will is to sign up for 24/7 security and a Defender that will never leave you nor forsake you. When tempted to take matters into your own hands, be still and know your Defender is near.

PARENTING AND GOD'S WILL

LUKE 2:49

> *"And He said to them, 'Why did you seek Me? Did you not know that I must be about My Father's business?'"*

Jesus, in his younger days, had great wisdom. He understood what life was all about. He recognized His purpose and focused His energies on that purpose. He knew life was short and that we had a limited time to do what could only be done while on earth. Jesus saw eternity as what to live for and that a fallen world with fallen people needed a Savior and a hope. We too must recognize that we exist for God and He doesn't exist for us.

Jesus told His worried parents that, "He must be about His Fathers business." They were worried about Him, not knowing where He was, not realizing themselves that He must be about His Fathers business. At the time Jesus was teaching in the Synagogue, astonishing the listeners with the truth He brought forth. Jesus' parents at the moment were concerned about His welfare while Jesus, even as a young boy, was concerned about reaching the lost with the truth.

We see here that parents are not to interfere with God's plans for their children. We care for, love, nurture, support and train in the scriptures and in the ways of The Lord. Most importantly, we teach them to love God and how God loves them. We do that not only by word but how we exemplify it by our actions.

The hard part is to realize that our children are not ours but the Lords. It's important to remember He has a plan for them and to be careful to stay out of the way of that. Of course, this applies to our children who are following The Lord and there are different ways to handle wayward children. In either case, we have to trust them into God's hands.

Parents must be prayerful about letting go. We must let the natural process of growth and maturing take place and not hold so tightly we squeeze the life our of our children. Knowing the right amount of authority and control at the particular place in a child's life takes much wisdom from God but He will give it if we ask. A good rule if thumb is that we should always want to give them more freedom, more trust and more responsibility. We should be looking for, and praying about, opportunities to do so. That is God's desire and should be ours as well. It's hard to do but in the end it's better to get on the bus than to get in front of it. It's better to trust than to control. It's better to guide than to squash.

. . .

THE LESSON here is the importance of "being about our Fathers business," especially when it comes to parenting children. Seeing your parenting as an opportunity to do God's will, to live for Him and to serve Him, trusting Him and trusting children to Him.

THE CURE FOR STRESS

PSALM 61:2

"From the end of the earth I will cry to You, When my heart is over-whelmed; Lead me to the rock that is higher than I."

Life can get overwhelming at times. There is much to think about, so many responsibilities, so many demands and too little time. Things can get thrown at us from every direction to where stress is the norm. Some may not even remember what it feels like to be stress free. Some may think it is impossible. However the Bible says that nothing is impossible for God.

There is an antidote for stress. We find it here in our text. David sure knew about stress and he also knew where to turn. He speaks here of feeling overwhelmed as if what was going on was too much to handle. The antidote was to cry out to God. In other words, he looked beyond himself to find help. He looked to the One who was above all his trouble and the One who was always there. I believe God wants us to cry out to Him. I believe He allows us to be overwhelmed so we know our weakness, our limitations, our need for God and our need to be depending on Him. When we cry out we are asking for help from the One who can and will. We are admitting we are weak but He is strong. He is our rock because He is "higher than I." So comforting to know our Rock is solid and unshakable.

. . .

THE LESSON here is to know that Jesus your Rock the answer to stress. Cast your cares upon Him. Stress is unnecessary and useless. Don't let one second more of stress eat you up. Cry out to God, put your matter in His hands. Stress is only overwhelming when seen in comparison to us, but nothing in comparison to the "higher than I." Trust Him, He's got it all under control.

MINISTRY

//

LUKE 3:23

"Jesus was about thirty years old when he began his public ministry."

Public ministry flows from private ministry, never the other way around. We will never be bigger than we are in private with God. We should be bigger on the inside than we are on the outside. A ministry that is merely external will not have lasting fruit. Our flesh can only reach others flesh, but the Spirit can reach that which is deeper and eternal. Jesus said, "Whoever believes in Me, out of his heart will flow rivers of living waters." When we are with the Lord in private, He will be seen in public. It will be natural and organic, not forced and contrived.

Luke records that Jesus' public ministry began at thirty years old. Now this is not a standard, that every public ministry should start at thirty, but a lesson in what is most important in ministry, our inner man. It's easy to grossly underestimate our readiness for ministry. We may have big dreams and big plans, we may have vision and enthusiasm and that's a great thing, but then the work must begin in us first.

The development of our inner man is so we will be fit and strong for the dreams and goals that God gives us. Don't despise these times, be patient and let patience have it's perfect work. God is forging a warrior, a vessel of honor capable of fulfilling those great dreams and goals. It always starts with the inner man and when that radiant inner man shines forth, public ministry will look like Jesus.

. . .

THE LESSON here is that your ministry is never greater than the depth of your relationship with God. Emphasize the private personal relationship and your outward ministry will grow from there. Be careful of an over emphasis on what you do instead of who you are. If you tend to the relationship, God will cultivate the fruit. After thirty years, Jesus' public ministry began and only lasted three years.

Spend time with Him, pray, meditate, read and study His Word for this private ministry will be your public ministry. Like the disciples, people will see that you have been with Jesus.

Numbers 30:1 31:54, Luke 4:1 30,
Psalm 63:1 11, Proverbs 11:20 21

BEING FILLED WITH THE SPIRIT

LUKE 4:1

> *"Then Jesus, being filled with the Holy Spirit, returned from the Jordan and was led by the Spirit into the wilderness."*

Being filled with the Spirit is a great desire and a great prayer. When we think of being filled with the Spirit we think of satisfaction, abundance, fruit, joy, love, peace and so forth. We think of it as the desired state of a Christian and the power of God to do what we can't do and to be what we can't be. This is all a part of being filled with the Spirit and it is right to pray for, but it goes deeper than that.

Here Jesus, being filled with the Spirit, was led by the Spirit into the wilderness. It begs of the screeching noise on a vinyl record. Wait a minute, we may say, the "Spirit" leads us to the wilderness? We can be filled with the Spirit and then led to a place where we will be tried and tested. Shouldn't we be led to the land of milk and honey? Shouldn't we be led to the land of big grapes and pomegranates? That may be, but the Spirit will also lead us to dry places, difficult places and even places of extreme testing.

This may seem so "un-Spirit-like" at first but is really very Spirit-like. You see, God fills us with the Spirit then puts us in places where all we can rely on is the Spirit. He will strip us of that which we can mistake for the Spirit, or substitute for the Spirit, so that we have the full benefit of being filled with the Spirit.

When Jesus was tested, He was physically weak and vulnerable. However, when the flesh is weak we must rely totally on the Spirit. As Paul the Apostle said, "His grace is sufficient and His strength is made perfect in our weakness." When we are weak He is strong. So the Spirit works in us to fill us, then leads us to experience the fullness by placing us in positions of deeper dependence.

· · ·

THE LESSON here is to see the beauty of the working of the Spirit, doing what you can't do and taking you where you would never go. Your part is to be obedient, His part is to take you to greatness.

MARCH 21

Numbers 32:1 33:39, Luke 4:31 5:11,
Psalm 64:1 10, Proverbs 11:22

GOD'S WORK VS. MANS' WORK

//

LUKE 5:5

> *"But Simon answered and said to Him, 'Master, we have toiled all night and caught nothing; nevertheless at Your word I will let down the net.'"*

There is a big difference between our work and God's work. Especially trying to do God work by our own strength. When God works it feels easy, like the wind is at your back. It feels like you're being carried along by a current in the ocean. It's supernatural and obvious that there is a power working that is not of yourself.

The disciples had been fishing all night without any success. They labored and toiled. This was their craft, their livelihood and what they knew best. With all their ability they still came up short. We too, when trying to bring in the Spiritual, will come up empty if we don't follow the Lord. Like the disciples, it's better to listen and obey than to try to do things our way.

It may seem counterintuitive to what we think is the best, like Simon (Peter) being told to lower his net after fishing all night and catching nothing. However, when we see the importance of obedience, then we will reap the fruit of God's power. It will be manifested in and though us. Jesus said without Me you can nothing but with Me you can do all things. He also said, "Abide in me and I in you and you will bear much fruit."

. . .

THE LESSON here is that it is better to let God work through you than to try and produce or manufacture that in which you cannot do. Rest in His goodness and put all your energies into what God is doing. Listen for His word and act upon His leading. Then you will be sure to have a full net, a full heart and a full appreciation of God's power. Gods' work, Gods' way, God's timing is always perfect.

Numbers 33:40 35:3, Luke 5:12 28,
Psalm 65:1 13, Proverbs 11:23

INTIMACY WITH GOD

LUKE 5:16

"So He Himself often withdrew into the wilderness and prayed."

There are times when it is important to withdraw. Not so much for physical rest, although that is necessary, but to simply hear from God more clearly. Our over stimulated senses can drown out that still small voice of the Lord. Withdrawing to a private place for a private time to hear the still small voice of the Lord brings refreshment, vision and insight.

Praying while withdrawing brings intimacy that our souls so desperately need. It will bring clarity and strength. It may even reveal some weaknesses in your relationship with God that would never be availed with too much commotion. Some may feel awkward during this time indicating that their relationship with the Lord may be shallow. This is common because activity can be mistaken for intimacy. There is no substitute for intimacy.

· · ·

THE LESSON here is that withdrawing to pray is essential to a growing and vibrant walk with the Lord. As Jesus did, do it often. Don't let the many and various distractions keep you from this very rewarding and enriching time. Shut off your phone, computer, TV or whatever it may be. Be still before Him. It may be hard or awkward at first, but as you grow in intimacy you will begin to crave these special times. They will be like the dessert of your day.

GOD'S WAY

//

PSALM 66:12

> *"You have caused men to ride over our heads; We went through fire and through water; But You brought us out to rich fulfillment."*

It is important to know where God is bringing us. Knowing that God has a plan and is working toward an end is extremely helpful in times of fire. We will feel like we are being overcome, like we are drowning and that things are out of control. In these times we must know God is working toward an end. He has a direction, purpose and a plan for His children. He takes responsibility for the believer and has a stake in the outcome.

We see this in our text. The Psalmist is reflecting back on the times where it seemed like all was against him and his people, and there was no hope. Then he recalls the end in which God was bringing them. He calls that end "rich fulfillment." This is always where God is taking us. We are always headed to this place in the Lords plans. God never takes us to places to hurt us, ruin us or destroy us. He is never making things less in the end. God is always making things better. He is always headed to addition and multiplication. This is God's way.

• • •

THE LESSON here is that no matter how things may look, God is taking you toward rich fulfillment. The fire is needed to purify, the deep waters for faith and the opposition for dependence. There is no other way to rich fulfillment but the way God has you going. Turn to Him, trust Him and depend upon Him for He is taking you to a place greater than you could have ever hoped but would have never chosen to go there on your own.

GIVING AND GETTING

LUKE 6:38

> *"Give, and it will be given to you: good measure, pressed down, shaken together, and running over will be put into your bosom. For with the same measure that you use, it will be measured back to you."*

Jesus said it is more blessed to give than to receive. An essential characteristic of a Christian is one who is a giver. The heart of one changed by God through a new birth in Christ is others before self and to consider others as more important than self. This is because, as Paul the Apostle said, "to live is Christ" and "it is no longer I who live but Christ who lives in me." If this is true, then we can see why a Christian has a giving, others first nature.

With this nature, a Christian finds great joy in the act of giving. A true giver does not need reciprocation of the giving to find joy because the joy is in the process of giving. A Christian can have no expectations of return, knowing that not only is there great joy in the giving process but also knowing that this is what Christ did and there is great joy that comes from the opportunities to be like Christ and display faith. The best giving is the giving that is unseen and unreturned.

The Christian will also find joy knowing that there is an added joy because God sees and rewards our giving. When giving with the right heart and attitude, which is simply to bless, we lay up treasures in heaven. Our giving here resonates into eternity.

Finally, a spiritual secret is that our giving will bring a return of what we give. If you want love, give it. If you want mercy, give it. If you want forgiveness, give. And, if you want a lot of it, give a lot. If God shares insight with you, give it and you will get more. Whatever it is, give it. This is one of a Pastor's secrets. The more they share the Word, the truth and Godly council, the more they get. So the giver gets to enjoy that which is shared.

· · ·

THE LESSON here is to see that you are to be like river channels, that what you receive is shared and as you do you will get more. Be careful of hoarding as you will become like the Dead Sea. Without an outlet the supply dries up, becomes stagnant and dies. Giving will free you from a selfish and self- centered heart that robs you of life and vibrancy. Give what you have been given and you will be given more. A giving person is a rich person.

MARCH 25

Deuteronomy 4:1 49, Luke 6:39 7:10,
Psalm 68:1 18, Proverbs 11:28

SEEKING AND FINDING GOD

DEUTERONOMY 4:29

> *"But from there you will seek the LORD your God, and you will find Him
> if you seek Him with all your heart and with all your soul."*

God is not hidden in a way to where He is not able to be found. However, He is hidden to those who don't care. As much as one wants Him, they can have Him. It really depends on the individual. Some only want a God that fits their terms or their own ideas of God that is not the God of the Bible. Others seek God in places that He won't be found, like false religions or cults.

In the text we find that God is found when sought. This says that if there is a person who truly and sincerely wants to find God, they will. There is a promise here that God will reveal Himself to that sincere seeker.

He also says that a true seeker will seek in a way that they will do it with all their heart, meaning it will be so important to them that they will want Him above all else. It means that they will want Him like they want air. It would be a matter of importance and even desperation. They will not only seek with their heart but also with their soul. From their innermost being they will want God. To this seeker, God will be found.

Maybe God has seemed distant or hidden to you. Perhaps you have been seeking God with little heart and little soul. Ask yourself how desperate you are seeking Him and if perhaps other interests have occupied your heart and mind to where they are crowding God out. Maybe you've been too busy for God.

. . .

THE LESSON here is to seek Him and don't stop until you find Him. There is absolutely nothing more important that being in a right relationship with God. Everything in life comes from the well of our fellowship. Go for it!

WISDOM

LUKE 7:35

"But wisdom is justified by all her children."

The value of wisdom is without compare. Of all earthy possessions, wisdom is the most valuable. We are to seek wisdom with all that is within us . Through wisdom the Lord set the earth in place and placed the boundaries upon the waters. Through wisdom He created the stars and the constellations. Imagine what we could do with a little wisdom.

Wisdom is not found in the earth but only in God. When we seek Him we will find Him and when we surrender to Him we will find wisdom. James says, "if anyone lack wisdom ask." The essence of wisdom is to fear God. This means we have God in the right place in our lives. We revere God as all powerful and all knowing. We see God as the Creator of the earth and everything in it. We see God as eternal and the source of all life. We see Him as the source of good and the One who is in control of our destiny. We see Him as the Judge who will judge all the living and the dead.

When we fear God then we will hate evil. All evil is destructive and harmful. It can be disguised as fun, entertaining and harmless but as Eve found out, this is not the case. Evil is opposed to God and therefore should be something one who fears God would reject and resist. God will ultimately destroy all that opposes Him and therefore evil will be no more. Wisdom says it does not want to have anything to do with that which will be destroyed. Evil takes away and robs one of God's goodness.

Finally, wisdom has an effect that will be seen in its results. As our text states, "wisdom is justified by all her children." We see that a wise life, one that fears God and hates evil, will bear fruit. It will be shown to all that wisdom has blessed, built up, added to and enriched the life of the wise person and those around them. Be careful about being wise in your own eyes but look though God's eyes.

. . .

THE LESSON here is to place God at the center of your life, walk in obedience to Him and enjoy the fruit of a wise life.

WORSHIP ATTITUDE

LUKE 7:38

> *"And stood at His feet behind Him weeping; and she began to wash His feet with her tears, and wiped them with the hair of her head; and she kissed His feet and anointed them with the fragrant oil."*

Worship is a powerful thing. Humans are made to be worshippers and when Jesus died on the cross for our sins, the path was opened for true worship. The call of every Christian, first and foremost, is to be worshipers. It's easy to get so caught up in activity and serving that we forget this.

The religious Pharisees were uncomfortable with this woman's worship. They wanted Jesus to send her away. We can get so caught up in religion that we are too prideful to be worshipers. Mere religious exercise will do that to us. Be watchful when what you do is more important than Who you worship. We can do nothing without Him. We are never stronger than when we are at His feet.

This woman worshiped because Jesus was all she wanted. She didn't need a class or seminar to learn to worship, for worship will come naturally to the one who sees Jesus. Just as many, when they realized who Jesus was, would fall at His feet. They would become aware of their sinfulness and when they feared, Jesus would say, "come, don't be afraid."

The flippant attitude of the Pharisees can be common amongst modern day Christians. We see this in different ways. Ultimately, if those in the Bible who knew Jesus responded with such a worshipful attitude, shouldn't we? Do we pick apart the music style, the arrangement, the song choice or voices? Or are we seeing Jesus? Is there perhaps something wrong with how we see Jesus?

Worship literally means to turn and kiss. It is not about us what we get, it's about Christ and what we give to Him.

. . .

THE LESSON here is to see that worship is humble, Christ centered, giving, costly, unashamed, from the heart, adoring, grateful, intimate, praising, Spirit led and pleasing to the Lord. It is a sweet aroma. Worship is the height of your Christianity. Be careful you haven't grown to big for it because if you have, you've grown the wrong way.

GOOD SOIL

///

LUKE 8:8

> *"'But others fell on good ground, sprang up, and yielded a crop a hundred-fold.' When He had said these things He cried, 'He who has ears to hear, let him hear!'"*

Jesus says our hearts are like soil. He says that what determines the type of soil our hearts are is the receptivity of God's Word and our acting upon it. This good soil is fertile for God to plant His seed knowing that a good crop will come from it. The evidence then of good soil is in the Godly things that come out of the soil. As Jesus said, "we will be known by our fruit."

Good soil is useful in that it brings forth things that others can enjoy. Primarily it will be love. God is love, therefore Godly love will be produced in us and through us. This love will be how we show the world we are different and set apart. This love will spring forth in action by loving others, even our enemies. It will be the main defining characteristic that shows God has taken root in our lives. This love is so different than anything of the world that it screams divine, supernatural, Heaven and God.

Our part is to simply receive God's Word and act upon it. The Holy Spirit is empowering us to do so and also activating the Word, or seed, so that God's Word is living and active. It's alive in us and working through us. When this takes place it's as if we are being carried by the wind. It feels like we aren't even doing anything. That's why Jesus said we are simply to abide in Him, like a branch would stay connected to the vine, and if we do we will bear much fruit.

What will spoil the good soil is Satan, persecution that leads to falling away and worldly concerns.

. . .

THE LESSON here is to see the importance of the soil of your heart. What might you need to watch out for that will not allow good seed to grow. There is such great simplicity in Christ and that is how He has created it. Simply take in His Word and simply obey it. The rest is up to God. That's good soil.

Deuteronomy 11:1 12:32, Luke 8:22 39,
Psalm 70:1 5, Proverbs 12:4

SUCCESS

DEUTERONOMY 11:22

> *"For if you carefully keep all these commandments which I command you to do—to love the LORD your God, to walk in all His ways, and to hold fast to Him."*

When a person becomes a Christian they face challenges that they never had to deal with before. They enter into the realm of Spiritual Warfare, as the enemy of our soul is not happy with losing his people. The best Satan can do is to render the Christian ineffective and rob them of enjoying all God has for them. God knows this and equips the Christian with spiritual weapons to conquer the attacks of the enemy. Using these weapons will ensure a successful Christian life.

Here in our text we have three simple instructions for a successful Christian life. The first is to love the Lord. Christianity is built on a personal relationship with Jesus Christ. That relationship is built on love. It's love that drives the Christian. It's love that restrains them. It's love that motivates them. Be careful not to leave your first love. Love is at the heart of everything a Christian does. Love never fails.

Secondly, a successful Christian will walk in God's ways. This means that God has a way to live and we are to order our lives in accordance to what God wants to do. The Bible says that, "there is a way that seems right to man but the end of that way is destruction." It also says, "God's ways are not our ways and our ways are not His ways." So, to walk in God's ways is to live by faith and not by sight. We do this by getting into the Word and by following the Holy Spirit inside us. The Bible says to, "not be conformed to this world but be transformed by the renewing of our minds." Satan wants us to walk in his ways but Jesus has set us free to walk in light rather than darkness. As we do we will be walking in God's love.

The last point here is to hold fast to Him. This means that there will be pressure to walk away from God, to walk in the old ways we used to and to do our own thing. Here we see that we are to simply not loosen our grip on God and the relationship with Him. It's really just keeping God as our center. When He is first in our lives, successful Christian living will come. There are many things to distract us from the Lord, that want us to loosen our grip, so beware. Many are very subtle, but anything that interferes with our relationship with God will loosen our grip. Be aware of your life and pay attention to compromise and neglect.

. . .

THE LESSON here is to see that you are already a success in Christ. Live out that success by loving God, living for God and holding onto Him. Success will be a life well lived, a life after God's own heart and a life that ends with God saying, "Well done my good and faithful servant, enter into the joy of The Lord." That is what success is.

TRUTH

DEUTERONOMY 13:1

> *"If there arises among you a prophet or a dreamer of dreams, and he gives you a sign or a wonder."*

God is truth and the devil a liar. Truth is what is and what is right, whereas lies are what aren't and what is wrong. A life built on lies and falsehood is a life without reality, without light and without any foundation. Truth sets one free while lies take one captive. A life built on truth is a life of strength and stability.

What is truth? All truth is from God. God's truth has been revealed to mankind in Jesus Christ and in His Word, the Bible. So in order to live in truth our lives must be lived according to Christ and the Word of God. Satan will use lies to manipulate people to do his will. Ultimately he wants to destroy people for all eternity by speaking against the way of salvation through Jesus Christ. The whole world is under the sway of Satan's influence keeping them in the dark. That is why Jesus is the light of the world. He brings truth into darkness.

In our text we see that people will arise supposedly speaking truth and speaking "the way." Think about all the musicians and celebs that have influenced the way people think and view life and the world. They can even come and do miracles even or say things that seem as if they are supernatural. The time just before Jesus comes back, called the "last days," will see an increase of deception and brain washing on a global scale. Things will be so believable and right except for one thing, the Word of God. It won't match up to God's Word. People, on a mass global scale, will believe the lie and eventually the Antichrist will come on the scene, deceiving the whole world. There will even be religious undertones pacifying the religious crowds who want faith without conviction. These religious liars will come like wolves in sheep's clothing, devouring the vulnerable through deceit and practical lies that tickle the ears of the hearer and give them a self-centered worldly religion so they can have all the world and think they can have God at the same time. The Bible says you can't love God and the world at the same time.

．．．

THE LESSON here is that no matter what you may feel, no matter what sign, no matter what wonder, no matter what may seem to work, if it doesn't match up to God's Word, get rid of it because it's a lie.

MARCH 31

Deuteronomy 16:1 17:20, Luke 9:7 27,
Psalm 72:1 20, Proverbs 12:8 9

FOLLOWING JESUS

LUKE 9:23

> *"Then He said to them all, 'If anyone desires to come after Me, let him deny himself, and take up his cross daily, and follow Me.'"*

Following Jesus is the smartest, scariest, most thrilling and fulfilling path anyone can take. Many of the disciples immediately put down what they were doing to follow Him. There must have been something about Him that caused them to leave all behind to follow.

What an adventure it was. Of course, most importantly, they found eternal life in Christ. They also found that Jesus was the way, the truth and the life. It definitely wasn't easy, but it was awesome. Following Jesus is awesome.

In order to follow Jesus, one must deny himself. We cannot follow ourselves, our impulses, our own agenda and follow Jesus at the same time. Jesus is going in the opposite direction of the world. It's an either/or thing.

Each person must ask themselves, "what am I'm living for and how is that demonstrated in what I do?" Some deceive themselves by thinking they are following Jesus, while at the same time living for themselves, or the world, while thinking church attendance, prayer, Bible Study or good deeds will suffice.

The Bible says God is looking for obedience over sacrifice. Obedience is a good indicator of the authenticity of our faith. There are a lot of things a nonbeliever can do without even being saved. Obedience out of love shows great faith. A good question to ask yourself is, "When have I ever said no to something, or myself, because I am a follower of Christ?"

Denial will take care of itself if we follow Jesus. If we are following Him, we will be denying self at the same time. Jesus is not going to lead us into evil, sin, selfishness and worldliness. Jesus said the kingdom of Heaven is not in eating and drinking but in righteousness, peace and the Holy Spirit.

So we are either living for self or living for God. Paul the Apostle said, "For me to live is Christ." He also said, "I don't count my life dear to myself," meaning he is not holding on to what he wants but embracing what God wants. He also said, "I have been crucified with Christ and it's no longer I who live but Christ who lives in me and the life I now live in the flesh I live by faith." This is what denying self is.

• • •

THE LESSON here is that you are to follow Jesus. As the disciples learned, following Jesus not only transformed their lives but transformed others lives. You are not asked to be in charge, but to follow. Like sheep, following is what Christians are good at. When you do follow you will discover life at its fullest. When Jesus is leading, you are succeeding.

INHERITING YOUR INHERITANCE

DEUTERONOMY 18:2

> *"Therefore they shall have no inheritance among their brethren; the LORD is their inheritance, as He said to them."*

What may seem like a punishment may actually be a reward. God oftentimes withholds good things so we can have the best things. What may be perceived, as a great disappointment is really God's appointment to so much better. Think about a dog being told by his master to stop eating crumbs off the floor. The dog may be disappointed but the master wants him to sit at the banquet table to dine like a king. Are you eating crumbs when God says dine at my banquet table? Don't settle children of God, your Father owns the cattle on a thousand hills. When we place our hope in God, that hope will never disappoint.

The Levites were the ministers. They were not given a piece of the promise land like other tribes. Instead, they would have the Lord in a very special way. Those with the land would not have the same connection with God, which is a much greater treasure and privilege. It comes down to, would we rather have God or a creation of God? Would we rather have the source or the product, the substance or the shadow?

In Psalm 84:11 it says, "God withholds no good thing from those who walk uprightly." This means that for the Christian, we have all we are supposed to have and that we have all that is good for us. Contentment, then, comes into play as we receive by faith all that the Lord gives with gratitude and thanksgiving.

It may be that we lack in an area and that is because God wants to give us Himself instead of what we think we need. God may be teaching that He is all you need and if you have Him you have it all. Maybe He wants to free you from the dependence on things for happiness. Maybe He wants to free you from bondage to material things.

There is a way to respond to our positioning in life. Acts 17:26-27 says wherever we are geographically in life, or whatever season of life we are in, that God has pre-appointed it. So God puts us in places, and it says the reason is so that we seek Him in an intense desperate way and the reward would be finding Him.

Jesus said, "Seek first the kingdom of God and His righteousness and all things will added unto you."

. . .

THE LESSON here is to ask, do I value what God values, a personal intimate relationship with Him? The proper response then in all of life is to seek Him in it. He is your exceedingly great reward. He is the treasure and what may seem like a loss or a lack is an opportunity to gain the greatest treasure, God Himself.

FIGHTING THE GOOD FIGHT

LUKE 9:54

> *"And when His disciples James and John saw this, they said, 'Lord, do You want us to command fire to come down from heaven and consume them, just as Elijah did?'"*

It's important to know the right fight to engage in. As Christians we are definitely in a battle. However, our battle is not against flesh and blood but against unseen forces of darkness. It's easy to mistake who and what we are up against. Identifying the enemy is the first step in being a successful fighter.

James and John, also known as the "sons of thunder" were identifying the enemy as those who would reject the message of Christ. No doubt they saw Jesus as a conquering King who came to set up His Kingdom on earth through strength and power.

They saw no further than what their eyes could see. They saw those who opposed the message as threats to God's Kingdom that needed to be taken out of the way. They asked Jesus if they should call down fire from heaven on them. The best thing they did in the whole scenario was ask Jesus.

Jesus' answer was that it wasn't the Spirit of God that told them to call fire from Heaven, that His mission was to save not destroy. What James and John did was mistake the enemy that was behind what they could see. Beyond the rejectors was the real enemy, Satan.

Jesus said that when someone doesn't receive the seed of the Word of God it is the devil who snatches away the seed. That doesn't negate personal responsibility but shows that the devil is behind the scenes working to prevent people from salvation.

Knowing that the enemy is Satan then gives us the right ammunition to fight the good fight of faith. So many times we fight against people when we should be fighting against Satan. The way we do this is through the Spirit. The Bible says, "Not by might, nor by power, but by My Spirit says the Lord."

The Spirit will always defeat Satan. When the Spirit is working there is love. Love never fails. When the Spirit is working there is prayer, righteousness, the

Word, the truth, the gospel, faith, salvation and ultimately power. In your battles remember the real enemy is Satan, and he cannot defeat the power of God working in and through your life.

When tempted to lash out, love. When tempted to back bite, pray. When tempted to give up, have faith. When tempted to doubt, take every thought captive. When tempted to hate, forgive. When tempted to return evil for evil , return evil with good. When tempted to shun, embrace. When tempted to gossip, praise. When tempted to lie, speak truth.

. . .

THE LESSON here is to see that the devil is no match for the Spirit of God but he will defeat you and your own power every time. Overcome evil with good using your Spiritual weapons of warfare remembering that Jesus wants to save and not destroy. Fighting the good fight is fighting the right one with the right weapons. You will win this fight every time.

Deuteronomy 23:1 25:19, Luke 10:13 37,
Psalm 75:1 10, Proverbs 12:12 14

STAY CLOSE TO JESUS

DEUTERONOMY 25:17-18

"Remember what Amalek did to you on the way as you were coming out of Egypt, how he met you on the way and attacked your rear ranks, all the stragglers at your rear, when you were tired and weary; and he did not fear God."

The most vulnerable targets of Satan's attacks are the stragglers. Those who casually follow Christ with a lethargic and complacent attitude are easy prey. Nearness to Christ is the place of safety where we are passionately engaging Him with our hearts. Especially when we are tired and weary, we must be ever so careful to stay close.

Peter told Christ that he would never deny him and yet with all his willpower to do so he fell to Satan's attack because he was following Jesus from afar. He didn't want to be too close otherwise people would know of his relationship with Christ. It's always best to make a clear and bold declaration of faith than to deny Him or hide your relationship with Him.

Peter thought it best to keep Christ in sight yet remain at a distance. This is the place where our willpower is no match for Satan's power. Staying close to Christ in and of itself is our defense as the power of Jesus is no match for Satan. Our power is in our nearness to Him.

In our text we also see those of the Children of Israel, who lagged behind, were the those who fell. The devil goes for the weak and weary Christian. This may include the self sufficient Christian who is weak in God's power but strong in their own. This person is also taking up the rear guard.

· · ·

THE LESSON here is to stay close to Christ. He is your best defense and place of refuge. Watch for the things that may cause distance between you and Him. Watch for the cares and concerns of the world. Watch for busyness. Watch for complacency in fellowship with other believers. Watch the company you keep and the entertainment you engage in. Watch for neglect of the Word. Watch for prayerlessness. Watch for persecution that makes you want to give up. Watch for pride and self righteousness. Watch for self sufficiency. Stay near to Jesus with simple faith and obedience. Let Him be your defense.

CHOOSING THE GOOD PART

LUKE 10:41-42

> *"And Jesus answered and said to her, 'Martha, Martha, you are worried and troubled about many things. But one thing is needed, and Mary has chosen that good part, which will not be taken away from her.'"*

Mary, being still before Jesus, sitting at His feet and enjoying His presence, chose the good part. She was enjoying time with Jesus. That sweet fellowship from the best place to see His face, which is at His feet. When you are in a position of humble submission to Jesus, you are blessed. What a great picture of relationship with The Lord.

Martha, on the other hand, was up, busy, preparing and wanting to make everything just right. On the surface it seems to be a good thing. To make sure your guests are taken care of and enjoying the hospitality provided. However, when busyness interferes with relationship, then you have erred. Martha was worried and troubled because she wanted everything to be perfect. That's what will happen when one is more focused on the work than on the Master.

• • •

THE LESSON here is that the best place you can be is at the feet of Jesus. Even when you are serving, serve from the feet of Jesus. His presence will always refresh you and refresh others. At the same time, be careful of missing the best place because of works. When you work in the flesh to try and please the Lord, like Martha, you will be worried, troubled, frustrated and angry. Take time to enjoy Him and you will enjoy everything else much more.

Deuteronomy 28:1 68, Luke 11:14 36,
Psalm 77:1 20, Proverbs 12:18

WORDS MATTER

PROVERBS 12:18

"There is one who speaks like the piercings of a sword, But the tongue of the wise promotes health."

Our words matter. What we say affects the hearer in one way or another. It's wise to use our words well by thinking about their effect before we say them. Words have a way of embedding themselves in the minds of others in a way that can often be remembered for a lifetime. This means we can help shape others for the glory of God by allowing the Spirit to direct our tongues. This is what a wise person does.

Our scripture speaks of the contrast between two people who use their tongues in opposite ways. One uses their tongue as a sword in a way in which it cuts and hurts people. Some have mastered their craft to a science and have a trail of verbal slashing in their wake. They speak from hate, selfishness, pride and ultimately the flesh. In the end they themselves lose because their own words are an indictment of their heart that is full of darkness.

The effects of the wise tongue bring health by bringing healing, by building up and encouraging. Sometimes they correct where it is needed. All their words are words of love. This takes a surrender to the Holy Spirit because what ultimately comes out of our mouth begins in our hearts.

. . .

THE LESSON here is to ask yourself what effect your words are making. Look around those close to you first and you will see your opportunity. Then look out further until your area of influence is being influenced for good. Make it a habit to speak no corrupt words but only that which speaks health and imparts grace to the hearer. Speak truth, speak love, speak life. Make it a prerogative to speak into others what goodness and grace the Lord has spoken to you.

SIMPLE FAITH

DEUTERONOMY 30:14

> *"But the word is very near you, in your mouth and in your heart, that you may do it."*

God has made things very simple for us. He has given one way, one Savior and one truth. He has proven these simple truths so that anyone who truly wants to know can easily see. He is a clear and simple revealer of His will and no one will be without excuse.

His simplicity is also close in proximity. He has brought truth to us in a way we can understand and in a way that is close. God hasn't kept His truth in heaven where it is inaccessible. He hasn't kept His truth in a vault or fortress. He has brought it near. So near it is in us, meaning we are wired to know the truth and it's source.

The Bible says that God has put eternity in our hearts. Every human is wired to know God, his Creator. They actually suppress the truth, or those innate instincts that tell them God is real and that they need to be right with Him. Sin is the barrier. One who rejects God ultimately does so for no other reason but that they love darkness rather than light. It's not as if one can't know Him, it's more like they won't know Him.

Like the thief on the cross, turning from sin to God with a simple act of faith, from the heart, is all that is needed for one to be saved from their sin and brought close to God the Savior. Faith in Jesus, the God who saves, the Eternal One, the Almighty.

. . .

THE LESSON here is to see that faith is simple. Not easy, but simple. Living out your faith with simple obedience to the Holy Spirit guiding and directing you from within. It's good to remember that at the end of the day, every man will bow and every tongue will confess that Jesus is Lord.

It's that simple.

Deuteronomy 31:1 32:27, Luke 12:8 34,
Psalm 78:32 55, Proverbs 12:21 23

TREASURE

//

LUKE 12:34

"For where your treasure is, there your heart will be also."

How we feel when we think about something will show us what we value. When we value something highly, we feel good when we think about it. We like to think about it and we think about it often. What we value will direct our paths in life. We will try and move in the sphere of that in which we value. It will be what we want and what we pursue. What we value will tell us where we will be.

Our scripture points out that what we value is where our heart will be. Value is like a bus that takes our heart to a destination. It pulls us in a direction. It sets aside the things that get in the way of what is valued. If we value our health, we will go to the gym and eat right. If we value education, we will go to school and do our best to learn. If we value music, we will practice and play.

If we value the Lord, our hearts will follow Him. We will want to be with Him, grow in our relationship with Him and honor Him in our lives. We will forgo the passing pleasure of sin so we can have the lasting pleasure of fellowship. He will be in our thoughts, in our hearts and on our tongues. Our affections will grow towards Him and we will serve Him and share about Him. Valuing Jesus as our great treasure has the greatest reward there is because then our hearts will be set on heaven and not earth. Our hearts will take us to Jesus and find all we need in Him. We will see heaven as our home and earth as our mission field. When our hearts are led by valuing Jesus, we will be rich in Him.

· · ·

THE LESSON here is to see that it all comes down to what is most important to you. When you value Jesus, you will have the greatest reward and that is Jesus Himself. Treasure Jesus, He is worthy of all your praise. Make Him your priority and focus. Keep Him before all-else and you will find that you are the richest on earth.

BE READY

LUKE 12:37

> *"Blessed are those servants whom the master, when he comes, will find watching."*

Are you ready to die? One day, everyone will stand before Jesus. When they do, they will confess that He is Lord. Some will confess as a testimony against themselves as to their rejection of His forgiveness. At that time they will indict themselves and head on into everlasting torment.

Those souls spent their lives burying their opportunities God had placed before them to receive full pardon of their sins. Over and over again they suppressed the truth. They denied, revolted and rebelled against the pleas of the loving Savior. They weren't ready to meet Him. Instead, they convinced themselves that this day would never come. They were too busy, too successful, too smart, too invested, too intellectual, too prideful. They were having too much fun and maybe too convinced God would accept them on their own terms and not on His terms. They weren't ready.

We are confronted with our mortality constantly. We see death all around us. Loved ones die, animals die, vegetation dies. Seasons change and days go by all speaking of our mortality. Yet, some ignore the reality of eternity. Some are not ready to meet their fate and are not prepared for what's next. When that day comes they won't be ready for eternity. They weren't watching. They weren't prepared. They weren't ready.

Our scripture points to the importance of meeting our Maker. We are blessed to be ready, the scripture says. Those who confessed Jesus as Lord, making Him their Lord and Savior this side of eternity. They are blessed because they are set. They have settled their eternity and made peace with God. They have made the most important decision there is in life.

They will be watching for Him. They will watch by thinking about eternity and keeping their eternity in mind as they live on earth. They will be watching what God says. They will be watching their lives. They will make sure they are ready.

There is really nothing more important than being ready for eternity. We shouldn't make any plans for the future until we've made plans for our eternity. We shouldn't have any goals until we've settle our ultimate goal. We shouldn't take one more step, take one more breath or have one more thought until we have reserved our spot in heaven.

. . .

THE LESSON here is to see how critical it is to be ready. Jesus says to watch. Make Him, eternity and salvation your priority. Be ready by admitting that you are a sinner. Sin is what keeps us from God. Settle that issue. One sin, one sinful thought or action, will keep us from salvation, but if you turn from your sin to Jesus, ask for His forgiveness He will forgive.

Settle the issue now, because then, it will be too late. Be ready!

DEALING WITH DEPRESSION

PROVERBS 12:25

> *"Anxiety in the heart of man causes depression,*
> *But a good word makes it glad."*

Depression is an "out of sync" disorder. Something gets "out of sync inside of us. There are different causes, for example, when our chemicals get "out of sync" or when life's circumstances get us "out of sync." As humans we have feelings and emotions and sometimes they get "out of sync." Many cases of depression are spiritual problems and often go undetected as such. One thing is for sure, depression is hard to live with. Some people struggle all their lives with it while others only have flashes of it throughout their lifetimes. The Bible gives us great help when dealing with depression.

Here in our text we see that anxiety causes depression. When we worry we get "out of sync." We are not equipped to worry so worry ends up short circuiting us. Anxiety stems from fear. When we fear something may happen or when we feel the lack of control over a situation. When this happens we get "out of sync" mainly with God.

Being "out of sync" with God will always lead to depression. The reason is, God is the source of life, the source of peace and the source of joy. He is the creator of all and the continuous cause of all. Being "out of sync" with God is being disconnected from all that is good.

The answer for depression then is to be "in sync" with God. The moment we put our faith in Him we have peace with Him. Immediately there is no more friction in the most important relationship there is. When we have peace WITH God we the have the peace OF God. No more friction and then a bestowal of supernatural peace bringing a rest in our heart.

We also receive forgiveness of the sin which burdens our souls. There is a heaviness the unforgiving sinner carries. Christ offers forgiveness which leads to a clear conscience. No more guilt or shame. In our innermost being we are clean and guilt free. We have rest.

· · ·

THE LESSON here is to see how important it is to be with being in sync with God. When you are "in sync" with God you are able to pray and give Him all our fears and anxieties. You can drop them off and unload the burden knowing that He promises to take them from you. Prayer is a great privilege that guards your heart and our mind when we pray in faith. You can then rejoice in the Lord because you are free and taken care of.

This is the good word of God that is the cure for depression.

THE DOOR TO ETERNAL LIFE

LUKE 13:25

> *"When once the Master of the house has risen up and shut the door, and you begin to stand outside and knock at the door, saying, 'Lord, Lord, open for us,' and He will answer and say to you, 'I do not know you, where you are from.'"*

Jesus says that He is the door. He is the opening to heaven. He is the road to eternal life. Jesus is the way, the truth and the life. No man comes to the Father but by Him. Only He could be the only way because only He died for our sins. No other but God Himself, come in the flesh, could be a sacrifice for our sin. Do you know the door?

There will be some who think they do but don't. This is who is being spoken of in the text. Not the outright rejector or the proclaimed atheist who reject God overtly. There will also be those who reject God religiously or self righteously. They substitute their thing for God's thing. These are the ones who do good things and even would be considered "religious."

The problem is that they trusted in what they did and not in what Christ did. As they worked to gain salvation they were denying Jesus' work for their salvation. They were blinded by pride to the point where they didn't even know that Jesus was the door. When it came to heaven they didn't even know who Jesus was. I'm sure they knew about Jesus, but they didn't know Him personally.

· · ·

THE LESSON here is to see that the question of eternal life is, "do you have a personal relationship with Jesus Christ?" Have you entered into the door by faith? Have you come His way and not your own? There is only one door that leads to everlasting life. Don't be surprised when it's too late. Enter in now and when the time comes to meet Him face to face He will say, "Well done my good and faithful servant, enter into the joy of The Lord." Much better words than "I don't know you."

PRIDE

//

LUKE 14:11

> *"For whoever exalts himself will be humbled, and he who humbles himself will be exalted."*

Pride is such a malicious disease. It eats away at all that is good. It is like cancer that eats away our souls and interferes with all other functions of our being. Pride is evil for it blinds one to their need for God. Pride is what caused the once beautiful angel, Lucifer, to fall from heaven and be damned forever. Pride is the strength of the flesh and is opposed to the Spirit.

There are many things that feed our pride giving us a distorted view of ourselves and of reality. Knowledge is one of those things that feeds the ego. The feeling of superiority may come when we know something others don't. The need to feed our minds with knowledge is not a bad thing in and of itself, but must be watched carefully as knowledge without humility puffs up, and God resists the proud but gives grace to the humble. Anything that makes us feel better than another is pride.

Talent can feed our pride, making us feel as if the skill or talent was our doing, instead of recognizing that we simply received the gift or talent from God. It's good to remember that everybody is uniquely gifted by God and perfectly equipped to be awesome at something.

Beauty can be a handicap to our spirituality. In a culture that emphasizes beauty to the point of obsession, beauty is rewarded like nothing else. A beautiful person is told they are beautiful so often that beauty can become their identity. One can begin to rely on the compliments and status to find their happiness and security. It's good to remember that anything we find our identity in, that can be taken away, is a false identity.

Success is very difficult to deal with. People worship successful people. Success can be such an idol that one would be willing to sacrifice their eternity for. Success can be a god that drives a person to be a slave to it. Success breeds pride and feeds ego. It's an endless road to nowhere.

There are many more things we could list but ultimately pride is our desire to "exalt" ourselves instead of God. It is where we want what is rightfully God's. The best way to deal with pride is to use whatever we have for God's glory recognizing that He made us and gave us what we have. It's not us, it's Him. We didn't choose our DNA and genetic make up. We didn't choose our looks, our talent, our size, our personality, our eye hand coordination, our ability to carry a note, our speed or our strength. We didn't choose our biological parents nor the place and time we were born. It's all part of our uniqueness that we are to embrace and use for God's glory. The real question is "what are we doing with what we have?"

. . .

THE LESSON here is to not make it about you, make it about Jesus. Realize that with what you are given comes responsibility. The more responsibility you have the more you have to give God the glory. What you do with what we have is really a test to see who and what you worship, God or self, humility or pride. He must increase and you must decrease. This is the secret of success. The humble will be lifted up by God, the prideful will be brought low.

REPENTANCE

//

LUKE 15:20

> *And he arose and came to his father. But when he was still a great way off, his father saw him and had compassion, and ran and fell on his neck and kissed him.*

There is a great joy in a homecoming. To be back with the one you love. Having sweet fellowship that was lost and restoration of that which was ruined. This is the joy of a lost one that comes home. This joy has it's own sweetness and reward for it is a joy that tastes the pain of loss first, then is followed by gain. That which is gained is valued so much because it learns the value of what was had.

Here in our text we get a picture of God running. This is the only time in scripture God is pictured in such a way. This is the way the father of a prodigal son, who had run away and taken all his inheritance only to lose it all, received the broken runaway at his return. This is the joy God has when a rebellious pleasure seeker feels the pain of sin and comes to their senses and returns to their first love.

How does one end up going from the riches of God to the pigpen of sin? It all has to do with the pull of the world on our flesh. The world is like a magnet that tempts us to walk away from God. It promises a better life, more fun, more excitement and happiness. When we take our eyes off Jesus we can start to believe the lies. Satan will inch in to our minds and whisper to our hearts if we let him. The appeal he puts forth is like bait on a fisherman's hook. Once we take it he has us and starts reeling us in until we find ourselves empty, lost and with the pigs.

. . .

THE LESSON here is to see that God is always ready for His children to return. Repentance is sweet as it will drive you back to God's love with a broken heart. God is near to the brokenhearted. This verse shows how happy God is to receive the lost child. He has compassion, He runs, He hugs and He kisses. The love of the Father for a repentant sinner is a love that makes a prodigal glad to be home and confounded why he left.

TWO MASTERS

LUKE 16:13

> *"No servant can serve two masters; for either he will hate the one and love the other, or else he will be loyal to the one and despise the other. You cannot serve God and mammon."*

Everyone has a master. A controlling influence in our life that is behind what we do and the decisions we make. No one is completely autonomous but rather all belong to someone or something. When you do something ask why you're doing it. Or when you are deciding something ask why you're making the decision you are making.

What your master is will be evident by what you do and why you do not do it. Jesus told Peter to feed His sheep if he loved Jesus. John the Apostle said, "This is love, that we keep His commandments and His commandments are not a burden." The question is, "What is your master?"

Some try and have two masters. They would like to serve Jesus and they would like to serve material things like money. Maybe in their minds they are not thinking that money is their God but their actions and attitude say different. Their life is dominated by accumulation of wealth and financial gain. Their mind dominated by thoughts of how to get more and what else can I buy. An attitude of more, bigger, better. The bible warns us over and over again about the negative effects of materialism and how difficult it is for the rich man to have a good relationship with God when wealth is their driving force in life.

The love of money and materialism is at the root of all evil. If one loves money they posses a root of evil inside. They will be slaves to their desire for more and money will be their God. When someone is a Christian, yet is driven by financial gain, they are in conflict with the Word of God.

· · ·

THE LESSON here is to see that when it comes to God it is not possible to serve God and money at the same time. Materialism and the world appeal to the flesh. They are opposed to spirituality and opposed to Christ. It is not possible to have two foes as masters. What will happen when you try is that you will hate the other. If money is your master you will hate Jesus. If Jesus is your master you will hate materialism. You can't serve both. Christ must be your Master otherwise you will be mastered by sin.

FAITH AND FORGIVENESS

LUKE 17:6

> *"So the Lord said, 'If you have faith as a mustard seed, you can say to this mulberry tree, 'Be pulled up by the roots and be planted in the sea,' and it would obey you."*

Faith is the hinge to the Christian life. Paul said that the life we now live, we live by faith. It is faith that drives us to do or not to do. Faith is trusting in the character of God and letting Him direct our lives. It is obeying the move of the Spirit within us. Faith is how we live with power and how God moves in our lives. Faith is how we abide in Christ and it is how we overcome. Faith is the key to inheriting the land God had has given us. Faith lets God choose for us and receives what God wants us to receive. Faith is the Christian's best friend.

In our text the disciples were asking for more faith. Not so they could fatten their wallets but in response to Jesus stressing the importance of forgiveness in relationships. We see here what Jesus values, the importance He puts on relationships. Jesus says that faith is the only way we can forgive and says that God's power is needed for forgiveness. We all know how hard it is to forgive. Unforgiveness is a prison we lock ourselves in. God offers His grace and blessing when we choose to forgive. God empowers us to forgive if we allow Him to.

Faith is powerful because of the object of our faith. He says that "mustard seed" faith will pull up the roots of the powerful mulberry tree. Not only is the quantity of faith important but so is the quality. Faith in God, in even small amounts like the tiny mustard seed, will uproot that which is beyond human ability and that is the root of bitterness. Faith will uproot even the deepest most stubborn roots. The faith to forgive is faith that restores and frees.

. . .

THE LESSON here is the importance of faith in your ability to forgive. You can forgive if you choose. Don't let bitterness and unforgiveness rule your life, have faith, forgive and live.

HEAVEN

LUKE 17:21

"Nor will they say, 'See here!' or 'See there!' For indeed, the kingdom of God is within you."

The kingdom of God is where Jesus rules and reigns. It is where His government of righteousness and peace reside. It is where love and joy are not something to achieve but the normal state of affairs. It is where people are complete and satisfied. The kingdom of God is home for the believer.

Jesus here tells the disciples the location of the kingdom of God. He says it's not a place we go but a place that comes. In other words, as we live on earth we are not in God's kingdom. The world is marred by sin and influenced by Satan. Observation tells us that this is not heaven.

However, through faith in Jesus Christ, His perfect kingdom will enter our hearts. It will be inside us. Heaven is in us. Enjoyment of life will be as we surrender to Jesus our King. As He rules in our hearts, heaven then will be our reward. The fulfillment will be within us not outside of us. We will experience the goodness of God internally not externally.

One day all Christians will wake up in God's kingdom. There will be no more faith because we will realize our faith. There will no more struggle between the flesh and the Spirit because the flesh will be no more. There will be no more struggle with sin and struggle to walk in the Spirit. We will be in joy, in peace, in love, in satisfaction. It will be the end of struggle because we will be in heaven.

For now, the kingdom is in us. When earthly life ends we will be in it. For now, we can enjoy heaven through walking in the Spirit and not in the flesh. One day we will be satisfied when we awake in His likeness.

. . .

THE LESSON here is to take heart, be encouraged by heaven knowing that one day the struggle will end, but for now the kingdom is within. Delight in God, surrender to His rule and heaven will be alive in you. As you wait for the day to be in God's kingdom, find your strength now in the Kingdom of God inside. There is a party going on, a celebration of grace and it is with you wherever you go. No use in looking in this world for heaven, look to Jesus and heaven will find you.

SALVATION

///

LUKE 18:11

> *"The Pharisee stood and prayed thus with himself, 'God, I thank You that I am not like other men—extortioners, unjust, adulterers, or even as this tax collector.'"*

The attitude of our heart will determine the receptivity of God's Word. Pride in the heart will cause poor reception. God is hard to hear on that wavelength. A prideful heart that thinks it is good on its own, is lost and hard to reach. It will deflect offers of help and reject rescue attempts, like one stranded in the middle of the ocean without a life jacket saying no to the Coast Guard extending a life preserver. Pride kills.

When it comes to salvation, the one who thinks they are better than others and have no need are the most lost. Success can be a major detriment to salvation, when success causes one to think that there is something inherently better about themselves compared to others. The Pharisee in our text was like that. He equated his ability to keep rules with greatness. He compared himself to others and thought, "My, I am good." He thought, "Look how bad everyone else is, if only if they were like me." His problem was one of "self righteousness" or thinking that God would be impressed with him because of his goodness compare to others.

In reality, the Bible says that, "There is none righteous, no not one," and "Our hearts are deceitfully wicked above all things," and "All our works are like filthy rags," and "It is by grace we are saved through faith, not of works lest any man boast." You see, it is only when we realize our righteousness compared to God's righteousness that we say, "Lord, have mercy on me a sinner."

Where pride blocks the seed of salvation, humility is fertile ground. Those who know how sinful they, are and know they can do nothing about it, cry out to God for mercy. Desperation often brings a person to this reality.

. . .

THE LESSON here is knowing how much you need a Savior. Realize that you are drowning, and reach out for the saving hand of Jesus Christ. Pride says, "Thank you God, I'm not like other men." Humility says, "Thank you God for saving a wretch like me."

ANSWERS TO PRAYER

LUKE 18:41

> *"Saying, 'What do you want Me to do for you?' He said, 'Lord, that I may receive my sight.'"*

Jesus is asking the blind man, "what do you want me to do for you?" The blind man was crying out for Jesus in a public place and told by the crowd to be quiet. He would not listen to the crowd but was intent on getting Jesus' attention. He knew Jesus could heal him and he knew this was his opportunity. The cure was right in front of him and he wasn't going to let Jesus pass him by.

Jesus asks us the same thing, "What do you want Me to do for you?" He is in front of us, He cares and He wants us to tell Him. Tell Jesus what you want, knowing He can do it. He can change any situation because He is all powerful and nothing is too Hard for Him.

What we ask for will reveal our heart. God is not a magic genie who is at our disposal to work according to our will. James says, "You have not because you ask not, and when you ask you ask amiss that you may spend it on your own pleasure."

We see the Apostle Paul praying that his thorn be removed from his side. He prayed three times and the thorn was not removed. The thorn was needed to keep Paul humble and dependent on God. God's strength would be made perfect in His weakness and God's grace would be sufficient for him. The thorn kept Paul strong in God's power and strong in God's grace, whereas the healing of the blind man's sight would make him strong in faith and spiritual sight enabling him to see Jesus as more than healer but also as Messiah. In each case, Jesus responded with the best and highest good for each man.

Here then we see the tension between the way God responds to our requests. The constant between the two men is faith. They both knew God could do it. In all our praying, faith is the key. They both had faith to ask Jesus, they both had faith in His power and His willingness. We too must pray with belief. They also both had a need. They had a reason to cry out and they were both desperate. They could do nothing to change their circumstances and they both needed a miracle.

The variable was the answer. God healed the blind man yet did not heal Paul. The question is why? Sometimes the miracle is in what we ask for, other times the miracle is in something bigger and deeper than we ask for. God's answers to our prayers will always be in the best interest of us, of His glory and for eternal reasons. Knowing this will help us to rejoice in whatever the answer to our petitions may be.

. . .

THE LESSON here is to remember that God works perfectly for your good, and that good will be the highest good, that also works for His glory and eternal purposes. You can rest assured, when you cry out to God, He hears and answers according to the best and highest good.

NEGLECT

JOSHUA 18:3

> *"Then Joshua said to the children of Israel: 'How long will you neglect to go and possess the land which the LORD God of your fathers has given you?'"*

Neglect is a condition that sneaks up on us with little notice. The reason is that neglect comes when we are noticing other things. Our attention gets divided and our mind gets filled with too many things. It is a silent killer that can go undetected until we start to experience the symptoms of neglect.

In our text we see the Children of Israel neglecting what was already given to them It was theirs, but they had to go and posses it. God's promises are like that, we must go and possess them. Like a coupon, we may have it but we must redeem it.

We will start to lose our joy, become frustrated, irritable and less loving. We will lose our peace and forget our purpose. We hurt and struggle and wonder why. Satan has now infiltrated our once passionate love for God and cooled it down to a chill. He has secretly robbed us of the fullness of God and has distracted us from taking the territory God has given us.

. . .

THE LESSON here is to recognize if there is anything you've been neglecting. Now is the time to stop neglecting the inheritance God has for you. It may be time to simply rid yourself of anything that takes your heart and soul away from your first love. It's better to neglect the unimportant to focus on the most important. It's time to surrender, press forward and obey. God loves you too much to let you feel comfortable neglecting Him. Come to Him for a fresh start and keep Him as your one desire. The Lord has good land for you.

DESPISING THE WORD

PROVERBS 14:13

> *"He who despises the word will be destroyed."*

The Bible is full of warnings. God sees what we don't and knows what we can't. He alone is wise, full of understanding and seeing all things. It is with this greatness that He instructs us as a wise Father wanting only the best for His children.

Gods intent is to guide us in the best paths. The Bible says that there is a way that seems right to man, but the end of that way is destruction. The best thing a person can do is listen to God's warnings and heed them.

Despising God's Word is ascribing no value to it. It is putting it down or ignoring it. Notice that to despise God's Word there has to be exposure to it. The problem isn't ignorance but rejection. By rejecting God's Word we are rejecting the right path, the right way and the safe road. We are rejecting the ultimate guide who always leads correctly. Rejecting God's Word is destruction.

It's not if, but when, the despiser will reap its own desire, life without God. The despiser will drink its own poison killing all that is good, right and true. Ultimately the despiser will find themselves destroyed for all eternity because they would not yield to God and His method of salvation.

. . .

THE LESSON here is that you are to value God's Word as our most important possession, as the most important priority and the most important path. Then you will travel safely on the road to eternity.

GOD'S WORD

JOSHUA 21:45

> *"Not a word failed of any good thing which the Lord had spoken to the
> house of Israel. All came to pass."*

There are not many guarantees in the world. Things that once seemed so certain
can easily fade away. Things change, people change and circumstances change.
In the midst of all the uncertainty in the world, God is the same yesterday today
and forever. He will never change and He has given us His written Word that
will never fade away.

God has proven the certainty of His Word through thousands of years of fulfilled prophecy with 100% accuracy. He has written the end from the beginning
and then has staked His authority on His accuracy. He said what could not be
known, and then when time caught up, He has always proven to be right. Many
naysayers and skeptics have come and gone but God's Word stands.

There is nothing that proves God's Word more than His working through the
nation of Israel. There is no human explanation for their existence and perseverance through history as a people, their reformation and establishment as a
nation after thousands of years of international exile, and the divine protection
of their nation.

. . .

THE LESSON here is that you have a guarantee in life that you can count on.
God will fulfill His Word and all will come to pass just as He says it will. When
you build your life on God and His Word you will be solid, never shaken and
firmly planted no matter what storm may come. God's Word will endure forever.

SPIRITUAL WARFARE

JOSHUA 23:10

"One man of you shall chase a thousand, for the LORD your God is He who fights for you, as He promised you."

The great exploits of God's people are beauty to behold. The Lord does for man what man cannot do for himself. Especially when it comes to Spiritual warfare. When we are with God we are a majority. One thousand to one odds are unfair to the one thousand, if the one is God. It doesn't matter what forces come against us, if God is for us then who can be against us. Christians have their confidence in The Lord and He will fight for them.

Our job is to be obedient to the Holy Spirit. We have no idea what is going on behind the scenes in the realm of spiritual warfare, so we must follow the Holy Spirits leading. That's why we may be confused and resistant to the Spirit's leading but what may not seem prudent and practical to our minds is really God orchestrating our safe passage through things unseen. There is safety in obedience and not in rebellion.

· · ·

THE LESSON here is that God will fight for you. He will not be defeated and neither will we. Put your confidence in His power and strength and not your own. He has promised His protection and no matter how bad things seem, let Him fight FOR you and not WITH you. In other words, you can step aside and say, "Lord, it's all yours." Whatever you're facing say, "Lord, it's Your problem, it's Your fight and it's Your trouble." Don't try to steer the ship because Jesus is already at the helm. The battle belongs to Him.

PERSPECTIVE

LUKE 21:13

"But it will turn out for you as an occasion for testimony."

Perspective determines what we see and how we see it. Looking at the ocean from the beach is much different than looking at it from a scuba mask from underneath. How one responds to the things that happen to them in life will reveal their view of things. A reaction is worth a thousand words.

Having a Biblical perspective gives the clearest view of reality. Without a Biblical view one will only see a tiny bit of reality and will miss the bigger and more important picture. Without a Biblical perspective the view is narrow and obscured by one's own blurry "self first" lens. A Biblical perspective sees beyond self to God, and this perspective gives a clear picture.

Seeing bigger is the Biblical perspective that allows one to see not just what is happening to them as the biggest view but then sees God has a purpose and plan in every situation that goes beyond the "self" lens. The Biblical view sees opportunity in all circumstances to glorify God and to testify to His greatness.

In our text we see an exhortation (or encouragement) that follows a warning. The warning was that Christians will be thrown in jail for being a Christian in the last days and the exhortation was that their circumstance will lead to opportunity. Having a Biblical perspective sees opportunity in tragedy, trial, hardship, loss and difficulty. God is using the circumstance for much greater purposes, like Jesus dying on the cross was for much greater purposes than could be seen by the "self first" lens.

· · ·

THE LESSON here is that having the right perspective in life is crucial, especially when you go through things that are different than you want or expected. The good news is that God is creating an opportunity. Look for the opportunities in your pain and you will find a much greater perspective. God is using you in the greatest way, to testify about Him and to bring others to the hope of Jesus Christ. With this perspective you will find your greatest purpose that your life could have. This is seeing life through God's eyes, the greatest perspective of all.

APRIL 23

Judges 1:1 2:9, Luke 21:29 22:13,
Psalm 90:1 91:16, Proverbs 13:24 25

NUMBERING YOUR DAYS

PSALM 90:12

"So teach us to number our days, That we may gain a heart of wisdom."

Wisdom will come if one understands the brevity of life. The Bible says, "Life is but a vapor." It may not seem like it but in comparison to eternity life is just a blink. The psalmist here is asking that the Lord would teach Him to be mindful of this reality.

There is nothing more tragic than a wasted life. One who lives as if they will live forever. Living as if this life is all there is and having a philosophy of life that says indulgence and pleasure are the height of one's existence. The psalmist wants to be free from that thinking, desiring to be aware of his limited existence in order to make the most of the time he has.

To live a full life is to know that there is a short time to do what can only be done here on earth. Once it's over, it's over, and there is no turning back. This is the time to live for Christ in a way we will never be able to in the future. Jesus said lay up treasure in heaven where moth and rust won't destroy.

The teaching of the Bible is that we are here as Christians on a mission. We are here to live for Him, serve Him and glorify Him. We are here to make disciples and to build His Kingdom. That is why we remain here on earth still and why God has not taken us home yet. We have work to do, so we must be about our Father's business.

• • •

THE LESSON here is for you to pray that God would teach you to be aware of your life's temporary and fleeting moments so that you would make your life count where it really matters, in eternity. You will never regret living your life for God, but you will regret wasting it for things that really don't matter.

JESUS OUR VICTORY

LUKE 22:31

> *"And the Lord said, 'Simon, Simon! Indeed, Satan has asked for you, that he may sift you as wheat.'"*

Satan is an opportunist looking to pounce whenever we are weak. He especially likes when we think we are strong and underestimate him. He loves when we don't rely on Jesus and try and stand on our own. He loves when we get complacent in prayer, God's Word, using our gifts and following the leading of the Holy Spirit.

Satan has no mercy and hates us more than we could ever imagine. Satan will lie, deceive, tempt and manipulate in order to steal, rob and destroy. He targets Christians in a special way knowing that he has already lost the war for their soul so he will try and win a battle or two in order to injure their walk and effectiveness.

Jesus spoke to Simon, or Peter, about this. He warned Peter about Satan's desire to sift him like wheat. Peter is not the only one being warned. Every Christian can put their names in there too. We must take this warning very seriously because of the dangerous intentions of Satan.

Following the warning, Jesus says in essence, Peter, don't worry because I am praying for you, that your faith doesn't fail. That should have been all the encouragement Peter needed, as well as all the encouragement we need. We have nothing to fear because Jesus is praying for us and faith cannot be defeated. Satan cannot beat faith so he will try to get us not to have faith. He will try and get us to depend on ourselves and our own strength. He will try and get us to be self-reliant and self-sufficient.

That is where it all went wrong for Peter. His answer to Jesus was basically, don't worry about it Jesus, I got this, I am ready and I will never fail. Resisting Jesus' help, he trusted in his flesh and ultimately learned a very painful lesson.

· · ·

THE LESSON here then is knowing that your flesh is no match for Satan, but Satan is no match for Jesus. Greater is He that is in you than he that is in the world. Your victory is in Jesus. Trust not in what you can do, trust in what He has done. Jesus is the victory that has already been won.

APRIL 25

Judges 4:1 5:31, Luke 22:35 53,
Psalm 94:1 23, Proverbs 14:3 4

YOUR WILL BE DONE

LUKE 22:42

"...saying, 'Father, if it is Your will, take this cup away from Me; neverthe-less not My will, but Yours, be done.'"

The secret to the Christian life is found in these seven words of Jesus, "not my will, but Yours, be done." Here we see what submission and surrender looks like. The Christian's strength is in his weakness.

Jesus, going through the agony of the struggle between the flesh and Spirit, finds power through yielding to the Father's will. This is where the battle is won and where Satan loses power. This is where the truth of who or what our master is, reveals itself. The pressure of retreat, the temptation of the easier way and path of least resistance is where the greatest victories are won.

The Christian is not asked to gain victory through might but through submission. There is a big difference in the two. Jesus said we are to abide not strive. Abiding is just staying connected to Jesus through faith, which is the connector. As we do, God works through us and accomplishes His purpose powerfully and supernaturally.

The difference is yielding vs. exerting. Think of someone pushing against your outstretched arm. You can resist or yield. When you resist you are using your strength and when you yield it is God's strength. His power is matchless and limitless. Our power is weak and limited. We get weary where God never tires.

. . .

THE LESSON here is that we are to be great at surrender, exercising our faith and not our might. God will bring the results as we yield to His will. When we are weak, He is strong. Make it a habit, make it a prayer, make it a reflex, make it a theme, when push comes to shove the answer is always the same, not my will but Yours be done.

When the battles rages and the pressure is on,
the flesh tempted and the Spirit strong,
say yes to God and no to I,
His will be done, my will die.
Victory gained and Satan crushed,
no power over me and threats hushed,
God's will be done no greater words,
the Christians power through surrender.

THE LORD IS WITH YOU

JUDGES 6:12

> *"And the Angel of the LORD appeared to him, and said to him, 'The LORD is with you, you mighty man of valor!'"*

"The Lord is with you," was what the "Angel of the Lord" said to Gideon before he was commissioned to free the Jews. Gideon was not anything or anybody special. He was the least in his family, belonging to the weakest tribe. He was well aware of his inadequacies as seen by his repeated requests for more confirmation that God would give him victory. Yet, he was the perfect candidate for greatness.

Notice that the "Angel of the Lord" was none other than a pre-incarnate appearance of Jesus. He calls Gideon "mighty" and "brave." Gideon was not that. However, "the Lord was with him," which made all the difference. No matter our weaknesses or limitations when God is with us we are mighty.

The Lord with us is all we need to know as we go out day by day and live our lives for the Lord. We carry the greatest weapon, the greatest power, the greatest ally and the greatest friend. So often we look at the enemy or obstacle in comparison to us, when we should be looking at them in comparison to the Almighty God. "The Lord with you" settles all our fears and worry. "The Lord with you" is our confidence and strength that we can never be overcome.

• • •

THE LESSON for you here is to know and remember that you are never alone and never asked to face life without the Lord. Whatever the calling, God is our enabling. As Gideon defeated a great army against all odds, you to will overcome all that comes against you because the Lord is with you.

THE GLORY

JUDGES 7:2

> *"And the LORD said to Gideon, 'The people who are with you are too many for Me to give the Midianites into their hands, lest Israel claim glory for itself against Me, saying, "My own hand has saved me." ' "*

God is very particular about the glory. Not because He is needy of attention and recognition but because of the truth. God, being God, needs no introduction nor does He need validation. He is self-sufficient and self sustained. His holiness is unchanged by mans' opinions. He is the Great "I Am" and will always be. He is not affected by anything man thinks about Him, but man is greatly affected by his own thoughts about God.

Throughout the Bible God is revealing Himself to man so that man would know Him correctly. He teaches us about who He is, His character and attributes, so that man would be oriented to Him properly. This is mankind's greatest privilege. Knowing Him on His terms is knowing Him truthfully and not erroneously. When one makes up a version of God that is acceptable to him, yet not truthful according to God's Word, then that person has made a God in his own image and does not know the true and living God.

Here in our text, Gideon, who is greatly overmatched to begin with, is told to get rid of more people. God wants the numbers to be so ridiculous that there could be no mistake that it was God and not Gideon who won the battle. God does this to show His glory and power to man and to show that He is altogether separate from man. Ultimately this is to show how much we need God and how much we need Him to save us. Seeing His glory defeats all attempts of man to approach God on his own merit and refutes any thoughts of self-righteousness. This is why it is so important that God gets the glory and not man. So we see Him properly and we see ourselves properly.

Notice that if Israel took the credit for the victory, or in some way thought that it was their greatness that accomplished the command, then the glory they claimed would actually go against God. There is no sharing of the glory but whatever was a gain for them was a loss for God and ultimately for their own salvation.

. . .

THE LESSON here is to never touch the glory. God is the only one who deserves the glory and the only One who is glorious. Be very careful with success and how Satan can use it to puff up your flesh to the extent that you enjoy the praises of men over the praise of God. Make sure God gets the glory!

NO MORE SEPARATION

LUKE 23:45

"Then the sun was darkened, and the veil of the temple was torn in two."

The veil represents separation. It restricts, hides and forbids. The veil is what separated the Holy place in the Temple from the most inner part of the Temple called the Holy of Holies. The presence of God was in the Holy of Holies, unseen but for once a year by only the High Priest and only through ceremonial washings and offerings that had to be performed flawlessly. The Holy of Holies was for the most part left alone, quiet and abandoned. All the work went in the Holy Place. That's where the High priest would change the bread, burn the incense, trim the wicks of the candles and refill the oil that lit the lamp stand. The Holy place was a place of activity, whereas the Holy of Holies was a place of glory.

When Jesus died on the cross, the veil was torn. We are told elsewhere that it was torn from the top to the bottom and not the other way around, indicating it was God who tore it and not man. It happened immediately after Jesus breathed His last breath, indicating that Jesus' sacrifice was sufficient to take away our sin. The veil is reported to be 60 feet long, 30 feet wide and 4 inches thick. A Jewish historian, Josephus, reports that two horses on either side could not pull it apart, yet that veil could not stand up to the love of God. So the power of God's love is able to do what man could never do, removing the barrier that separates man from God.

Here we see that Jesus' darkest moment was our brightest moment. His death granted our access. The separation now gone, by faith we can come into His presence. That's what the gospel did for us. It removed the barrier, which was sin, that we could come in.

• • •

THE LESSON here is to see that you have full access to God. Is there anything keeping you from God's presence? Are you drawing near and enjoying His presence? The veil is now torn, what once was an isolated room can now be your home. Jesus says come in and bask in My glory of God.

Judges 9:22 10:18, Luke 24:13 53,
Psalm 100:1 5, Proverbs 14:11 12

THE POWER OF THE HOLY SPIRIT

LUKE 24:49

> *"Behold, I send the Promise of My Father upon you; but tarry in the city of Jerusalem until you are endued with power from on high."*

Jesus didn't want the disciples rushing into ministry yet. They were filled with joy at the realization that Jesus rose from the dead. They were filled with hope and expectation. They understood now the importance of salvation and that Jesus truly was the Savior of the world. They understood their mission was to share Jesus with the world as ambassadors of Christ and as those with the ministry of reconciliation. They we expedited and ready to go, yet Jesus said to wait.

What they didn't understand was that they were on a mission that required power that they did not have. It would take more than just teaching and explaining what happened. It would take more than eyewitness testimony. It would take more than clever arguments. They needed power because they were sent on a mission to do what only God could do.

Many times we rush into ministry and service with good intentions but lacking in power. Good intentions will not accomplish the work of God, only God's power can do that. Ministry without God's power is like a car without an engine. It will go nowhere.

It's easy to forget the most important part of ministering and serving the Lord and that is the dependence upon the Holy Spirit. Be careful of becoming a ministry robot that can kick on cruise control because we are following a system or program. Don't get too caught up in trying to do everything so perfectly that you forget you can do nothing without the power of the Holy Spirit.

· · ·

THE LESSON here is to see that the Holy Spirit can do through you what you cannot do on your own. Rely on His power through surrender. Better to wait for the Holy Spirit to move than to proceed without Him. God can do in a flash what you cannot. It's not a matter of speed and quickness to make things happen, it's a matter of obedience that allows God's thing to happen. When you go in His power you will be amazed at what God can do and thankful that He lets you be a part of it.

JESUS

JOHN 1:1

> *"In the beginning was the Word, and the Word was with God, and the Word was God. He was in the beginning with God. All things were made through Him, and without Him nothing was made that was made."*

Who is Jesus? Scriptures foretold of a Savior that would come and take away the sins of the world. Over three hundred scriptures spoke of the Messiah and what He would do. There was much anticipation of the Savior and hope that He would change things.

With all the anticipation of Jesus' coming, what was most important was that Jesus would be correctly identified. It's not only important to believe in Jesus but also to believe correctly about a Him. John makes it very clear in the very beginning of his gospel who Jesus was.

FIRST Jesus is called the Word. Essentially, Jesus is the communication of God the Father to man, in man's language. Just like our words are used to share with others what is inside us and unseen, so Jesus came to share what was in the Fathers' heart and unseen. Seeing Jesus was seeing the Father in our language.

Man could not know God nor understand God unless He became human. The second member of the triune God (one God in three persons) took on a body of flesh and blood to reveal God to us. This is why He is called the Word.

SECONDLY, it says that Jesus was in the beginning. This means that Jesus was already here when there was a beginning. He was before the beginning. Jesus, being God, had no beginning. He always was and always is. Jesus never didn't existed but always existed. He wasn't created and He didn't become God. He is eternal. This is a very important point as Jesus could not be the Savior unless He was eternally God.

THIRDLY Jesus, the Word, was with God in the beginning. Again speaking of His deity or how much He was God. He was there with the Father, at the same time, at the beginning of creation. This shows His equality with God the Father and that they are one, but separate.

FOURTHLY, not only was He with God, Jesus was God. There could not be a more clear statement as to who Jesus is. He is plain and simply God. He cannot be lowered to merely a Teacher, Prophet or religious leader but beyond that, and the most important life saving identification of who Jesus is, is to know that He is God.

FIFTHLY, John says all things were made through Him and nothing was made without Him. So Jesus was the creator of all. This again stresses His Deity, as Jesus is separate from creation as the Creator. He brought all into being and there is nothing in existence that He didn't make. This puts Jesus in a category all to Himself and was necessary for Him to be the Savior.

. . .

THE LESSON here is to make sure we know the Jesus of the Bible. Jesus, the communication of God to man, the preexistent One, equal with God the Father, second member of the Trinity, creator of all and God Himself in the flesh.

BEHOLD THE LAMB

JOHN 1:29

*"The next day John saw Jesus coming toward him, and said, 'Behold! The
Lamb of God who takes away the sin of the world!'"*

Jesus is called "The Lamb" by John the Baptist. It's noteworthy that John would
refer to Jesus as "The Lamb" when he first sees Jesus. There are many ways to describe Jesus and He Himself used many different descriptions. For example He
says that He is The Door, The Light, The Bread of Life, The Vine and The Way.
Why does John the Baptist see Jesus as The Lamb of God?

John is not just greeting Jesus but he is also making an announcement. John's
role was to be the forerunner of Christ, meaning he would prepare people to
meet Jesus. John would remind people of their need for repentance as he prepared people to turn from sin to God. He would baptize them preparing them
for their need to die to themselves and be made new. He would live a holy and
righteous life preparing them for their need for holiness. John was sort of a
warm up band for the main attraction. Then when Jesus finally arrived he, by
preparing others, was the most prepared to see Jesus.

The moment John lays eyes on Him he saw the realization of all his work. He saw
the fulfillment of the Passover Lamb that for centuries had been slain to cover
the nation of Israel's sins. John saw not "a" lamb like all the endless number of
lambs that were slain but he saw "The" Lamb. The one and only Savior of the
world. The reality behind all the shadows of Old Testament life. John saw the
most important aspect of Jesus' role as the incarnate God, a sacrificial lamb, a
soon to be murdered Savior. John saw the answer to sin, the innocent blood that
was required and the perfect sacrifice to be offered.

John's announcement was the greatest announcement the world has ever heard,
Jesus the Lamb had come and He was going to take away the sin of the world.
There has never been a more loving description of God who created the universe
and all that is in it, yet came into that world in human flesh to be slaughtered for
us. Jesus, The Lamb of God, sinless perfection made vulnerable to sins punishment for a sinful race of humanity. The irony of it all yet perfectly perfect for a
loving God and demonstrating that love.

· · ·

THE LESSON here is that you too can "behold the Lamb" rejoicing, as your sin
through Jesus has been put away forever.

MAY 2

Judges 15:1 16:31, John 2:1 25,
Psalm 103:1 22, Proverbs 14:17 19

BELIEVE

JOHN 2:23-24

> *"Now when He was in Jerusalem at the Passover, during the feast, many
> believed in His name when they saw the signs which He did. But Jesus did
> not commit Himself to them, because He knew all men."*

There is a certain type of belief that Jesus looks for. Not all belief is the same. Not all belief is saving belief. It is true that belief is required for salvation, but the object and quality of belief is what saves. Not that those who believe the most are saved, but those who believe in Jesus as He is revealed in scripture and that belief rests in His work to save.

There is a belief that does not touch heaven. The demons believe in Jesus. They even believe in Him as the Bible says He is. They believe Jesus is God, is the Creator of all, is sinless and all powerful. They even have a fear of Him. Yet they are not trusting in Him for salvation.

There are others who are trusting in Jesus for their salvation but have made Jesus in their own image, not accepting Him as He is. The may say Jesus "became" a god through His good works but he was born a man like every other man. Others may say he is a god like many other gods. Nothing special or unique other than he was an exalted human being.

Others may believe Jesus is who the Bible says He is yet are trusting in a combination of His work and their own good works for salvation. This too misses the mark for all our works are like filthy rags the Bible says. We are not going to present to God our "filthy rags" and say "here you go God, let me in."

In our text we see that there were some who believed in Jesus because of the signs He did. They were fascinated by the supernatural working and wanted to see more of that. They saw Jesus more as a novelty than a Savior.

Some may have seen these "believers" as genuine but Jesus knew their hearts. He saw that they did not have a genuine belief but a circumstantial and superficial belief. They had a belief the suited themselves more than suited Jesus. They had a belief that would not accept a suffering sacrificial Savior but a belief that said

I want Jesus to give me stuff and be my personal genie in a bottle. As a result of their misguided belief, Jesus didn't commit Himself to them.

· · ·

THE LESSON here is to really think about what you believe in. It's very pertinent, not only to our day and age but also to a western cultural brand of non-Biblical Christianity that centers more around self then it does around God. This "form of Godliness" is self-centered and world centered. It takes it cues more from pop culture than from Almighty God and His Word.

Only belief in the Biblical Jesus, that is resting their eternity fully on what Jesus has done, and who He is is a belief that Jesus commits to.

THE KING

JUDGES 18:6

"In those days there was no king in Israel; everyone did what was right in his own eyes."

Jesus is the King of Kings. He has all authority and rules and reigns from on high. When He is our King we live according to His government, submitting to His ways. His Kingdom then rules us, bringing the fruit righteousness, peace and joy in the Holy Spirit. There is order and no need for constraint, for love will rule the day and constrain in the man.

In our text we see the effects of essentially each person having their own standard. They will not submit it to any authority, making themselves their own king. They set up their own rules which accord to their own ideas of what is right and those rules will be determined by "what is best for me."

Those without a king ultimately make themselves the king. There is no order because they have no absolute truth but a functional truth that changes depending on the circumstances and situations. One sees "right" from a different lens as another's "right." Not only can a society not work this way, individuals cannot work this way.

Those without a King will think that what they are doing is right, with great abilities to justify their wrongness. How can anyone have any correctness in their lives without a clear understanding of what really is right and really wrong? There is no standard which transcends them but only what their own eyes perceive as correct.

· · ·

THE LESSON here is to thank God for His truth that sets you free. Living for King Jesus means you don't do what the world tells you is right but you follow the Holy Spirit and look to God's Word for direction. When you submit to the Holy Spirit, you are led by His hand and ruled by love and order. You are anchored in truth and stable in the rock of Christ. Love will fill your heart because our King is awesome in power and deeply loving. Jesus is your King and you are ruled by love.

GOD WORKS IN MYSTERIOUS WAYS

JOHN 3:23

"Now John also was baptizing in Aenon near Salim, because there was much water there. And they came and were baptized."

John the Baptist had a calling to baptize people. He was to prepare people's hearts for the coming of Jesus. It may sound obvious but his location was dictated by his need. John needed water so he was in Aenon near Salim where there was much water. Here is a key to God's will.

God works in mysterious ways for sure, but He also works in obvious ways at times. As we see in our text, God leads us to where we can be successful. In other words, He leads us to where the water is. John needed water to baptize so God led Him to where the water was. When God leads He not only prepares the person He is leading, He also prepares the place where He is leading them. He makes the place fit for arrival of those carrying out His plan. Like John, God will make our destination fit like a glove.

We also see that God also provides. God will take us to where everything we need to fulfill HIS calling will be found at the place He brings us. It's all there if we will follow the Lord. Like the disciples who were sent out and told to take no food, bag or money for their journey. They had all they needed in their commission itself and all the provisions needed would be where they went.

Next we see that there was MUCH water where God led John. Water in the Bible is a symbol of the Holy Spirit. Wherever God leads us, there is an overflow of power and fruit of the Holy Spirit. We can do nothing without this empowerment and God knows this. The great thing about ministering in God's power is that not only do those we are ministering to get to experience the power of the Holy Spirit, so do those in whom God is pouring out the Spirit through.

Finally we see that God takes us where we will find fulfillment. Sometimes we can fear God's will and wonder if we submit all to a Him that we will be miserable at the place He takes us. This is not the case. God will take us to where we will be most satisfied. To the missionary in Haiti, to the preacher in Africa, to the teacher in Japan, to the construction worker in Mexico or whatever. This will be our paradise. God knows what best fits us for how He made us and equipped us. This is where He will lead us. Paradise then is being in God's will.

. . .

THE LESSON here is that God knows exactly what you need and if you have Him, you have all you need. He will lead you where you can be successful, where the provisions are, where the Holy Spirit empowers and where you will be most fulfilled. No need to fear what God may do through your surrendered heart, rather fear what you may miss by resisting.

WHAT DOES THE FOLLOWING CHRIST LOOK LIKE?

RUTH 1:16

> *"But Ruth said: 'Entreat me not to leave you, Or to turn back from following after you; For wherever you go, I will go; And wherever you lodge, I will lodge; Your people shall be my people, And your God, my God.'"*

Following Jesus is what a Christian is to do. This means we have given our lives to Him and we are not living for ourselves but we are living for Him. Only a true Christian would follow Jesus because following Him means giving up our own ways and our own lives. It means we have given our goals to Him and our aspirations are now His. He is our life.

Ruth gives us an example of what following Jesus may look like. She tells her mother in law that she would rather leave all her hope in this world just to be with her. This is the attitude of a follower of Christ. The Apostle Paul said that what was a gain to Him was a loss for Christ. He also said that he counted all things he lost as rubbish that he may gain Christ.

A follower not only is willing to leave world hope to follow Christ, but they also will continue on no matter the temptations to quit. For Ruth, she was told by her mother in law to go back and even her sister in law did go back. We too will face many challenges to our faith to go back to what's comfortable and more promising by the world's standards. However, a true follower of Christ doesn't live by the world's standards but by faith in God. When tempted the true follower continues on.

Next, a true follower will go where Christ goes. Where is that? It is where the Holy Spirit directs us from within. A true follower knows God's voice and is obedient to His leading. A true follower has an inward guide taking the follower to where Jesus wants to be and where He would go if He was here physically again. Jesus is wanting to reach people with His love and that is where He will lead us. Listen to His direction and be obedient to His call. We then will find ourselves where He is.

A true follower will live where Jesus lives. This means, like Ruth, we will live in God's will. This is the home of the Christian. This is where the Christian is most comfortable and this is where the heart is. When we become Christians, our heart is to be in God's will.

A true follower also will be with God's people. This is where Christ is. He is with the church, the body of Christ. If Jesus were here physically, He'd be in church. The book of Revelation, chapter one verse thirteen tells us He is in the midst of the seven lamp-stands. Not that He wouldn't be out in the world also, but that His home is with the body of Christ, building it up, encouraging it and blessing it. This is where the follower will be and this is what the follower will be doing.

Finally, a follower of Christ will have the God of the Bible as their personal God. We follow the God of the Jews and even though one may not be a Jew, we worship their God which is the one and only God for all to worship.

· · ·

THE LESSON here is that a true follower of Christ follows the God that was from the beginning, that led Moses and the Jews out of Egypt. The God that helped David and Solomon build the temple. This is the God of Jerusalem and Israel. Their God is your God and by faith we all come through Jesus Christ.

This is what it means to follow Christ.

GOD'S PROVISIONS

RUTH 2:16

> *"Also let grain from the bundles fall purposely for her; leave it that she may glean, and do not rebuke her."*

God is gracious and full of compassion. He is good to all, and His tender mercies are over all His works. We see how God loves to care for us in the most wonderful ways. He knows what we need and His delivery and timing are always perfect. He will never let us down and we can rest in His love. He rewards those who walk by faith through perfect provisions.

In our text we see an example of God's perfect provision. Ruth, leaving her worldly hopes behind to follow Naomi, didn't know where her provisions would come from but she knew she was to be with Naomi. Faith is like that, we may not know where provision will come from but we know who our provider is. As long as we are His, then we know He will provide.

Obediently following is the key. We don't have to know all the answers and have everything figured out, we just need to know what God is leading us to do. He will take care of the rest. As Jesus said, "Seek first the Kingdom of God and His righteousness and all these things will be added unto you." The provider will always provide.

The hungry foreigner, Ruth, was allowed to glean, or take any wheat that had fallen to the ground. Boas, the land owner tells his servants to "purposely" let grain fall. In other words they were to make it intentionally fall not just randomly fall. This was an order of the master. God purposely lets what we need fall our way.

So often we strive and struggle to make this happen. We push and press to see our desires. However, it's not like that with the Lord. He will purposely throw down what we need. Not that we don't work or that we are irresponsible, but that we do everything we do for the Lord then we trust He will take care of us.

Finally we see here that when we walk by faith God throws things into our laps. He loves to bless us and will give those blessings, showing He is gracious and full of compassion.

. . .

THE LESSON here is knowing that God is a rewarder of those who diligently seek Him. The greatest part of walking by faith is waking up each day knowing that surprises are waiting for you and God loves to give them. The reward of waking by faith is the supernatural provision God will provide for you each and every day.

GETTING OFF THE MAT

JOHN 5:8

"Jesus said to him, 'Rise, take up your bed and walk.'"

It's easy to fall into a rut and not expect God to do great things in our lives. When we do, we can get our eyes off Jesus, forget the hope we have in Him and doubt that He has made all things new for us. We can lose sight of His plan for our lives and that He wants to do great things. When we fall into this rut we are negative, skeptical and often depressed. This is not what God wants for us. He says that He wants to give us life, and that more abundantly. He wants to give us passion, power and purpose so that our days are filled with awe and wonder.

Perhaps we have become like the lame man in our text. Jesus asked him if he wanted to be made well. This man had suffered from an infirmity for thirty eight years. He was hanging around a special pool called Bethesda in which an angel would occasionally stir the water and the first one in would be healed. Well, not such a good plan for a lame man. He could never get in before the others.

When Jesus asked Him if he wanted to get well he said he couldn't because he couldn't get in fast enough. He really didn't answer Jesus' question. All he could think about, and see, was what he couldn't do, missing Jesus Himself standing right in front if him. Jesus was ready, willing and able to help him but he could not see that. This is how we can be when we lose sight of Jesus because we are looking at the problem.

Jesus answers back and says to, "rise, take up your bed and walk." He says that to us today as well. Basically, "get going." You have been made well. You are a new creation in Christ, endowed with the power of the Holy Spirit. You are healed and anointed to bring comfort to the broken hearted and encouragement to the weak. You are not the old self you are healed.

The first step is to rise. You may not feel like it. You may feel hurt, lame, incapacitated. You may feel forgotten or treated unfairly. Whatever it may be, it's time to rise. You are made well. Jesus will get you through but you have to take that first step. Get up and you will find your strength. Rise and you will find your purpose. But you must first rise.

Next, take up your mat. In other words, take away the things in your life that keep you from rising. The mat was this mans refuge and comfort. It was also his bondage and trap. Take away the darkness, the habits, the self pity. Take away the excuses and options to go back. Once you rise keep going forward. No need to look back or keep that old bed that kept you in a place of oppression and uselessness.

Finally, you are to walk. Walk in the newness of life which is walking by the power of the Holy Spirit. Walk surrendered to God's power. Walk in grace and love. Walk in confidence and in your spiritual gifts. Serve, pray, get into the Word, encourage others. Get the focus off self and on to the greatness of Christ. Forget what's behind and live for today. Do something that takes faith and requires you to get out of your comfort zone. Plug in to your church body and be a contributor and a blessing. This is what God has called you to do. God will bless you and make your life useful and a blessing.

• • •

THE LESSON here is that you are not called, healed and anointed to stay on your mat, you are called, healed and anointed to go with the strength and power of the Holy Spirit. You have been made well, now rise and walk.

ENVY

PROVERBS 14:30

"A sound heart is life to the body, But envy is rottenness to the bones."

Envy takes away from the beauty of one's uniqueness. It also robs God of His magnificence by denying His creative wisdom and omniscient plan. Envy says God is deficient and lacking. It is one of Satan's best tools.

In our text we see the comparison of a sound heart to envy. A heart is at the core of life. It gives life to the rest of the body through pumping blood which contains oxygen and nutrients. A healthy heart delivers life. On the other hand, envy spreads disease to the rest of the body. It poisons and makes everything in us rotten, even to the innermost structural support like the bones. Envy cannot be compartmentalized but will harm the whole person. Happiness and envy cannot coexist because one comes from health, the other disease.

We see here the all encompassing effects of envy. Like a metastatic cancer, envy will spread and destroy the person who carries it. The solution is then to be thankful to God for everything. How you look and what you have is a good place to start.

. . .

THE LESSON here is to learn to accept that God has made you perfectly for the calling He has in your life. He has put you where should be and given you what you need to have. Knowing this you can thank Him, rest in His perfect plan and look to Jesus for satisfaction and not to others for comparison. Embrace who you are and what you have as a gift of God knowing He knows what He is doing. Envy ends when thanksgiving begins.

1 Samuel 5:1 7:17, John 6:1 21,
Psalm 106:13 31, Proverbs 14:32 33

SOUL FOOD

//

PSALM 106:15

"And He gave them their request, But sent leanness into their soul."

God's perfect will contains within it everything you really ever want. All you crave and desire is found right there. Nothing material can fill that void and bring the fullness like God's perfect will. This is what you should aim at.

In our text we see that it is possible to get some things you want but when you do it won't deliver what you desire. This is the disappointment one can feel when fulfillment is not attained the way they thought it could be. If you could have as much money, possessions, power or position you wanted but could never be fulfilled or satisfied, would you take it? What if you were offered 10 billion dollars but if accepted you would have to forfeit any chance of joy, peace or love. Of course not, because the material object is really not what you are after but what you think the material object will bring. Well, we see here from our text that fulfillment can only come from the Lord and being in His perfect will.

. . .

THE LESSON here is that it is not about the getting, but about the submitting. This is where you will find fulfillment. Submitting to God, His plan, His will and His way. When you do you will find fatness in your soul. There will be an abundance of satisfaction because God's will is satisfying. Don't settle for the unsatisfactory and empty cravings of the flesh, which never satisfy, but rather, let God do that. You will be rich and full where it really matters, in your soul.

SEPARATE

1 SAMUEL 8:5

> *"And said to him, 'Look, you are old, and your sons do not walk in your ways. Now make us a king to judge us like all the nations.'"*

The nation of Israel was called by God to be separate from all the other nations in order for other nations to see the goodness of God. Other nations would see God's blessings and miraculous care given to those who follow Him. Their purpose was to be a light in a dark world and give hope to all the world in pointing to the goodness of God. They were to be different, not the same, so all the world could see.

However, Israel as a nation desired to be more like the world than separate from it. They saw their calling as a burden and not a privilege. This was the beginning of the end for them. In the same way, Christians are called to be separate from the world, not like the world. Christians are called to be ruled by God as their king and not by the ways of the world. Christians are called to live by faith and not by sight. When a Christian does this they are fulfilling their purpose and glorifying God.

Like the nation of Israel, when you want to be ruled by the world instead of God there will be great difficulty. You will not experience the power of God to live above circumstances and all the trappings of the world. You will fail to point to God's goodness and provision for your life as God promises to those who let Him. There will be no fruit, no light and no salt.

· · ·

THE LESSON here is that God has so much better for you. It all starts with surrender. He will do all the work, you just have to obey. He will lead you to green pastures and beside still waters. He will exceed your thoughts and plans for your life. Goodness and kindness will follow you all the days of your life. God will prove His goodness to the world through His care for you. Those around you will not be able to deny God's goodness that they see in your life. Live for Him and not for the world. God has called you and you are not of this world. Shine brightly for Him and you will the poster child of grace as you live in His love.

1 Samuel 10:1 11:15, John 6:43 71,
Psalm 107:1 43, Proverbs 15:1 3

DEALING WITH ANGRY PEOPLE

///

PROVERBS 15:1

> *"A soft answer turns away wrath, But a harsh word stirs up anger."*

The wisdom found in the Bible gives insight in dealing with many situations. One such situation is dealing with angry, hot headed people. You may come across these people along your path, and if not handled properly, it can turn into a very ugly situation.

The natural impulse is to match or exceed another's intensity level. When a mad person comes your way and is aggressive toward you, you will feel your own anger and aggression rising up. You will have a surge of emotions that want to dictate the way you respond. Then you have two angry emotional people going at each other which won't have a pleasant ending. This is how and why arguments escalate to boiling points of anger. When in an emotional state, the flesh takes over. The flesh is hard to tame and is never satisfied so it will go further and further. Maybe you or someone you know has problems with their anger and is suffering the consequences as a result.

Pride is at the center of this anger with an unwillingness to yield to another. You may feel as if they are getting the better of you and that you must stand up for yourself and defend yourself. You don't want to look foolish or let someone have any advantage over you, so you won't ever give in or compromise. It is impossible to ever have any healthy, good relationships with such a prideful attitude.

The answer here and works amazingly well. Instead of a prideful and emotional response in the flesh, catch yourself. When you feel your temper rising and your blood boiling, stop and pray. Give God control and then answer back in a soft tone. Acknowledge the other person, give kindness in place of their anger.

· · ·

THE LESSON here is to give good in place of other's bad. When you do, in most cases the situation will be diffused and who knows, you may win a soul to Christ.

COURAGE

PSALM 108:13

> "Through God we will do valiantly, For it is He who shall tread down our enemies."

Courage is so rare to find. We see it in movies and read about it in books, but real courage, courage to do right, to stand for Godly principles and go against the flow, takes real corsage. The enemy is pressing toward compromise by selling an easier way. He wants a less offensive cross, more cheap grace and Christ-less religion. It takes real courage to be follower of Christ in a fallen, Christ rejecting world.

In our text we find the key to courage in the words "through God." When the Almighty is our power and strength we have nothing to fear. All enemies will fall when God is on our side. Threats and intimidation are laughed at by God. When we live through Him we are valiant and able to face all that comes against us.

Fear comes from uncertainty of the possible outcome. When we see things "through us" instead of "through God," we cannot be certain if our strength will hold up. We know we have weakness that can be exploited and therefore we fear.

"Through God" however, there is never any uncertainty because He will always be victorious. The Bible says "no weapon formed against us shall prosper."

· · ·

THE LESSON here is when you go in God's power, victory is certain. You will find the courage to press on in faith "through God." This is how the ordinary do the extraordinary.

RIVERS OF LIVING WATER

//

JOHN 7:38

> *"He who believes in Me, as the Scripture has said, out of his heart will flow rivers of living water."*

Water speaks of life, refreshment, abundance, satisfaction and purity. What a great picture we have here in our text of what happens when we believe. The moment we put our faith in Christ we are given the Holy Spirit. He is our helper, counselor, power, guide and strength. He makes all things new and gives us a dynamic that sets us apart.

Jesus says that this "water" will come from inside us. That it will flow from us. It will not just trickle but rush like a mighty river. This means that there is movement, life and activity. This is how the Holy Spirit works. He works from within, which means we get to enjoy His work as He flows from us and that others get to enjoy His work also.

All ministry and Christian service, if done right, is merely the outflowing of the Holy Spirit that takes on the form of an activity or service that ministers the love of Christ. When the Holy Spirit is flowing there is the fruit of love which blesses and shows God's will toward man.

. . .

THE LESSON here is to let the Holy Spirit work powerfully through you by surrender and obedience. Pray for the Holy Spirit to move, to empower and fill. Don't grieve or quench the Holy Spirit by sin and disobedience but allow the supernatural to work. Belief is the key. God will do exceedingly abundantly according to the power within you. Apart from Him you can do nothing but with Him you can do all things. The Holy Spirit is the difference between good works and God works.

LITTLE IS BIGGER

1 SAMUEL 15:17

"So Samuel said, 'When you were little in your own eyes, were you not head of the tribes of Israel? And did not the LORD anoint you king over Israel?'"

Humility is essential in God's people. John the Baptist said, "He must increase, I must decrease." We can never go wrong by exalting Christ in all we do. In fact, that should be the goal. The question we must ask ourselves, "Who am I doing this for, who is getting the glory?"

In our text we see the importance of humility. The greater the responsibility, the greater the need for humility. Positions of power influence require much humility because of the greater temptation of pride.

In our text, Saul, who initially felt inadequate and cowered from his mighty calling, was in a better place than when he experienced the power and influence of being the King of a Israel. The temptation proved too great as he felt empowered to do his own thing, which was in rebellion to God's thing.

The power of Saul's life was in His humility, which forced him to depend on God. He was given position by God, as opposed to getting it himself. All anyone has is a gift from God and our responsibility is to be good stewards of it. This means that we whatever we have, whether it be talents, opportunities, possessions or whatever, they are gifts that we are to take care of for God. We are to use all our resources not for self but for God's glory.

Saul's anointing, or empowering, to fulfill His calling was alive through his initial humility. As he thought little of himself he knew he needed God to work through him. Saul would simply listen to God and do what God said. When pride set in, he depended more on himself than God, which ended up to be inadequate for what God had called him to do. He thought he knew better than God and used his position for himself instead of God's glory. The anointing or empowering was stifled through his pride.

. . .

THE LESSON here is to remain absolutely dependent upon God. Watch out for the subtle slip from that dependence to a self-sufficiency. Watch for the business like approach to life that relies more on techniques and skill than the Holy Spirit. Watch out for that little feeling of entitlement that says," I deserve this" or "I earned this." Watch for the attitude of superiority over others. Remember, everything is a gift and the more you know you need God to properly take care of it the better you will. God gives grace to the humble but resists the proud. Humility is the soil in which God's grace grows.

IT'S ALL IN THE PREPARATION

1 SAMUEL 17:37

"Moreover David said, 'The LORD, who delivered me from the paw of the lion and from the paw of the bear, He will deliver me from the hand of this Philistine.' And Saul said to David, 'Go, and the LORD be with you!'"

All our experiences in life amounts to who we are. Each and every thing that we go through chisels the raw material into something distinguishable and unique. We truly are one of a kind. No one can be who we are, not even close.

David, the little shepherd boy, had no idea at the time that not only was God grooming Him to defeat Goliath, but also to be King of Israel. What may seem like an ordinary thing is actually God preparing us to fulfill His calling.

David here, promoting the idea that he, of all people can defeat the giant, explains to King Saul that that he has already been delivered from the lion and the bear, so a Philistine will be no different. When David was all alone out tending to his sheep, those frightening moments where his life was in jeopardy, were actually giving him confidence. You too may be going through something frightening or very difficult and God is preparing you for something great.

Notice what he learned. His confidence was in the Lord Who delivered him. He experienced God's hand of protection and deliverance. Had he not been put in a situation where his life was threatened, he would have never known this and he would have never had the confidence to face the giant. He learned where his help came from. He learned that God is with him. He learned not to be afraid and that God was greater and more powerful than any foe.

David was prepared through his experiences and all of that preparation came to a head when he took Goliath's head. Because of his preparation, only he could do what God had called him to do. When others doubted him, they had no idea that God had been getting him ready for this moment. They only saw the boy and not God with the boy and his preparation.

. . .

THE LESSON here is to embrace everything in your life as God's unique equipping to uniquely carry out the unique plan God has for you. Every little bit of your life will factor into God's. Don't despise the small things and miss the present because you're so occupied thinking of your future. God is preparing you for something great, and every lesson and experience will contribute to that. Not one thing less or one thing more, but exactly what you need. It's all in the preparation.

SALVATION

//

JOHN 8:44

> *"You are of your father the devil, and the desires of your father you want to do. He was a murderer from the beginning, and does not stand in the truth, because there is no truth in him. When he speaks a lie, he speaks from his own resources, for he is a liar and the father of it."*

There is war going on in the spiritual realm. We can't see it but we sure experience the effects of this war. The battle is ultimately for the souls of mankind. He is held in check by the limitations put on him by God. The nature of this conflict centers around free choice. God didn't make us robots that are programmed to say and do what God asks. He made us so that we have the capability to deny him, as well as chose Him. This makes it about love because in order for it to be about love there has to be the capacity to choose.

Satan comes into play as the other option. He is the other choice. There is no in between, as we see here in our text. Either God is our Father or Satan is. That's right, if God is not our Father, by faith in Christ which gives us a new birth as a child of God, then Satan is. Every human being is given what is needed to make that choice, so it really comes down to an active determined rejection rather than a passive inability. Hell is a place where its inhabitants reside because of their stubborn determination to reject God. We are either for Him or against Him. To not be for Him is to be against Him.

Satan has tactics. His nature is that of a murderer who does not stand in the truth. This means he lies to people through various means to take them away from God and into his murderous trap. Truth is so important because that is where the battle is won or lost for souls. Satan speaks lies to willing hearts and minds, giving them just what they need to reject the truth in their hearts. Romans chapter 1 says that they suppress the truth in unrighteousness and they exchange the truth for a lie.

Ultimately, we either belong to God as our Father or Satan is our Father. Truth does not change and is given to us in God's Holy Word, the Bible. We will not escape hell inventing our own way to heaven. We will not get there by good works or good behavior. We will not get there through religion or church attendance.

· · ·

THE LESSON here is to remember that there is only one way to get to heaven. God has only gone remedy, one road and one truth. Jesus said, "I am the Way, the Truth, and the Life. No man comes to the Father but by Me." That is the truth and your eternity rests on how you respond to it.

THE SWORD

1 SAMUEL 21:9

> *"So the priest said, 'The sword of Goliath the Philistine, whom you killed in the Valley of Elah, there it is, wrapped in a cloth behind the ephod. If you will take that, take it. For there is no other except that one here.' And David said, 'There is none like it; give it to me.'"*

David here is on the run and in great danger. The angry Saul was after him in hot pursuit and had every resource at his disposal. Saul had bad intentions toward David and his anger was fueled by jealousy. David had nothing as he had to flee quickly with only the clothes on his back. David here in our text comes across a Priest and asks for a sword.

The sword in the Bible represents the Word of God. David knew the power of the sword first hand as he used it to lop off the head of Goliath. The Word of God will destroy the power and dominion Satan, just as it did Goliath. David would need that weapon, as do we. David knew the importance of the sword in defeating the enemy and we should too.

Jesus used the sword against Satan when tempted three times in the wilderness. He answered Satan with, "It is written." The truth is what kills Satan's attacks because he uses lies. Satan's lies cannot stand up to God's truth.

One important point was that David believed that God's Word, or the sword, would be sufficient to defeat the enemies and protect him. We too must not only read God's Word but we must also use it, believing it will kill all threats to our walk with Christ. It's not just reading, it's applying and then resting and believing in it. Mere reading in and of itself is of little value if not mixed with faith.

Notice also there was just one sword. David said, "There is none like it." There is nothing like God's Word, the Holy Bible. It is the truth revealed and given by God. There is none like it. The same sword David used to kill the Philistine is the same sword that will be useful to him in his trial with Saul. It's the same with us, the same scriptures David used, Jesus used, the disciples used and all the church following has used to fight the good fight of faith, will also give us the victory over Satan and sin.

Finally, notice it had to be taken out. Maybe your Bible has been tucked away somewhere and you've been looking for answers. Maybe you're in trouble or having a hard time. The answer is right there in God's Word. Get it out, take it up, put it to work. Read it with a prayerful heart letting God speak to you.

· · ·

THE LESSON here is to see that everything you need, like David, will be found in God's Word. The sword of the Spirit, which is the Word of God. Take up God's Word and you'll have all you need for the journey.

GOD'S MIGHTY ARMY

1 SAMUEL 22:2

> *"And everyone who was in distress, everyone who was in debt, and every-one who was discontented gathered to him. So he became captain over them. And there were about four hundred men with him."*

David, here, gains an army. It has been said that beggars can't be choosers, and that was certainly the case with David. However, when God chooses, things can't always be measured by their appearance. When we put our lives in God's hands we can rest assured that there is always more than meets the eye.

The four hundred who gathered around David were in distress, in debt and discontent. This is not the top quality candidate. These people would have a hard time getting any type of job. They were desperate and had no hope. Their only option was David and his only option was them. A match made in heaven. They were fit for each other and could share their desperation. Funny how God often brings people together like this.

In the end, God met David's needs as well as the four hundred men. Like Jesus' disciples, God chooses the foolish things to confound the wise. He can always take humble and desperate people to great heights when they surrender to Him. God loves to do the impossible through His people. He did this for David and the four hundred and He will do it for you.

· · ·

THE LESSON here is to simply depend on Him, no matter if you are in distress, in debt and discontent. God will turn things around and show His might through your mess. God's mighty army consists of weak people that are humble enough to lean on God.

1 Samuel 24:1 25:44, John 10:22 42,
Psalm 116:1 19, Proverbs 15:20 21

GOD'S PERFECT WILL

1 SAMUEL 24:4

> *"Then the men of David said to him, 'This is the day of which the Lord said to you, 'Behold, I will deliver your enemy into your hand, that you may do to him as it seems good to you.' And David arose and secretly cut off a corner of Saul's robe."*

Just because you CAN do something doesn't mean you SHOULD do something. We are presented with opportunities all the time and it takes real wisdom to either do or not do the right thing.

David was confronted with such an issue as he hunted down like an animal by King Saul and his men. It was unjust and malicious. The Lord had anointed David to be King yet Saul was occupying that role. Now David was presented with an opportunity.

David came across Saul sleeping in a cave. It seemed as if it may even have been God's will that David found Saul this way. It seemed as if David would have been justified in taking Saul's life. Even David's men were saying it was God's will. What pressure!

David did not take Saul's life. Instead he cut off part of Saul's robe to show Saul that he could have taken his life. Even that provoked David's conscience. You see, David knew his time had not come. Yes, he was anointed King but it wasn't time.

. . .

THE LESSON here to not take matters into your own hands. David will reign as King, but that was up to God, not only to anoint him, but also to place him in that position. Just as God was preparing David for the position of King, you never want to cut (pun intended) God's preparation in your life short.

SIN KILLS

JOHN 11:39

> *"Jesus said, 'Take away the stone.' Martha, the sister of him who was dead, said to Him, 'Lord, by this time there is a stench, for he has been dead four days.'"*

Sin stinks! It kills everything it comes in contact with. It spoils all that is good by spoiling it with its toxin. We often don't see sin this way because Satan can put it in an attractive package and wrap a bow around it making it look good. Make no mistake, sin always kills.

In fact, death is a result of sin. Before sin entered the world there was no death. Jesus, seeing Lazarus dead made Him weep. He was weeping over the sadness of how sin brings so much misery.

In out text we see the pain, the death, the stench and the agony of sin in the dead body of Lazarus. Not only does sin kill physically it also kills spiritually. Sin will kill the fruit of the Spirit like a fruit fly will kill a banana. It will eat away at one's love, joy, peace, patience, kindness, goodness, faithfulness, gentleness and self-control. It will kill fellowship with God and relationships with other people.

The good news is, like Lazarus, Jesus gives life when we are dead. He is the resurrection and the Life and though we may be dead we will live, if we believe. Jesus came so that we may have life. He makes all things new and like Lazarus, He will raise us to eternal life, that when we pass from this earth we move on into eternity with Jesus.

Maybe you have been dead. Maybe your attitude stinks or you joy is dead. Maybe your peace is gone and your love is buried in a tomb. Maybe you have never been made alive spiritually and are still dead in your sins. Whatever the case, Jesus will give you life and make the dead alive.

· · ·

THE LESSON here is see that the way to have this new life is to turn from the direction you are going and believe. Believe, meaning to believe in Jesus Christ, as Lord and Savior, the eternal God and promised Messiah. Believe in what He did, living a perfect, sinless life and dying on the cross in our place. Then being raised from the dead in the resurrection. Believe in Jesus and you will be saved. Believe Him not only for salvation, but to live powerfully, full of life and fruitfulness. Sin kills but Jesus gives life.

THE BODY

//

1 SAMUEL 30:24

"For who will heed you in this matter? But as his part is who goes down to the battle, so shall his part be who stays by the supplies; they shall share alike."

The body of Christ is an amazing thing. Every Christian is a part and every Christian has a role. All individual parts are important to the whole body just as a human body has many parts that all work together for the whole. Every part is unique in its function and when it is not functioning the whole body suffers. Each part of the body is not in competition with the other but is one and should have the same overall goal, which is to glorify God. When the body works together in harmony then God is glorified and Christ, who is the head, is controlling and directing things, just as a brain controls the human body.

In our text we see that some of David's warriors went to war, some stayed home and some stayed behind and watched the supplies. It would seem as if the ones who put their lives on the line and actually killed the enemies would be more important and have a bigger reward. David, however, makes a really important statement when he says that those who went to war and those who stayed behind shall share alike. This shows that each part of the body of Christ is important and when one part benefits the whole benefits. It shows that what is really important is being faithful to what we have been given, no matter how big or small. It shows that we all have a vital role no matter what it may look like.

. . .

THE LESSON here is that you are to see the whole body of Christ as important and not just what you or an individual member of the body is doing. There is no room for competition and jealousy in the body of Christ. Be a contributor and not a detractor.

SEEING JESUS

JOHN 12:24

> *"Most assuredly, I say to you, unless a grain of wheat falls into the ground and dies, it remains alone; but if it dies, it produces much grain."*

The Greeks were asking to see Jesus and this is the answer Jesus gave to His disciples who brought Him the message. What an interesting answer to their inquiry. What Jesus said gives us amazing insight into how we are to view Jesus and how we are to view our own lives.

What Jesus was saying was that in order to see Him correctly one would have to see Him in light of the cross. The cross would display the fullness of who He was. You see, at the cross is where we see love poured out. Just as a grain of wheat planted in the ground to bring forth a harvest, Jesus' life would also bring a harvest. Death would be required for more than one stalk to come, so Jesus died for many who would come. Never can we doubt this amazing love of Christ.

. . .

THE LESSON here is that you must never take the cross out of your view of Christ. You must never forget His love and although you may not understand everything going on, all you need to know is that Jesus gave it all for you. Whatever you are facing, Jesus faced it for you. See Him and watch your fears die in Jesus' undying love.

YOUNG MEN AND THE WORD OF GOD

PSALM 119:9

"How can a young man cleanse his way? By taking heed according to Your word."

Sin is a problem at any age but it can be especially difficult for young men. The strength and passion of young men, the adventurous spirit, the easily bored nature and impetuousness of actions make for a vulnerable state. Scientist have discovered that a male brain is not fully developed until the age of twenty five and that part of the brain still developing is the part where rational decisions are made. Then adding alcohol, drugs and/or pornography on top of that, it's a wonder they even survive.

There is an answer to the sin problem and it's found in our text. The most important thing to implement into a young man's life is the Word of God. This foundation will keep him safe. A young man will know the difference between right and wrong and have a biblical perspective pertaining to life. He will know God's heart and be able to identify danger and traps laid out so they know what is the right path and wrong one. He will be trained in righteousness as his mind is renewed and transformed. The Word bypasses all the predispositions young men have toward sin giving them real and effective ammo to fight the good fight of faith. It really works.

The book if Hebrews chapter 5 and 6 tells us that when one is not mature in God's Word they are not able to tell the difference between good and evil. We live in a day where it's hard to tell. Evil comes in all sizes and is very pushy, to say the least. Add peer pressure into the deceptiveness of sin, where good is called evil and evil good, and you have an intoxicating drink of destruction. The Word of God brings clarity and sobriety for a young man. It brings light into darkness.

The most important thing for a parent, mentor, coach, teacher, older sibling, Pastor, Youth Pastor or any person in the place of influence in a young mans life is to see the importance of imparting the Word. Do it often, do it urgently, lovingly and patiently. The investment may not be seen right away but those seeds will not return empty. They are working underneath the surface and doing more than you could ever imagine. You will never regret, you will never go wrong teaching the Word of God to a young man. It's tragic when this is neglected thinking they are too young or they won't be interested. Young men are hungry for truth and will eat it up if they will be fed.

The text says that it is the young man "taking heed" to God's Word which cleanses his way. This means we need to teach young men not only the understanding and meaning but also how to obey God's Word. It's one thing to know it, it's another to obey it. The Bible says that the wise man who builds his house on the rock is the one who hears the Word and DOES it. Teaching how to follow is important but exemplifying it is MOST important.

. . .

THE LESSON here is to see that we are losing our young men because we are neglecting the importance of God's Word in their lives. Have you outgrown the Word of God? Have you found more profound ways to train up our boys? Is their success in athletics or academics or whatever becomes more important than their success as a Man Of God? Society tells us different. The neglect of the Word of God is to the neglect of our young men . The answer is right here in this one little verse, so profound, so true and so needed today! God's Word, the hope of our young men's future.

2 Samuel 4:1 6:23, John 13:31 14:14,
Psalm 119:17 32, Proverbs 15:31 32

THE WONDER IN GOD'S WORD

PSALM 119:18

"Open my eyes, that I may see Wondrous things from Your law."

The Psalmist knows that God's Word contains wonder. He knows that God's Word is much more that an academic study. He knows that this is where truth is found, along with wisdom and meaning. He knows that all the splendor he can see with his eye doesn't compare to the wonder in God's Word. Everything else is magnified when we see it through the lens of scripture. The sky becomes more blue, sunsets become more magical and stars become more heavenly, because we see the wonder of God in them through corrective lenses.

The Psalmist asks for his eyes to be open because the wonders of God's Word are revealed, not found. God must show them to us or we will not see them. They are spiritually discerned not intellectually figured out. God's Word is an endless well of Spiritual riches and the humble in heart, who will be good stewards of these treasures, are those in who see the deepest gems.

. . .

THE LESSON here is that you would see God's Word as a wonder filled book to be pursued with all your heart. There is nothing like it on all the earth. It will endure forever when all else is passing away. Seek God through the book, not just information. Pray over it, meditate upon it, share it and obey it. When your eyes are open you will see more of God and less of you. God in all His wonder may be too much for the naked eye to see, but to the Spiritual eye God will reveal His magnificent wonder.

VISUAL PURITY

PSALM 119:37

> *"Turn away my eyes from looking at worthless things, and revive me in Your way."*

Here the Psalmist, having a great desire to stay pure and Holy, asks God to turn his eyes away from things that have no value. He has a great understanding of the destructiveness of sin, which is easily lost in our day. He deeply understood how hurtful sin was. He saw it as evil and darkness and something to passionately stay away from.

Next, he knew that in his own flesh were passions and desires that were not of God pulling on him. He felt the pressure and needed a focus upon God with all the good things of God. He needed God's power over his own willpower to have a life that was victorious over sin. This was very serious to him.

Finally, he realized a strategy of Satan that is used so well to bring people into sin and that was through the eye gate. He knew that his flesh, which was already polluted with sinful lusts, would be enticed through what he saw. His eyes would see something that his flesh desired. His eyes were an entryway to sin. This would trigger a response in his flesh. So he asks God to turn his eyes away from these things.

Avoid putting yourself in situations where you know you will see sinful things. You cannot UNSEE something and Satan will use every possible mental image to harm you. If you have seen a lot of bad images ask God to clean your mind, heart, soul and spirit. The Bible tells us if we confess our sins He will be faithful and just to forgive us. Then make it a habit to set no unclean thing before your eyes. Great peace will come when you have clean eyes, clear vision and a pure heart.

. . .

THE LESSON here is to practice visual purity. Don't think you can see that which is not Godly and Holy without any effect. Visual temptations are all around you and hard to avoid. This is no mistake. Satan lurks around every corner with visual candy wanting to draw you into sin with it. Make it a habit to have pure eyes as best you can.

2 Samuel 9:1 11:27, John 15:1 27,
Psalm 119:49 64, Proverbs 16:1 3

THINKING RIGHT

//

PROVERBS 16:3

"Commit your works to the Lord, And your thoughts will be established."

Our thoughts affect our actions. Our thoughts also reveal what is important to us. They will affect the way we feel as well because our thoughts affect our emotions. The Bible tells us we are to direct our thoughts instead of letting them direct us.

Naturally, we don't think right. The mind without God is a mind that leads to destruction. We think self first, God thinks self last. We think here and now, God thinks there and then. We think get, God thinks give. We think earth, God thinks heaven. We think control, God thinks let go. We think it's up to me, God thinks it's up to Him. We think works, God thinks relationship. We think religion, God thinks relationship. On and on we can go with a mind devoid of God resulting in thoughts devoid of truth.

How can we think right? The Bible says we are to have the mind of Christ. In our scripture here it says our thoughts will be right and stable by committing our works to the Lord. This means that if we first give what we do to the Lord, He will give us what to do. This takes surrender. Without a complete surrender we will be incomplete in our understanding.

It's clear from our text where true vision comes from. It comes from the Lord working through one who wants the Lord to work through them.

· · ·

THE LESSON here is that the starting point of thinking right is to first be right with God by giving to Him your all. Maybe your thoughts are unclear at best. Maybe you're fuzzy about things. The answer is to say, "Lord, I commit my works to You. I want Your will and I want to use whatever resources I have for You." God will begin to work in your thoughts so that you will both want to do and do what things God has placed before you. Thinking right is thinking what God thinks.

WHERE TO FIND PEACE

JOHN 16:33

"These things I have spoken to you, that in Me you may have peace. In the world you will have tribulation; but be of good cheer, I have overcome the world."

Jesus was telling the disciples that He was leaving them for a time and that they would all be scattered around, to each their own. It was very hard news to accept. A big reason for their difficulty receiving the news was their mindset that focused on this world. They thought the time had come for Jesus to establish the Kingdom on earth when in reality He was establishing His kingdom in heaven.

We can also fall prey to great disappointment, which takes away our peace, if our hope doesn't rise above this world. Jesus was changing that mindset with the disciples, as well as with us, by pointing them to where real hope comes from. He establishes two principles that will determine our experience of peace.

First, He says "in Me" you may have peace. He tells them where true peace comes from and it is in placing our confidence or trust in Christ. We will never be disappointed, never lose hope and never be let down. No matter how things may look, if our faith is in the unseen and not the seen, we have our faith in the unchanging, everlasting all knowing God. He will never leave us nor forsake us and has a plan that He is working out, that He guarantees is good.

The second principal is that "in the world you WILL have tribulation" (emphasis mine). This is a statement of fact and will ALWAYS be true. Whenever, whatever and whoever we put our trust in outside of Jesus will in some way negatively affect our peace. No doubt about it. All that is tainted by sin cannot be relied upon like Jesus with His bloodstained guarantee.

· · ·

THE LESSON here is, to be mindful of, what you place your faith in. Jesus for peace or the world for distress.

Put your trust in Him and know that He is in control so you don't have to be. True faith finds peace in Him.

ONENESS

JOHN 17:21

> *"That they all may be one, as You, Father, are in Me, and I in You; that they also may be one in Us, that the world may believe that You sent Me."*

The three members of the Holy Trinity, God the Father, God the Son and God the Holy Spirit, were complete in and of Themselves. A difficult doctrine to understand yet clearly told. God, in three persons, equal yet distinct, one yet three. They were completely sufficient in and of Themselves. They shared love, fellowship and communication.

Here we find the most amazing prayer of Jesus, which gives the Christian incredible insight into the depths of our blessings through faith in Christ. In essence, He prays that we would be "one." Not that we become God, nor that we become another member of the Trinity for there is only one God who is the Creator and all else is the creation. However, we are grafted into unity with the Lord as a branch is united with the vine.

This sweet unity we have with the Trinity is the great blessing of Christianity. Fellowship with the Creator is why we were created. When we enter into a relationship with Christ we enter into the reason for our existence. Fellowship with God is where we are complete and filled with joy. Fellowship with God should be the aim of every believer. It's not by accident that there are so many traps Satan sets to prevent this. He will attempt to make Christianity about everything and anything but simple fellowship. He knows this is where Christians find their strength and so, like in the garden, he will attempt to make a Christian feel that simple fellowship is inadequate. He will say, "You have to DO more, you have to BE more, you have to try more." He will say, "God is keeping things from you" and that "relationship with God is inadequate."

Oneness with God, Jesus prays, will result in oneness with other Christians as well. Jesus wants unity within the Body of Christ. This is most beautiful to God and brings glory to His name. It also reveals who He is to others, who are not Christians. This oneness amongst believers is only possible through yielding to God and allowing His will and not our own. Just as there is no division within the Trinity, there will be no division when yielding to the Trinity. Division occurs through the flesh where envy, pride and selfishness exist.

. . .

THE LESSON here is that oneness with Christ should be your aim. Put away anything and everything that interferes with that and you will find everything you want, along with oneness with others who desire the same thing. In the end it's not about you, it's about Him. Seeing things this way is seeing the greatness of God's glory in your life.

TRANSFORMATION

JOHN 18:11

> *"So Jesus said to Peter, 'Put your sword into the sheath. Shall I not drink the cup which My Father has given Me?'"*

Making Jesus into a mold that we are comfortable with is a slippery slope leading to nowhere. Jesus said some hard things that would cause the casual follower to turn back where they came from. Others would make assumptions about Him based on their own preferences and when their assumptions were incorrect they would also turn back. Peter could not fathom a suffering savior so he did all he could to hold on to his misconceptions.

The next step in making Jesus into our own image is then taking matters into our own hands in order to force our perception of Him. When we do, we end up compromising who He is. Peter did this when he could not submit to God's will for Jesus. The result was a bloody mess that Jesus had to clean up. We see that God's will is going to be completed and it's up to us if we will be in compliance or defiance. When confronted with our misconceptions about Jesus, it's always best to surrender to His truth than to force our error.

When we understand that God is transforming us, we can allow Him to mold and shape us the way He wants. This is especially true when it comes to our understanding of who Jesus is and what His will is.

• • •

THE LESSON here is, don't fight against but fight with Him. Transformation is painful but the end is beautiful.

2 Samuel 15:23 16:23, John 18:25 19:22,
Psalm 119:113 128, Proverbs 16:10 11

TRUTH

JOHN 18:37

> *"Pilate therefore said to Him, 'Are You a king then?' Jesus answered, 'You say rightly that I am a king. For this cause I was born, and for this cause I have come into the world, that I should bear witness to the truth. Everyone who is of the truth hears My voice.'"*

Truth is really all there is. It is reality, what is and what is right. Man has gotten to the point where truth isn't the standard, which comes from God, but relative depending on one's own feelings about it. This is ironic because truth is truth whether we think it is or not. Truth doesn't bow to opinions, but all opinions bow to truth.

When man determines what truth is, he essentially is putting himself in the place of God. This is the height of arrogance that a limited finite being would put himself in the position to make such a judgment. Man cannot even determine when he was born, where he is born and to whom he was born. This in itself shows that man is in no position to be the authority on truth. We make mistakes all the time and change our opinions frequently. This proves that truth must come from a higher source and authority.

In our text, Jesus reveals to Pilate that He is that authority. He says that He was born into this world for the very reason of bearing witness to the truth. He should know because He was there before the beginning. He is the creator of all, even truth. He knows all, is unchanging, all-powerful and everlasting. He is the definition of truth as Jesus said, "I am the truth." He qualifies to be the truth.

Everything must be measured by Him. He is the gold standard. Jesus finishes His statement saying, "Everyone who is of the truth hears His voice." Truth then is revealed to those who are "of the truth." Pilate, like many, didn't know truth when it was standing right in front of him. Truth was talking to him, looking at him and confronting him. It seems as if he was pricked in his heart about the truth yet was determine to not be effected by it because of political reasons.

· · ·

THE LESSON here is that you must never harden yourself to truth by turning from that inward testimony of it. You must never violate your conscience for worldly gains and concerns. Truth is the supreme commodity to be had and you should seek it and conform to it above all else. The truth will set you free where everything else will take you prisoner.

2 Samuel 17:1 29, John 19:23 42,
Psalm 119:129 152, Proverbs 16:12 13

IT IS FINISHED

JOHN 19:30

> *"So when Jesus had received the sour wine, He said, 'It is finished!' And bowing His head, He gave up His spirit."*

Grace says, "It is finished." The end of human performance and continuous effort to gain God's favor. The end of any barrier between man and God. Grace says I did the work and you receive it. Grace ends the restlessness in trying to attain and brings restfulness knowing it is already gained. It is finished is one of the greatest statements in the Bible.

Temptations will come that say, "There is more." Satan tempted Eve with this enticement. The carnal mind loves this appeal to pride that says you can have more and become like God. We love to feel important and that we have something others don't. Satan says come and get more, come and see more and come and experience more. He will have religions set up to accommodate those who take his bait. Be very careful of anything that says there is something more outside of Christ.

When Jesus said, "It is finished," He gave complete and total sufficiency. You are complete in Him. He has given you everything pertaining to life and Godliness in Christ Jesus.

. . .

THE LESSON here is to rest in knowing that ALL requirements for salvation have been met in Him. The righteous requirements of God the Father have been satisfied in God the Son. Rest in the comfort of His finished work. Faith in His work is what makes it yours. When you have it you have everything you will ever need. Learn to go to Christ for everything. Let Him be your all and all. Jesus is all you need.

THE TREASURE OF GOD'S WORD

//

PSALM 119:162

"I rejoice at Your word As one who finds great treasure."

If there was one thing, one point, one message you could give someone important to you before you died, and they would actually take your advice and do it,
what would it be? I got to thinking about that one night as I was preparing for a
family devotion. I sat with my open Bible resting in my lap, praying for just the
right thing to share and thought, what would be the one thing I would want my
kids to know if this were the last thing I ever shared with them. Like a pendulum swinging back and forth, many thoughts came to mind but my heart kept
resting on this one thought, "the treasure of God's Word." As I began to pray
about this thought it was like the pendulum stopped and was at rest. The other
thoughts were gone and the Lord gave me peace that this was the message I was
to share with my kids that night.

During the teaching and prayer, I felt the Lord speak to me about what a great
treasure His word is. I began to reminisce about how the Word has gotten me
through so many things in life. I remembered times when God had unveiled
truth to my specific situation as if He was right there speaking to me face to face.
I thought about how I have grown through being taught the Word and through
my own time in the Word. I thought about the times when I didn't know what
to do and God spoke right to me through His Word. I remembered the times
when God gave me just the right verse or scripture to share with someone in
need, who desperately needed more than I could give them. I remembered how
I have grown closer to the Lord through His Word and those special times of
sitting with my Bible in a quiet place with no agenda, no study to prepare for,
just wanting to spend time with Him and how His presence was so near, as if I
was the only one who existed in the world. I remembered how my friend at the
age of 16 showed me verses in the Bible that spoke about God's power, might
and strength and thinking to myself, "Wow, this isn't at all what I thought it
was." Then my friend took me through what I now know as "the Romans Road
of Salvation" which is the gospel that is presented through various verses in the
book of Romans. I remember God speaking to me through those verses and my
friend asking me if I would like to ask Jesus into my heart. I had no hesitation
as God had been speaking the truth to me and my heart was overjoyed with

the answer to my feelings of dissatisfaction and emptiness, despite having many achievements. I now will have all eternity to enjoy that one little decision I made to receive Jesus Christ as my Lord and Savior. What a treasure indeed, this book is to me.

. . .

THE LESSON here is to open your heart and mind to God by getting into His Word in a way in which you come to it as the most important thing there is. Come prayerfully, expectantly as you are coming to God Himself, because you are. He will meet you there, He will speak to you, and He will touch you. Let Him minister to you through His Word and I guarantee, by the power of the Holy Spirit and the authority of God, that you too will rejoice at His Word as on who finds great treasure. There is nothing like it, nothing comparable and nothing can substitute for it. It is our greatest treasure.

THE HIGHWAY OF THE UPRIGHT

PROVERBS 16:17

> *"The highway of the upright is to depart from evil; He who keeps his way preserves his soul."*

The Christian life is compared to a race by the Apostle Paul. We can also compare it to a path we walk or a journey we take. The Bible says to take the narrow road. Here in our text we see the Christian life compared to a highway. It is true that we face many challenges to faithfully following Christ while at the same time we have been given every tool to be successful.

The key to the journey is to recognize and depart from evil. It may seem obvious but it is not always so. We live in a world that calls evil good and good evil. It's hard to know sometimes. The best way to recognize evil is to know good. When we know good it's easy to distinguish it from bad. The best way to know good is the Word of God, the Bible.

A minimal understanding of the Bible will minimize our view of good and evil. It's not only knowing the Word, it's being consistently in the Word. We never want to be on the wrong side of sowing and reaping, meaning that if we spend 5 minutes a day on the Word and 3 hours looking at useless or sinful things, we have no chance. A regular, steady diet in God's Word is vital.

Finally, it takes faith to depart from evil. This is where we simply obey and, by faith, act upon what we know.

• • •

THE LESSON here is to see that at some point it just comes down to simple obedience. This is where you will really start to grow. God has given you everything needed to obey; it's just a matter of doing it. When you do, you will reach new heights in your relationship with God for it is he who obeys that finds God's riches.

HELP

//

PSALM 121:2

"My help comes from the Lord, who made heaven and earth."

We all need help. There are times when we feel very helpless, even desperate. We need to be very careful when we do because we are vulnerable to making very bad decisions. A desperate person is a vulnerable person. When we have the Lord in our life there is never a need to feel helpless and desperate. That's why the Bible tells us to be still and know He is God.

Our Psalmist recognizes this great help he has in the Lord. He isn't looking for his circumstances to change, he isn't trying to fix everything, he is simply looking to the Lord for help. He knows the Lord is truly the One who can and will help. The Lord will teach us this through various trials. We need to be trained in "looking to the Lord." Through trial and error, we come to this place of saying "my help comes from the Lord."

Notice also that the Psalmist notes that his hope comes from the One "who made heaven and earth." In order for us to learn where our help comes from we need to know His capabilities. If He made heaven and earth, He can help us. This means that He has the power and strength to help. He is above all and so we can rest in his power and not our own. When we truly see God for who He is we will rest in all our circumstance. He truly is able.

• • •

THE LESSON here is to go to God for help. Learn to go to Him knowing His power, and knowing that He is willing. God cares about all that goes on in your life and invites you to come to Him. He is an ever -present help in time of need. God is ready, willing and able to help His children. Having the Lord on your side is all the help you ever need. He loves when you call on Him.

THE SIMPLE CHURCH

ACTS 2:42

"And they continued steadfastly in the apostles' doctrine and fellowship, in the breaking of bread, and in prayers."

There was an unusual energy surrounding the early church. Imagine years of ritualistically obeying rituals and commandments devoid of the relational connection that they pointed to. There would have been such uncertainty in the continuous sacrifices that had no end or finality. The harsh religious leaders would put heavy burdens on the people to follow the religious ordinances and laws, which they themselves could not adhere to themselves.

The law pointed out their sin, demonstrating God's unattainable righteous requirements. Then Jesus put an end to all this by fulfilling the law and setting the people free. He did what the laws and ordinances couldn't do and offered free of charge the greatest gift man could ever receive, the forgiveness of sins, eternity in heaven, a personal relationship with God based on love and the imparting of the Holy Spirit to empower.

The early church didn't need a lot, they had Jesus. The Holy Spirit was moving and it was a blessing. Gratitude filled their hearts and meeting together to share their faith with one another was a great joy. I don't imagine too many showed up late or had to be coerced to attend service. The Holy Spirit was being poured out in their lives.

They continued moving forward with purpose and intention. They were all about Jesus and when He is in the center there is incredible wonder. The Holy Spirit, of course, was to lead people to Jesus and when you have groups of people being led by the Spirit you will have unity, life and love.

Notice they didn't do a lot of things. It wasn't about numerous activities; it was about one activity, worshiping Jesus. This may take different forms but it all centers around Jesus. The early Church was not into gimmicks or circus acts, Jesus was all they could handle. Their enthusiasm was inspired by the Holy Spirit and led their simple activities that would all honor and value Christ. It was simple, powerful and fulfilling. When we have Jesus, sideshows are unnecessary and even distracting.

. . .

THE LESSON here is that Jesus must always be the main thing. He is the reason we gather together. All we do is for Him and to give Him honor and glory. We lift His name on high. You must be careful about other things that may creep into your life that may hinder the pure worship of God. The flesh is easily entertained. Don't confuse fleshly pleasure with pure worship. Having Jesus is more than you can ever handle. Keep it simple, keep it relational and keep it personal. When you do, when you gather together with other believers centering their hearts on worshiping Jesus it will be completely out of this world and lacking nothing.

2 Samuel 23:24 24:25, Acts 3:1 26,
Psalm 123:1 4, Proverbs 16:21 23

CHOOSE MERCY

2 SAMUEL 24:14

"And David said to Gad, 'I am in great distress. Please let us fall into the hand of the Lord, for His mercies are great; but do not let me fall into the hand of man.'"

When given the choice of punishments, David preferred to fall into God's hands versus man's. His reason was that David knew God was merciful whereas man was not. In this we see the greatness of God's mercy as well as the severity of man's ways.

David says the Lord's mercies are great. Mercy is when God withholds what is deserved. If we did, we would immediately suffer judgment and wrath. This is what the sinning, rebellious heart deserves yet God is slow to anger. He is not willing that anyone should perish so He gives opportunity after opportunity for us to allow Him to take our place in punishment. God will do that for us, which shows how tenderhearted He is toward us. Instead of that mean man in the sky looking to strike us down, God desperately wants to love and forgive us. This is who He is and what His nature is. He is great at being merciful.

On the other hand, man is harsh. The nature inclination of man is to be over another. Man is not compassionate or tender hearted like God. Man cannot love like God can and left to himself, will step over another to get what he wants. The epitome of this was at the cross. Mankind crucified an all loving, all merciful and sinless Man. They persecuted the one in whom did no wrong. He never hurt or harmed another and only did what was right and good. Not one action of His was selfish or self-serving. Completely others-centered, Jesus went about doing good and demonstrating His love. Man put Jesus on the cross. An innocent man who also was willing to die for those very ones who put Him on the cross.

At the cross we see man's heart as well as Jesus' heart. Mercy beat injustice. Love beat hate. Kindness beat anger. Good beat evil. Jesus beat sin and death. David was right, God is merciful and man is not.

· · ·

THE LESSON here is that when you turn to God in faith you will find what David found, that God delights to show you His mercy. Choose mercy.

LIKE CHRIST

///

ACTS 4:13

"Now when they saw the boldness of Peter and John, and perceived that they were uneducated and untrained men, they marveled. And they realized that they had been with Jesus."

How much time do you spend with Jesus? If you spend that amount of time with your spouse, how would your marriage be? If you spent that much time at your career, how successful would you be? If you spent that much time learning a skill, learning an instrument or learning another language, how good would you be at it?

Education and training are no substitute for spending time with Jesus. Getting to know Him and grow close to Him relationally is the best thing one can do to be an effective witness for Christ. When we spend time with Him we are transformed into His disciples to the extent that others will see an obvious difference in us that points to His glory.

In our text we see this effect. The time Peter and John had been with Jesus translated into boldness. People saw that Peter and John were bold in a way that could not be explained by some type of learning. Their boldness was who they were, not what they were trying to be. It was natural to them because they had BECOME bold witnesses for Christ. They had been changed into something they were not. This is especially significant in Peter's life as he once denied Jesus three times out of fear. Now he is standing for Jesus in boldness.

Typically, what we spend time doing is what we will be good at. We will never waste our lives spending time with Jesus. This is the best use of our time and the most impactful way we can live. When we do it becomes natural to be like Christ and do the things Christ did, after all, the first Christians were named "Christians" by others because they noticed that these "Christians" were like Christ, which is what "Christian" means.

. . .

THE LESSON here is, make sure you're spending time with Jesus. Whether alone or not, practice His presence wherever you are. Pray, read your Word, talk to Him, talk about Him, praise Him, thank Him, utter His name and His truths. Meditate upon Him and think about Him. Occupy your mind with Him. Spend time with Jesus and you will become like Him.

NO SWEAT MINISTRY

ACTS 5:38

> *"And now I say to you, keep away from these men and let them alone; for if this plan or this work is of men, it will come to nothing; but if it is of God, you cannot overthrow it—lest you even be found to fight against God."*

The work of God cannot be stopped. One trap we can fall into is thinking that ministry work is up to us. We may think that if we're really good at God's work it will succeed. We may think that if we have a good strategy, good planning, a good team with good staff, a good budget, a good location, a good building etc., then people will come and ministry will happen.

It is possible to have all that and no real ministry is happening at all. Now there is nothing wrong with quality in ministry, in fact we should strive to be the best we can be and have those gifted and anointed to do God's work. The difference is, we don't rely on those things to bring God's fruit.

It's important to know the difference between God's part and our part. When we mix these roles up we will not have spiritual fruit and we will get frustrated. We will feel as if we are on a treadmill of fleshly striving in order to manufacture God's results. We are taking God's role when we do this.

Instead, when we understand that results are up to God and we are privileged to be a part of what He is doing, then we can be free to enjoy, be thankful and watch God work. This is the thrill of ministry, knowing if anything is going to happen it's going to be the Lord, the awe and expectation of allowing God to work in order to fulfill His plan.

Knowing that we are not responsible to make or produce but merely to abide and follow. No matter what the results, we can enjoy all of ministry because everything will be exactly the way it's supposed to be. As long as we are faithful, knowing that's our part.

This is what the Pharisee Gamaliel advised his angry cohorts to do. They wanted to kill Peter and John. He said that if it's the Lord, it cannot be stopped and if it's not, it won't continue.

• • •

THE LESSON here is to take heart, relax and know that if the Lord has called you, if He has sent you, if He is working, then nothing will stop Him and the work He is doing through you. It might not be perfect and it may seem unsuccessful but hold on, take heart, and stay faithful because God is working out His unstoppable plan.

JUNE 8

1 Kings 3:3 4:34, Acts 6:1 15,
Psalm 126:1 6, Proverbs 16:26 27

HEARING HEARTS

1 KINGS 3:9

> *"Therefore give to Your servant an understanding heart to judge Your people, that I may discern between good and evil. For who is able to judge this great people of Yours?"*

If you could ask God for anything, what would you truly ask for knowing God would grant it? The answer to this question will tell you a lot about what is going on in your heart.

Upon taking the throne, God asked Solomon what he wanted. God would grant whatever Solomon asked for. In Solomon's Divine response, we see the heart of a great leader, and great man of God and a great servant of God. Solomon felt the pressure of the responsibility God have given him to lead the people of Israel. He was afraid of this daunting responsibility and wanted to do well.

Solomon asked for what literally translates to "a hearing heart." Of all that he could have asked for, he asked for the most important thing. He knew that no amount of training could properly prepare him. He said he felt like a child in his position without even the slightest ability to make the right decisions. Solomon knew what all good leaders and people of God know, that he needed God to continually direct him.

God's promise throughout the Bible is that He will be with us. This would be all the child of God would need to know in order to do God's work. Solomon wanted God's direction, he wanted to hear God's voice and he wanted to have a heart that is receptive to God's direction.

· · ·

THE LESSON here is to live in such a way to where you look for God's direction. A life lived in constant communication and sensitivity to the Holy Spirit is a life lived wisely and effectively. The most important prayer you can pray is for a heart that hears the Lord and is surrendered to his will. A hearing heart is

1. Humble, knowing it needs God's direction.
2. Willing, knowing it must follow His direction
3. Attentive, knowing it can be easily distracted.

Pray for a hearing heart and everything else will fall into place.

UNLESS GOD BUILDS THE HOUSE

//

PSALM 127:1

"Unless the Lord builds the house, they labor in vain who build it."

How much labor or energy is spent for nothing? The value of hard work is noted in the Bible and laziness is condemned, yet effort must be directed in what God is doing, otherwise it is useless. Connecting to God's work is the key to effective ministry and restful meaningful effort.

In the text we find this amazing principle of labor. We see that it is not what we do for God but it's what He is doing that He lets us join. As Jesus said that His "yoke is easy," we get a picture of how it looks to work WITH, not for God. We are yoked or connected with Him like a farmer with his ox plowing the field. God is doing the work and we are along for the ride.

It is possible to have "results" but those "results" may be merely a work of the flesh that has no eternal benefit, that the only reward is the praise of men, elevation in the eyes of men but not in God's eyes. Man's work recognized as God's work. It's important we don't get those confused.

. . .

THE LESSON here is to join God's work and not to ask God to join your work. Knowing that it's not just the "work" that is important, randomly doing things for the Lord but instead, it's "work" that is directed by the Lord. It is meaningful, blessed, effective and unstoppable. God's work is not in vain and will resonate into eternity.

REAL STRENGTH

PROVERBS 16:32

"He who is slow to anger is better than the mighty, And he who rules his spirit than he who takes a city."

True strength is not power that is out if control, but power that can be controlled. This is also called "meekness." It is the ability, or strength, to use strength for good purposes.

We see in our text this truth expressed. First is the truth about anger. Anger is an emotion that can cause much damage. Many can be hurt by anger when it is not controlled. Whether it is physical anger or otherwise, when anger turns into sin it is destructive. Many have trouble controlling their anger and that is a weakness, not a strength.

Next, the Proverb speaks of the strength it takes and the value of being able to control our spirit. This is true strength. A person who is the boss of their feelings and emotions is a strong person. A person who is not a victim of what their flesh tells them but is in total control of themselves. This takes great strength and a person with this strength has a great asset.

The strength to control anger and to rule one's Spirit is not found in man himself but in a Man higher than himself, Jesus Christ. Jesus, the God-Man, came to set us free from our flesh and slavery to it. Jesus gives us power beyond ourselves through the Holy Spirit. When we are surrendered to Him and walking in the Spirit, our flesh will not be in control.

· · ·

THE LESSON here is to see what real strength is. Jesus is your strength, He transforms your heart and gives you a constant source of power to overcome your weakness and make you a mighty instrument in God's hands. Having control of your anger because Jesus is in control of you, that is what real strength is. His strength is made perfect in your weakness.

DON'T GIVE UP

ACTS 7:55

> *"But he, being full of the Holy Spirit, gazed into heaven and saw the glory of God, and Jesus standing at the right hand of God."*

Stephen, the first of many who would be killed for their faith in Christ, shows how to stay the course in the midst of great difficulty. He will soon be a martyr by stoning, yet he did not fail in his calling to preach the gospel and faithfully follow Christ. How did he do this?

First, He was filled with the Holy Spirit, meaning he was directed by God and given supernatural ability to continue in patient endurance. He was given boldness to proclaim truth even if it would cost him his life. Being filled with the Spirit is vital to persevering because the Holy Spirit won't quit and won't tire, but the flesh and willpower has it's limits. The Spirit is willing but the flesh is weak.

Next, He gazed to heaven as He focused on the eternal and not the temporal. He lifted his perspective as we must do when face with trials. When we look to God, focus on Him, we rise above our trouble like Peter walking on water. We will stay on top of our trouble as we fix our gaze upon Jesus but like Peter, when we look at our "waves" seeing only our problem, we will be sure to sink. Faith that keeps focused on Jesus will never sink.

Finally, when Stephen looked to Jesus He saw His glory and power. We too must see Jesus as all-powerful and all in control. He, in proper perspective, will morph our trouble into light afflictions that are not worthy to be compared to our future glory. In comparison to Jesus nothing is too big and nothing is too difficult. Jesus is over all, He is incomparably awesome, full of mercy and gracious care.

. . .

THE LESSON here is, don't give up. When you are filled with the Holy Spirit, focused on Jesus and knowing His power, you like Stephen and all the countless martyrs that followed, will be able to meet anything that comes your way, with great power to faithfully continue on, following Jesus all the way to the end.

1 Kings 9:1 10:29, Acts 8:14 40,
Psalm 130:1 8, Proverbs 17:2 3

GOD'S LEADING

///

ACTS 8:26

"Now an angel of the Lord spoke to Philip, saying, 'Arise and go toward the south along the road which goes down from Jerusalem to Gaza.' This is desert."

The leading of the Lord is often impractical. What we may think is right, God may not. This is because God is doing MORE than meets the eye. He has a bigger plan than we have. Not only that, but God is also working from many different angles. This is why it is so important to follow His leading even if it doesn't make sense.

It is important to be clear of His leading as we are prone to move upon emotional or fleshly reasons. We can want something so bad we imagine God must be in it and leading when in reality it's just our own plan that we want God to bless. The best way to avoid this is to ask yourself if you would be okay with a yes or no answer. Ask yourself if what you really want is God's will. Pray through things and don't make impetuous decisions. Don't force things to happen for if it's the Lords will, it will happen without forcing things. Enlist Godly friends who can pray also and ask for their advice. Those who are not emotionally involved in a situation and are mature spiritually will be a big help. Ask the Lord for confirmation and be in the Word. This will all help in discerning the Lord's leading.

In our text we find Philip with clear leading but with unclear reasons. He may have wondered why he was supposed to go to the desert and what awaited him. I'm not sure what his thoughts were, but maybe he was excited to see what the Lord was going to do, knowing that God always has something extraordinary at the destination of His leading. This is exactly what happened to Philip. While God was leading Phillip, He was also leading an Ethiopian man to find salvation. As God is leading the Ethiopian, He led Phillip right to him to explain what the Ethiopian was reading in the book of Isaiah. In the end, the man gets saved and baptized. God's leading was God's blessing.

. . .

THE LESSON here is follow God's leading. There may not be a pot of gold at the end of the rainbow, but if you follow the Lord through simple obedience, you will find much better. The most satisfying part of the Christian walk is walking in harmony with God. Matching Him step by step will lead you in constant fulfillment and joy. God is at the end of every step and where the Lord is, there is fullness of joy and pleasure forevermore. God's leading and your following is the ultimate life there is.

KNOWING JESUS PERSONALLY

ACTS 9:4-5

"Then he fell to the ground, and heard a voice saying to him, 'Saul, Saul, why are you persecuting Me?' And he said, 'Who are You, Lord?'"

Saul, also known as Paul, maybe one of the greatest Christians to have ever lived. God used him to write most of the New Testament. He planted many of the first churches and gave us much of our Christian doctrine. He was just a man like you and I, a man that God used mightily. His beginning however, was not so great.

He was a persecutor of the church. He hated Christians and Jesus Christ whom they served. He thought he was doing God a favor by freeing the earth of these "Christians" not knowing he was actually against God. Religion will do this very thing. When it takes the place of a personal relationship with Jesus Christ, all that is done in the name of religion is destructive.

Saul's (Paul's) whole problem can be found in this verse when he says, "Who are you Lord?" He didn't know God personally, he only knew Him religiously through ceremonial traditions or good works, which he hoped would satisfy God and make him acceptable to God. This effort leads to frustration, disappointment and never ending attempts at self-righteousness to the point where he was actually willing to kill Christians. That all changed the day he met Jesus and found acceptance through Jesus' sacrifice and not his own efforts.

The secret to Paul's success as a Christian is very simple, He met Jesus. As we see in our text, Paul was stopped in his tracks with one simple question proposed by Jesus when He asked, "Why are you persecuting me?" Paul knew that he didn't know Jesus and asked, "Who are you?" Jesus introduces Himself and all was changed for Paul there. He came to know Jesus personally.

Paul's response says it all when he said to Jesus, "What do you want me to do?" Paul, now knowing Jesus personally, had the only reasonable response to someone can have when meeting Jesus. To know Jesus is to serve Him and live for Him.

• • •

THE LESSON here is that Christianity is knowing Jesus personally (there is no salvation without this) and to serving Him unreservedly. You, like Paul, no matter what your past has been, can be extraordinary through ordinary obedience to the Lord.

JUNE 14

1 Kings 12:20 13:34, Acts 9:26 43,
Psalm 132:1 18, Proverbs 17:6

TRUE WORSHIP

1 KINGS 12:28

"Therefore the king asked advice, made two calves of gold, and said to the people, 'It is too much for you to go up to Jerusalem. Here are your gods, O Israel, which brought you up from the land of Egypt!'"

Worship is the high privilege of all believers in Christ. We are made to be worshipers and we find great strength in our worship. We will be worshiping in all eternity as a natural response to the glory of God. Worship is an outpouring of a heart that knows God and when one is intimately connected to God, worship is as natural as breathing. He alone is worthy!

Worship is not random, nor is it at the whim of the worshiper, to worship anything and everything he wants. This is not TRUE worship but idolatry. TRUE worship has the right object of its affection. Since only God is the creator, above all creation, only He is worthy. We are to worship in Spirit and in Truth so only worship that is in truth, directed by the Holy Spirit, is true worship.

In our text, "the King" of Israel, Jeroboam, was concerned the people would turn from him to his competitor Rehoboam because the place of worship prescribed by God was in Jerusalem, which was not part of Jeroboam's territory. He didn't want people to go into Rehoboam's territory. His solution was to imitate the prescribed worship in Jerusalem in his own territory. The problem was his imitation was false worship. It wasn't in truth and wasn't in Spirit. It was man-made and selfishly motivated. It was not sacrificial and falsely identified two calves as the object of worship instead of the one true God. It falsely glorified a creation over the creator, even ascribing credit to the two golden calves for the miraculous work God did on behalf of the nation of Israel by bringing them out of Egypt.

. . .

THE LESSON here is that true worship concerns itself with the correct identity of what is being worshiped. It also is concerned about the holiness, purity and reverence of worship. True worship centers on one thing, the one true God revealed in three persons. We worship driven by the Holy Spirit and in simple truth of who He is and what He has done. Worship is not something we decide in our own way what it is all about, worship is all about adoring the only one who died for our sins and loves us unconditionally. Worship is easy when worship is about Jesus. He is easy to worship.

UNITY

PSALM 133:1

> *"Behold, how good and how pleasant it is for brethren to dwell together in unity!"*

It is true that a house divided cannot stand. Division is something Satan uses to weaken the body of Christ and must be fought against vigilantly. The stakes go beyond personal reasons for unity, to the bigger picture of God's glory and evangelism.

The Bible tells us that it is our love for one another that testifies to our relationship with God and that how we behave with other believers shows the non-believer that we are truly different and transformed by the grace of God.

Unity then is a priority in the life of a believer. Unity in the essentials of Christianity will bring love and grace in the non-essentials. It seems that in many cases, it's the non-essentials, which are so easily manipulated by Satan.

We don't have to have our way or push for our rights when Christ is our Lord. We can yield to others in matters of personal preference and points of view when they don't violate the truth of God's Word. The key to unity in the body of Christ is yielding to the Holy Spirit. When we do this, the Holy Spirit will always lead us to glorify God.

No two people yielded to the Holy Spirit will behave antagonistically with forgiveness, jealousy, rivalry, spitefulness, hate and selfishness. These are all sins of the flesh and involve the work of Satan and not the Lord. They divide and don't unite, they destroy and don't build. Always remember when we feel these feelings, that it is not the Lord, and the bigger picture is God's glory and not ourselves.

. . .

THE LESSON here is to make unity with other believers a priority. To value unity above any self interest and gain. To put away pride and allow the Holy Spirit to work. To do whatever is possible, as much as it is up to you, to be at peace with all men. As we see in the text, unity is seen by God as good and pleasant. He loves unity, the devil hates it. Whose side do you want to be on? Whatever is preventing you from unity, if it's not compromising the truth of God, it's not worth it.

1 Kings 15:25 17:24, Acts 10:24 48,
Psalm 134:1 3, Proverbs 17:9 11

COVERED BY LOVE

PROVERBS 17:9

> *"He who covers a transgression seeks love, But he who repeats a matter separates friends."*

God's love is the reward of faith. To know the love of Christ which passes knowledge is to enter into the greatest relationship of life. God's love is so deep, so wide, so high that nothing can separate us from His love. God's love should also overflow our hearts like lava spewing from a volcano, and when it does we will love others as Christ loves us.

We can interrupt God's love with selfish acts that interfere with what God wants to do. God puts a high premium on loving one another and here in our text He points out one of those love blockers. The Proverb says that, "One who seeks love COVERS a transgression" (emphasis mine). This shows that we have to have some "intention" in loving others.

We must make it a point, a priority and a goal. We must endeavor to keep the bond of peace. In doing so we will value others so much that we would not want to make them look bad or emphasize to others their weaknesses or sins. We would see the person as Christ does and that means we would see the best in them, resisting the carnal, fleshly urges to tear others down. This is what love does, it covers not exposes.

• • •

THE LESSON here is to value God's love so much that we extend His love to others the same way He gives it to us. God's love is forgiving, patient and merciful. God's love protects and will never injure or even diminish another. Instead, you must build others up, cover them and allow God to work on their weakness just like He does with us.

Let your love be seen in how you keep the unseen. Love covers all our sins, Jesus is the ultimate cover, hiding the repentant sinner in His robes of righteousness.

DECILE

I KINGS 18:21

> "And Elijah came to all the people, and said, 'How long will you falter between two opinions? If the Lord is God, follow Him; but if Baal, follow him.' But the people answered him not a word."

At some point we all have to make a decision. We must be definite about what we believe. We all have enough information to believe in God through creation itself that bears witness to a creator. Everyone knows that where there is a creation there must be a creator. Some even "dabble" in "religion" or "God things" yet still come short of deciding to the point of believing and trusting.

Elijah was bringing the Children of Israel to a point of decision. The good news is that God will reveal Himself to any sincere inquirer. He will take whatever simple faith we have and reveal more and more. He will show us the way and light the path. He does this with the people who were going back and forth between God and the false god, Baal. God proved He was the one true God by bringing fire down from heaven to light the altar of sacrifice. The point is, what are you doing with what you know? How sincere are you to want to know the truth?

In reality, one who rejects God does so because they don't want to have to answer to a higher authority. They want to be their own authority and stay in darkness. The Bible says that people love darkness rather than light and to have to be held responsible for their lifestyle is not what they want. The sad truth is that those who reject God do so intentionally to the damnation of their own soul. Instead of following the Lord they follow their own god that is a figment of their imagination.

· · ·

THE LESSON here is to decide. Jesus said you are either for me or against me. To be undecided is to decide against God. There is no middle ground in eternity for the undecided. The Bible says that we die once and then comes judgment. The moment you pass from this life your eternity will be sealed in one of two places that no one will be able to change. It will either be heaven or hell.

THE CHURCH CAN'T BE STOPPED

ACTS 12:7

> *"Now behold, an angel of the Lord stood by him, and a light shone in the prison; and he struck Peter on the side and raised him up, saying, "Arise quickly!" And his chains fell off his hands"*

The early church was in constant awe of God's work. With nothing to rely on but God Himself, they were moved by the Holy Spirit to do God's will. The church might have been it's purest then, being without many of the modern churches tools and techniques. Every day was like watching a parade, wondering what exciting encounter would come next. Things were growing, things were happening and souls were being saved.

Their formula was simple, let the Lord work. Watch what He can and will do. Follow and don't lead. Follow step by step, walking in agreement with the Lord. The church was powerful and many came against it, trying to stop God's work. Many were killed, starting with Stephen and all throughout the history of the church and that continues today.

However, persecutions are fertilizer for church growth whereas times of ease and comfort seem to bring about complacency and lethargy in the church. We see here in our text that persecutions didn't cause the church to give up, it caused them to pray and depend on God. This is exactly what they did when Peter was put in prison.

Satan's plans backfire when we meet his attacks with our spiritual weapons. No plan of Satan's attacks can stop the work of God. In fact, Jesus said "the gates of Hades will not prevail" against the church, and now over two thousand years later the church has spread across the whole world and is thriving despite all attempts to stop it.

. . .

THE LESSON here is to take confidence in the power of God. When you set out to serve God, nothing will be able to stop you. Press on and persevere despite all obstacles, because obstacles are merely opportunities for God to do amazing things.

POWER

1 KINGS 21:2

> *"So Ahab spoke to Naboth, saying, 'Give me your vineyard, that I may have it for a vegetable garden, because it is near, next to my house; and for it I will give you a vineyard better than it. Or, if it seems good to you, I will give you its worth in money.'"*

Power is a dangerous thing in the hands of one who is not capable of handling it well. Not many can, for power is something that must be controlled or else it will control you. Men naturally lust for power as it is a commodity earth dwellers see as highly advantageous to their existence.

Power, it is thought, gives control, authority and independence. Power gives one the impression that they do not have to be accountable to anyone which goes with the natural inclination of not being told what to do or not being "bossed" around. Power is also viewed as an instrument of superiority over others, which men naturally strive to obtain. It is at the heart of a human heart that is deceitfully wicked. Here in our text we see an example of this.

Ahab, the King of Israel wanted something he didn't have. To the one with all the power it is not good to be denied a desire. Spiritually we know that it IS good to be denied desires that are not in God's will. We learn to see a denial, as Christians, as something that God wants to do in order give us the better thing, which is not of the flesh.

Those with power, having the capability to use their power to get whatever they want. They have great difficulty with self-denial so they end up with more of what they want and less of what God wants, if they are not able to control their power and use it for good.

Ahab said to his neighbor Naboth, "Give me your vineyard." Naboth's only problem was that his families vineyard was next to the King's palace and he was unwilling to give in to Naboth's power. He stood his ground, which is suicide when it comes to doing so to one that has power and is willing to use it. Being near to people like that is not wise if one can help it.

Power sees what it wants and is unable to see people who get in the way with understanding, compassion and empathy. Power dehumanizes all individuals who are in the way of what they want because they are blinded by their power. When a powerful person doesn't get what they want, they cannot rest in God's perfect will but can only think about what they don't have. These thoughts, when unrestrained by higher purposes, will eat away at the powerful persons heart causing deep sorrow and frustration.

Eventually, with the help of his evil, power hungry wife Jezebel, Ahab got what he wanted through manipulation and deceit. Power will use whatever means necessary to get what it wants because it doesn't rest until it does. The problem with that is power never rests. It always wants more and is never satisfied. As it has been said, "Power corrupts and absolute power corrupts absolutely." Such was the case with Ahab.

. . .

THE LESSON here is to use whatever power or position you may have well. Never take decisions lightly and always remember to have compassion and great value in people and never lose sight of their humanity and that God loves them so much that He died for them. While seeing the overall good, also see the individual good and make decisions that benefit both if possible. Like Jesus, never use power for personal gain but only for God's gain. Have great integrity in all you do knowing the God will raise up if that's His will. In the end, when God grants power remember what a great responsibly it is and use it to do good.

TRUTH

1 KINGS 22:8

"So the king of Israel said to Jehoshaphat, 'There is still one man, Micaiah the son of Imlah, by whom we may inquire of the Lord; but I hate him, because he does not prophesy good concerning me, but evil.'"

Truth is a constant. It is what it is, it does not change to suit the situation or to fit the circumstance. Truth has one source, God Himself. Truth is what builds lives, relationships, foundations, integrity and freedom. It is the truth that sets us free.

While truth is a constant we are the variable. What we do with the truth depends on us. In our text, the King of Israel was more interested in want he wanted than the truth. He surrounded himself with prophets that told him whatever he wanted to hear with the false endorsement from God. As long as they told him fairy tales he was in his own fantasy land. Living in fantasy land is not sustainable. Like Humpty Dumpty, it all comes crashing down.

There was one man that would not conform to the King's fantasy land but was more interested in telling the truth of God. He would not compromise, yet the King hated him because he didn't want the truth. The King went so far as to say the Prophet of truth was evil because the King thought He was the constant and his way was the only way. He set himself up as the standard of truth instead of God.

. . .

THE LESSON here is that you are to conform to the truth and not the other way around. It may be hard at first, when things don't go your way, but in the end the truth will lead you right to God. There is no other way because Jesus is the "Way, the Truth and the Life." Look for the truth and receive it for this is God "the Potter" shaping you "the clay" into a glorious vessel of honor. There is nothing better than the truth because God is truth, and to have truth is to have the heart of a God.

THE VALUE OF A LIFE

PSALM 139:13

> *"For You formed my inward parts; You covered me in my mother's womb.*
> *I will praise You, for I am fearfully and wonderfully made;"*

It is clear from the Bible that we are handcrafted. God, the master craftsman, takes time in making us just so perfectly and uniquely. Out of the approximately 7.13 billion people on earth, no two are exactly alike. God sees us as special because He makes us special with a special plan and calling on our life.

In His detailed work, God designs every cell, every chemical, every organ and system. He works from head to toe, from skin to bone. He wraps our insides with skin fitting everything together with a purpose. He does His work inside a mother's womb allowing her the privilege of being a part of His work.

God uses material from mother and father allowing them to be uniquely connected to the precious miracle of life. We see mother and father having roles in the creation of life as the great privilege of bringing a life into the world. The whole process is a testimony of God's love and grace, touching lives though the miracle of a new life.

· · ·

THE LESSON here is to see the value God places on your life. You are priceless. You are made "fearfully" or with great respect and value. You are made "wonderfully" or individually distinctive. If God sees you this way, how should you see yourself? Made in His image, touched by God's hand, personally handcrafted with a unique plan and calling. Embrace who you are, thank God for how He made you and be the best in the world at being you. God thinks the world of you and He should know, He made you.

JOY

PROVERBS 17:22

"A merry heart does good, like medicine."

Joy is a theme that runs throughout the Bible. The Bible stresses the importance of joy in what we do and what we go through. In so many ways, joy is a gift and a blessing. This is why the enemy, Satan, wants to steal our joy. He will attack us so that life becomes one big drag, rendering us complacent, lethargic and indifferent.

Joy, as our text states, has healing properties. It's like medicine. Joy will heal us physically, emotionally and spiritually. This also suggests that perpetual sadness is the opposite of medicine and actually is harmful. There are however, scriptures that speak of sadness, sorrow and mourning as good things. This is true to a certain extent. Jesus was a Man of sorrows yet the book of Hebrews tells us that Jesus was anointed with gladness above His companions. Jesus was a joyful Man, yet also sorrowed.

We can reconcile these two by understanding that joy and sorrow both have their place, but sorrow that comes from our flesh, or sin nature, is not Godly sorrow. Godly sorrow is beneficial and actually contributes to joy. Godly sorrow is the sadness we feel over our sin, which leads to repentance and then joy. Sorrow that leads to brokenness regarding ourself or self-desires frees us to truly live in joy if we turn to God through them. Sorrow over others eternity and hardness of heart to God will lead us to pray, evangelize and trust God. This is how sorrow can be productive by leading us to Jesus, the source of joy and removing self-centered bondage and worldly attachments from our lives.

On the other hand, sadness that stems from the lack of faith, sin, selfishness, self focus, jealousy, envy, bitterness and/or unforgiveness is a sadness that is debilitating and destructive. This type of sadness can lead to hurting oneself and possibly others. Satan will use this emotion to control people and keep, them in darkness.

There are cases of chemical imbalances and mental disease that are physical problems. However, this is not the discussion here. Let me add however, that self focus, worldly focus, resisting God's will and forcing our own will, along with a sinful lifestyle, can and will cause chemical changes to the brain and the rest of the body. So, in some cases it is a matter of the chicken and the egg. As we see in the text, joy can heal many of these cases regardless of the cause. With that said, we should make room for those who truly have need of medication but even then joy will help heal.

The question comes, how do I do it? How do I have joy? The answer is provided in the scripture. The first step is to know where joy comes from. Joy has one source, God. There is no true joy outside of God. Knowing this then, we have to know that His joy is given and experienced freely, simply by being in a right relationship with God. Starting with turning from our sin to Jesus by faith in order to be forgiven and to have peace with God. Before we do this, we are enemies of God, which means we are against the only source of joy. When we are "born again" by turning to God in faith, trusting in Jesus and His work in dying for our sins and raising again from the dead, we are forgiven.

Then the Holy Spirit comes and lives inside of us and when we surrender to the Holy Spirit we will be filled with the fruit of the Holy Spirit, which is love. God's love, when experienced, gives joy that is unspeakable. So ultimately joy simply comes from God to man through ones faith and trusting in God allowing Him to have His way. When we surrender to God we are surrendering to His love.

. . .

THE LESSON here is the importance of joy. Inject joy into all you do by doing all you do for The Lord. It's not about what you are doing or what you are going through, it's about faith, trusting that God has a plan and is working everything out for good.

GRACE

//

ACTS 15:24

> *"Since we have heard that some who went out from us have troubled you with words, unsettling your souls, saying, 'You must be circumcised and keep the law.'"*

Understanding grace and applying it to our lives is no easy task. Grace is an affront to our "American Way" that wants to earn things. In one sense it is good to work hard but when we apply working hard to earning God's favor or blessing we have stepped away from grace on into law. To think that Jesus has paid it all, that there is nothing more to do or to get in regards to our salvation, is challenging. The temptation is to add something that we do to our experience with God. When this happens we are legalists.

Legalists "add" to God's grace a work, effort or requirement that extends beyond scripture. It puts a yoke on people that Christ has already removed. Usually, when we encounter a legalist we feel troubled and unsettled in our souls instead of freedom and release that grace brings. This was the situation going on in our text.

. . .

THE LESSON here is to live in God's grace knowing all debts have been paid. Be free to love God which is what you have been freed to do. Grow in grace and not self-righteousness or bondage. Watch for the traps of legalism that say, "Now you need to do this or that." Instead, simply follow the Holy Spirit in simple obedience and He will lead you to what you should do. The key is "abiding" not "trying." Abiding says, "Stay connected to the vine by faith," whereas trying says, "If I do this better or try harder then I will be more Holy and/or Godly." Rest in God's FINISHED work and you'll find that God will do more than you could ever hope or dream of, especially by your own efforts.

LED BY THE SPIRIT

//

ACTS 16:6-7

> *"Now when they had gone through Phrygia and the region of Galatia, they were forbidden by the Holy Spirit to preach the word in Asia. After they had come to Mysia, they tried to go into Bithynia, but the Spirit did not permit them."*

The secret to Paul's success was that it was the Spirit working through Him. He was "led by the Spirit" in what he did and the Spirit led him to fruitfulness and effectiveness. Paul was a man on a mission, led and fueled by God. We can also have great success if we will let the Spirit lead.

In our text we see an example of this. Paul didn't just do whatever he wanted or go wherever he felt like it. Even with noble intentions to save the world, we must be led by the Spirit. Seems odd that the Holy Spirit would forbid the preaching of the Word. Wouldn't God want everybody to hear? We can convince ourselves that more is better but if the Spirit is not leading, it's never good to proceed.

Paul was even held up by the Spirit once again after being held up from preaching in the region of Galatia. What he didn't know, and what we may not know, is that God's roadblocks are actually God's green light to His perfect will. His denial is His road to higher ground. His disappointments are his appointments to better things.

This is exactly what happened as God was leading Paul to go to a city called Philippi, which was in Macedonia. In Philippi he met Lydia, who received the Word, and then many other encounters resulted in an incredible and fruitful time of ministry there. All because he was led by the Spirit.

. . .

THE LESSON here is to see that you must be led by the Spirit. Be watchful for open doors and sensitive to closed ones. God is working out His plan and it much better than ours. He knows what He is doing and will be faithful to complete what He started. Letting the Spirit lead is a life of adventure and excitement. Doing things beyond what our capabilities are and God being glorified through it all. Don't force, push or muscle your way through but by simple obedience follow the Lord's leading and He will do the rest.

FREEDOM IN CHRIST

ACTS 16:26

> *"Suddenly there was a great earthquake, so that the foundations of the prison were shaken; and immediately all the doors were opened and everyone's chains were loosed."*

We are never freer than when we are free in Christ. Our chains are broken to sin and selfish desires. We are free to live the way God intended us to live which is in fellowship with Him, walking together in the cool of the day. What a great feeling it is to break out of the prison of self and the power of sin which controlled our lives.

Freedom in Christ is so liberating that no matter what may be our confinement here on earth, it is merely a place to enjoy our freedom. This may seem counter intuitive but our freedom in Christ lifts us higher than all circumstances of our earthly existence to a place of greater fulfillment of God's higher purposes in our lives. We are no longer victims of circumstances but sons and daughters of the most-high King, Jesus Christ. He is in control and working out His great plan for our highest good.

In our text we see this attitude on display. While doing God's work, proclaiming the truth and preaching the gospel, Paul and Silas were arrested for casting a demon out of a slave girl who was making money for her masters through this evil spirit which possessed her. While in jail, they praised God and sang hymns to the Lord. They knew that even though they were in prison, they were free because God was in control. They knew they were not subject to men's desires but to God's will. Therefore they knew God was up to something. That's true freedom. Knowing that no man or earthly circumstance is in control of us but the most-high God is. God miraculously freed them, leading them to an opportunity to preach to the jailer who was saved along with his family.

· · ·

THE LESSON here is that when Christ sets you free, you are free indeed. All things in Christ are merely opportunities not confinements. No man is free until he is free in Christ. When you are free, use that freedom to walk with God. Your freedom in Christ is your daily gift to be used and enjoyed. It gives God much pleasure when you do.

JUNE 26

Psalm 144:1 15, Proverbs 17:27 28

MEASURING TRUTH

ACTS 17:11

> *"These were more fair-minded than those in Thessalonica, in that they received the word with all readiness, and searched the Scriptures daily to find out whether these things were so."*

The "Bereans" were a people from a place called Berea. They were preached to by Paul and Silas. They no doubt knew of Paul and Silas and heard of their message. They no doubt were excited to hear what they had to say, as much of the region was all a buzz with this new movement. Our scripture says they, "Received the word with all readiness." Their hearts we open and anxious to hear. However, they didn't just blindly receive what they said, they checked it out according to scripture. This is what makes the Bereans' so great.

The Bible is the standard. All else is measured by it because it is the revealed truth of God handed down to us and proven to be divine, written by God Himself through the hands of men. It has proven to be true over thousands of years and has transformed the lives, families, communities and nations who have embraced it. God's Word will endure forever and therefore is the measuring stick by which all should be measured.

We all have a tendency to give too much worth to what human "authorities" have to say. We value degrees, certificates and diplomas. Imagine the credibility the Apostle Paul and Silas brought to town with them. Imagine the experiences, miracles, church plants, souls converted and demons cast out. Yet, the Bereans' are commended for checking what was said by the Word of God.

. . .

THE LESSON here is the importance of the truth. Throw out anything that doesn't hold up to Biblical truth. Don't be deceived by the many deceivers that are out there and are getting worse. Don't fall prey to the "experts." If it's not lining up with the scriptures it is not true. Make it a habit to know the Word and to be able to use it to dissect truth from error. When you measure truth by the Bible, you will never be a lightweight.

RELATIONSHIPS

PROVERBS 18:1

> *"A man who isolates himself seeks his own desire; He rages against all wise judgment."*

God made the human race to be relational. We are beings who thrive in connecting with others and sharing life with others. Life was not meant to be lived alone. There are times to be alone, to think, to spend time with the Lord, to rest and to pray but not as a lifestyle of isolating.

God is a relational being, communicating and sharing love within the Trinity even before the human race was created. Then, God created man to have a relationship with Him and one another. This is why love is so important. Love is relational. We are to love God and love others as a fulfillment of God's law. Love is the rule and love is relational. Healthy humans are relational and unhealthy humans are isolationist.

In our text we see the importance of relationship. In regards to making decisions and judgments about things, someone who withdraws from others counsel and wisdom really only wants what they want, regardless of if it's the right thing or not. That's why the Bible says, "There is wisdom in a multitude of counselors." Godly advice, from Godly praying people filled with wisdom and the Holy Spirit is invaluable, showing humility in listening and taking in what others may say or points of view they may have.

This doesn't mean they are right, as we see in the book of Job with his "miserable counselors" but it helps our point of view. However, when we "fly solo" in life and don't see the value of others, we really are missing the value of relationships that God has provided because of simply wanting what our desire is and not caring about others. This is an unhealthy and destructive attitude that isolates us from God and others.

• • •

THE LESSON here is that a healthy relationship with God will result in a healthy relationships with others. That doesn't mean you will necessarily have a lot of friends or that everyone will like you, quite the contrary, but it will mean that you, like Jesus, value people, involve ourselves with them, embrace them, love them and do your best to be at peace with them.

JUNE 28

2 Kings 13:1 14:29, Acts 18:23 19:12,
Psalm 146:1 10, Proverbs 18:2 3

IT'S ALL ABOUT JESUS

//

ACTS 18:28

"For he vigorously refuted the Jews publicly, showing from the Scriptures that Jesus is the Christ."

Scriptures are a testimony of Jesus Christ. Layer by layer we see Christ and at all His different angles. Like a prism, Christ is multifaceted and multidimensional. His grace is manifold or diverse. We can grow in it and still not come close to seeing it all. He is the revelation of the Father and revealed in God's Word. The imagery and pictures in the Old Testament all point to Christ, as He is the fulfillment of the anti-types or pre-examples of Him. The volume of the book is written of Him.

There are over 300 prophecies of Jesus Christ in the Old Testament, all being filled exactly as stated. John the Baptist announced Jesus as, "The Lamb of God who takes away the sins of the world." Jesus was the fulfillment of the sacrificial lambs that were slain by the High Priest as an offering for sin. Jesus is not only the central figure in the Bible, He is the central figure in all of Human history.

In our text, Apollos used the scriptures to show who Jesus was. He knew the scriptures to be a testimony of Jesus Christ and used them to show the truth about His identity. He showed them that Jesus was the One in whom scriptures spoke about. He came just as scriptures said, where scriptures have said, when scripture has said, in what manner scripture has said and He fulfilled what a scripture has said. Jesus is who He said He was and proved that He, and only He, could be the one true Savior of the world.

· · ·

THE LESSON here is to know that it is really all about Jesus. He is the main thing. Jesus is the Alpha and the Omega, the beginning and the end. Your life must reflect this if you believe it to be true. All your life must be yielded to Him. All your hopes and dreams, goals and ambitions are His. Give all to the Good Shepherd for He is all. Nothing is right without Him, with Him everything comes into focus. With Him you have everything, without Him you have nothing. It's all about Jesus.

AUTHENTIC CHRISTIANITY

//

ACTS 19:15

"And the evil spirit answered and said, 'Jesus I know, and Paul I know; but who are you?'"

Does Satan know your name? In our text there were some Jews trying to cast out evil spirits in the name of Jesus. They saw the power of the disciples and all the miraculous works and figured they would get in on the action. They tried to duplicate the disciples authentic experience with God and real conversion to Christ. The source of the disciples power came from the in dwelling of the Holy Spirit at their conversion. Their power flowed from the Holy Spirit within, which the Jews who were trying to cast out demons did not possess. The true working of God cannot be duplicated, a fact that became obvious to the Jews.

The demons were not moved by these spiritual "cons." The demons said they knew "Jesus and Paul" but not the impostors. When one is numbered with Christ, Satan takes notice. We become public enemy number one to him. True believers are a threat to Satan, a force he cannot contend with. The disciples would be able to cast out demons by the name of Jesus because Jesus was in them. They were one with Christ and so the power they had over Satan's was in their relationship with The King of Kings. There is no way to duplicate a real authentic relationship with Him. One may be able to fool people but not God and certainly not Satan. In the spirit realm true Christians are known and eventually true faith will be found out for what it is, just as fake faith as well.

· · ·

THE LESSON here is to be an authentic Christian. Duplication without authentication is worthless in the eternal realm. Knowing Christ shakes the foundation of hell. Satan and his demons have no power over God's children. They can be bold with nothing to fear. Does Satan know who YOU are?

JOY

///

ACTS 18:24

> *"But none of these things move me; nor do I count my life dear to myself,*
> *so that I may finish my race with joy, and the ministry which I received*
> *from the Lord Jesus, to testify to the gospel of the grace of God."*

Speaking about his upcoming suffering and imprisonment, leading to his eventual death for his faith in Christ, the Apostle Paul shared these words with his followers. This statement reveals the heart of Paul and the secret of joy. How can one have joy when all seems lost? How can one have hope when the future seems bleak? Paul shows us the secret of joy.

First off, he says, "None of these things move me." This means that whatever the circumstance, he is still the same. Whether good times or bad, he has leaned to be stable through all. This is important to understand yet impossible to accomplish. Yet Paul truly was stable in the face of torture, imprisonment and death. How can we be stable regardless of the problem that confronts us? Before we see how, know that we need stability that is not conditional upon circumstances but independent from them.

Secondly, he says that, "he doesn't count his life dear to himself." Now we see the anchor. Paul is not holding on to anything that could be lost. He had a dependence upon that which could never be lost, Jesus Christ. He had turned over all rights to himself over to God and therefore was able to rest in God's lap. The more we hold on to our life the more we are attached to changing circumstances. It's impossible to have true joy until we detach from ourselves and attach to God. Notice he says, "So I may finish my race with joy." There is a direct relationship between joy and losing our lives to God.

Lastly he says he doesn't count his life dear to HIMSELF, not only so he could finish his race with joy, but also, "the ministry which I received from The Lord Jesus." The last piece of the puzzle is to know that our joy comes from living for God and fulfilling the ministry He has given us.

That's why Paul could be grateful in prison, being stoned, persecuted, arrested and tried. He saw all of that not in regards to his life, which would seem bad, but in regards to God's plan. Those events lead to Paul finishing his ministry and that was what he saw life to be about. He lived for something bigger and better than himself, which in turn was also the best for himself. All his life was meaningful and nothing was ever lost or taken away because all was given to a God. Joy flowed from Paul like a white water rapid because he was God's therefore joy was his and it is yours also.

. . .

THE LESSON here is to see that joy is vital and is directly related to your relationship with Jesus. All life that we live for His glory and His will results in joy. This is why we are here and where we find fulfillment.

2 Kings 18:13 19:37, Acts 21:1 17,
Psalm 149:1 9, Proverbs 18:8

ATTITUDE

ACTS 21:13-14

> *"But he said, 'Why all this weeping? You are breaking my heart! I am ready not only to be jailed at Jerusalem but even to die for the sake of the Lord Jesus.' When it was clear that we couldn't persuade him, we gave up and said, 'The Lord's will be done.'"*

When confronted with suffering how do we respond? There are many irritants in the Christian life looking to irritate us into the flesh and away from God. What makes the difference is not what the irritant is but how we respond to these irritants. Not that it's easy, and there are things we deal with that seem unbearable, however, we can do it with God's help and God's strength by turning to Him in times of need.

In our text, Paul was being told to avoid Jerusalem where he would be bound. It was a sad day for his friends who didn't want Paul to go. His attitude was one of readiness. He was prepared to finish the race. The overriding attitude of Paul's life, which was also Jesus' attitude, was, "The Lord's will be done." When this is our attitude we are ready for anything. As long as it's the Lord's will we know there will be all the provision needed to face and finish whatever is before us. God will never allow something to cross our path unless He has equipped us to handle it. Yes, He will never give us more than we can handle.

· · ·

THE LESSON here is to let your attitude be dictated by your eternal perspective, making God's will your desire. When you do, you come into that which is much bigger than yourself, joining with the greater plan. When this issue is settled you will be settled. The Lord's will be done, the attitude Satan has no answer for and the power of every believer to finish well.

PRAISE THE LORD

PSALM 150:6

"Let everything that has breath praise the Lord. Praise the Lord!"

All the living owes praise to the Lord. It's good to know the difference between the Lord and man. Only He is worthy to receive praise because only He is the One above all as the Creator of all. He is self-existent and existent. Without beginning and end. All life comes from the Lord and we do not create anything other than what the Lord has already given us and done. When we get confused about who is who, God and man, Creator and creation, we lose perspective of everything else in life.

The best way to express the difference between ourselves and God is through praise. We are told in our text that, "Everything that has breath praise The Lord." The very breath God has given us is to give it back to him in praise. Because He is God we can praise Him knowing He is working all things together for good. Praise puts our perspective back on His goodness and abilities instead of on our weakness and incapability's. Praise says, "You are bigger, you are better and you are the One who blesses." Praise says, "You are a God and I am not."

· · ·

THE LESSON here is to remember that you are to be a person of praise. Your lifestyle should reflect the greatness of God through your praise. The more you grow in the Lord the easier it is to praise Him.

THE BOOK

//

2 KINGS 22:8B

"I have found the Book of the Law in the house of the Lord."

What a day that was, the day "The Book" was found. God's house, the Temple, had been neglected and upon it's restoration the book was found. It's no mistake the correlation between God's Word and the "House of God." They go together in that when God's Word is front and center, God's House is strong and vibrant. When "God's Word" becomes negligible, so will the "House of the Lord." The house may stand, it may be popular, it may look good and have a lot of money but it won't be "God's House," it will be "Mans' House" with no eternal merit or worth.

The recovery of God's Word, "The Book," would bring the people back to the Lord. No amount of repairs to the structure of the Temple could have brought the hearts of the people back around to God Himself. It's easy to mistake outward activities for inward transformation when in reality it's only superficial and empty. God's Word is the instrument that has power to restore people, families, communities and nations. There is no other way for God's Word to reveal God's heart, God's way, God's truth, God's love, God's mercy, God's Salvation and most importantly God's Son, Jesus Christ.

Have you "found The Book?" Has it been lost gathering dust somewhere? Have you been missing the voice of the Lord?

• • •

THE LESSON here is to "find The Book," open it, pray about it, and do it. All of God's people are to be people of "The Book." It will change you into the man or woman God wants you to be. Don't ever let the book depart from you, stay close to it, and it will keep you from sin, plant you firmly like a tree beside the water, and establish your life on the unmovable rock. Find "The Book" and you will have found life's greatest treasure.

LORDSHIP

PSALM 2:2

> *"The kings of the earth set themselves,*
> *And the rulers take counsel together,*
> *Against the Lord and against His Anointed, saying,*
> *'Let us break Their bonds in pieces*
> *And cast away Their cords from us.'"*

Man naturally resists authority. Rebellion is at the heart of our broken nature. Those who reject God, and hate those who represent God, do so ultimately because they don't want anyone to rule over them. Ironically, those who rebel against God's authority are the ones in the most bondage. The Lordship of Jesus is the most freeing thing there is.

Jesus came to set the captives free. He came to give life and liberty. He came to loose the chains of sin and self which held us captive. His Lordship is submission to love, to grace, to mercy, to peace and joy. His Lordship is light and easy because He works in us and through us. His Lordship gives fulfillment and purpose. We are not forced to comply but transformed to comply to that which builds us, strengthens us and stabilizes us. His Lordship adds and edifies. Submitting to His Lordship is submitting to greatness and is not hard.

On the other hand, the bondage of the world takes away from us. Sin destroys and hurts. It is a harsh task-master with no love or mercy. Without the Lordship of Christ, we are imprisoned by our own lust and carnal desires that can never give what they initially promise, leading to eternal damnation. The Lordship of the world is deceiving, making its slaves robots programmed to do Satan's will. There is no freedom without Christ.

· · ·

THE LESSON here is that rebelling against God is rebellion against your own soul. The desire to "break bonds" and "cast away cords" is the world's way of thinking that being free from God's Lordship is being free. In reality, the dominion or power of darkness is holding them captive like a pardoned prisoner remaining in jail. Let God be the Lord of your life and you will be the most free.

JULY 5

1 Chronicles 1:1 2:17, Acts 23:11 35,
Psalm 3:1 8, Proverbs 18:14 15

HELP FOR A BROKEN SPIRIT

PROVERBS 18:14

> *"The spirit of a man will sustain him in sickness, But who can bear a broken spirit?"*

That which makes up our inner self, our spirit, is capable of injury just as our outer self. The spirit, however, is much harder to fix. The wounds to our spirit are unseen yet they affect our whole being. These wounds run deep, causing deep pain, which are unbearable.

In our text we see the importance of a healthy spirit. When it is healthy it will sustain us through physical sickness and all other maladies we go through. It is our spirit that carries us through. A strong spirit will withstand any storm. A broken spirit is like a broken dam. It cannot handle any pressure the comes it's way. A broken spirit is a broken life.

There are no medicines for a broken spirit. Not much human intervention will help a broken spirit, for only God can reach it. The answer to a broken spirit is an Everlasting God who can reach into the human heart and heal and restore the sickest and most damaged of people. God is a restorer specializing in restoration. Even the slightest damage needs to be fixed and that is why we are to come to God and allow His healing power do its work deep within us.

. . .

THE LESSON here is the knowing importance of a healthy spirit. Be careful of accumulating wounds without applying the balm of the Holy Spirit. Are you hurt in your inside? Are you withdrawn, bitter, unforgiving, jealous or just plain hurting inside? God is ready to heal you. Turn to Him, receive His love, ask for His help and you are on your way to a healthy, strong spirit. God the healer is ready to help.

GOSPEL LIFE

ACTS 24:24

> *"And after some days, when Felix came with his wife Drusilla, who was Jewish, he sent for Paul and heard him concerning the faith in Christ."*

Every encounter is an opportunity. Christians are placed where they are for purposes beyond the seen. The gospel message is the ultimate reason we are placed where we are and also the reason the people in our lives are placed there. Sometimes God has to put us in places that can be difficult to be, in order for the gospel message to reach the people who need to hear the message. Another reason is so that those around us can see what the gospel message looks like as we live it out in front of them.

Paul in our text is before a Roman official and his wife. Felix is to make a determination about Paul's punishment. He is being pressured to condemn Paul, who is really innocent. Felix's motivation is bribe money he was hoping Paul would give him. He was also wanting to do the Jews a favor so he left Paul in prison. The motives of Felix were completely evil and selfishly motivated. Yet the innocent Paul was there for a bigger reason. Felix and his wife listened to Paul's message concerning faith in Christ.

· · ·

THE LESSON here is to see every occasion in light of the gospel. To realize God has placed you where you are and has placed those around you so that they would also hear or be encouraged concerning the faith in Christ. Never see your situation as something that is about you, see it as a situation that is about the gospel.

1 Chronicles 4:5 5:17, Acts 25:1 27,
Psalm 5:1 12, Proverbs 18:19

WHEN WE ARE OFFENDED

PROVERBS 18:19

> *"A brother offended is harder to win than a strong city."*

The devil thrives in contentions. He loves to see people tear each other apart. Whether it be with their tongues, their fists or in their hearts, contentions are the devils best friend. He knows "a house divided cannot stand" so he works from inside the house to make it fall.

In our text we see an example of this. When we are offended it is easy to develop animosity toward another. An offense is when we get attacked or slighted personally. Our pride gets hurt and when our pride is hurt we have a hard time recovering. We will put up a barrier between ourselves and the offender and that's why an offended brother is "harder to win than a strong city."

Jesus provided the answer to this at the cross. This is where He died and by faith we die with Him. This means it is no longer us who lives but Christ who lives in us. Since we are dead to ourselves we need not be bothered by offenses because dead people don't care if they are offended. Love may be poked, but it is not provoked. All our insufficiencies have been taken care of at the cross. We are free to keep the bond of peace even when Satan attacks it.

. . .

THE LESSON here is that you are not to be touchy and sensitive in regards to the way others treat you. Your sufficiency is in Christ so it doesn't matter what others think or say. The only opinion that matters is Jesus', and He thinks the world of you.

ALMOST A CHRISTIAN

ACTS 26:28

> *"Then Agrippa said to Paul, 'You almost persuade me to become a Christian.'"*

An "almost" Christian is not a Christian at all. There are many who hear the Word, feel it's truth resonating with their heart and still resist it. There are some who do Christian service, sing Christian songs and are considered "part of the fold" by those who know them, yet still remain dead in their sins. Many churches even cater to "almost Christians" by tailoring their services to meet their needs. Minimizing the Word of God while insisting on "relevance," avoiding speaking about sin, sacrifice and suffering in order to keep things "positive" and assuring congregates of their salvation in order to ensure church growth and financial prosperity.

In our text, King Agrippa was given the opportunity to have eternal life. The opportunity came to him because of God's dying love for him. The message of truth in Jesus Christ, the free gift of forgiveness of sin and eternal life if he would respond by faith to the message Paul brought to him. For whatever reason he came close. Could there be a more tormenting knowledge in hell as to know you almost didn't go there? Imagine what he and many others live with in eternity knowing they were that close to escaping their condition. "Almost" in hell means nothing more than torment.

Don't make that mistake when your eternity is at stake. Be sure, be certain now, by believing in Jesus Christ and trusting in Him alone for you salvation. Don't trust in man, false teachers with false gospel that center on a false view.

. . .

THE LESSON here is to put your hope in God as revealed in His Word. Know that you have eternal life because of what Jesus said. Settle the issue now by surrendering your life to Him. Jesus knows whose are His and will not let one of His be snatched out of His grip. Don't be an "almost Christian," be a born again Christian for that is the only Christian there is.

THE WICKED

PSALM 7:16

> *"His trouble shall return upon his own head, and his violent dealing shall come down on his own crown."*

The Bible has much to say about the wicked. Man, at the core, is wicked and probably much more than he even thinks. The heart of man is deceitfully wicked, the Bible says, and "who can know it?" We are so wicked at heart that we are even tricked by our heart, thinking we are good. The Bible says there is not one righteous. This is why we need a Savior to forgive us of our sins.

In our text, David is speaking about the wicked. He is being pursued by them and describes their own problems as that which will come back to hurt themselves. Ironic how when evil attacks the righteous, it ends up with that evil attacking themselves. One can never get by with wickedness and evil for it will consume everyone in the end. Evil has no mercy and no discrimination. It is a destructive force.

· · ·

THE LESSON here is to remember that Jesus is the remedy to evil. At the cross He took the destructiveness of sin upon Himself in your place. He has given the you new life, forgiveness, freedom and protection. Sin and its power have been destroyed by the power of God. You are no longer in their sins being destroyed; they are in Christ being renewed. Rejoice in that today.

INVINCIBLE

ACTS 27:24-26

> *"Saying, 'Do not be afraid, Paul; you must be brought before Caesar; and indeed God has granted you all those who sail with you. Therefore take heart, men, for I believe God that it will be just as it was told me. However, we must run aground on a certain island.'"*

Each person has an appointment made by God. He has a calendar in heaven with our name on it and a date when we will be finished in this life. "It is appointed man once to die and then comes judgment," the Bible says. For the Christian, our time is up when our calling is fulfilled. God leaves us here for a specific purpose, which He has laid out perfectly, and once we completed it's like we cross the finish line into eternity. Until that time, we are invincible.

In our text Paul was hitching a ride on a ship. When they came across some bad weather the Lord spoke to Paul and said they should wait out the storm. His words were rejected and now they were all in big trouble. As scary as it was, Paul was invincible because God's plan was to bring him before Caesar. Nothing could happen to Paul because God wasn't finished. We too are invincible until God is finished and when that time comes we will cross our own finish line on into eternity.

· · ·

THE LESSON here is to keep your eyes on the prize. Your existence itself is proof that God is not finished. You have a divine purpose that God is still working out. Nothing is random or insignificant and God wastes nothing. As you keep your eyes on Him, follow His lead in obedience until that day when you hear Him say, "Well done my good and faithful servant, enter into the joy of the Lord." Life is very short in comparison to eternity and we only have a short time to do now what we will enjoy in heaven. Don't fear death for you are invincible until your race is complete.

GRACE

ACTS 28:4

> *"So when the natives saw the creature hanging from his hand, they said to one another, 'No doubt this man is a murderer, whom, though he has escaped the sea, yet justice does not allow to live.'"*

Rational thinking says that one gets what they deserve. A murder deserves death. A thief deserves prison and a liar deserves punishment. The reason we know this is we all have a sense of justice that comes from our creator. God made man in His likeness and because God is a just God, we too know instinctively that there should be a consequence from our negative actions.

However, when it comes to applying justice to our own lives we also have a tendency to not see our own condition as clearly as we see others condition. We are not typically objective when it comes to our own sins. The Bible says that our "hearts are deceitfully wicked" so that even we can be tricked by our hearts. So our system of justice is flawed unless we are completely honest with ourselves.

In our text we see that Paul, and those on board the ship with him, had come across some unusually kind hosts that welcomed him when he was shipwrecked in Malta. They made a fire for the distressed group but when Paul grabbed a bundle of sticks to throw in the fire, a viper came out and latched on to his hand. The natives figured Paul had done something to deserve this attack and since he escaped the sea, now the hands of justice will have their way. This is how a Christ-less theology thinks. Without Christ, all will pay the penalty for sin and it will be fair and just. However, by grace we are unscathed by venom of sin.

· · ·

THE LESSON here is to embrace God's grace, just as Paul was not killed by the viper, you also are spared justice in lieu of grace. Jesus took your place in judgment. He was killed by the snake of sin so you wouldn't be. All those who are in Christ no longer get what they deserve, but get what they don't deserve. That is how grace works.

ENCOURAGEMENT

ROMANS 1:11-12

"For I long to see you, that I may impart to you some spiritual gift, so that you may be established—that is, that I may be encouraged together with you by the mutual faith both of you and me."

Encouragement is one if the most powerful tools we have to build the body of Christ. Some Christians are especially gifted at it but all Christians have the potential to do it. Barnabas in the Bible was a great encouragement to many. In fact, his original name was Joseph, but when he sold all his goods and gave the money to the Apostles, they changed his name to Barnabas, which means, "Son of encouragement." What a great thing to be known as.

In the text we see how important encouragement was to Paul. He wrote of his longing to visit the Roman Christians so that he and they would be encouraged by each other. Even the strongest and most successful believers need encouragement, maybe even more. Encouragement can be just the thing to get someone over the hump or to just get going. When one is beat up, battered and bruised, a word or act if encouragement may be just what they need to heal and be restored.

You can be a huge blessing right away. No training is needed. You are ready. If you look at whose around you right now, you will find your mission field of encouragement. Blossom those around you through your words and acts of encouragement and you will find yourself very encouraged as well. Encouragement goes a long way in the kingdom of God. Who knows, you may be encouraging the next Paul. Who are you going to encourage today? Are you going to be an encourager?

. . .

THE LESSON here is that you can have a powerful ministry of encouragement. Make it a point to be an encourager. Look for opportunities to encourage. Encourage often and lavishly. Encourage skillfully with the perfect words for the perfect person on the perfect occasion. Be good at it by emphasizing it, looking for opportunities and praying about it. Don't flatter or insincerely praise, but notice the good about people, especially the things of God in them.

LET JESUS SHINE

//

1 CHRONICLES 15:29

"And it happened, as the ark of the covenant of the Lord came to the City of David, that Michal, Saul's daughter, looked through a window and saw King David whirling and playing music; and she despised him in her heart."

Not everybody will understand a personal relationship with Jesus Christ. From the outside looking in, it can be hard to understand the joy that comes from having a personal relationship. To the outsider, the joy of a Christian can look silly and even fake. It doesn't make sense to the outsider because of the supernatural component of a life lived in Christ. The outsider can become cynical, jealous and even hostile when they see something they don't have. A personal relationship with Jesus Christ is completely out of this world.

In the text we see the outward expression of David, a man after Gods own heart, to the inward reality of God's presence. The Ark of the Covenant represents God's presence and David was elated. His joy overflowed as he played music and whirled around. This is often how the presence of the Lord makes one feel.

One should never be ashamed of this joy and never try and cover it up, for it speaks of God's goodness and demonstrates to others that there is something they may not have. Many will long for this relationship through the manifestation of God's presence in our lives. However, we also see David's wife Michal's reaction. When she sees David responding this way, she despised him in her heart.

. . .

THE LESSON here is the importance of your personal relationship with Jesus Christ. To know the joy and its fullness that comes from His presence walking in His love and faithfulness. There is nothing better than God's presence in your life. No matter what others may think or how they may react to your personal relationship with Jesus Christ, always make it your aim to let Jesus shine and may Jesus shine so brightly that you light a path for them to know Him personally.

EXALTATION

1 CHRONICLES 17:7

> *"Now therefore, thus shall you say to My servant David, 'Thus says the Lord of hosts: "I took you from the sheepfold, from following the sheep, to be ruler over My people Israel."'"*

Exaltation comes from the Lord, the Bible says. When we place our lives in His care, God sees fit to bring about the right place in life for us. Since He is the One who lifts up, we are free from human strivings to try and be superheroes. We can rest in His care as we entrust our future to Him. We can be confident that we are where we are suppose to be and when God sees fit, we will be raised up. It's good to know that the Lord does that and He gets all the glory.

The Lord, speaking through the profit Nathan, reminds David of the incredible work that has been done on David's behalf. From shepherd boy to King, is David's story and it was God who sought David out when David was not expecting it. He was going about his business, doing his job faithfully when the call came. He was the least likely for the promotion, at least in man's eyes, but best qualified in God's.

Over the years God had prepared David through his service as a shepherd. Learning how to lead the sheep, protect them, take care of them and find the lost ones, taught David about how to lead people. Having time alone to think, pray, meditate and see God's glory in the splendor of nature taught him how to follow God.

· · ·

THE LESSON here is to just be faithful with what God has given you right now. Be faithful to what you have and what is right in front of you. Don't worry about what you don't have for God will bring about all we are supposed to have. When we are faithful in the little things, He will raise us up. God will take you to places you never could have imagined.

A NEW HEART

ROMANS 2:29

> *"But he is a Jew who is one inwardly; and circumcision is that of the heart,
> in the Spirit, not in the letter; whose praise is not from men but from God."*

The reference here is one of a change of heart. True change that changes the selfish fleshly person into a selfless Spiritual person. This is what "circumcision of he heart" means. It's amazing to see this transformation. We are not talking about the development of a person by achievement, personal growth, maturity, education or whatever micro changes people may have. We are talking about the birth of something completely new, where there was no life and substance, where there was no substance.

As we see in the text, nothing made of material can create the spiritual. No flesh can reproduce the spirit, as flesh gives birth to flesh but only the Spirit can give birth to the spiritual. This is why Jesus said, "You must be born again." Not that we need to be born human again, but that we need to be born spiritually. This is why with the new heart one receives makes a person a whole new person. They become whole, more of themselves than they ever were, yet more a citizen of heaven than of earth.

We see then that when this transformation occurs we find, "Praise not from men but from God." In other words, our relationship with God changes from enemies to family. God is pleased with us, accepts us and takes care of us. He is our Father and we His children. We inherit His kingdom and are co-heirs with Christ. The cry of our heart changes from me, myself and I to Father, Son and the Holy Spirit. He becomes our goal, ambition and desire. We are satisfied in Him and He is always with us. The new heart is a heart filled with love, joy and peace.

The Bible tells us how to have this new heart. When we recognize we are sinners and turn from our sin to God and ask His forgiveness. We put our faith in Jesus Christ, the preexistent God who become man to save the world from sin by living a sinless life, dying on the cross for OUR sins and raising from the dead just as the Bible told us beforehand.

. . .

THE LESSON here is to remember that a simple step of faith in Jesus Christ is the remedy to your sinful broken heart. Turn to Jesus if you haven't already and rejoice in His goodness always.

THE PURE WORD

PSALM 12:6

> *"The words of the Lord are pure words, Like silver tried in a furnace of earth, Purified seven times."*

It's hard to know these days who's telling the truth. Things can be slanted and twisted in so many ways that one has to sift through and "read between the lines" to make sense of things. Even then we are left with trying to decide who and what we can believe. Society has perfected the "white lie" and substituted the truth with what is convenient. It's exhausting to say the least.

That is what is so refreshing about God's Word, the Bible. It is truth, straight from God to man. It is unadulterated, pure and clean. It will always be right and we can trust it. It is God-breathed, written through mans' hands onto the pages of the Bible. It stands the test of time, fulfilling all it's promises and prophecies. It will endure forever while the ways of man will pass away. It conforms to no one but will transform all who read and obey it by faith.

You will stand strong in every storm of life, be free from the lies of man and the vain changing philosophies of the world. You will be blessed, refreshed, strengthened and wise. The purity of God's Word stands above all the world has to offer, keeping you safe in its steadfast unchanging truth.

· · ·

THE LESSON here is to remember that you have been given the greatest of treasures in God's Word. Build your life on its truths and accept what lines up with it. You are not to impose your views upon the standard of truth nor blend your opinions or ideas with "some" scripture. Take it as it is, all of it, as God's Word, and build your whole life on it.

RIGHTEOUSNESS

ROMANS 4:3

> *"For what does the Scripture say? 'Abraham believed God, and it was accounted to him for righteousness.'"*

How can one be right with God? God is holy and righteous and a perfect judge. Sin must be judged because it is against God's holiness. The requirements for one to be right with God are "righteous requirements" meaning that we are to be holy as God is Holy. How is He holy? He is perfectly holy. That is the standard and the requirement for our acceptance.

As sinners, the Bible says that "all have sinned," we cannot produce the righteous requirements of God. His demands not only include our actions but also our thoughts. One bad thought proves we have bad, or sin, in us. We lack the perfection God requires. This means that it is impossible for God to accept us based on our own imperfect righteousness. He wouldn't be a just God if He did.

Abraham, in our text, was a righteous man it says here. Notice what made him righteous, his belief. Even before the law came about with Moses, which pointed out God's perfect requirements, righteousness came only one way. It has always been that way, as we see here. There is not one bit of good work that can merit our forgiveness. There is not one thing WE can do to erase our sin. It is beyond our power, as people dead in sin, to "un-die." We need help. We need an outside source. We need One who is over and above sin's power.

Not only is God a just God, He is a merciful God. He is willing to forgive anyone who wants His forgiveness. What are the terms? It's believing in HIS RIGHTEOUSNESS and accepting HIS FORGIVENESS. However, God doesn't just forgive because sin requires punishment. The punishment for sin is death. So God sent His only Son, Jesus Christ to live the perfect life without sin. God became a man so He could do what we couldn't. This gave Him the right to be our sacrifice. Jesus died in our place so that forgiveness is based on justice and mercy. This is called grace.

. . .

THE LESSON here is to keep your eyes upon the cross and remember where your righteousness comes from. The cross was greatest display of love man has ever known. Jesus loves you that much. Believe on The Lord Jesus Christ and be saved. Rejoice in your salvation an in your Savior today.

WHY ATHEISM?

PSALM 14:1

"The fool has said in his heart, 'There is no God.'"

It takes quite a leap of faith to look around and say there is no God. A child will naturally know there is God. God is seen in the creation. We all know that when we see something made that it has a maker. It's normal, natural and logical to think that. It's normal to think an effect has a cause. So why do some say in their heart there is no God?

It is the most foolish thing there can be and it takes a great work of active forceful ignorance to un-know something. To deny something that is already inside of us naturally. We are wired to know there is a Creator. God has set eternity in our hearts. So to deny that is an active suppression of what they know to be true. They have to detach from the obvious. They have to keep a cover on what their instinct tells them and keep convincing themselves over and over again, even though all that is in them says the opposite.

The reason they do this is that ultimately they do not want to be accountable for their sin. They love darkness rather than light and don't want to have to change. Their pride won't allow for humble submission and so they live a life if resistance which creates constant friction inside of them. They resist brokenness that leads to surrender even though they feel empty and broken inside.

What a terrible way to live. One day every knee will bow to Jesus. Better to do it now and be forgiven of sin in order to spend eternity in heaven than to reject God and spend eternity in hell. Maybe that is really what this life is all about. An opportunity for faith, to choose God for all eternity.

· · ·

THE LESSON here is to remember that there really is nothing more important than your relationship with Jesus Christ. You will never live or know life until you have one. Choose Jesus and you're choosing life.

GOD'S LOVE

ROMANS 5:8

> *"But God demonstrates His own love toward us, in that while we were still sinners, Christ died for us."*

The most valuable thing we possess is our lives. Our lives are precious and a gift from God. When life is lost we feel pain because we can never replace it. Knowing this should help one to value every moment we have and enjoy our time with those around us. It is true that each moment is precious, a gift and to be enjoyed.

Everything we need to know about how God feels about us is seen in what Jesus was willing to give, His own life. He didn't just "say" I love you, He proved His love. Now to give your life for someone is an undeniable statement. Think about it like this, when you make a purchase you are saying that you value something by the amount you will pay for it. If you buy a car you are saying in monetary terms that, "I value this car this much." If you value a car less than the price, you won't buy it saying, "It's too much." Jesus paid the ultimate price for our salvation. In dying for us He is saying, "I love you to the highest possible degree, I am willing to pay the highest price for you."

God's love is truly the greatest love the world has ever seen. It is a proven love, an undeniable love and a satisfying love. It is a love that was undeserved and unmerited. This unconditional love came while we were enemies of God, against Him in every way. To die for a loved one or friend is nothing compared to dying for someone who is against us and hates us to the point of hurting us.

· · ·

THE LESSON here is, whenever you doubt God's love, whenever you wonder if you are lovable, whenever you wonder if there is anyone who can love you, remember the cross. All of life's question marks were replaced by the cross. At the cross all your doubts will be resolved and all questions answered. Jesus loves you more than you can ever imagine.

THE HARVEST OF BLESSING

PSALM 16:6

> *"The lines have fallen to me in pleasant places; Yes, I have a good inheritance."*

A Christian life is a pleasant life. When living in God's will things always fall in place. The Bible says that, "All things work together for good," and when we are in sync with God's plan they surely do. God is a good God and His desire is to bless. The only way we can be blessed is to be like Jesus the blesser.

This is why even the Christian may experience difficult things. In God's great desire for our greatest welfare, He must break us from that which hinders His greatest work. This can be painful but the results are glorious. To be free from ourselves and from wanting to control every situation that comes our way. God will teach us that He is in control and we are not. It is when we learn this that we are free to be free.

· · ·

THE LESSON here is to remember that all goodness comes from God. Being in a right relationship with Him is where the lines fall in our favor. God's favor will be your happy place, not a geographical location. Everything flows from our relationship with God. Tend to that and the harvest of blessings will take care of itself.

MARRIED TO CHRIST

ROMANS 7:4

> *"Therefore, my brethren, you also have become dead to the law through the body of Christ, that you may be married to another—to Him who was raised from the dead, that we should bear fruit to God."*

The essence of Christianity is in a personal relationship with Jesus Christ. That relationship is not just a casual friendly relationship, but it is a marriage. Wow, as a Christian, we are in the most intimate and unhindered connection possible. The joy of unhindered free exchange of love with the God of all creation.

Think about what this marriage took. Jesus had to die for us to be married to Him. How much did He want us? The maximum amount. He held back nothing, giving up all to restore relationship with Him. The motive was love. Love drove Him to the cross as He experienced the excruciating pain of our own sin that kept us apart. His death brought union.

Are you experiencing His love today? Is His love overflowing your heart? Is it displaying His character and nature for all to see? If not then maybe you have left your first love. Maybe you have regressed into the law. Maybe you have stopped trusting, stopped obeying, stopped loving. Maybe today it's time to just enjoy Christ and receive a His Love. After all, He can't wait to share it with you.

. . .

THE LESSON here is remembering that you have the most incredible union that fills the heart and produces and abundance of love (fruit) that displays His goodness in and through our lives.

NO CONDEMNATION

ROMANS 8:1

> *"There is therefore now no condemnation to those who are in Christ Jesus."*

Condemnation is a terror that haunts mankind. The feeling of guilt is a burden to our souls. We are all guilty before God and the friction caused in our hearts is why many turn to unhealthy and destructive things without even realizing it. Think about it, a heart at rest does not seek rest, it already has it. A heart in guilt must seek relief.

A Christian has the relief of condemnation. No more guilt to contend with because we are "in Christ." This means that we are seen by God the Father as Christ's sinless perfection. He sees us but as those who are hidden. Because Christ died for us, He sees our old sinful self as dead and our new self as alive without sin. He sees us as Holy and blameless.

If God sees us this way, it's important for us to see ourselves this way. Yes we struggle and are still in sinful bodies practically. We grow through a lifelong process of "sanctification" or separation from sin. However, our position in Christ is secure and settled as the price has been paid.

. . .

THE LESSON here is to remember that there is now no more condemnation for you because Jesus took your place. See yourself as God sees you, and also see others Christians as God sees them. Let that truth be the meditation of your heart.

PERSPECTIVE ON SUFFERING

ROMANS 8:18

> *"For I consider that the sufferings of this present time are not worthy to be
> compared with the glory which shall be revealed in us."*

Suffering is a part of being alive. It is part of the human experience in which
no one gets a free pass and there is no immunity. How one suffers then will
determine the quality and effectiveness of their life. The extraordinary life of a
Christian gives great victory over suffering, allowing a Christian to live WITH
suffering and still have great joy, peace and strength.

The Christian does not need to run from suffering but can embrace it because
of the understanding they have regarding it. Suffering adds to the Christian life
whereas suffering diminishes the life of a nonbeliever. Suffering is seen as good
for the Christian whereas it is seen as bad for the nonbeliever.

A Christian is not a robot, emotionally detached from their feelings and reality,
but it is quite the opposite. A Christian can feel all the emotions of life without
being controlled by them. That's why a Christian can experience life to the fullest without having to numb themselves from those feelings. A Christian can feel
emotions without being controlled by them.

The negative manifestations of painful feelings like anger, depression, frustration, codependency, lashing out at others etc. or destructive behaviors such as
addictions and/or unhealthy relationships are all a result of being controlled by
unpleasant emotions. If one's life never rises above a higher motivation than
"self" they will remain in a rut of despair with no escape. Nothing will "fix" a
nearsighted selfish person but to turn to God in faith and live for His glory and
not their own. As Paul said, "For me to live is Christ" and "I don't count my life
dear to myself so that I may run my race with joy." Jesus even said to the Father,
"Not my will, but yours be done" as an example to us.

The whole problem then is "self" and Jesus died to free us from "self." Until we
die to "self," "self" will kill us. On the other hand, a Christian can "feel" these
emotions and instead of a negative manifestation or unhealthy coping mechanism, by faith can experience God and relate to others in a much greater way.
These "suffering" feelings contribute, not deter the Christian life. They add to

our experience of love, joy and peace. They make us feel alive and inspire passion when seen in light of God.

In our scripture here we see this. The word "compare" is the key. This word is not in the original text and was added for clarity but the point being made is the same. The point is that our suffering here on earth is made tolerable, "doable" and even embraceable by what we compare it to. If we only look at things by how they relate to ourselves and/or our lives in this world, we are guaranteed to be most miserable. If we see them in comparison to eternity, God, heaven and a higher purpose we will see our suffering as contributing to our experience of life here and our life in heaven.

. . .

THE LESSON here is knowing that all of your life can be embraced when you compare it to eternal things. The greatest of your suffering will seem light compared to eternity. You are free from circumstantial control when you embrace the God of all good in all circumstances who is in total control. Ultimately then, you must die to start living. See behind, see beyond, see bigger and live better.

2 Chronicles 11:1 13:22, Romans 8:26 39,
Psalm 18:37 50, Proverbs 19:27 29

IT IS ALL GOOD

ROMANS 8:28-30

> *"And we know that all things work together for good to those who love God, to those who are the called according to His purpose. For whom He foreknew, He also predestined to be conformed to the image of His Son, that He might be the firstborn among many brethren. Moreover whom He predestined, these He also called; whom He called, these He also justified; and whom He justified, these He also glorified."*

We all would like good to come our way. Good things, good people, good circumstances or good places. However, we don't always know what is good for us. Not to mention our definition of good can be misleading. We don't know the future and can't predict how things will turn out. We are so limited in our understanding, so our efforts are feeble at best.

Good has only one source. All good flows from God. There is no good outside of God and all that is good is good because of God. Knowing this then helps us to find good. For a Christian, as our text states, "All things work together for good."

This means that over and above all our circumstances in life is God working on them. He takes all our circumstances like ingredients and works them into a great masterpiece. Every single thing, with nothing left out, when it's in God's hands, He applies good to them.

Not that "all things ARE good" because they are not. Living in a fallen world broken by sin, we experience what would have never been experienced by Adam and Eve in the Garden of Eden. All things were good then and in Heaven and the New Heaven and New Earth all things will be good again, but not now. So God works it all for good.

The important thing to see is that there is a certain classification of people to whom He "works all things together for good" for. It's for "those who love Him and are called according to His purposes."

Every Christian "loves Him and is called according to His purposes" because when a person becomes a Christian they are responding to God's love toward them first. "We love Him because He first loved us" the Bible says. When we become a Christian we are given the Holy Spirit, which the fruit of the Spirit is love, and we are give an internal thirst for God that cries out to Him "Abba" (Daddy) Father. The evidence that we have the Holy Spirit inside us is the desire to obey Him as scripture says "if we love Him we will obey Him."

Not that we are perfect but that we "want to" obey and do His will. A Christian then places His life in God's hands and allows God's plan to unfold. This requires a surrendering of our own plans for our lives. This is why it says that, "God works all things together for good to those who love God and are called according to His purposes." So then, it is to those who have given their lives to Christ, allowing Him to work out His plan that "all things work together for good."

Finally, at the end of verse 30, we have the target that God is heading toward, glorification. When God takes all our "stuff" and works it, what He is doing with it is glorifying us. What does that mean? It means He is conforming us into the image of His Son, Jesus. What "good" is then, is making us like the source of good, Jesus Christ. How much better to be good then to just have good given.

That's why being "made good" can hurt and why we don't always get what we want. Good is not us getting every earthly desire, it is getting Jesus and being made like Him. Whatever gets in the way of our ultimate goal, glorification, God works to remove.

· · ·

THE LESSON here is knowing what real good is. The process of God "working all things together for good" will not seem "good" if you don't see the importance and priority of glorification making you like Jesus. However, when you do, you can trust that all things "are working" for your highest good. It is true then, that for you "it is all good."

2 Chronicles 14:1 16:14, Romans 9:1 24,
Psalm 19:1 14, Proverbs 20:1

THE JOY GIVER

PSALM 19:8

"The statutes of the Lord are right, rejoicing the heart;"

Following God is not restricting but freeing. It is a lie of the devil, going back to the Garden of Eden that says God is a "withholder," thinking that there is something more than God or something that needs to be added to our life that God hasn't already freely given. This lie has been accepted and promoted from the beginning of mankind to the demise of all who traffic in it.

Our scripture gives us a great teaching on the higher life given by God. He, being the creator of the universe and everything in it, knows how things work. God designed man to fit into the world He created so that man would experience the goodness that comes from God. Part of that goodness is joy. The feeling of joy is the experience of God's goodness and blessing He gives. It comes from being closely connected to Him. There is NO other way for us to have joy other than that.

So when we read that God's "statutes" or "ways given to man to live" are "right" and "rejoice the heart," it is God telling us how to be filled with joy. His statutes can be seen as a highway of joy. God wants this for us and also knows that sin is a joy killer. He knows we don't always see what's up ahead so He says trust Me and stay on My road. Follow the signs (statutes) that point to joy and keep you in joy. "Off the road is only danger and I don't want you to get hurt," God may be saying, as this is His heart in instructing us. God loves us that much.

· · ·

THE LESSON here is that following the Lord is to live in joy. Embrace Him with all your heart with faith, believing that He loves you and wants to bless you. He will lead you beside still waters and make you lie in green pastures. He wants to bless you and overflow you with His living water. He wants to show you His loving-kindness and abundance of life. You will never regret following God and putting His will above your own because God knows how to do things right. He is a giver of joy and tells you how to walk in it. God's way is the way of joy.

FAITH—GOD'S BLUEPRINT

PSALM 20:7

> *"Some trust in chariots, and some in horses; But we will remember the name of the Lord our God."*

Every person has a blueprint they work from in the way they live life. The blueprint is a belief system, which frames the way they see the world. Life will take shape according to the blueprint one has, just like a house will be designed according to the designer's blueprint. As time goes by, what is seen on paper will become a reality. The closer one sticks to the blueprint, the more true reality will be to the design.

God has designed an incredible life for each Christian. Each blueprint is specifically designed by God for a life that is both fulfilling and meaningful. Ultimately the blueprint is drafted in such a way that the life brings glory to a God and displays His goodness for others to see. Jesus said in His Word to, "Let your light shine before men that they may see your good works and glorify your Father in heaven."

On the other hand, there is another blueprint given for each person. This blueprint is an empty and incomplete blueprint because it is designed without God. This is where a person tries to create their own reality by "building their own house" without any expertise, experience or know-how. They don't even have the proper building materials and they have no money to buy what is needed. This is how people who live without God approach life. Their blueprint is merely what THEY "think" and what "seems" right to them. The trouble with this blueprint is that the Bible says, "There is a way that seems right to a man, but the end if that way is destruction."

Even Christians can get the blueprints mixed up when they forget God's master plan. We can forget to follow God's lead and then revert back to the old plan. We venture into trouble by taking steps without God. We can give practical reasons and justify our actions, but is God leading or is it a feeling or emotion leading? Do we then we ask God to bless when we are following the wrong blueprints?

. . .

THE LESSON here is to be living off the right blueprint. The blueprint that sees God over and above the material things of life and sees a better plan that builds a life on God's Word and trusts in His way. You will not moved or shaken by worldly circumstances but rather knows God is in charge and will be faithful to finish building His masterpiece, your life. You will say "you can have all this world, just give me Jesus." You will step out filling the blueprint of God's master plan even when it may be hard. You will trust in God and not anything else. When that blueprint takes shape, God's work will be proven to be a winner every time.

THE FRUIT OF FAITH
AND THE WORD OF GOD

ROMANS 10:17

"So then faith comes by hearing, and hearing by the word of God."

Among other things, God's Word is a builder of faith. To hear what God thinks, what He has done, what He is doing and how He works and then relating that to His interest in mankind, leads to the logical conclusion that we can trust Him. Lack of faith is not knowing and understanding God. To know Him is to trust Him.

God's Word then should be a central part of the Christian life, since faith is how a Christian lives. A personal devotional life of delighting in the Word is vital to a fearless life of following God's plan. Then to be in a church body where the Word is taught and emphasized will bring health to our spiritual condition.

Any deviation from the Word in a Church body creates a vacuum for all sorts of philosophies of men, traditions of men and works of men. God's Word dismantles those idols by shattering them with the truth and setting it's captives free to enjoy a simple relationship with Jesus Christ.

It's not by accident that Satan wants to minimize the Bible and even cause it's extinction in order to undermine our faith, which undermines our relationship which God that is built on faith. Satan can create a powerless and ineffective church if He can get the Bible out of the people's hands and have the church operate in their own powerless ways that are no match for the power of darkness.

· · ·

THE LESSON here is to see the importance of faith and it's connection to the Word. The more of God's Word, the more faith. Remember, however, that it's not JUST reading but then it's believing and doing. The divine interaction of God and the human soul takes place in this garden of intimacy. God relating to man through faith and the Word, by the power of the Holy Spirit, grows the roots of Godliness in the depths of the human heart, bringing forth the FRUIT of Godliness throughout the entirety of the whole being. That is the fruit of faith and the Word of God.

A WORK IN PROGRESS

//

PSALM 22:1

"My God, My God, why have You forsaken Me? Why are You so far from helping Me, And from the words of My groaning?"

David here is writing prophetically the words of Jesus as He was bearing our sins on the cross. One might think it was the excruciating pain Jesus was experiencing that caused Him to cry out, but it as also the feeling that God the Father wasn't helping Him. We can all experience this as Christians.

It's hard to come to the understanding that God hears and God cares but sometimes doesn't "immediately" change our painful situations. Yes, God uses pain and suffering to bring about His gems. As an all-knowing God, He sees better things for us that we cannot see at the time. He is working a better "good" for us that is also good for others and for His glory. That's why He doesn't immediately rescue us from the cries of our heart, even though He hears our cries.

· · ·

THE LESSON here is to recognize that God strengthening you through your trial. If God seems silent or His rescue seems distant, the good work is not finished. Don't take the cake out of the oven too soon because when it is ready it will be worth the wait. In the meantime, God will be right with you, never allowing you to be burned. He will watch the temperature and keep it at just the right amount knowing what you can handle. Be still, you are a work in progress and God is not finished yet.

A LIVING SACRIFICE

ROMANS 12:1

> *"I beseech you therefore, brethren, by the mercies of God, that you present your bodies a living sacrifice, holy, acceptable to God, which is your reasonable service."*

To understand the goodness of God is to WANT to give oneself to Him. Notice the urgent heartfelt cry of Paul's heart to call the Christians in Rome to give themselves over to God. After spending 11 chapters of speaking about how wonderful God is, and explaining all that God did on our behalf, He now says to give themselves over to Him.

Their surrender to a loving God was based on His argument of God's mercies. To know that, as Christians', we don't have to be afraid of God and that He will not hurt us. His mercy was proven on the cross where He took the punishment so it could be withheld from us. This act of mercy shows that we can feel safe with God. Giving oneself over to Him is hard and frightening until we know that His intentions toward us are only good.

Knowing the nature of God and His intentions toward us leaves one with only one "reasonable" response. That is to give oneself to this goodness of God who accepts us just as we are. We are free to be ourselves and to know that God actually likes us just as we are. This is the best feeling one can have and motivates one to WANT to give of themselves.

· · ·

THE LESSON here is knowing that your sacrifice is really giving up the bad to get the good. Giving up the bondage to have freedom. Giving up the loneliness to have relationship. Giving up doubt to have hope. Giving up fear to have confidence. A living sacrifice is ultimately a living surrender to God's goodness that He wants you to have.

LOVE LIKE JESUS

ROMANS 13:8

> *"Owe no one anything except to love one another."*

The basis of Christianity is love. God is love and He acted upon His love by dying on the cross for us. He has set His love upon us and His love fills all the cravings of our heart. God's love must be received in order for us to encounter God in our hearts. The great thing about His love is that no one is beyond its reach.

Having received God's love, every Christian is obligated to love one another. Our scripture here says we actually "owe" love. Think about those God puts in your life and remember that reason they are there is for you to love. It's not easy to do but God will enable when we take that step of faith.

· · ·

THE LESSON here is to know and remember HOW much you are loved by God and to make sure that is how you are with those around you. Like God's love, your love is to be unconditional, always wanting the best for others. Taking in consideration that love is what builds and edifies. Especially a love that gives, protects, honors and respects like Jesus does with us. Loving like Jesus will change lives, especially your own.

THE LAW OF LOVE

ROMANS 14:21

> *"It is good neither to eat meat nor drink wine nor do anything by which
> your brother stumbles or is offended or is made weak."*

There is an overriding principle in the life of a Christian called "love." All our
actions should be motivated by love. Whether it is what we do or in what we
don't do, our actions should be rooted in love. This is the heart of a Christian.

In our text we see the importance of love over liberty. There are a lot of things we
CAN do, but that doesn't mean we SHOULD do. We have liberty as Christians
and we always have to be concerned how what we do may affect another. This is
a greater priority considering that Christ died for them.

. . .

THE LESSON here is that you have been bought with a price, and you are no
longer your own. True love is the example Jesus set for you and that is to consider another as more important than yourself. This may cost you some personal
freedoms, but the greater freedom you have is to forgo your freedoms to give
love to others, especially in areas where another might be hurt or stumbled in
their relationship with God. Choose the greater freedom to love, for love is the
most freeing thing

2 Chronicles 30:1 31:21, Romans 15:1 22,
Psalm 25:1 15, Proverbs 20:13 15

OTHERS FIRST

///

ROMANS 15:1

> *"We then who are strong ought to bear with the scruples of the weak, and not to please ourselves."*

A true sign of strength is in how we interact with those who are not strong. Strength in our scripture is demonstrated by the ability to control oneself for the purposes of edifying another. This means that a stronger person is able to put up with the irritations of one who needs to mature in order for a greater good to occur.

We are all works in progress and some are further along than others. Those further along were once those not so far along and needed others who were further along to put up with them. Strong Christians are able to put their selves aside for the enrichment of others. This is no easy task and only by the grace of a God can we deal with irritations so that the weak can become strong.

. . .

THE LESSON here is that true strength comes by putting others before yourself. When you can see that it is not about "self" but about Jesus, you will become considerate of others and conscientious of their sensitivities in light of the ultimate prize, the glory of God. When strength is exercised in selflessness by living to please God and not self, you have the strength to turn the world right side up for Jesus Christ.

PRAYER AND PEOPLE

ROMANS 15:30

> *"Now I beg you, brethren, through the Lord Jesus Christ, and through the love of the Spirit, that you strive together with me in prayers to God for me."*

Paul ends this epic letter to the Romans focused on prayer (chapter 15) and people (chapter 16). Prayer and people are at the core of Christianity because we are relational beings. God made us in His image and God is a triune God meaning He is One but in three persons, The Father, The Son and The Holy Spirit. Before man was created, God was sharing fellowship and love within the Holy Trinity. When we were created we were made to also crave for relationship, especially relational intimacy.

Prayer is the language of intimacy that connects the divine God with the soul of man. Through prayer we find that connection which God has opened up through His Son Jesus Christ. Paul is asking for those he loves to pray for him because he knows that prayer will make a difference. Maybe God leaves results in the prayers of the saints because He wants to include us in the process of His unfolding plan. Whatever the case, prayer makes a difference and moves the hand of God.

Notice the urgency with which Paul asks for prayer by "begging" them. He also "begs" them to pray through Jesus who has opened the door to the throne of God for us. He also begs them to pray through the "love of the Spirit" so that our prayers are driven by the Holy Spirit and not our selfish flesh. When we pray through the Spirit we will pray for the things God wants and the things that are His will for His Kingdom. This is effective prayer.

Finally we see that Paul is including himself in praying for himself but in regards to God's will. He sees himself as just part of the Body of Christ and that all believers are together in this one goal of glorifying God, spreading the Gospel and building the Kingdom of God.

· · ·

THE LESSON here to learn that prayer is relational, with God and with people, uniting hearts to God and to one another all at the same time.

FALSE TEACHERS

///

ROMANS 16:17

> *"Now I urge you, brethren, note those who cause divisions and offenses, contrary to the doctrine which you learned, and avoid them."*

"A house divided cannot stand," the Bible says. It's no wonder Satan, like a mathematician, wants to reduce the body of Christ to the lowest common denominator. In order to do so he needs willing participants, so he works to provoke the flesh of his subjects to react to his enticements.

Paul, in our text, warns about this threat to the church at the conclusion of his letter to the Christians in Rome. Threats to the body of Christ lurk in every corner. The unseen principalities and powers that take aim at the destruction of God's church.

The good news is that the church will never be destroyed and the "gates if Hades will not prevail" against God's mighty body, the church. However, it is possible for him to win smaller battles and his most effective strategy is to work from within the church.

Satan does so by planting "his" people inside the church to teach contrary doctrines to God's truth. There are preachers, church influencers and leaders who know what and how to say things that appeal to people who want a Christianity that looks more like the world than it does like Christ.

These false teachers subtlety, and often skillfully, mix lies in with "some" truth. Their teaching emphasizes a bigger and inflated "self", which reduces God to something lower than He is. Their teaching is self-centered, world centered and man centered. It involves a compromise and manipulation of the clear teachings found in God's Word.

Watch an over emphasis on money, as that seems to be what false teachers like to talk about. Watch teaching that denies Jesus as the only way to salvation, teaching that denies Jesus as God who eternally exists and a gospel message that includes something we must do to contribute to salvation. Watch teaching that denies sin, suffering, sacrifice and a denial of an eternal hell where those who reject Christ will go.

Be careful of prideful and arrogant teachers who love to talk about themselves more that Christ and that love to parade themselves more than champion Jesus.

. . .

THE LESSON here is to be highly sensitive and aware of false doctrine sticking to the simple Word. All you need is what's in God's Word and what is clearly revealed. Don't adjust truth to fit your lifestyle, wants and desires but adjust your lifestyle, wants and desires to God's word. Go to a church that "teaches" God's Word and allows God's Word to dictate truth instead of sprinkling scripture over man centered, materialistic greedy, culturally compromising babble.

FIGHTING FEAR

//

PSALM 27:1

> *A Psalm of David.*
> *"The Lord is my light and my salvation;*
> *Whom shall I fear?*
> *The Lord is the strength of my life;*
> *Of whom shall I be afraid?"*

If anyone had reason to fear it would certainly be David. A fugitive from the most powerful man in the Nation of Israel, King Saul, David was in danger for his life. He was a man of war who was under attack, and threats of attack, constantly. Yet he writes how he was able to deal with his fear.

He didn't see any reason to fear because of where his help came from. This wasn't a mere concept for him, it was what he had experienced in his life. Time and time again God would rescue him from danger. He learned through experience that he could trust God. Even going back to the days of shepherding sheep, David would experience God's help in fighting off lions and bears.

His experience taught Him that not only can God help, but also that God is willing to help. But, at some time David had to actually take that first step of faith. He had to believe in the character of God when he had no experience with God. Then he would have to take whatever little experience he had with God, and add that to the growing understanding he gained with God, to grow in his confidence to the point of being the Giant slayer and one who feared no one.

. . .

THE LESSON here is, fear is conquered by faith. Learning that the battle belongs to the Lord and to trust in His unfailing love. Taking the first step and saying, "Lord, be with me, fight for me and help me." All it takes is that first step and God will meet you, building your faith to face bigger battles ahead.

THE SMOOTH PATH

PSALM 27:11

> *"Teach me Your way, O Lord, and lead me in a smooth path, because of my enemies."*

Life is really complicated when we appoint ourselves as the CEO's of our own lives and all that happens in the world. Like a plate spinner trying to keep each plate spinning along with all the others all at the same time. Trying to manage and control what we can't control is unsustainable and will lead to frustration and "broken plates".

Here David cries out to God asking for help to run his life. What he asks for is not a better way to do things his own way, but that He could learn to do things God's way. In that prayer, we find the answer to a wonderful and smooth life.

David sees that there are many enemies that get in the way of a smooth life. Just as every movie has it's protagonist, every life has it's potholes that can make for a bumpy ride. No one gets out unscathed in this fallen world, tainted by sin. With a fallen world there are fallen people, tainted by the lust of the flesh, lust of the eye and the pride of life. Satan and his fallen comrades work around the clock to use every tool and trick at their demonic dark disposal to steal, kill and destroy. Ultimately, there is no chance for a fallen person in a fallen world run by the most fallen of all, Satan. That's why the Bible says that there is a "way" that seems right to a man, but the end of that way is death.

God has a better path for those who choose it. His way is smooth, even where it is rocky. He makes things really simple and for those who choose, they will find this path to be the "path of life." It all comes down to simply doing what is clear in God's Word. Life becomes very simple when we get out of the way, stop fixing and controlling, and just let God do what He does best, lead us on the smooth path.

· · ·

THE LESSON here is to simply let God have His way by letting Him lead the way.

Ezra 3:1 4:23, 1 Corinthians 2:6 3:4,
Psalm 28:1 9, Proverbs 20:24 25

SOMETHING NEW

///

EZRA 3:12-13

> *"But many of the priests and Levites and heads of the fathers' houses, old men who had seen the first temple, wept with a loud voice when the foundation of this temple was laid before their eyes. Yet many shouted aloud for joy, so that the people could not discern the noise of the shout of joy from the noise of the weeping of the people, for the people shouted with a loud shout, and the sound was heard afar off."*

Not everybody can rejoice in what the Lord is doing. Some can't depart from an old frame of reference. Some can only see things through an old lens. Some only have one grid of personal, preconceived perception. Some sabotage their own sense of wonder and surprise by holding on to the past in a way that doesn't allow for the new.

When we are children, we discover the wonder of discovery. So many things are new and so much about life is exciting. Children carry a sense of awe with them into each day. Losing this sense of wonder is when we become stale; life is predictable and sad when the predictable becomes our accepted paradigm.

God is a God who delights in surprising us. Like a parent watching their child open a gift on Christmas morning, God delights to fill each day with wonder and unpredictability. That's what makes things interesting, exciting and fun. The unpredictability of life keeps us sharp, engaged, and creative. It gives us a sense of anticipation and keeps us looking for God's things in the midst of the mundane and predictable.

In our text we see two different reactions to the rebuilding of the Temple. One of joy and one of sorrow. The ones who can appreciate the past, yet anticipate today, are the ones who rejoice in the work of God in present time. The ones who live in the past and compare all that happened then to how things should be now, will always be sad because the past can never be relived.

· · ·

THE LESSON here is to embrace each day completely on that days own merit. Don't let the past be the only standard for the current. Enjoy the blessings of the Lord in real time moments. Live in present time, and rejoice for this is the day that The Lord has made. He has something new for you.

GOD WILL GIVE THE INCREASE

1 CORINTHIANS 3:7

"So then neither he who plants is anything, nor he who waters, but God who gives the increase."

God is not impressed by what we "do" for Him. He doesn't see our work like others might and say, "Wow, how do they do that?" It is God who gives ability and God who gives ambition and God who accomplishes all through us. "Without Him we can do nothing," the Bible says. God "…works in us to will and to do," meaning that God works in us to desire and to fulfill the desire or to want to do, and to do what He wants us to do.

We "do" according to God's "done." In other words, we walk in the power of His finished work. We are participants in His glorious plan, bringing about such glory that God will be seen and known for all He is. Maybe not today, but one day as His plan is an unfolding plan. It is God who "gives the increase," bringing about the "results" of His glorious plan. To see Him working through us, not us working to "produce" His will, is the key. God is the producer, we are the distributer.

· · ·

THE LESSON here is to "walk" in what God has prepared for you. "You are His workmanship, created in Christ Jesus for good works that He has preordained, that you should walk in them." You are not responsible for producing good works, just walking in them. By allowing God to work, you will experience freedom from the frustration of trying to do what you cannot do and the excitement of experiencing what God can do through you. In the end, He gets all the glory and you get all the fun. Look for those good works He has put in your path today and walk in them.

AUGUST 8

Ezra 7:1 8:20, 1 Corinthians 4:1 21,
Psalm 30:1 12, Proverbs 20:28 30

GOD'S POWER

1 CORINTHIANS 4:20

"For the kingdom of God is not in word but in power."

God's kingdom is our kingdom when He becomes our King by faith. We enter into His eternal Kingdom at the moment of faith; we live for and to our King Jesus. His Kingdom comes with benefits. One of those benefits is the power of the Holy Spirit.

Most other things in life are done in our own power. We work, we strive, we labor to the point of exhaustion to achieve things. The Kingdom of God is not like that.

Not that we don't work hard but that we are working with the supernatural power of God. The difference is that there is a divine power when God is working, versus a limited human power when we work. It's important to know the difference.

God's power is unlimited and inexhaustible. When Peter was struggling to pray Jesus said, "The Spirit is willing but the flesh is weak." Jesus said that, "Without Him we can do nothing," meaning nothing in the kingdom of God and in the realm of the Spirit can happen without the power of the Holy Spirit.

God's power gives life and restores. When God's power is at work there is a strange fingerprint of the eternal in all it touches. His power doesn't deteriorate but invigorates. Unlike human power, which tires and fades, God's power gives back to the vessel as it is poured out.

Finally, God's power is how a Christian is able to live the Christian life. It's a life of surrender, which brings transformation from the inside. It's the power to become what God has intended, that is not left up to us to live up to standards we have no capacity to achieve. His power does the work when we let go of our own efforts.

. . .

THE LESSON here is to be patient, let go, give God your heart, and His power will do what you can't. It is something beautiful to behold God's work in your own life as "He" makes it something beautiful.

MISPLACED COMPASSION

EZRA 9:11-12

> *"Which You commanded by Your servants the prophets, saying, 'The land which you are entering to possess is an unclean land, with the uncleanness of the peoples of the lands, with their abominations which have filled it from one end to another with their impurity. Now therefore, do not give your daughters as wives for their sons, nor take their daughters to your sons; and never seek their peace or prosperity, that you may be strong and eat the good of the land, and leave it as an inheritance to your children forever.'"*

All of our natural bents or feelings must be guided by the Lord. God gave us feelings and emotions, which are a blessing, but they can be misguided or misplaced. In others words, the way we feel, in and of itself, is not a good gauge for what is right. They must match the way God feels as well.

In our text we see that the children of Israel were not to compromise with those who were against God and actively in rebellion against Him. The land was filled with false idols and false gods. The children of Israel were not to seek their prosperity or peace. That surprising statement shows that God actually wanted the higher good, a right relationship with Him, which a continuance in material wealth and peace would actually hinder. Not only that, as was the case, the Children of Israel were affected by their involvement and association with them which profoundly and negatively impacted them and their own calling and purpose.

God feels right about everything. Whenever we read the Bible and think, "that sounds mean" or "that doesn't seem fair," the problem is that we are not feeling the right way. We must pray that our heart and mind will be in sync with God's so that we would feel the same way He does. We are prone to error when we are misaligned with God's heart and make decisions based on what we think and feel instead of what God thinks and feels.

Some people are wired to be very compassionate, caring and sensitive towards others. People wired this way feel other peoples pain and are intolerant of cruelty and unfair treatment, as God is. They have this attribute of God and feel as God does in this regard. While this is good, it is important to be balanced and surrendered with these feelings.

We are not more compassionate than God and we don't love more than Him. So when we over extend compassion above God's compassion, we can fall into sin and become enablers that hides the work of God, instead of contributing to the work of God.

. . .

THE LESSON here is to make sure your compassion is placed where God's compassion is. We are all wired a certain way and that we need to yield all to the Holy Spirit to make our feelings, bents, emotions thoughts and ideas holy, Godly and usable for His kingdom. Your part is yielding, His part is transforming. Then your compassion will be right in line with Christ, the most compassion the world has and will ever see. He is the compassionate One.

BOUGHT WITH A PRICE

///

1 CORINTHIANS 6:20

"For you were bought at a price; therefore glorify God in your body and in your spirit, which are God's."

Jesus paid a debt we could not pay. A ransom was needed to purchase back our freedom that was lost to sin. The price was so high that nobody could pay it but for the price of the life of the very creator of the universe, Jesus Christ. This shows how valuable we are and how much God loves us. He was willing to pay the price; he gave everything for you and me. The incredible love of God will bring joy to our soul.

The correct response to our debt that was paid is to then live for Jesus and to forsake that in which He saved us from. The high price of love shows how bad and destructive selfishness, pride and self-indulgence can be. The perfectly loving, compassionate and self-less One gave no reason to harm Him other than outright hatred of truth, hatred of light and hatred of good. He went around loving people, healing people and helping people. The end result was death to the perfect One, at the hands of those who hated an innocent man. The heart of man is truly wicked.

When we come into a personal relationship with Jesus, we then have a whole other reason to live. We have not only been saved "from," we've been saved "to." Our trajectory is now toward the One who saves. We see the priority of glorifying the One who loves us. Now we belong to the most gracious Savior, wearing our salvation as a garment of praise. We belong to the most high King and the banner over us is love. We now belong to Jesus, we are His, and He is ours.

· · ·

THE LESSON here is to remember "Who" you live for. Make Jesus your aim and glorify Him in your choices, your actions and your devotion, remembering that your life is His. It's easy when we know that the nature of God is good and that He wants to bestow that goodness upon you. May God's love drive you to God's rest in His perfect will and plan for your life. Be anxious for nothing, you have been bought with a price.

PRIDE BLINDS

PROVERBS 21:4

"A haughty look, a proud heart, and the plowing of the wicked are sin."

Pride is the ultimate sin for it exalts "self" above God. There is nothing more indicative of sin than one who thinks that they have no need for God, when God is actively causing every breath, every heartbeat and every life sustaining activity of the human body. God is keeping everything running in His world by His wisdom and power. God is performing acts no man can understand, with ease. He is directing the events of the world and all things are in His control.

He knows everything and there is nothing He does not know. If one were to take everything there is possibly to know in the world and beyond, how much would one human really know? What percentage would the smartest human ever to live know in comparison to all there is to know? I don't think it would even register on any scale of measurement because it would be so minuscule in comparison. Yet there are those who think they know better than God, Who proves His limitless power day after day simply by one look at the rising and setting of the sun.

The sin of pride refuses the forgiveness of God, which is the most tragic effect of pride's blindness. To think that one would be willing to bet their eternity on what "they" think and what "they" believe apart from what God has said and demonstrated throughout the history of man, can only be classified as sheer ignorance. For the one who says "there is no God" as they stand in God's own creation.

. . .

THE LESSON here is to remember how dangerous pride is. It blinds the greatest intellect from the simplest of truths. Don't hold on to your pride, let it go and you will see that pride is a burden not worth carrying.

JUST SOME THOUGHTS ON DEPRESSION

PSALM 32:10-11

"Many sorrows shall be to the wicked; But he who trusts in the Lord, mercy shall surround him. Be glad in the Lord and rejoice, you righteous; And shout for joy, all you upright in heart!"

Depression is mostly seen as a physical condition that requires chemical support from an external source (medication), in order to supply physically what is thought to be lacking in the body, which is said to cause depression. Basically, depression then is said to be a malfunction or imbalance of chemicals in the human body and the common approach is altering or balancing those chemicals should help the depressed person not be depressed.

As a whole, is doesn't seem like there are less depressed people and less manifestations of depression's effects, like suicide. In fact, it seems to be just the opposite, that there are more depressed people and more suicides, while at the same time more medications being used, at least in the U. S. Is this the answer?

Maybe there is more than just the physical approach. Maybe depression has a deeper cause. Or, to look at it another way, maybe happiness is not found at the physical level. Maybe happiness just manifests itself at the physical level as well as depression. Maybe happiness is not merely a chemical adjustment. Even those who do take medications for depression are not overall "happy people" but just "not depressed people." It seems to me that happiness, the cure for depression, goes deeper.

We are not just bodies walking around. Our bodies are not "us" but vehicles for "us" to interact with the physical world. What is "us" then? According to the Bible, "us" is our souls and is the unseen immaterial part of "us" or the real "us" that will exist beyond our bodies physical existence.

When the spiritual aspect of our humanity is neglected, happiness is neglected. Maybe depression is the physical manifestation of the core of our being in a poor state. Maybe medication is just putting paint on an already condemned house that really needs foundation repair. Maybe some people do need medication, but I think it's worth looking at the possibility that depression has a deeper root and that maybe the cause is a spiritual problem and not a physical one. Maybe no matter what physical approach one takes, the results will be minimal at best, if the soul is neglected. For whatever it's worth, I think it makes sense to look at the spiritual side of "us" and see what the book that addresses the spiritual side of "us" says.

. . .

THE LESSON here is that when you look at depression, you should look to Jesus; receive His forgiveness, His healing and His happiness. He is the answer the broken sad world is looking for. Pray that more people can find relief from guilt, purpose for their life, value in who they are and strength that comes from deep internal happiness in Christ. We can only hope and pray that those hurting souls will find peace in Jesus.

KNOWLEDGE AND LOVE

1 CORINTHIANS 8:1

> *"Now concerning things offered to idols: We know that we all have knowledge. Knowledge puffs up, but love edifies."*

It's a trap to make knowledge supreme in the Christian life. After all, knowledge is important. We need to know, to understand, to search the depths of the Godhead. Knowledge is sneaky however, because it may start out as noble but also has the potential to spark a flame of pride.

Knowledge in and of itself is not the problem; it's what can happen when handled improperly. Since pride is one of our biggest pitfalls in the Christian life, Satan lurks around our pride button tempting us to flip the switch when we feel the temptation to appropriate something to ourselves instead of God.

The pride button stays off when we say "thank you Lord," "praise You Lord," "all things come from You Lord," "may You be glorified Lord." Winning the pride battle is a matter of knowing that all things come from Him and all glory goes to Him. When God is glorified is when love and knowledge are working together, as we use Our spiritual gifts the way Jesus said in Matthew 5:16, "Let your light so shine before men, that they would see your good works and glorify your Father in heaven."

Ultimately, where knowledge fails, love never will. The target of our faith in Christ will be love. Love is supreme, triumphing over all else. Love will build and strengthen. So knowledge should run on love and when it does, knowledge will be sweet, helpful, Christ-like, self-less, full of grace and mercy. Love will lift others above one's own self. Love will die to personal gain for others gain. Love is how one should view their decisions and personal interactions. With love, the devil has no answer but to try and get one to not love. Love is so powerful that it can't be stopped.

· · ·

THE LESSON here is to never let knowledge depart from love. Knowledge will not build the Kingdom of God without love, so let love rule you and guide you and you'll be sure to live an impactful life. Knowledge, when bathed in love, makes for a sweet recipe of building God's kingdom

Nehemiah 7:73 9:21, 1 Corinthians 9:1 18,
Psalm 33:12 22, Proverbs 21:11 12

THE JOY OF THE LORD IS YOUR STRENGTH

NEHEMIAH 8:10

> *"Then he said to them, 'Go your way, eat the fat, drink the sweet, and send portions to those for whom nothing is prepared; for this day is holy to our Lord. Do not sorrow, for the joy of the Lord is your strength.'"*

A joyful person is a strong person. They are able to deal much better with struggles, enjoy blessings and pour into others. Joy is an attribute of God that He shares with His children so that they can feel His love. Joy sort of feels like the experience of God's pleasure deep inside us.

In our text we see the importance of joy. The children of Israel were told to not sorrow because they needed to be strong. They were in no position to be weak as enemies who did not like them rebuilding the walls up around the temple surrounded them. Sorrow would make it very difficult for them to do God's work at this time. The best solution to weakness is joy.

Notice that it was God's joy and not theirs. We are not the generators of joy, but God is. It's His joy so we know where to find it. We find it in Him. This brings us back again to "Him." It all comes back to "Him" and when He is the center of our life we are centered in so many innumerable blessings. He is the fount of all blessing. His goodness He desires to share with those who will allow Him to.

· · ·

THE LESSON here is to see the importance of joy. Embracing God wholeheartedly is to embrace His joy and to be strong for life. It seems clear that joy is a choice and that it is always available and it is found in Him. Choose joy today by letting go of all that is not of God, surrendering circumstances, fear, the future and whatever it is that is making you weak and stealing your joy. Choose joy and be strong.

AMBITION FOR THE GOSPEL

1 CORINTHIANS 9:22-23

*"To the weak I became as weak, that I might win the weak. I have become
all things to all men, that I might by all means save some. Now this I do
for the gospel's sake, that I may be partaker of it with you."*

A good question to ask yourself is, "What is my all consuming passion?" In
other words, what is it that you are ambitious about? What drives you and motivates you. To find out what your passion is, look at what occupies your thoughts.
What is it that when you think about it, it excites you? How you feel when you
think about something says a lot about what you value? Think about how you
spend your time, your energy and your resources. These will all help in discovering what it is that may be your passion.

As Christians, we are wired in our new spiritual D. N. A. to be passionately ambitious for Jesus Christ. To know Him and to make Him known. This is what a
healthy Christian does. Jesus said that we are to go into all the world and make
disciples. This is the primary activity of the Christian, doing what Christ did,
what the disciples did, and what the Apostle Paul is saying in our text, that he
did. Is that what our passion in life is? Are you ambitious for the gospel?

Paul is saying that he would do, whatever it took to reach people with the gospel of Jesus Christ. He was ambitious for the gospel. He said "by all means win
some." Paul is not saying that he takes a salesman approach, pitching Jesus thinking that great sales skills and techniques would win people over. His approach
was to connect with people right where they were and give the "truth" that leads
to Christ. No doubt, like Jesus, He would try to understand where people were
coming from, he would connect with them and appreciate how they may view
things in life. What a great example for us.

The gospel is relational. It is the way to a personal relationship with Jesus Christ
and it is to be shared "by" people, "to" people. What we see here with Paul is the
importance of acceptance in sharing the gospel. Accepting people where they
are in order to bring them where they need to be.

It's not denying or compromising scripture, may that never be. It's not saying
that there are many ways to heaven and that it doesn't really matter what you

believe as long as you believe. It means that we have tender hearts for where people are in life and care how they got there. It means we care enough to listen and hear where they are coming from. It means we pray for them. It means we respect them as human beings and are humble.

Paul did this because he genuinely cared for people and their eternity. Evangelism is messy when done this way. It requires involvement in lives that are messy. It requires a dependence upon the Holy Spirit to do what no human can do without Him.

. . .

THE LESSON here is to remember that the gospel is every Christian's responsibility as we are "stewards" over the most precious news the planet has ever know. Maybe today your passion for the gospel has run a little cold. Maybe today is a time to remember that there is nothing more important than the salvation of the human soul. Maybe it's time to passionately pray for the lost and how God may use you to share with them. There is no greater calling and no greater responsibility. There is nothing more "Christian" than winning souls. May we be, like Jesus, like Paul, doing with all our means whatever it takes to win people to Jesus Christ. Eternity is forever, the gospel is for now.

USING OUR LIBERTY

1 CORINTHIANS 10:23

> *"All things are lawful for me, but not all things are helpful; all things are lawful for me, but not all things edify."*

There is an incredible freedom in the Christian life. When one is walking with the Lord, there are only green lights. We don't have to worry about red lights. All the promises in God are yes and amen. It's all go when we are going in God's perfect will.

It's such an amazing feeling to walk in the Spirit because where the Spirit is, there is liberty. Loving God and having Him as your ambition matches what we want with what He wants. There is no friction and when our will rises up, it does so in competition to God's will. Friction enters, liberty is compromised and repentance is the answer.

The most freeing thing about our freedom is how we use it. To use our freedoms for the highest good is to be free to the highest degree. In other words, having no restrictions to do God's will, being empowered by the Holy Spirit to do what we can't do in our flesh, and do what builds people and God's kingdom, is the highest use of freedom because there is no friction in that. That is, what God wants to do and what we want matches, we stay free to the highest degree. We also avoid the freedom-stealers of self, sin and worldliness which we were once slaves to and now we are free from.

· · ·

THE LESSON here is to learn that just because we CAN do something doesn't mean we SHOULD do something. Remember the highest use of freedom is to serve God, to help, love and to edify. When you are doing that, you are free, blessed, being blessed, filled and living at the highest level of human existence. Stay out of the personal prisons of self and live to serve God and others. Freedom has no limits when it's used God's way.

FAITHFULNESS

NEHEMIAH 13:13

> *"And I appointed as treasurers over the storehouse Shelemiah the priest and Zadok the scribe, and of the Levites, Pedaiah; and next to them was Hanan the son of Zaccur, the son of Mattaniah; for they were considered faithful, and their task was to distribute to their brethren."*

Faithfulness is the character of an individual to be consistent in taking care of what has been placed in their care. This is an attribute God is pleased with and actually requires. It is an attribute that is easily overlooked, or minimized, but anyone who deals out responsibility to others knows the importance of a faithful person.

Faithfulness in a Christian's life is toward many things like the gospel, ministries, people in our lives, opportunities we have, our Spiritual gifts, church fellowships, families, jobs etc. Basically it's whatever God has given us or put in our lives. What we do with those things is our faithfulness to it. Seeing the things we have as from God is the first step in being a good and faithful steward. It's not our stuff, it's God's, and we are just to take good care of it.

The Holy Spirit empowers a Christian to be faithful. The Apostle Paul lists "faithfulness" as a fruit of the Spirit in Galatians 6:22. Another way to look at faithfulness is to see a lack of it as a lack of walking in the Spirit. In our own personal walks with God, and in our service to Him, our success basically comes down to just being faithful. If we would stop looking at mere outward measures of success, which really belong to The Lord, and look, to be faithful, we will find that is where success lies.

Paul also said in 1 Corinthians 4:2 that the requirement for a "steward," or one given responsibility for "God's things," is to be faithful. Understanding then, that it is God who gives the increase and it is us who have the responsibility of being faithful with the power that God has already supplied.

It's not uncommon to be stuck in a rut of unfaithfulness, going only so far until we won't go any further. One may hop from church to church when they get challenged and end up never progressing. Faithfulness will involve two things, quality of care and quantity of care. In order for us to grow, we need both.

Quality of care is taking care of "God's stuff" well. It means we see whatever it is that is in our care as so valuable that we make sure it's in a good state. Like a collector would take care of a classic car, a faithful steward will make sure their treasure is in good shape. It won't be neglected or in disrepair. It will be nurtured, watched over, healthy and strong.

The other aspect of stewardship is quantity of care. This means that it will be seen through to the end. It will be patient, it will persevere, endure and be seen through. It doesn't give up or look to bail out, it finishes and doesn't move on unless God moves, and when He does it is usually not to nothingness but to bigger things that the present faithfulness has equipped for. Quitting never prepares for bigger things, it only teaches the importance of not quitting.

Have you committed to something and bailed out? Or have you neglected that which God has placed in your care? Don't make excuses but acknowledge that you have not been faithful and start being faithful right now to what's right in front of you. When you do you are on the road to be a successful Christian. God isn't looking for the "next big thing" or the "next great talent," He is looking for faithful people.

. . .

THE LESSON here is to focus on faithfulness and not merely results, for it is God who adds the increase. In the end, faithfulness is what counts. Live for the day when God says; enter in my good and <u>faithful</u> servant.

WAITING

PSALM 35:17

> *"Lord, how long will You look on? Rescue me from their destructions,
> my precious life from the lions."*

"How long" is a sentiment a lot of Christians feel. The line of thinking is, "God, I know You are powerful and strong, You are mighty to save, and I'm Your child. Don't You want to help me? How can You let me keep going like this? Why aren't You doing something?" It seems logical that a loving God would rescue us in our time of need, yet sometimes it doesn't seem like He is.

Patience is one of the hardest things about being a Christian. In order to wait well, we need to know that God's timing is most likely not ours, but it is perfect. We need to know that waiting isn't inactivity, it is unperceived activity. God is never inactive, but He does work under our radar at times. He is preparing the harvest like a farmer who plants a seed and works the soil to prepare it for the right time.

Sarah was promised a child, yet she got impatient and took matters in her own hands. She thought she could hasten God's promise, getting impatient and tired of waiting. We must watch the temptation to take matters in our own hands when we can't see what's in God's hand, but God is working, don't worry. When the time was right, Sarah had her promised son and it was according to God's "set time."

You too may be saying "how long Lord?" You may be wondering why God seems silent, why He doesn't seem to be helping and why it doesn't seem like He cares. In times like that the answer is "faith."

. . .

THE LESSON here is to learn to not take matters in your own hands but by faith, trust that God will bring it to pass. Don't focus on the end, focus on Him. Good things take time, and God is giving you His best. Be still, rest in Him, trust in Who He is and His character. God has not forgotten, He's just working a better thing than you can perceive.

FOR SUCH A TIME AS THIS

ESTHER 4:14

"If you keep quiet at a time like this, deliverance and relief for the Jews will arise from some other place, but you and your relatives will die. Who knows if perhaps you were made queen for just such a time as this?"

Nothing in life is random, without meaning and purpose. There is a reason we are where we are, whether it's our geographic location, station in life or season in life. God has preset all of that for a reason.

The important thing is WHAT we do with where we are. To miss the purpose behind our existence and placement is to miss out on what God has in store for us. God's plan will still be accomplished, as we see in our text, it's just that we will miss our role in it, which is to miss the purpose for our existence. Life without purpose is meaningless.

. . .

THE LESSON here is to know that you are where you are "for such a time as this." An amazing amount of "God-ness" has you situated where you are right now. Seeking God and surrendering to His plan will bring to life the spectacle of God's radical, supernatural, divine grace that calls "people" to carry out heaven's program. Like Esther, refusal will kill your connection with eternity while acceptance brings life. You "are" for such a time as this, go live for Him and what He has called you to do.

THE SUPREMACY OF LOVE

1 CORINTHIANS 13:13

"And now abide faith, hope, love, these three; but the greatest of these is love."

The supremacy of love is the theme that runs throughout the entire Bible. One could say that the Bible is the greatest love story ever told. Taking into account the countless portrayals of love in all different forms of expression in life, one could surmise that humans crave love and are made for love. Without love one will suffer from stunted growth and development. A baby deprived of love has little chance of having a healthy mental and emotional state.

Since we are made in God's image, we were created in love, through loving hands, to be connected to love. Considering that God is the only source of love, we ultimately crave to be connected to God. Without that connection a person will have a felt void that often wonders, "is this it?" There may be superficial connections that fill shallow and superficial wells but nothing exists that can fill the bottom of the deepest well, all the way to the top and overflowing, like the love of God.

This divine romance was set in motion by God, lost through Eve, and recovered by Jesus. As we read in the Bible, "that God so loved the world that He gave His only begotten Son." Jesus was sent on a rescue mission to reconnect us to His love by dying on the cross, taking our place and bearing the penalty of our sin. This was the ultimate love. All doubts were answered as to how God feels about us at the cross.

This recovery of love fills that deep longing and quiets our restless hearts. This love, called AGAPE, is an intense, unconditional, sacrificial and intimate love. When one comes to faith in Christ, they have come into the love of Christ. The connection to God's love then is the greatest delight of humanity.

As we see from our text, love is to be the driving force in our lives. Without love, all our activities are without the supernatural life behind them, leaving us dry and stale. Loveless service is unproductive and even irritating. Loving service is invigorating and puts the passion and joy in the service.

. . .

THE LESSON here is to remember the supremacy of love in all you do. You are to pour out the love of God as you serve Him. Every attribute or characteristic you have must be bathed in love in order for it to be a work of God and not of man. No matter what great attribute you have, even faith and hope, without love it is nothing. Make sure love is your motive and you will never fail. The supremacy of God's love will conquer all.

CHOSEN TO SUFFER

JOB 1:8

> *"Then the Lord said to Satan, 'Have you considered My servant Job, that there is none like him on the earth, a blameless and upright man, one who fears God and shuns evil?'"*

Many are familiar with the story of Job. It is the oldest written book in the Bible and chronicles an episode in the life of Job that is heart wrenching. He suffered greatly. He lost his 10 children, his wealth and his health. He was subject to shame and condemnation by his friends and even his wife. What did he do to deserve all that suffering? Why so much pain? Our text tells us that it was God who actually suggested that Satan consider Job for his target of affliction.

Was God mean? Is He cruel? He even sent His own Son to be crucified. What may seem mean to us is only because of our severe case of nearsightedness. The story of Job is actually one of love, grace and mercy, just as is God's Son dying on the cross for our sins. Our nearsightedness has a tendency to look too closely and place too much emphasis on the temporary, while God sees the eternal.

This great book shows that it was because of the goodness of Job, not the evil, that God pointed Him out to be afflicted. He had a heart that desired God. He had a faith that trusted God and a hunger to be right with God. He was the perfect candidate for suffering.

Job was permitted to suffer in order to deepen His relationship with God. The suffering had a purpose and that was intimacy with God. Suffering works wonders in our lives to bring about the greatest treasure of intimacy with God. Suffering is given to God's best in order to bring out God's best. When one finds the riches in God suffering brings forth, they will see the privilege of suffering and the goodness of it.

When we value God and our relationship with Him above all else, then we will suffer well. In the end, Job told God that, "Where he once heard now he sees." Suffering transforms our relationship with God from a concept to a reality. God then becomes real to us, close to us and valuable to us. Its not that He wasn't before, but suffering brings a fellowship that goes beyond. This is why God chose

Job to suffer. The greater good God brought forth could have never happened without it. It will be the same for you.

. . .

THE LESSON here is to see that all your suffering will be worth the result if you turn to God in faith and let Him bring you through to the finish line. Stay the course when going through a trial, for like Job, God is working the deep things of eternity into your heart. God's peace will sustain you, His presence will overwhelm you and His power will strengthen you. Greater is He that is in you, than he that is in the world.

MOTIVES

PROVERB 21:27

> *"The sacrifice of the wicked is an abomination; How much more when he brings it with wicked intent!"*

Motives are important when it comes to God. He sees our hearts and He cannot be manipulated. He knows why we are doing something and is not fooled by false motives. People can be fooled and manipulated, but God can't.

In our text we see how God feels about those who try and manipulate Him. It speaks of those who have no intention of knowing God or bowing down to Him, yet offer sacrifices as if they do. Their motives are to get God to conform to their wishes and not the other way around. God is not a God who we order around, He is a God we fear.

• • •

THE LESSON here is that the only acceptable motive is to come to God with an honest and sincere heart, to worship Him and submit to His will, to put Him on the throne and take yourself off. He alone is worthy to be praised. Come to Him humbly and He will respond graciously.

THE MEDIATOR

JOB 9:33-35

> *"Nor is there any mediator between us, Who may lay his hand on us both. Let Him take His rod away from me, And do not let dread of Him terrify me. Then I would speak and not fear Him, But it is not so with me."*

Recognizing the vast gulf between God and himself, Job sees his great need. He knows God is too big, too holy and too wise to even approach. In his sinful condition, the great gulf is magnified. Hopeless and helpless, he ponders the solution.

A mediator would be able to understand him and present him to God, Job thought. "If there could be someone like me but also like God! One who is holy yet able to condense to the level of a sinner," Job hoped. "One who was without sin yet could be with sinners, One who could understand the plight of sinners and relate to them and go to the Father for help, "Job would imagine. "If there could just be a mediator, I could be right with God."

"Not only would that mediator go to God on my behalf," Job continued, "a mediator could come to me on God's behalf. A mediator would be able to communicate the heart of God the Father in a way that I could understand; He could come and speak in my language. With a mediator I could know the heart of God, what He is like, what He thinks and what He feels. I could know God, relate to Him and He with me. A mediator is the answer."

Job's answer would come thousands of years later when, "the Word became flesh and dwelt among us." Jesus filled the role of the mediator that Job longed for when God Himself took on the flesh of humanity as a human being. He humbled Himself so we could know God as Jesus is the "express image" of God the Father. All we could ever know about God has been revealed in His Son. As Jesus lived His life He went through what we do, He suffered, was tempted, abandoned and had feelings like we do. He gets it, He gets us and He gets life.

. . .

THE LESSON here is to know that Jesus is your Mediator, the go between for you and God the Father. He is your hope as He died for your sins and rose again from the dead. He was able to bridge the gap that could not be crossed. He is the bridge divine upon which you pass from this life into God's loving embrace. He is your Savior who understands, forgives and welcomes. He is your ever-present help in times of need. He is all you need, your go between, your Great Mediator who presents you to the Father by His own blood. Jesus Christ, your great Mediator, the answer to all your prayers.

WORKING FOR THE LORD

//

1 CORINTHIANS 15:58

> *"Therefore, my beloved brethren, be steadfast, immovable, always abounding in the work of the Lord, knowing that your labor is not in vain in the Lord."*

Working for the Lord is different than any other work. It's not just ministry work per se; it's whatever we are doing and how we do it that counts. The key is to see that everything we do is to be done "to" Him. This extends the reach of our motivation past ourselves to a much higher motivation, God. When we do that we never lose passion for what we do.

Passion will come and go depending on the reward. When our passion reaches no farther than ourselves, then when the cost is greater than ourselves, we begin to think "what's in it for me," or "what's the point?" We start to look at things as either worth it if "self" is benefited, or not worth it if "self" is not benefited. When the cost to "self" is higher than the benefit then passion runs dry.

The reward to "self" must outweigh the cost in order to sustain passion. "Self" likes pleasure, prestige, fame, glory, reputation, honor, comfort, higher levels of living standards and so forth. People will be willing to sacrifice the "self things" as long as somewhere down the line their efforts will end in the restoration of "self" things at a higher level.

Working for the Lord is different. Our motive shifts from self to God and we see a greater purpose and calling in all we do, we can continue to be passionate no matter what the personal cost. We can do this because of what our text says, "knowing that our labor is not in vain."

All we do for The Lord has eternal benefits. No matter what the activity, that's not important as Who we are doing it for. Keeping our focus on the Lord and off ourselves will fuel all our efforts with passion.

· · ·

THE LESSON here is to serve the Lord wherever you are and in whatever you are doing. Stay the course, don't complain, ask God for strength and power and He will fill your cup. Let the love of Christ "abound" in and through you, and you will have an infectious passion that will glorify the Lord. Look at each day as an opportunity not for yourself, but to glorify God. See that as the purpose of your day and you will find great joy in all you do as you do it for the Lord.

SEEING ETERNITY NOW

JOB 19:25-27

"For I know that my Redeemer lives, And He shall stand at last on the earth; And after my skin is destroyed, this I know, That in my flesh I shall see God, Whom I shall see for myself, And my eyes shall behold, and not another. How my heart yearns within me!"

After recounting his dismal condition and feeling of hopelessness, Job has a moment of clarity. A spark of sunlight of eternal hope enters into his desperate situation bringing comfort in his darkest hour.

We too need comfort in our darkest hours. Shifting our trajectory slightly upward makes all the difference. No matter how dark, the light of God is always there. When we see life through an eternal lens, we gain proper perspective. Nothing in life should be looked at without it, for to do so misses the reality of eternity, which brightens all of life.

Exactly what was in that eternal lens of Job's? He said, prophetically, that, "He knows that my Redeemer lives." Through the darkness, Job saw a risen Savior. He saw the risen Savior as His Redeemer. The One who rose from the dead to bring to life all those who believe in Him. He saw hope in that Redeemer, hope for now and hope for eternity. He saw One that was in darkness come to life and he saw that his Redeemer would do that for him too.

He saw his Redeemer standing on the earth at last. Job knew that no matter how dark it was on earth, God would redeem all things. He knew God would make the earth right again and dispel the darkness once and for all.

He saw that his body was breaking down but that one day when his body breathed it's last breath that he would see God face to face. He was encouraged to know that no matter how bad things got, he was still headed toward his home in heaven. He thought about the glories of heaven and the unhindered presence of Jesus that would never end.

Finally he recognized a longing in his heart for that day. No doubt, in our dark days the longing for heaven grows. Job recognized that his heart had bigger longings than anything in this world could fill. He knew he was made for bigger things, better things and satisfying things. Job knew that his afflictions were but for a moment compared to eternity.

. . .

THE LESSON here is the importance of an eternal perspective on life. Letting God in is letting the light in. Everything compared to eternity is nothing. As the Apostle Paul said, "these light afflictions are not worthy to be compared to the future glory revealed in us." There has to be the comparison. When eternity is in view, the temporary, no matter how bad, is swallowed up and reduced to something not worth your time worry about. In eternity, you won't have time for it.

Job 20:1 22:30, 2 Corinthians 1:1 11,
Psalm 40:11 17, Proverbs 22:2 4

COMFORT

///

2 CORINTHIANS 1:3-4

"Blessed be the God and Father of our Lord Jesus Christ, the Father of mercies and God of all comfort, who comforts us in all our tribulation, that we may be able to comfort those who are in any trouble, with the comfort with which we ourselves are comforted by God."

Life can be unbearable at times. The struggle is hard and our coping abilities limited. Some look for comfort in all the wrong places, finding themselves in a worse place than they started in. In times like these it so good to know that God is the great comforter.

There is nothing beyond the reach of His comfort. It is always bigger than the wound and is available at all times. God's comfort is better than anything one can buy; yet it's free. He is the God of "all" comfort so His comfort is all-inclusive. Whatever comfort is needed, God has. He will heal all wounds with the "balm of Gilead."

When God comforts us in our tribulation something happens. We change. His comfort is so amazing that we are so blessed by His comfort that we can then comfort others with God's comfort. That's one of the reasons God allows tribulation in our lives, so He can comfort us. We then in turn are able to comfort others in the way God has comforted us.

This also means that without tribulation we would never experience God's comfort and we would not be much good in helping others. The most tried Christians are the most able to help others. What a gracious God then, that allows tribulation so we can experience His comfort.

• • •

THE LESSON here is to look to God for your comfort. When you suffer, the reward is always greater than the pain. He will come in a way that is so gentle, delicate and soothing. His comfort will not only heal you but also change you. Look for opportunities to comfort others for they are all around.

CHRISTIAN LEADERSHIP

2 CORINTHIANS 1:24

"Not that we have dominion over your faith, but are fellow workers for your joy; for by faith you stand."

The goal of Christian leadership is to work for other people's joy. A Christian leader is one who is surrendered to God's will, trusting in God's will and being empowered to do His will. A Christian leader is one who has given up the rights to himself so that all his rights are in God's hands. Christian leaders must be humble, seeing themselves as servants and not those who want to control others in order to bring about their own desires.

This is why a Christian leader is so different from one who is not. There are those, even in ministry, who have selfish motives and take advantage of people. They are in it for themselves and therefore want to "have dominion" over others faith. In other words, they want to control people. They place their authority on a level equal to or above God's. Watch out for people like this.

In all great Christian leaders there is a great humility. This means that they don't have an elevated view of themselves as "God's gift to the world" but they feel the weight of their responsibility to care for others and be good stewards over the areas of responsibly they have been given. They see the privilege of serving God and serving others and so they know the importance of relying on God and being empowered by Him.

Ultimately then, a Christian leader will work side by side others as "fellow workers" and not "superior workers." They will work toward building others in faith and do what God has asked them to do in order to help others live by faith. Paul saw that as the target of his authority, to lead people and build people in faith.

• • •

THE LESSON here is to see what a Christian leader is, a servant. The greatest in God's kingdom are the servants of all. When God uses you, He will equip you to encourage faith. The result of those walking in faith will be joy. What could be better than being appointed by God to help people have joy by walking in faith? Christian leadership is not easy, but if called, there is nothing more fulfilling.

TRIUMPHANT VICTORY

2 CORINTHIANS 2:14

"Now thanks be to God who always leads us in triumph in Christ..."

The Christian always has something to be confident in. When a Christian is walking by faith, surrendered to God's will and focused on Kingdom work, he will walk in triumphant victory. The Bible says, "The gates of Hades will not prevail against His church." Nothing has, and nothing will, stop what God is doing. The church of God has been under attack from its inception 2,000 years ago, yet continues to flourish around the world. Nothing will stop God's church.

It's important that God is leading, however. He is the One who leads us in victory, so when we are following His agenda and not our own, He will be leading us into victory. It's when we veer from His path that we fail. It may not look like failure because there still may be thriving ministry, according to mans' standards and human opinion, yet God sees things by His standards. What seems like success, when measured by the world's measures of success, may in God's eyes be a complete failure. God sees the heart.

. . .

THE LESSON here is that victory comes from simple obedience. Be careful of using the wrong measures like the number of people, the amount of money and the number of programs. God looks for obedience and that in and of itself is the victory. Then you can leave the rest to Him.

OUR SUFFICIENCY

2 CORINTHIANS 3:5

"Not that we are sufficient of ourselves to think of anything as being from ourselves, but our sufficiency is from God."

When God calls us to a task He also provides the ability. Nothing is impossible for the one who serves God and is surrendered to His will. The Bible is full of accounts that display God's greatness through weak and inadequate people. No one is able to do God's work without Him.

However, nothing is impossible with Him, the bigger the odds, the greater the glory to our Lord. When we think we need more, God will often reduce so there will be no doubt as to the source of power. Naturally people will want to attribute success to man, and this is something we need to be careful about. God will use instruments that rely on Him and give Him all the glory.

• • •

THE LESSON here is to never measure what can be done by what you can do. Rather, measure what can be done by what God can do. The results are unlimited when you don't limit God. Let God work so that people will have no other explanation but to say, "It's the Lord." Just be available and God will prove Himself mighty. Your sufficiency is from God.

AUGUST 30

Job 34:1 36:33, 2 Corinthians 4:1 12,
Psalm 44:1 8, Proverbs 22:10 12

THE TREASURE INSIDE US

2 CORINTHIANS 4:7

"But we have this treasure in earthen vessels, that the excellence of the power may be of God and not of us."

The gospel is a treasure. It reveals to God's heart to us. The gospel is love in action speaking louder than mere words as God "walked the talk" by showing His true character and nature. His love is amazing, supernatural and generous, reaching out to any man that will receive it. The Christian is one that has this treasure inside of them.

The treasure of the gospel transforms us so that what we have inside is clearly not "normal", its "supernormal" or beyond normal. We, through the work of God, possess a power that can only be determined to be God and not ourselves. God's power is what a Christian should live with. The magnificence of a "normal" vessel containing the divine contents is the glory of the gospel.

· · ·

THE LESSON here is to let God work through you. It is God, and not you Who has the power. When you let God work through you, there will be power that shouts supernatural. Look for God to great things, above all you can ask or think, and people will be drawn to God's love. You will be a vessel filled with power and nothing will be impossible. Stay out of the way and God will do the rest.

FIGHTING DISCOURAGEMENT

2 CORINTHIANS 4:16-18

> *"Therefore we do not lose heart. Even though our outward man is perishing, yet the inward man is being renewed day by day. For our light affliction, which is but for a moment, is working for us a far more exceeding and eternal weight of glory, while we do not look at the things which are seen, but at the things which are not seen. For the things which are seen are temporary, but the things which are not seen are eternal."*

Discouragement is something every Christian who really cares about God's work, His Kingdom, the lost and the body of Christ, has to contend with. To the one who really cares, this attack is one of Satan's best weapons. The Christian who cares will have to deal with feelings of failure, fruitlessness and lack of "success."

Fruit will not always abound and be plentiful the way we often think. It is not always linear the way we want. There are times it will seem like nothing is happening. There will be dry seasons where we question our calling, wondering if we missed something or we wonder if there is a point to all we are doing.

The question then is, are you simply being faithful? When you are, you can see things as God sees them. You will see that even though you may be faced with difficulty, the difficulty is nothing compared to eternity. Your inward person is growing while the outer is dying. Emphasizing the outward is how you may be getting discouraged, emphasizing the inward or unseen will encourage. Fighting the battle of discouragement is simply a matter of seeing the eternal through the eyes of faith.

· · ·

THE LESSON here to learn that you must fight against discouraging feelings by standing on the truth by faith. No matter what you perceive, God is still at work. Fight discouragement by seeing all you do in light of eternity. The things that discourage you are short term. They are not the measure of who you are, or how God sees you. Other people's perception of you and/or your ministry is not what matters. If it did Jesus would have not gone to the cross. Its what God sees that counts.

THE FRUIT OF SUFFERING

//

JOB 42:5

> *"I have heard of You by the hearing of the ear, But now my eye sees You."*

At first glance it would seem that Job was allowed to be treated unfairly by God when he was living such a Godly life. It seemed like God was mean in his dealings with Job, especially by not bailing him out of his pain. Now, at the end of the book we see that God was blessing Job by "suffering out" more impurities in his life and making his faith real and personal.

Job states the difference his suffering made. His great faith went from hearing to seeing. In other words, it became real. It's the same with us. There is a big difference in reading the Bible than seeing it. There is a big difference in hearing about God than seeing Him.

Suffering makes our faith real. It makes God real and our need for Him real. We experience His presence in a different way as we "fellowship with His suffering" (Philippians 3:10). He meets us in our sufferings in a unique way that His presence becomes our reward.

· · ·

THE LESSON here is to see the blessing of suffering. It is needed in your life. You don't have to be afraid but instead you can walk through it by faith, knowing there will be a great return on the other side. Suffering has fruit that bears God's blessing and there is a special fruit that comes through suffering. You don't have to go looking for suffering, just keep seeking God and He will do what's best to give you the best. Suffering will bring God's best in the end. Like Job, the end will be better than the beginning.

EVERYTHING BEAUTIFUL

ECCLESIASTES 3:11

"He has made everything beautiful in its time. Also He has put eternity in their hearts, except that no one can find out the work that God does from beginning to end."

God is an artist. He is a master craftsman that specializes in restoration. He makes beauty for ashes, the oil of joy for mourning, and the garment of praise for the spirit of heaviness. We are his workmanship or more literally, His poem. He is writing the poem of our lives.

We are also co-laborers with Him in building His Kingdom. Yet, God also works on a schedule. His own schedule and not according to our schedule, unless we are on His schedule. One thing is for certain; God has and will make everything beautiful "in it's time."

This is a great confidence we have in the Lord when we place ourselves in His hands. Two key words for us are "beautiful" and "time." God could do everything immediately, but He chooses instead to work on an ever-unfolding schedule. As He does, we get glimpses of beauty all around us. When we make it a focus to look around at the beautiful things He places in our paths, we will get glimpses of Heaven.

These glimpses of heaven resonate with something deep in our hearts because as the text says, "He has put eternity in our hearts." This means that we are wired for eternal things. Material things point to something bigger, and it's when we see the Master Creator behind the creation that we see the deeper meaning of beauty, and that is to be connected to the beautiful One who makes all things beautiful in its time.

· · ·

THE LESSON here is to let God work according to His timetable. Remember that you can't always see all that God is doing, but your eternal heart will be filled when you fill it with the eternal God. In your life you may be having a hard time seeing the beautiful. Maybe it's still in the process. Maybe all you see is the ugly. Maybe you're brokenhearted. Be encouraged, God is making everything beautiful in His time, and it will be worth the wait.

Ecclesiastes 4:1 6:12, 2 Corinthians 6:14 7:7,
Psalm 47:1 9, Proverbs 22:16

OPINIONS

ECCLESIASTES 5:2

> *"Do not be rash with your mouth, and let not your heart utter anything hastily before God. For God is in heaven, and you on earth; Therefore let your words be few."*

Opinions are everywhere these days. I guess they always were, but now we have access to everyone's opinions it seems. The trouble is, when other people's opinions become our own opinion. Opinions are just that, they really don't mean anything unless they are based on God's truth. His are the only ones that count.

When it comes to eternal things, opinions can lead people to hell. Or maybe there is no hell in one's opinion. Even though God says there is, and Jesus died so we wouldn't have to go there. But opinions are like that, giving a false sense of reality.

Just because someone THINKS something doesn't mean it is. "How do you know, where do you get that, where is that in the Bible?" are all good questions to ask. How many people have gone to hell because the based their eternity on what they "thought" to be true, or someone else's opinion, rejecting God and His truth, while at the same time many of those opinions have proven to be wrong over the years.

• • •

THE LESSON here is to be careful with your words. Remember that God has never been proven wrong, and has spoken the truth in His Word, the Holy Bible. Let your words, your opinions and ramblings; be few in the presence of an Almighty God. Be quick to hear and slow to speak. God doesn't have opinions, only truth.

TWO TYPES OF SORROW

2 CORINTHIANS 7:10

> *"For godly sorrow produces repentance leading to salvation, not to be regretted; but the sorrow of the world produces death."*

Not all sorrow is the same. As we see in our text, there are two kinds of sorrow we need to know about. One is good and one isn't. One points us to God and one doesn't. So not all sorrow is bad, it depends on what it produces in our lives.

Godly sorrow is when we feel so terrible about something that we actually go in a different direction than the direction we are going that has caused the sorrow. Sometimes we are like moths to a flame and keep coming back for more.

Godly sorrow is when we are broken from what we have done and finally come to a place where we actually look beyond ourselves and to God. This sorrow has a way of hurting us to God. Most people need this sorrow to actually come to God at all. Some might call it "the end of the rope" or "rock bottom." The end result is salvation when one puts their faith in Jesus Christ and His finished work on the cross.

For a Christian it is important to be sensitive to when we have Godly sorrow, or an insult to our relationship with God, turning the moment we feel the sorrow of sin or whatever is causing there to be a problem in our relationship with God. Otherwise we risk the terrible condition of a hardened heart. Pray that you would never get comfortable or desensitized to sin. Keep a short account with God without letting sorrow from sin continue to the point where that becomes your "new normal".

The other kind of sorrow is the sorrow of the world. This sorrow is the terrible feeling that comes when you get caught or have some negative consequence from your actions, and yet still continue on in the same direction. There is no softness of heart and no sensitivity to God. Worldly sorrow actually has an compounding factor that comes with it, in that the sorrow is compounded because there will be a greater need for relief, which will only be found in things that bring more death and destruction. The sorrow of the world digs it's own grave and climbs in all by itself. Without coming to the end of oneself and turning to God, the sorrow of the world strives to keep the dead alive.

. . .

THE LESSON here is that sorrow is only productive when it leads you to God for the answer. He is the only remedy. Don't let pride or stubbornness keep you from love and forgiveness. God is ready to forgive and abundantly pardon. Let your sorrow do something, let it be effective and don't waste it. Sorrow can be the greatest source of joy you may ever have if it causes you to look to Jesus. Sorrow is not bad if it kills you to life.

WHAT IS LIFE ALL ABOUT?

ECCLESIASTES 12:13-14

"Let us hear the conclusion of the whole matter: Fear God and keep His commandments, For this is man's all. For God will bring every work into judgment, Including every secret thing, Whether good or evil."

When all is said and done, all of life boils down to, "fear God and keep His commandments." This is what life is about. It's sort of like a testing place so we can choose God or choose against Him. Sometimes it's hard to see the point of life on earth. Yet through it all, God communicates Himself to us and has given us everything we need to know in order to know Him. No man will have an excuse.

This life then is to come into a right relationship with God which all begins with, "fearing God." To "fear God" is to know He will bring every work into Judgment as verse 14 states. It means knowing that there is an Almighty Creator that we are responsible to and will be held accountable to. It means we have respect, reverence and awe for One that is infinitely higher than us and that will judge us for our actions, if they are good or evil.

"Fearing God" then will show in how we keep His commandments. God's commandments are the standard for good. All that is good will be in line with these standards and all that is evil will not. God is perfectly good, a perfect light with no darkness in Him. He created us in that light, without sin and with a perfect connection to God, in harmony with who He is. Man would enjoy the unhindered presence of God that came with His sinless nature. That all changed.

In order for perfect communion with God there had to be a perfect union of natures, a Holy God and a sinless man. When given the choice, man chose evil in the Garden of Eden and, ever since, mankind has been tainted with sin. Man was tempted to not fear God, to believe more in the creation than the Creator, more in the creature than the Creator. The choice presented brought failure to man's purpose, severed the connection to life itself.

God didn't give up, having a plan to restore what was lost. The plan showed the incredible love of God for us and His desire to reconcile man back to Himself, and do what man could not, be perfect.

It would take a perfect man to make a perfect sacrifice in order for reconciliation to occur. No man could do this, being infected with sin, only a pure Holy man could. God Himself, would have to die for mans' sin, demonstrating His love for us that while we were still sinners Christ died for us (Romans 5:8).

. . .

THE LESSON here is that life all boils down to being in a right relationship with God. You do this by choosing to put your faith in Him and what He has done to restore your relationship with Him. Remember that life never even begins until you are born again, with life in the Spirit. Now that your sins HAVE been judged and accounted for, as Jesus was judged in your place, life boils down to choosing God. It boils down to this being a place where you choose your eternal destiny. This life is where you choose eternal life; now and forever more.

HIS BANNER OVER ME IS LOVE

SONG OF SOLOMON 2:4

> *"He brought me to the banqueting house, and his banner over me was love."*

There is nothing that stakes it's claim more to a Christian's life than love. God parades His love over us so the world can see. He is proud to wave the banner that shows His feelings and He is proud to be our God.

As recipients of His love, a Christian should feel comfortable knowing they are loved and cared for. There is a certain way that a secure person carries himself or herself. God's love is like an anchor that allows them to be safe and stable. When a Christian knows they are cared for, they will feel free to just be. This security let's them blossom in who they are because then they aren't forced to be who they aren't when driven by insecurities.

Notice in the scripture "he brought me to the banqueting house." Speaking of a groom wanting to be alone in a private place to spend time with his bride. God, too, wants to manifest His love to us personally and intimately. This speaks of the importance of getting away with the Lord to a quite place at a quiet time. The need for this is a desperate one because we desperately need to experience God's love and be satisfied and secure in it.

. . .

THE LESSON here is to be secure in God's love for you. To rest in it knowing that you are uniquely special, passionately cared for and deeply adored. Faith is what grasps on to this. Believing what God says and what He has done. Knowing He accepts you just as you are, no matter what we have done or haven't done. He flies the banner high, "this is my loved one." Let those words sink in, "you are madly loved." God is crazy about you.

Song of Songs 5:1 8:14, 2 Corinthians 9:1 15,
Psalm 51:1 19, Proverbs 22:24 25

THE JOY OF REPENTANCE

//

PSALM 51:12

> *"Restore to me the joy of Your salvation, and uphold me by Your generous Spirit."*

Joy is a byproduct of God's salvation. It can only be found in connection with the fountain of joy, God Himself. Our joy is really God's joy simply received when we receive Him and His gifts of grace. It's all part of God restoring that, which was broken, our relationship with Him. When sin enters our relationship, joy leaves.

David here in our scripture, was struggling. Joy had been replaced by sorrow. Sin's price is death, death to joy, death to love, death to peace and anything good. There is an answer to this painful goodbye to goodness, and it is repentance. Turning to God with a sorry apologetic heart brings instant restoration.

• • •

THE LESSON here is to repent if you need to. Maybe like David, sin has sapped your joy. Repentance is the medicine for the soul as we see in our text. God has a generous Spirit. He waits for your return and will restore you to the joy of His salvation. Sin hurts but repentance restores. Don't waste another moment without joy. Life is too short to live without it.

MENTAL PURITY

//

2 CORINTHIANS 10:5B

"Bringing every thought into captivity to the obedience of Christ."

Our minds are a target for the enemy. He throws unseen fiery darts, laced with lies, into the synapses of our brain in order to dictate what he wants us to think. The thoughts don't become ours until we agree with or accept them. Then they dictate to our emotions so that we are attached to lies not only mentally but also emotionally.

This strategy can be, and has been, effective in derailing many well meaning Christians, leaving them in a heap, broken down on the side of the road. Truth is always what is attacked, for truth will set us free and keep us free. Satan's lies keep us in bondage. There is a way to have victory over Satan's infiltration of our minds as we see here in our text.

The solution is to take any thought that is not of God and imprison it. Quarantine the false demonic lie so it doesn't spread to our emotions. Don't accept it but reject it like you would reject the plague. Make the thought bow down to truth by relegating it to where it belongs, as a thief to a life focused on God, His love, His grace, His goodness, His truth and whatever else is from above.

• • •

THE LESSON here is to control your thought life so it doesn't control you. Have a very disciplined mind that stays focused on the right things and quickly apprehend false things. Use your mind as a weapon to keep it connected to God and by initiating thoughts of Godly things. Practice mental purity and not just outward purity. When your thoughts obey Christ, so will your life, and you will enjoy a transformed mind. May your mind be a weapon for God's glory.

Isaiah 3:1 5:30, 2 Corinthians 11:1 15,
Psalm 53:1 6, Proverbs 22:28 29

DON'T BE DECEIVED

///

2 CORINTHIANS 11:14

> *"And no wonder! For Satan himself transforms himself into an angel of light."*

If there is one characteristic of Satan that should stand out, but seems to be less thought of, it's deceiver. Satan is typically thought of as an ugly terrifying monster type, which he is, but he doesn't always present himself that way. The horns and pitchfork Satan is not his usual attire.

Satan's mode of operandi from the beginning was to come in a Godlike disguise while at the same time questioning God's goodness. Usually in very subtle ways, he speaks with soft, kind and tender words, which are full of poisonous lies. People are much more accommodative to the soft approach. This is the warning in our text.

Like a chameleon, Satan is adaptable to different environments and knows how to get our ear. He is a flatterer and is most dangerous in the religious settings as he speaks of an "all loving God" who would never send anyone to hell. Flattering the righteous by great swelling words, telling them how good they are and how humanitarian and benevolent are the works.

As chests puff and heads swell with pride, the need for brokenness and humility flee and man's religion becomes made up in their own minds, usually with man in the center. Elevating mans' thoughts above God's, mans' way above His ways and mans' truth above the Almighty's truth.

. . .

THE LESSON here is to know that Satan is a deceiver. The answer to his sly attacks is to stick with the truth in God's Word. Look at what Jesus did and how He did it. Look at the disciples and what they did and how they did it. Glean from and study all of God's Word, for it is all-profitable (2 Timothy 3:16).

I SAW THE LORD

ISAIAH 6:1

"In the year that King Uzziah died, I saw the Lord sitting on a throne, high and lifted up, and the train of His robe filled the temple."

King Uzziah brought great wealth and comfort to the nation of Israel. The Israelites would enjoy the material delights of prosperity along with security and peace. However, when anything material becomes our focus, taking the place of God in our hearts, an idol has emerged.

We all have potential "Uzziahs", things that replace God on the throne in our hearts. Things like success, selfish ambition, money, hobbies, relationships, career and even ministry can usurp God's place as our soul's King. We must be careful, for God is a jealous God and when He is not at the center of our lives, He will work to remove those idols.

As with Isaiah, it is when our own "King Uzziahs" die that we "see The Lord". Seeing the Lord is the most important thing there is for a Christian and should be the aim of every Christian's life. Sometimes OUR dreams have to die before we can see the Lord and His bigger dreams begin.

. . .

THE LESSON here is to be aware of anything that takes the place of God in your life. Those "little foxes that spoil the vine," (Song of Solomon 2:15) will eat away at the fruit that comes from abiding in Him (John 15:1). Like a gardener, take good care of your soul by nurturing it with "God things," keep the soil healthy and pick out the weeds. Seeing begins when the things that blind, die.

SEPTEMBER 11

Isaiah 8:1 9:21, 2 Corinthians 12:1 10,
Psalm 55:1 23, Proverbs 23:4 5

STRENGTH IN WEAKNESS

2 CORINTHIANS 12:9

> *"And He said to me, 'My grace is sufficient for you, for My strength is made perfect in weakness.' Therefore most gladly I will rather boast in my infirmities, that the power of Christ may rest upon me."*

The message here in our scripture is, "all we need is grace." When faced with whatever comes our way, God's grace is enough for the task. Grace is favor from God, the all powerful God. His favor comes as a benefit of one who has come to know Him personally by faith, and will carry us through. His grace is enough.

God's strength operates through faith. Trusting in Him, looking to and leaning upon Him to accomplish His will through us. It is His power, or strength, that works in our weakness. When we try to do things in our own strength we short-circuit the work of God. However, plugging into His strength manifests His power.

When God's power is working through us, He gets the glory. Our boasting then is of Him and what He can do, not what we can do and us. So often we fight against our weaknesses instead of embracing them and yielding them to God. In the end, it is the most amazing thing to be a vessel for God's glory.

• • •

THE LESSON here is to remember that when you are weak, He is strong!

THE VALUE OF A SOUL

2 CORINTHIANS 12:15

"And I will very gladly spend and be spent for your souls;"

The suffering and hardship of Paul was considered the price for other's souls. Understanding the nature of eternity and the importance of our souls, which are eternal, Paul was willing to suffer whatever was necessary if it benefited another's soul.

This was the same attitude of Jesus. It was for, "the joy set before Him that He endured the cross" (Hebrews 12:2). A willingness to be used up for souls was the attitude of an eternal mindset. A selfish life of indulgence and pleasure is a waste, if souls are perishing. We will have all eternity to enjoy pleasure, and only now win and care for souls.

What would you be willing to do for another's soul? How much would you give, sacrifice and be spent? Souls of men are the most valuable thing there is, so much so that Jesus died for them. Are you investing in souls? Are you willing to spend and be spent so another soul can be won?

• • •

THE LESSON here is to make the souls of men your life's work. Let nothing interfere with your mission, for there is no better way to use your life. Love souls and give them Jesus and have no regrets. You'll have all eternity to enjoy the fruits of your labor.

SEPTEMBER 13

Isaiah 12:1 14:32, 2 Corinthians 13:1 14,
Psalm 57:1 11, Proverbs 23:9 11

I WILL OR THY WILL

ISAIAH 14:13-14

> *"For you have said in your heart: 'I will ascend into heaven, I will exalt my throne above the stars of God; I will also sit on the mount of the congregation On the farthest sides of the north; I will ascend above the heights of the clouds, I will be like the Most High.'"*

How did "Satan" become "Satan?" Was he always like that? Was he born that way? Did he come with red horns and a pitchfork? The answer is no. Satan was a most beautiful created angel charged with the task of making beautiful music. It was pride that caused his most tragic fall from grace.

As we see in our text, his glory was his shame. He thought he was greater than God. Talent, good looks, intelligence, fame, success and wealth can all be things that give people a false sense of reality. Selfish ambition got a hold of him and when that happens it is hard to see straight. Blinded by his lust for power and greatness he proclaims, "I will" instead of "Thy will."

It's good to remember who God is and who we are. A created being will always be inferior and subject to his Creator. There is no limit to God's greatness and without Him we are nothing. It's only by His grace that we live, enjoy, relate and connect to God's greatness. We must always remember that.

The key is to live your life in subjection to your Creator. Everything will come in line when you are in line with God. Seek Him first and His Kingdom, and all things will be added to you (Mt. 6:33). He will, not "you will" bring forth what is right and true for your life. Don't be like Satan, resist your will by saying "thy will be done." When you do that, you will walk with God.

· · ·

THE LESSON here is to watch those "I wills" in your life. Watch the feelings of superiority to others and especially God. You may not articulate that you feel superior, but your actions may say otherwise. When you can't trust God over yourself, His ways over your ways, and His plan over your plan, in essence you are saying "I will" instead of "Thy will."

DON'T MESS WITH THE GOSPEL

GALATIANS 1:8

"But even if we, or an angel from heaven, preach any other gospel to you than what we have preached to you, let him be accursed."

The gospel is perfect. Nothing needs to be added or subtracted to an already perfect piece. In fact, tainting the gospel by changing it is to be accursed. It's so serious because only evil would change the only means of salvation. There can be no sterner of a warning than this.

The key is the message and not the messenger. Sometimes we can lose sight of the message because we like the style, delivery or personality of the messenger. We can be "lured in" by the package and touched emotionally, and yet, the gospel is being compromised. This is the strategy of the devil, and when we don't pay attention we can fall prey.

Satan can disguise himself as an "angel of light" (2 Corinthians 11:14), looking like the real thing. There will be wolves, dressed like sheep we are told. People will love hearing these false teachers omit, add to, or manipulate the gospel so that people will have their ears tickled and hear what the want to hear instead of what the need to hear, truth.

The gospel is this; eternal God became a man, lived a sinless life, died as a sacrifice for our sin, rose again from the dead and whoever believes in Him (trusts in Who He is and what He has done) will be forgiven of all sin and accepted into His presence, now and forevermore in heaven with Him for all eternity.

The Bible says, "By grace we are saved through faith, not of works, lest any man boast" (Ephesians 2:8). Adding to the gospel would be anything that includes something we must do in order to be saved, beyond faith. Taking away would be anything that says one doesn't need to come to Jesus by faith but there are other ways to heaven. Or saying Jesus wasn't eternally God or didn't fully pay for our sin, for example.

· · ·

THE LESSON here is to pay attention to the message and don't be deceived by the messenger. Our text states that even if the Apostles, or an Angel, preach another gospel than what is clearly and plainly taught and revealed in God's Word, no matter who or what it is, must be rejected and even accursed. In essence, don't ever mess with the gospel and don't ever accept one who does.

SEPTEMBER 15

Isaiah 19:1 21:17, Galatians 2:1 16,
Psalm 59:1 17, Proverbs 23:13 14

JUSTIFIED, NOW WHAT?

GALATIANS 2:16

"Knowing that a man is not justified by the works of the law but by faith in Jesus Christ, even we have believed in Christ Jesus, that we might be justified by faith in Christ and not by the works of the law; for by the works of the law no flesh shall be justified."

Justification is a term that means to be declared righteous. Imagine being in a courtroom standing trial for something you are guilty of and the judge brings down the gavel and declares you innocent. This is what is called justification.

Why is it important to be declared "righteous?" The reason righteousness is important is because without it, no one can see God. Our sins keep us from God and His righteous requirements of "perfect righteousness" are beyond our grasp.

This verse tells us how we can be justified or declared righteous.

Justification can be thought of as, "just as if I've never done it." How can this be for a guilty sinner? Like our courtroom scene, it would be unfair for our sin to go unpunished. That creates a whole other set of problems with injustice. Instead of just being let off the hook, Jesus paid our fine for us.

The cross is where justice and mercy meet. The cross is where we are justified. The cross is where Jesus actually took our punishment and paid our debt. His act of mercy brings God's favor and blessing to guilty sinners. When Jesus said, "it is finished" from the cross, He was saying the debt of our sin has been paid.

In order for His sacrifice for our sin to become ours, we have to put our faith in Jesus and His finished work on the cross. This is how His work becomes effective in our life. We can do nothing but receive it by faith, and when we sincerely do, we are declared innocent and can never be charged again. This is why we are "saved by grace through faith, and not of our works." (Eph. 2:8) Good works can never save because good works can never erase sin.

. . .

THE LESSON here is to be thankful for your standing before God, fully justified in His sight. Now live a life of gratitude and thanksgiving. Now that you're justified, live free; live with a purpose, live for God!

FAITH

GALATIANS 2:20

"I have been crucified with Christ; it is no longer I who live, but Christ lives in me; and the life which I now live in the flesh I live by faith in the Son of God, who loved me and gave Himself for me."

Faith is the currency of heaven. It is what grabs a hold of salvation and secures entrance into heaven. One single act of faith removes sin and guilt once and for all and for all eternity. Faith makes us righteous.

Faith is also how a forgiven, righteous, justified Child of God lives. Once forgiven the walk of faith begins and just like faith saves us, faith also guides us. Sometimes we can think that we had to exercise faith to be forgiven, and then we put aside faith and live by our own strength and power. Nothing could be further from the truth.

Faith is also how we live our life. Every minute of every hour we are to listen and obey God. This requires us to trust Him with our lives and with our futures. Relinquishing control is not easy but when we know the nature of God, Who loves us and proved His love for us, we can let our hands off our lives and put them in His hands.

. . .

THE LESSON here is that living by faith is the way you are to live as a "Child of God". Trusting in His goodness, you can rest in His faithfulness. It's not about "you" anymore; it's about "Him" and "His" plan. When He is working His plan through your faith, you will be blessed to know a goodness and satisfaction that you didn't know existed before. Living by faith is what will bring heaven into your soul.

Isaiah 25:1 28:13, Galatians 3:10 22,
Psalm 61:1 8, Proverbs 23:17 18

THE SIMPLE WORD

ISAIAH 28:13

> "But the word of the Lord was to them, 'Precept upon precept, precept upon precept, Line upon line, line upon line, Here a little, there a little,' That they might go and fall backward, and be broken And snared and caught."

The Word of God is the foundational to the Christian life. It is essential in order for growth and to be strong and healthy. Without it, there is no growth, strength or health. It's just the simple.

It is not an accident God's Word is often minimized and even denied within the pale of Christianity. Satan attacks that which works and is effective for the Christian. The Word is front and center of his assaults, knowing that if a Christian stops reading his Bible, he stops growing and becomes vulnerable to all the other attacks he has in his arsenal.

In our text we see the rebuke to those "Men of God" who refuse to teach the Word of God. This "oxymoron" was common in Bible times as it is today. A "true Man of God" will teach the people the "Word of God" without compromise. The Word of God brings rest and refreshing as vs. 12 states, but it also rebukes those who deny it or compromise with it "they fall backward and be broken" snared and caught."

The way to teach is simply, where the hearer can hear and understand, then to teach in order, systematically, building truth upon truth, like a child's building blocks. There is an order to it and a flow where the Word is speaking for itself and not man speaking. The teacher is to present God's truth and not their own version.'

Be leery of a Pastor or Church fellowship where the Word is not regularly taught. As we see in the text, there has to be a place in the "Body of Christ" where the whole congregation is going systematically through the Word, verse-by-verse, line-by-line. This is called expository preaching.

There is a big difference in teaching "from the Word" and "teaching THE Word." Make sure the Word is being taught and make sure you are prayerfully seeking God and allowing the Holy Spirit to minister and transform your heart. There is just no substitute for God's Word.

. . .

THE LESSON here is to see the importance of God's Word in your life. Nothing can really happen for you as a Christian until you have an appetite for God's Word.

THE LAW

GALATIANS 3:24

> *"Therefore the law was our tutor to bring us to Christ, that we might be justified by faith."*

If faith is the way to access God's grace, then what is the point of the law? Why were the Ten Commandments given to Moses on Mt. Sinai? Why all the other additions to the law? Is the law useless? Is there a point to it?

In our text we see the point of the law. Like a schoolteacher, the law teaches us that we cannot be good enough to be saved. The law tells us the righteous requirements of God are moral requirements. The law tells us what God is like, perfectly holy and that we cannot be perfectly holy through the law. Ultimately, the law teaches us we need a Savior.

The law then is good. We would never know that Salvation must come through another without it. Considering it's standard is perfection, the law shows us what we are not. Anyone trying to get to heaven through the law or good works will have to be perfect. Not just in their actions but also in their thoughts.

Just thinking about another lustfully is a sin. Thinking about wanting something someone else has is a sin. Thinking we are better than someone else, feeling hateful thoughts or jealous thoughts is a sin. It goes on and on and on. The law tells us we are sinners.

The law is a tool to lead us to Christ. When the law points you to God and His grace it is good. When the law becomes your salvation, you are already damned. Good works can't, and won't, save because you can't be good enough. The law is an excellent teacher but a terrible Savior.

· · ·

THE LESSON here is to see the law for what it is, teacher that shows us we need a Savior. You can never be good enough so Christ did it for you. He fulfilled the law because you could not. He was perfectly sinless and therefore met the requirements that you could not and took your place in judgment.

Isaiah 30:12 33:9, Galatians 5:1 12,
Psalm 63:1 11, Proverbs 23:22

LOVINGKINDNESS

///

PSALM 63:3-5

> *"Because Your lovingkindness is better than life, My lips shall praise You. Thus I will bless You while I live; I will lift up my hands in Your name. My soul shall be satisfied as with marrow and fatness, And my mouth shall praise You with joyful lips."*

There is great joy in God's presence. The Psalmist here is expressing how good God is and how thoroughly he is enjoying Him. What the Psalmist is experiencing is God's "lovingkindness", which is character trait of God's that makes God so pleasant and enjoyable to be with.

Lovingkindness is the gentle touch of God that comes from His deep love for us. He is so "nice" that "nice" is too limited of a word. When love is expressed in kindness we feel adored, appreciated and cared for. This attribute is better than life itself.

The Psalmist wants to respond to God's lovingkindness so he praises Him. All he knows to do is to respond to those feelings he feels, and praise then finds itself blessing God, lifting up hands and giving himself over to Him. It's easy to surrender when the surrender is to such lovingkindness.

Finally, lovingkindness satisfies him. The food for the soul, which satiates so deeply that more praise springs forth of joy, is the final result.

· · ·

THE LESSON here is to know and enjoy God's lovingkindness. God is enjoyable and has made the way possible for you to enjoy Him through a personal relationship with Him. God's lovingkindness is better than life itself, it brings God's goodness to man's emptiness and will fill you to the full of heavenly delight.

THE FRUIT OF THE SPIRIT

///

GALATIANS 5:22-23

> *"But the fruit of the Spirit is love, joy, peace, longsuffering, kindness, good-*
> *ness, faithfulness, gentleness, self-control. Against such there is no law."*

Fruit is an outgrowth of what's inside. It's the goodness seen and enjoyed of healthy growth. The English word for fruit comes from a Latin work "fruit" which means, "to enjoy" (Merriam-Webster dictionary).

We all have enjoyed a good piece of fruit for its taste, color, texture and nutrients keeping us strong and healthy. The product of God working from the inside out in our lives is compared to fruit, to be enjoyed.

The fruit of the Spirit is really one thing that manifests itself in different ways. The word "fruit" in our text is singular and refers directly to "love." The fruit of the Spirit then is "love" and then expresses itself in the other ways mentioned, "joy, peace, longsuffering, kindness, goodness, faithfulness, gentleness, self-control". These qualities are a good way to know if God is in control or if we are. The difference is the Spirit's control versus our flesh being in control.

The fruit of God then is love, in which He gives us and wants it to be shared. We see then that the fruit of the Spirit is the goodness of God that manifests itself in a human life and the earthly realm, showing that there is something divine to be had. When the Holy Spirit directs our actions we sprinkle the world with God's love.

· · ·

THE LESSON here is that as you enjoy God, then others would enjoy Him through you. It all comes down to the freedom you give the Holy Spirit to have in you. It may be hard to let go, but when you do, there will be a great reward for you and to those around you.

MANASSEHS'

///

ISAIAH 38:4-5

> *"And the word of the Lord came to Isaiah, saying, 'Go and tell Hezekiah,*
> *'Thus says the Lord, the God of David your father: I have heard your*
> *prayer, I have seen your tears; surely I will add to your days fifteen years.'"*

Hezekiah was a good King for Judah. He was a rare leader in those days who turned his nation back to God in honor and dignity. He loved the Lord and wanted his people and nation to turn from their false gods to the living God.

Despite Hezekiah's reforms and devotion to God he had a huge problem with some bad news he received. A Prophet of God told him that his life would soon end. He prayed for more life and God granted him fifteen more years. In those years his son Manasseh was born, one of the worst Kings Judah has seen.

· · ·

THE LESSON here is when God's plan is not your plan, even when it's hard, it's always best. When you fight, resist and rebel against God you are fighting against what's best. Like Hezekiah, you may force your will and bring forth you own Manasseh. Better to have God's will than yours because Manassehs' always show up where your own will is alive.

RELEVANCE

ISAIAH 40:8

"The grass withers, the flower fades, but the word of our God stands forever."

There is a lot of talk about "relevance" these days in Christian circles, with conversations about how to reach our culture for God in the best way. Season's change, generation's change and cultures change, it's true, but one thing will never change, God's Word.

No matter the culture or generation, God's Word remains relevant. It speaks to the hearts of men and women, cutting through all barriers of time and culture to speak to the deepest need of mankind. God's Word stands forever.

· · ·

THE LESSON here is to know that God's Word is ageless and timeless and therefore always relevant. It should never be replaced or minimized, for it has power like nothing else to change the heart of man. When you make God's Word a priority, you will never be out date. His Word is for all generations and will stand forever.

THE GIFT

EPHESIANS 2:8-9

> *"For by grace you have been saved through faith, and that not of your-*
> *selves; it is the gift of God, not of works, lest anyone should boast."*

There can be no clearer statement about "salvation" than the one we have here. No "deeper" theological revelation can change "not of your selves." No honest enquirer can get another meaning out of "not of yourselves," yet many do.

God has not made salvation some esoteric, ethereal equation that only the spiritual elite can understand. He made it so simple a child can explain it. There are no hidden doors, no secret passageways to truth. He put it all out there, plain and simple.

He goes on to say "not of works." Very clearly we see that we cannot do anything to earn salvation. No amount of good deeds, good religious works or good behavior adds anything to salvation. "Not of works" closes the door to any human effort that is thought to save.

So why do people make it so complicated? I believe its pride that wants to contribute something to salvation or pride that can't admit we can do nothing in and of ourselves. Our verse goes on to say, "Lest anyone should boast." Salvation takes "us" out of the equation and places it solely on Christ.

Salvation then is simply "a gift." Like any gift it must be received. This gift of God is a gift of "grace," meaning it is something we receive that we haven't earned. Otherwise it wouldn't be a gift. It is God saying, "Here, this is for you."

Inside is the greatest gift of all, a gift that Christ paid for with His own life, with His own blood. It is the most expensive gift there is and only Christ could have paid for it. However, not everyone opens the gift.

Our part in receiving the gift and making it our own is faith. Faith says I believe Jesus is the eternal God, Who came as a man into this world to die for my sins. Faith says I will trust in Christ and not myself. Faith is our participation in the plan of God to save us. We are saved "through faith."

· · ·

THE LESSON here is to know that salvation is a gift. It's all of Him, and none of you. Grace is God's work and God's gift to you, it is how you are saved from sin and to eternal life with Christ. "Not of yourself," "not of works," but of faith in Jesus' work. Jesus paid it all, and all you do is receive it by faith. Have you opened His gift to you and are you offering it to others?

Isaiah 43:14 45:10, Ephesians 3:1 21,
Psalm 68:1 18, Proverbs 24:1 2

GOD'S LOVE

EPHESIANS 3:19

"To know the love of Christ which passes knowledge."

The greatest inner need of all humans is love. We are wired to have it and intrinsically we know when we don't. "Love lack" will manifest itself in many different behavioral issues whether we realize it or not. The need for love is so powerful that one will do almost anything to get it. Even if they don't realize it's actually love that they are craving.

There are many substitutes for real heart satisfying love that only comes from God. Many "love substitutes" act as temptations, looking to take true loves place. Without God's love, however, the heart is in a constant state of restlessness, searching like a lost child does for their parent. This frantic heart, untamed by God's love, will be consumed by its need for satisfaction.

A heart without God's love tries to survive by embarking on endless quests to find love, because like a body dying of thirst isn't concerned with anything beyond water, a heart without God's love is only concerned with making the "love lack" feeling go away. Many unhealthy and even diabolical behaviors are rooted in this lack of God's love.

In our text Paul is praying for the church, that they would know this love in an ever increasing and deeper way. What a great prayer, going right to the oxygen of the Christian life. Notice that he wants them to know something that is passed knowledge. How can that be? Perhaps this is why so many can't find it, yet need it.

This love, God's love, cannot be reduced to intellectual understanding, it cannot be attained by reason and it cannot be contained by formulas. Without coming to God, Who is the fountain of this love, there can be no calming of our hearts. Resisting God is refusing the deepest need of the human heart, love.

· · ·

THE LESSON here is to know that God's love is beyond human comprehension and can only be given, as a gift of God's grace, and that can only come by being in a right relationship with Him. When you come to Christ you are coming to the fountain of love, which tames the heart. It takes humility to receive this gift, but you are most blessed of all when you do. God's love is the hearts medicine.

Isaiah 45:11 48:11, Ephesians 4:1 16,
Psalm 68:19 35, Proverbs 24:3 4

RELATIONAL WARFARE

//

EPHESIANS 4:3

"Endeavoring to keep the unity of the Spirit in the bond of peace."

Relationships take work. Satan attacks them because he hates relationships. God has made us relational, like He is, and we are made in His image. However, since the fall, relationships have become a battlefield.

Sin has made us selfish and self-serving, which are contrary to what it takes to have a healthy relationship. Whatever the relationship may be, our quality of life is greatly affected by the health of our relationships.

We can't control how the other side of our relationships may respond to us, but we can control our own role in them. If we approach our relationships Biblically, we can have peace and freedom, regardless of the response we get.

In our text we see the way to win in relational warfare. The battle for healthy relationships is really a spiritual issue. When God redeemed us at the cross, He also gave us the potential to have redeemed relationships. It all comes down to the working of the Spirit in our lives and how that carries out into how we relate to others.

So Paul here, after laying the groundwork for all God has done for us, and all He has given us and blessed us with, and all the Spiritual power and grace, now says to endeavor, or make an effort to, "keep the unity of the Spirit and the bond of peace."

This is obviously important, as our Christianity is often played out in the battlefield of our relationships. So we are to unleash all the power of the Holy Spirit in our relationships in order for there to be unity, bond and peace. We can also say that breakdowns in relationships occur when the flesh, not the Spirit, is in control.

When the Spirit controls two people, in any type of relationship, there will be harmony, connection, bonding and peace. There will be a willingness to yield and submit to one another. The Spirit won't fail in a relationship, but the flesh always will.

. . .

THE LESSON here is to know that you have the power to win the relational wars you face through Christ. When you submit to Him, you will love others with His love. You will be others-centered instead of self-centered. You will have care and compassion and not jealousy and bitterness.

RELATIONSHIP BUILDERS

EPHESIANS 4:32

"And be kind to one another, tenderhearted, forgiving one another, even as God in Christ forgave you."

There are behaviors in relationships that build health into them, things that are building blocks to strong relationships, bringing strength and stability. Without them, a relationship will be weak and eventually break down. Healthy relationships have them, unhealthy relationships don't.

There are many, but in our text we have three vital ones. First of all, we see kindness. We are told here to be kind, so it's something we have to do. It will take intention, determination and focus. This is something that may not be natural for us, but something necessary for relational survival. Kindness is something we CAN do, with God's help, and a good first step to focus on.

The next is tenderhearted. This is keeping "softness" towards one another. Relationships are like a dump truck that can accumulate dirt and weigh us down. When we keep accumulating unwanted things from the other person in a relationship, we will put up walls and barriers so as to protect ourselves from more accumulation.

The key is to make sure there is no dirt accumulating. Keep your heart clean from negative clutter by loving, open, direct communication, praying with and for one another and surrendering hurts and agitations to the Lord.

While it may be healthy to have boundaries with some people, be watchful of a hardened heart that refuses to give the love, honor and respect that Christ would give. Watch the tendency to gossip, lash out and/or entertain hateful or angry thoughts.

The last one is to forgive. Maybe the hardest because it implies that there has been a wrong committed against us. Un-forgiveness is a relationship killer and a Holy Spirit quencher. It robs us of so much and brings one into a place that the devil would like us to stay. Since our whole salvation is based on Christ's forgiveness, we cannot ever withhold forgiveness from those who wrong us.

. . .

THE LESSON here is to make sure your attitude is right in what you are putting into your relationships. It will take an intense dependence upon God's help, but He will give you the grace to be what He has called you to be in your relationships.

Make sure your relationship with Christ is being played out in your relationships with others.

Isaiah 51:1 53:12, Ephesians 5:1 33,
Psalm 69:19 36, Proverbs 24:7

LIGHTS IN THE DARKNESS

EPHESIANS 5:11

"And have no fellowship with the unfruitful works of darkness, but rather expose them."

As Christians we are lights in the darkness. The world is a place of darkness that Jesus, the Light of the world has rescued us. There is now a responsibility for those of the light, and that is to shine brightly in this dark world so people will see the hope of Jesus in us and through us.

What is our relationship with the world to be as lights? How are we to interact with the conflicting world of darkness? In our text we see that we are not to have "fellowship" with it. In other words, we are not to be connected to it in a way that we would be part of it. We are not to join in the darkness and the works of darkness, which produces darkness. As "light shiners" we are to be "in" the world brightening it up, not "in" the world contributing to the darkness. We are also called to be involved and engaged in the world not isolated and hidden. This is the tension that exists for Christians that are in the world. Understanding that we are here to shine helps us to have the right perspective as to our role as "ambassadors" of Jesus Christ.

We are no longer one of its own but we are now children of the light. Our lives should show a difference in what we believe and Whom we serve. Good should be the fruit that comes from us, the good of God that shines a path to Him.

• • •

THE LESSON here is to stay disconnected to the darkness. To cut the umbilical cord to the world and stop feeding on it's bad food. To feed on the goodness of the Lord and His faithfulness, that you may light a path to Jesus Christ for others.

Isaiah 54:1 57:14, Ephesians 6:1 24,
Psalm 70:1 5, Proverbs 24:8

THE REAL BATTLE

//

EPHESIANS 6:12

> *"For we do not wrestle against flesh and blood, but against principalities, against powers, against the rulers of the darkness of this age, against spiritual hosts of wickedness in the heavenly places."*

Our real battle is invisible, in the spiritual realm. We experience the effects of it in the physical realm, through our senses, but what we experience physically is merely a symptom of the real cause.

The symptoms of evil are seen and felt in our world as hate, corruption, sexual immorality, anger, hostility, envy and the like. Things like terrible addictions to terrible things, sex trafficking, children abused, domestic violence, marital strife, family problems, kidnappings, gangs, cartels, corrupt government systems, injustices and things make us feel outraged because we know it's not right, proving that we all have an innate sense of right and wrong which comes from God and being made in His image.

Frustrations come when we feel helpless to do anything about it. What we are really longing for is a world without evil. The good news is, one day there will be such a world and that day is when Jesus comes back to rule and reign on earth once again in what is called The Millennial Kingdom. This is where Satan and his evil demonic workers will be bound up and unable to operate. During this thousand-year period Jesus and His followers will enjoy a perfect world on earth, ruling and reigning in righteousness. This is why is vital to be a follower of Jesus Christ.

In the mean time, Satan and his evil workers are wreaking havoc on this world and they are what is behind all the evil we see. This is why there really aren't any earthy solutions to evil and why evil will never be eradicated on earth until Christ comes. However, there are great weapons for the Christian in dealing with this darkness.

Until the day comes when evil is gone, we fight against evil with "spiritual weapons". Satan has no answer for the power of God. It's really not even a fair fight. That's why Satan tries to get us to fight him in the flesh and not in the Spirit, because he can beat us, but he can't beat God. So when evil knocks on our door, remember what is behind what is seen. Satan and his forces are the real cause behind it all.

. . .

THE LESSON here is know what you are really fighting, spiritual forces of darkness. Never fight these forces with your own weapons, your own strength or your own power, but fight with the weapons God provides which always win. Cover yourself with the spiritual weapons of truth, faith, righteousness, the gospel, your salvation, and the word of God, and above all that prayer. You will never lose when you fight against the real enemy with unbeatable weapons.

Isaiah 57:15 59:21, Philippians 1:1 26,
Psalm 71:1 24, Proverbs 24:9 10

TO LIVE IS CHRIST

PHILIPPIANS 1:21A

"For to me, to live is Christ."

What is life all about? Many spend their lives trying to figure it out. Struggling through the issues of life without a compass to direct us is like building a building without a blueprint. To "just wing it" so to speak is to be tossed like a ship on the sea without power. Eventually you will hit the rocks or sink.

Experimenting with different ideas on "why I am here" will take us to various ports, all empty of meaning and value. Our hearts will feel the effects of life centered on "self" or other attempts to gratify these longings. We all have them, for God has "put eternity in our hearts" (Ecclesiastes 3:11). We are wired for an eternal connection, we are made for more.

Paul the Apostle was one who looked to "religion" to fulfill this internal desire, doing whatever he could in his "religion" to find life's meaning. The more "religion" he had the more empty he became, fueling the mistaken desire for more "religion". That all changed the day he met Jesus (Acts 9).

All of life is to know Jesus and live for Him. Until that day, we will feel like fish out of water. When we can make this statement, "for me, to live is Christ," we have come into harmony with God's purpose. Our hearts are connected to God and to eternity. Life makes sense, has purpose and is heading somewhere amazing.

. . .

THE LESSON here is to make a clear and definite decision about your life. Be clear about what you live for and what your life is about. Once you do, then life is simple. It is then merely a life of empowered obedience to God, with fruitful labor for the King of Kings, the Author and Finisher of your faith. Live for Christ, it's the only life that counts.

OTHERS

//

PHILIPPIANS 2:3-4

> *"Let nothing be done through selfish ambition or conceit, but in lowliness of mind let each esteem others better than himself. Let each of you look out not only for his own interests, but also for the interests of others."*

The effects of God's work in the human heart are meant to reach beyond our heart, overflowing to others. When God is at work in us, we must also allow Him to work through us. When the transforming work of God is at work inside of us it will also change the way we think. We will have the "mind of Christ" (Philippians 2:5) by cooperating with God's work of transformation.

How does "the mind of Christ" think? Christ thinks that humility is good and as we see in our text, living unselfishly, without a self-centered outlook is divine. Christ thinks that real strength is the ability to use strength for greater purposes than mere self-interest, which will have greater effects that reach outside of us. When we look beyond self to others with the eyes of Jesus, we touch the world for eternity.

Christ thinks it's much greater to think of others as better than self. A Christ-like mind is not competing with others in order to feel superior or better than them, but helps others to be the best they can be, especially when it comes to the gospel and knowing Christ.

Lives surrendered to God will also be a lives surrendered to others. The highest life is when we are low for others. Not being over others but being under and lifting them up. It takes great strength to do this, a strength that comes from God and not us.

· · ·

THE LESSON here is to see the importance of the way you see others. That you would truly value others the way Christ does and to love them and serve them unconditionally. The life of a Christian is about God and then others. When your priorities are in the right place you will be too.

OCTOBER 1

Isaiah 62:6 65:25, Philippians 2:19 3:4,
Psalm 73:1 28, Proverbs 24:13 14

FORGIVEN

ISAIAH 64:6

> *"But we are all like an unclean thing, and all our righteousness are like filthy rags; We all fade as a leaf, and our iniquities, like the wind, have taken us away."*

How good can a person be? Can they be good enough to be accepted by the Lord? Can they be more good than bad? How good is good enough? These are questions we ask and have to come to conclusions about.

Typically, we make assumptions about these things. We come up with some sort of standard of what is good and what is bad. Even lifelong criminals have their own standards of acceptable behavior and we are all good about justifying our behavior.

The Bible gives us God's standard. He says in our text that we are all "like and unclean thing." Every one of us is a sinner. Degrees of sinfulness doesn't excuse sin. One may have more sin than another, but regardless of that there is still sin, which makes one unclean by God's standards.

Whether there is a little stain on your shirt or a big stain, the shirt is still stained. That's why the verse goes on to say, "all our righteousness is like filthy rags," meaning all our efforts to be good only make us dirtier. That's because a sinner can't remove his own sin. It takes a sinless One to do so. Trying to get rid of our own sin is life-rubbing mud and a stained shirt and hoping the stain will go away.

When we recognize our sinful condition and inability to do anything about it, we can see our great need for Jesus' forgiveness. Take heart, we have all sinned. What makes a "Christian" a "Christian" is that they are forgiven. Only by God's grace have we been set free.

. . .

THE LESSON here is to rejoice in God's grace. Be careful of trying to earn God's forgiveness or obtain righteousness by your own merit. Instead, receive God's forgiveness and stand in His Righteousness. His mercy will surround you and your sins are no more. Your new name is "forgiven," walk in that!

LIVING OUT THE CROSS

PHILIPPIANS 3:18-19

"For many walk, of whom I have told you often, and now tell you even weeping, that they are the enemies of the cross of Christ: whose end is destruction, whose god is their belly, and whose glory is in their shame—who set their mind on earthly things."

What is an enemy of the cross? Without the cross there is no Christianity, no salvation and no forgiveness of sins. The cross is where Jesus made the ultimate sacrifice demonstrating the ultimate love offering, the ultimate gift. The cross is where He died, so we can live, where He suffered, so we could be comforted and where He was bound so we could be free.

It's no wonder that the cross is such a point of stumbling for those who reject God. At the cross is where the truth of our heart's convictions reside. Like Jesus, the cross is also where we die to self so we can live for God. Jesus said that, "If anyone desires to come after Me let Him deny himself, take up his cross and follow me" (Matthew 16:24).

To follow Jesus is to deny self. One cannot follow Jesus and self at the same time because they are mutually exclusive. At the heart of all our problems is our propensity toward self and selfishness. One who denies denying themselves is denying the cross and following Jesus, thinking no further than "setting their mind on earthly things."

· · ·

THE LESSON here is to walk out the cross in your daily life. As a Christian, you live for God and not self. You live for the eternal and not the temporal. You live for heaven and not earth. The cross is your path, heaven is your home and God is your reward. Take up your cross.

Jeremiah 1:1 2:30, Philippians 4:1 23,
Psalm 75:1 10, Proverbs 24:17:20

THE CURE FOR ANXIETY

///

PHILIPPIANS 4:6-7

> *"Be anxious for nothing, but in everything by prayer and supplication, with thanksgiving, let your requests be made known to God; and the peace of God, which surpasses all understanding, will guard your hearts and minds through Christ Jesus."*

This text gives the Christian's cure for anxiety that really works. We have the power of God residing in us to do all things through Him that He has made provision for us to do. Being free of anxiety is one of those things. Unleash the power to live stress free and enjoy God's goodness. Here's how:

1. Be anxious for nothing – this is a command, so this is what we are called to do. Anxiousness is not a gift of the Spirit but a work of the flesh that is not trusting God. First step is to make a decision that being anxious is not God's plan and that you will not accept it as okay, but will battle it Biblically with the enabling given by God. He has given you the grace to not be anxious. When God commands, He also provides.

2. Pray – once you refuse anxiousness, then you go to God in prayer. This connects you with the source of all power. God wants you to come to Him, and when you do you are redirecting responsibility for your life and whatever you are going through. You are asking for help from the One who can and will.

3. Give Thanks – this is a huge key in curing stress. When you pray, you are not just saying a whole bunch of things over and over again thinking that the more you do then eventually feel better. Instead, here in this text, we see that when we are stressed we bring our specific issue or issues to God in prayer, knowing that He can and will help. When you give thanks you are saying that you have faith, that God will do what's best and that you are resting in the fact that He will, no matter what happens. This is unconditional faith, trusting God's will, God's way in God's time. Giving thanks says now you are done with the issue or issues because they are going to be dealt with by God in the best way. Giving thanks is like the period on the end of a sentence. It says it's finished. Faith trusts God, shifts responsibility to Him and leads to giving Him thanks.

4. Let your requests be made known to God – whatever it is that bothers you or stresses you out, just tell God knowing He hears, cares and responds.

5. Peace of God – when we do 1-4, the result it God's supernatural peace. It is not a natural or man-made peace. It is divine and can only be had by trusting God. It goes beyond the human realm as it "surpasses understanding." It guards the two most important places Christian's need peace, their hearts and minds. The two battlefields where peace is contended.

. . .

THE LESSON here is to see God's provision for you when it comes to anxiety and apply His prescription. If you still have anxiety then the wrong person is carrying the load. Give it to God, be free, find rest for your heart and mind and let God do the worrying. After all, it's not your problem, it's His now.

WHO IS JESUS?

///

COLOSSIANS 1:15-18

> *"He is the image of the invisible God, the firstborn over all creation. For by Him all things were created that are in heaven and that are on earth, visible and invisible, whether thrones or dominions or principalities or powers. All things were created through Him and for Him. And He is before all things, and in Him all things consist. And He is the head of the body, the church, who is the beginning, the firstborn from the dead, that in all things He may have the preeminence."*

The correct identification of Jesus is vital. He is not just a good teacher, a good person or a religious figure comparable to other religious figures. What we think about who Jesus is will actually determine our eternal destiny. So who is Jesus?

Jesus is:

1. The image of the invisible God—He is the visible incarnation of the invisible God. In other words, Jesus is God that came in the flesh.

2. Firstborn over all creation—As Jesus came into the world, born of a virgin, placed in her womb by the Holy Spirit, He then is the "firstborn" in priority. His miraculous birth into His own physical creation showed His place over it.

3. Creator of all things—Jesus was not created. He is eternal, the Alpha and Omega, the Beginning and the End. He is the great "I Am." Jesus always existed so there was never a time when He didn't. He is eternally God, second member of the Holy Trinity.

4. Before all things—As Creator, Jesus wasn't created. Therefore he was before "all" things. There was nothing that came before Jesus. Jesus came before "all."

5. Sustainer—Jesus holds everything together. Only God can hold the very biggest to the very smallest of all creation together. Without His sustaining power nothing could exist. If He can hold the universe together He can hold us together.

6. Head of the Church—The church is simply all believers in Jesus Christ worldwide. The church became a church through faith in Jesus Christ and what He did on the cross, dying for our sins. He is the Head, in control, empowering it,

guarding it and continuing it. The church is not controlled by man but by God. We just follow Him.

7. The beginning—Since Jesus is the Creator of all things and before all things, He is the beginning. As Genesis one says, "in the beginning, God." Jesus was in the Beginning, He is God, always was God and will forever be God.

8. Firstborn from the dead—Jesus wasn't the first to be raised from the dead, but He was the first of many who would be resurrected in the newness of life after Him. Since He was eternally God and sinless, He qualified to die as a sacrifice for our sins. When He rose from the dead, He conquered sin and paved the way for those who would put their faith in Him to also be forgiven and rise with Him as born again people with the indwelling of the Holy Spirit. No longer dead in sin, believers are new creations in Christ who will live with Jesus forever.

9. Preeminent—This means that Jesus is number one. He ranks above all else. Without Him we are nothing, with Him we are everything. Jesus is above all and every knee shall bow and every tongue confess that Jesus Christ is Lord.

· · ·

THE LESSON here is to see Jesus correctly and to respond accordingly. The only proper response is to surrender to Him, put your faith in Him, serve Him and worship Him with your life. He is absolutely amazing and wonderful. Big enough to hold the universe in His hands, and caring enough to hold your tears in a bottle.

OCTOBER 5

Jeremiah 4:19 6:15, Colossians 1:18 2:7,
Psalm 77:1 20, Proverbs 24:23 25

CALLING IT WHAT IT IS

///

PROVERBS 24:23-25

> *"These things also belong to the wise: It is not good to show partiality in judgment. He who says to the wicked, 'You are righteous,' Him the people will curse; Nations will abhor him. But those who rebuke the wicked will have delight, And a good blessing will come upon them."*

Wise people are those who are able to apply Biblical knowledge to practical situations. One of the places that can be difficult is deciphering between good and evil. In this day and age, those lines are becoming increasingly blurred.

In our text we see that part of the problem with determining good from evil is our tendency toward partiality, or favoritism. In other words, we have some things that don't seem as bad as other things because we have compromised with them. Some things of evil may have crept up into our hearts to where we don't see them for what they are.

Another problem we may have with seeing good and evil for what they are is that we may put personal experience with someone or something over what the truth in God's Word declares. We may have blurred vision because were using the wrong lens of experience over the correct lens of scripture.

· · ·

THE LESSON here is to call things as they are based on truth. Be careful about calling the wicked righteous for in the last days everything will be backwards. Good will be called evil and evil good. Let scripture be your guide and don't try and guide the scriptures to your pre-determined blurry point of view. Call a spade a spade, call evil, evil and good, good. Then, as our scripture says, you will have delight.

RELIGIOUS PHONIES

COLOSSIANS 2:8

> *"Beware lest anyone cheat you through philosophy and empty deceit, according to the tradition of men, according to the basic principles of the world, and not according to Christ."*

Fraud is everywhere, especially when it comes to religion. There are many "rip offs" and "counterfeits" to the real thing. Satan is a liar and a thief, looking to "steal, kill and destroy" (John 10:10). He desperately wants to take what Christ has given.

We are warned here, to "beware" of people that want to "cheat you." There will be those who try and alter our understanding of our relationship with Christ. These attacks center around the "additions" to the free grace of Christ. They will say Christ isn't enough and that there is more to be had. By doing so, they take away from grace.

They will use "philosophy" to appeal to men's intellect. They will propose "deeper thoughts," "higher insights" developed by "greater understanding." They will write books and hold seminars in appealing wrappings. It will all be deceit, empty contents of no real value, other that to exalt themselves and their followers over Christ and His Word.

Their ideas will be more in line with "traditions of men" which put more worth on what man does versus what Christ did. They will be disguised in religious clothing, which appeals to those who want to "feel" they are doing something to contribute to their salvation by earning it or deserving it, which is all "self-righteousness," an abomination to God and an affront to Jesus' sacrificial death on the cross.

Their teachings will be more in line with the way the world sees things and does things rather than the way God sees things and does things. Worldly success, self glory, pleasure and self-centeredness will be emphasized over sacrifice, suffering and God's will. These greed driven deceivers will do their "fleecing" in the name of God using "worldly principles" so those who want to feel better about denying the cross will be able to.

· · ·

THE LESSON here is to follow Christ and not man. Follow Him and not man made things, even religion. Walk by faith, seek intimacy knowing that if you have Jesus you have everything. Jesus paid it all, He is all you need, He is sufficient and you are complete in Him. Anything more than Jesus is less, for Jesus is all.

OCTOBER 7

Jeremiah 8:8 9:26, Colossians 3:1 17,
Psalm 78:32 55, Proverbs 24:27

GLORYING IN GOD

//

JEREMIAH 9:23-24

> *"'Let not the wise man glory in his wisdom, let not the mighty man glory in his might, nor let the rich man glory in his riches; But let him who glories glory in this, that he understands and knows Me, that I am the Lord, exercising lovingkindness, judgment, and righteousness in the earth. 'For in these I delight', says the Lord."*

This is a warning to the wise, strong and rich. Three characteristics of people that make humility very difficult. Those with what the world so values and even worships are viewed as God-like beings. To accept these traits as something other than a gift can leave these "super-humans" incorrectly feeling God is unnecessary, which makes them the least fortunate of all.

Whatever interferes with understanding and knowing God is not a blessing but a curse. No talent, intelligence, good looks, fortune or fame is anything without the One who bestows such things. The worst off, with God is the best off. Whenever we see ourselves by what we have or do, we are now slaves to those things which will ultimately fade away. It's sad to miss God and all eternity by glorying in the gift and not the gift giver.

The greatest riches are found in Christ and His attributes. There is no greater glory than to glory in the Lord, Who is worthy of all praise. When we glory in Him we will enjoy everything else. When we glory in Him we enjoy His lovingkindness, which is far better than our wisdom. When we glory in Him we glory in His judgment, which is far better than our might. And when we glory in Him we glory His righteousness, which is far better than our riches.

· · ·

THE LESSON here is to glory in the Lord Himself and not the stuff. Everything we have is a gift from God, enjoy it as you bless and praise God for it. Never trade the temporal for the eternal and never live for that which will never last. Live for Christ, delight in Him, and all else will fall into place.

SERVING GOD AND NOT MAN

//

COLOSSIANS 3:23-24

"And whatever you do, do it heartily, as to the Lord and not to men, know-
ing that from the Lord you will receive the reward of the inheritance; for
you serve the Lord Christ."

Here is a great thought, "whatever you do can be an opportunity for a reward."
We see this in the text. Sometimes it's hard to get motivated. We lose heart, we
lose hope and we lose interest. When we do, it's because our motivation is too
low and the reward is not great enough.

Nearsightedness is a trap all Christians can fall into. Failing to see the big picture
of all God is doing. Sometimes we can't, but we know by faith God is working
bigger things than just "the thing" we see.

When our motive is self, glory, riches or whatever it is that has an ending point,
is when the cost outweighs the benefit. Thats when motivation stops. We need a
higher motivation that has no stopping point and one where it's cost can never
outweigh its benefit.

Doing things for others is a good motivation, higher than self. Yet this also has
a cap to it. In our text we see a motivation that is eternal and endless, and that
is doing whatever we do for the Lord. Every task, every endeavor, every job etc.
can be done with ALL our heart when we do it for the Lord.

It's not so much about what we do, it's about WHO we do it for. We have a
tendency of gaging the work by what we consider important. This gives us levels, degrees or measurements that we self impose our own significance toward.
Some big, some small, some important, some not. This can determine our level
of effort and motivation.

However, doing something for the Lord is different. We can put our whole self
into whatever it is, and God empowers us to do it well, for His glory. Don't think
about the task, think about serving the Lord in it. Cut out the middleman, so
to speak, and remember God is the real boss. Do right by others by doing right
by Him.

There is a "reward" for EVERYTHING we do for The Lord. No matter what it is we are doing, no matter the results, win or lose, success or failure, when we do it unto the Lord we will never go wrong. He will reward us in Spiritual treasures that reach beyond the greatest worldly riches on into eternity. It the best benefit package there is.

. . .

THE LESSON here is to start right away doing everything for the Lord and not to man. You will find great delight, great satisfaction, great empowering and great joy in serving Him. You will be able to withstand great trials, mistreatment and lack of appreciation. You will be rich in Christ and His love, and you will discover great riches in heaven as well.

THE POWER OF THE GOSPEL

///

1 THESSALONIANS 1:5

> *"For our gospel did not come to you in word only, but also in power, and in the Holy Spirit and in much assurance, as you know what kind of men we were among you for your sake."*

The gospel is the "good news" that God came into world, died on the cross for our sin, rose again from the dead and that all who put their faith in Him will be forgiven of their sin and go to heaven. They will be filled with the Holy Spirit and given full access to God. They will be His children and He will be their God. It's the best news ever.

This gospel message is to be taken into all the world to be preached so men can be saved. The gospel is the hope of the world and is what every man and woman is looking for and needs. The apostle Paul here was ambitious about the gospel. He lived to share it and preach it with whatever opportunity God provided. He prayed and asked for prayer that God would open doors of opportunity.

As we see in our text here, Paul knew that it wasn't skill, technique, salesmanship or pressure that would draw people to receive the gospel. That's why he had so much confidence and excitement to share. He knew the opportunity to share the gospel would come with powerful and supernatural help and it wasn't dependent upon him.

He mentions three things that accompany the gospel. First is "power." The words of the gospel are laced with God's dynamite. They will affect the human heart and soul like nothing else. They will touch a person where no human can touch. Inside of those who hear the message, there is a dramatic moving or stirring because of this power. We have this confidence when we share.

The second is the "Holy Spirit. The third member of the Trinity comes with the gospel bearing witness to the truth, drawing hearts to Christ and convicting of sin. He is like a special agent that supernaturally facilitates the bringing together of a soul with the truth. He is working the gospel into the heart.

The third thing is assurance. The gospel, exploding with power, facilitated and confirmed by the Holy Spirit, tells the recipient and the proclaimer, that they can have confidence that the gospel works. Not that everyone will receive it into their hearts for salvation, but that it will work deeply. In other words, it will have an effect. God will do everything to bring people to salvation, except violate their free will. Even rejecting the gospel is an effective work because no man will have an excuse and say they never heard or were given the opportunity.

. . .

THE LESSON here is to have confidence to share the gospel. Make it a point of emphasis, a place of prayer and part of life. Pray for open doors, proceed through them and share the way of eternal life. Share it lovingly, compassionately and liberally. Opportunities are all around and you have the words of eternal life. Take a step of faith and pray today for the gospel to go out through your lips. You can be sure, it won't be just words, it will be accompanied by the ingredients of heaven.

GOD'S WORDS

JEREMIAH 15:16

> *"Your words were found, and I ate them, and Your word was to me the joy and rejoicing of my heart."*

God's words are living, breathing things and full of goodness. They affect the receptive, soft hearted heart. God's words change and transform in a restorative way, healing wounds with soul medicine and building strength with truth girding. God's words transcend all that is human and material, taking one to the eternal realm.

There is an attitude or approach to God's words that receives its benefit. The causal sampler won't benefit like the hungry feaster. We see in our text, Jeremiah says he "ate" them. He took them all in, integrated them with who he was. Like food, God's words became a part of him, making up the fabric of his being.

He saw God's words, in desperate and dark times, as vital to his very being. Like food, God's words sustain our spiritual life, bringing spiritual nutrients to strength. It's exactly what our souls need and without it, our souls famish.

The result of an approach to God's words, that "eats" them, is joy and rejoicing in our hearts. Nothing else can do this like God's words. Nothing can reach the depth of our being and nothing can incite joy filled passion like God's words.

· · ·

THE LESSON here is the importance of God's words in your life. Give yourself fully to it. Devour all you can. Be a man or woman of the Word. Eat it, rejoice in it, and celebrate it. Walk it out by faith, and by faith believe in it. May God's words become your life.

Jeremiah 16:16 18:23, 1 Thessalonians 4:1 5:3,
Psalm 81:1 16, Proverbs 25:6 8

TRUST AND HOPE

JEREMIAH 17:7-8

> *"Blessed is the man who trusts in the Lord, And whose hope is the Lord. For he shall be like a tree planted by the waters, Which spreads out its roots by the river, And will not fear when heat comes; But its leaf will be green, And will not be anxious in the year of drought. Nor will cease from yielding fruit."*

There are not many certainties in life. In fact, things are very fragile. So much is out of our control that one slight change can completely alter our whole life. Things like the weather, health, the stock market, jobs, the economy or other people's poor decisions all can affect us yet we have no control over them.

Jeremiah was a prophet in difficult days for the nation of Israel. There was nothing they could look at that would make them feel safe, secure and protected. In the midst of all that, this statement emerges, a certainty out of the chaos.

He says "blessed" or "happy" is the man. It would be difficult to find much to be happy about in their situation. However, looking beyond their situation to God would change everything. God is unchanging, all-powerful and all knowing. He is in control and nothing is out of His control. Coming back to Him brings peace.

When we come back to God we put "trust" and "hope" in Him. It's not just mentally acknowledging God, it is saying that I am believing in Him, His plan, His character and His way. It's saying that I am not looking or trusting in the world which changes but in God who doesn't.

The effects of putting our trust and hope in Jesus is that we will flourish, even though the conditions are poor. It means we will always have God as our supply and that we will be fresh and thriving. It means we will grow and become stronger, even though everything may be against us. It means we will not fear, even though there are scary things we are dealing with. It means we will have peace, even though things may be bumpy. It means we will thrive, even though everything else is barely surviving.

· · ·

THE LESSON here is to put your full trust and hope in God. When you do, you won't have to worry or fear because God will be your side. If God is for you, nothing can be against you (Romans 8:31). He will never fail you and will never leave you or forsake you. Nothing is too hard for God and nothing is out of His control. All it takes is trust and hope, and you will be happy and secure.

OCTOBER 12

Jeremiah 19:1 21:14, 1 Thessalonians 5:4 28,
Psalm 82:1 8, Proverbs 25:9 10

WE KNOW

///////////////////////////////////////

1 THESSALONIANS 5:4

> *"But you, brethren, are not in darkness, so that this Day should overtake you as a thief."*

A Christian is different from a non-Christian in many ways. One of those ways is that a Christian knows the end from the beginning (Isaiah 46:10). In other words, a Christian knows what is going to happen on earth. A Christian knows why the events of the world happen the way they do and that certain events will be signs that lead to the rapture of the church, the tribulation, the millennial kingdom and the new heavens and the new earth. These signs will increase in frequency and intensity as we get closer to the end.

It's all in the Bible, spelled out for us to know and respond accordingly. All throughout history the Bible has told what would happen, and then it did, exactly as it said. It spoke of Jesus coming to earth and His ministry in over three hundred prophecies, all fulfilled exactly.

· · ·

THE LESSON here is to be encouraged because you know what is going to happen and how it's going to happen. . Nothing is random, but all working toward an eventual new heaven and new earth. A day where there will be no more sin, struggle, hurt and pain. Be encouraged to live all out for Jesus and take as many people with you as possible. Who knows, it might be today. Are you ready?

FAITH AND LOVE

2 THESSALONIANS 1:3

> *"We are bound to thank God always for you, brethren, as it is fitting, because your faith grows exceedingly, and the love of every one of you all abounds toward each other."*

Paul is giving thanks for this group of Christians in Thessalonica. He says he feels "bound" or obligated to do so. He says it is "fitting" to do so. What would be so commendable about the Thessalonican Christians that giving thanks would be an actual duty?

"Growing faith" is an attribute that warrants "thanks." It's God working in and through a Christian, with their cooperation that puts the awesomeness of God on display. Faith is a heavenly trait that shouts there is something greater, bigger and beyond. To see faith working in a life is so different from the normal, practical, pragmatic way of thinking that one has to see faith and say, "there is something different about him/her."

When faith is growing, love will abound. When God works through faith, there will be love. Love is the test of faith. Faith opens the channel of our hearts for God's love to flow in us and through us. Love will flourish and increase. Without faith, the Love of God is stifled and all there will be is a manifestation of the flesh. There is no love like God's love, and to see it is a sight to behold. Heaven touches earth when God's love is working. It's so "other-world," one has to give God thanks.

· · ·

THE LESSON here is to see the connection between faith and love, and to see how faith results in love. You can measure your faith by your love because it takes faith to love like Jesus. When you are surrendered, letting God work through you, you will cause people to thank God. He will be glorified as people see Him shining through you. Take steps of faith, obeying the Lord, love others and watch "God things" grow.

LOVE THE TRUTH OR DIE IN DECEPTION

2 THESSALONIANS 2:9-10

"The coming of the lawless one is according to the working of Satan, with all power, signs, and lying wonders, and with all unrighteous deception among those who perish, because they did not receive the love of the truth, that they might be saved."

What is the condition of a heart that will fall prey to Satan? In our text we find this one all important answer, that it is one who "did not receive the love of the truth." There it is, when the truth would set them free, secure their hearts and protect them from Satan's deception, they did not receive it.

Without the truth in Jesus, a void is left for all other "untruths" to fill. It's natural for this to happen without God's truth. The heart searches for something to fill the emptiness. This person is a sitting duck for satanic deception. No one will be able to prevent themselves from following after Satan's first man, the Antichrist, without the truth.

Our text tells us the Antichrist is coming, that's a fact. He will come to work, rolling up his sleeves as an agent of Satan. In essence, he will be Satan in the flesh, working against God's plan to make captives of all he can.

His tool chest will include four tools. The first is power. Satan will have power that is greater than man's power. It will be supernatural and no one will be able to overcome him on their own. His power will be activated in the human realm and mankind will be mesmerized.

Not only will he have power, he will use signs. This means that Satan can work his power in the human domain so that people think he is God. It will be hard to deny these signs, as people will think that only God could do what Satan will do. It's important to remember that supernatural signs, in and of themselves, do not prove its origin is from God. We are told to "test the spirits" (1 John 4:1).

He will also use "lying wonders." People will be astonished at the apparent miracles and supernatural occurrences. Yes, the Satan can do this. There are things happening now in the spiritual realm that are not of the Lord but of Satan, attracting people to himself with powerful supernatural manifestations. The problem is, they will be lies that are difficult to detect for those who reject truth.

The final tool we see here is "unrighteous deception." This is where we see moral integrity, which is at the heart of God's holiness, attacked and good will be called evil and evil will be called good (Isaiah 5:20). Moral compromise, and even a complete denial of moral good, will degrade the heart of men like a backed up sewer. All the while, they will be deceived into thinking their immorality is good while they are being destroyed.

. . .

THE LESSON here is to see how vital the truth is. To stand on it, not compromise with it, and share it with those who don't have it. Hold truth up, champion it and let it be your light of life. Ultimately, love the truth. Don't be casual with it but embrace it with all your heart. When you do, it will save you, and many others that God puts in your path.

OCTOBER 15

Jeremiah 26:1 27:22, 2 Thessalonians 3:1 18,
Psalm 85:1 18, Proverbs 25:16

LIVING FOR A MISSION

2 THESSALONIANS 3:1-2

> *"Finally, brethren, pray for us, that the word of the Lord may run swiftly and be glorified, just as it is with you, and that we may be delivered from unreasonable and wicked men; for not all have faith."*

Paul was a man on a mission. His prayer request here reflects his deep desire to make disciples for Jesus Christ. Notice, of all the things he could have asked the Christians at Thessalonica to pray for, his request centers around that which he would need God to do, in order for his calling to be fulfilled. He knew prayer would do it, and without prayer he was lost.

The first thing we have to ask ourselves is "are we on a mission?" Do we see our lives the way Paul did or the way Jesus did when He said, "I must be about my Father's business" (Luke 2:49)? Do we have a passion for the lost? Are we ambitious for the gospel? For Paul, it was all consuming, as it was for Jesus. They were here on earth to serve the Lord in their calling, and they were focused and disciplined in that endeavor.

A major part of our battle is just figuring that out. Realizing that we are to live as missionaries on a mission. As Paul said in Philippians 1:21, "for me to live is Christ." When we know we are here to serve God then He will direct us into our specific calling. We are to be all in, completely committed and "lay aside every weight that hinders us" (Hebrews 12:1). Our life, what we do, how we do it, will reflect our commitment to our calling. This is especially seen in our prayers.

Paul wanted prayer for the effectiveness of God's Word. He was committed to proclaiming it and teaching it. He was desperate for it to work in the lives of those to whom He proclaimed it. He wanted the Word to run, spread and hit the hearts of those who would listen, and he wanted God to be glorified through it. All work of God will be according to His Word, as "faith comes by hearing, and hearing by the Word of God" (Romans 10:17). He knew prayer was the key to the Word's success and he pleaded for it.

He also prayed to be "delivered from unreasonable men." Paul knew that much opposition would come to steal the seed of God's Word away. He needed prayer to break through the opposition. The stakes were high and prayer would win the day. Every good work of God comes with great opposition.

. . .

THE LESSON here is to live as a missionary, fully committed to God's work. Pray and ask for prayer, that your calling will be fulfilled. Make sure your life is free from ambitions for comfort, glory, fame and riches. Simply dedicate yourself to God and His work, for this life will resonate into eternity. "Only one life, soon to pass, only what's done for Christ will last." (Jim Elliot)

THE SAVIOR

1 TIMOTHY 1:15

> *"This is a faithful saying and worthy of all acceptance, that Christ Jesus came into the world to save sinners, of whom I am chief."*

Why did Jesus come? To teach? Show love? Demonstrate kindness? Explain the Ten Commandments? While He did all those things, Jesus came to save sinners. He was on a mission, as the "Lamb of God" to take away the sins of the world. If there could be another way, or if man could earn his own salvation through good works, God wouldn't be very smart to come and die for those who didn't need Him to. There would be no point to His coming.

The reason we need a Savior is due to the disease of our soul called SIN. What separates us from God is SIN. What condemns us to hell is SIN. What keeps us in bondage, robs us of fulfillment, steals our joy, keeps us in darkness, quenches love and blinds us from seeing God is SIN.

What we need is our sin to be taken away. We need a medicine for our soul and panacea for our disease. This is why Jesus came. There is no other remedy, and we all have the SIN disease. We are all infected. We are all sinners plagued with SIN. "No one is righteous." (Romans 3:10) Sin has tainted all mankind, all His creation and all this world we live in. We need a Savior!

. . .

THE LESSON here is to know that Jesus came to do what no one or nothing else could, to save Sinners. Are you saved? Are you born again? Have your sins been forgiven? This is all one in the same question. Jesus paid it all and faith makes it ours. Put your faith in Jesus if you haven't already, and if you have, tell someone who hasn't that Jesus came to save sinners.

SALVATION IS A CHOICE

1 TIMOTHY 2:4

"Who desires all men to be saved and to come to the knowledge of the truth."

There can be no doubt about what God wants. He wants "all" men to be saved. He will do, and has done, everything necessary to bring men to salvation, yet not all men are saved. If God wants all men to be saved and has done all to save them, why aren't all men saved?

God will not violate mans' "free will." He gave man that mechanism so that salvation would require men to use their free will to choose God. Without free will, man would be mere robots programmed to do whatever God programmed them to do. There is no love involved when a pre-programmed subject "chooses" to be saved without a real choice. Love requires a choice and that is why God gave man free will.

I know that gets into some controversial territory in Christian theology. I also know God chooses us. So how does God choosing us and man choosing Him reconcile? I believe it's due to foreknowledge. God chooses those that He knows will choose Him, or those who will respond to the faith God has given each man, enabling them to enact upon the ability He has given to respond to His invitation to be saved.

Rejection of God then is a direct rejection, not a vague misunderstanding. It is purposeful and intentional. God, being a just God, desires all men to be saved, made the way of salvation, and gave each man the ability to choose Him. This then gives man the ultimate choice.

· · ·

THE LESSON here is to choose salvation in Jesus Christ. No one is without excuse. We all have to choose. We are either for Him or against Him (Matthew 12:30). We are either saved or not saved. Make sure you have chosen Jesus and you will have chosen to be saved. Jesus has done all, you just need to receive Him by faith. That's Jesus' desire for you, do you desire Him?

THE MYSTERY OF GODLINESS

1 TIMOTHY 3:16

> *"And without controversy great is the mystery of godliness: God was manifested in the flesh."*

Justified in the Spirit, Seen by angels, Preached among the Gentiles, Believed on in the world, Received up in glory.

From the days of old there was a mystery unfolding. Glimpses of grace that pointed to the wonders of God. Seeing the shadow, without the image, gave puzzle pieces of something to come. Jesus was the fulfillment of the mystery, the essence of the shadow and the missing piece of the puzzle. He was "the mystery of Godliness."

The "mystery of Godliness" was a person and His work, that would embody God, putting Him on display in a way which man could relate to and understand. It was the communication of God in man's language. All man could know about God would be revealed in His Son and the His work. Here is the Man and the work of the "mystery of Godliness."

1. God was manifest in the flesh—There can be no doubt about who scripture says Jesus is, God. The eternal Creator Who added flesh to His deity. He, Jesus, is God in the flesh.

2. Justified in the Spirit—Jesus was perfectly sinless. Untainted by the fallen condition that affects all creation. When Jesus was baptized, that sinless condition was declared to the world as the Holy Spirit descended upon Him (Matthew 3:16).

3. Seen by angels—Angels themselves, those heavenly beings, hovered around Jesus. They had never seen love like they had in the person and work of Jesus.

4. Preached among the Gentiles—Jesus was a Jew, the Lion of the tribe of Judah, but He was the Savior of all. His work was made now and made available to all.

5. Believed on in the world—The "mystery of godliness" was made known and required belief. Jesus was received and still is in all the world. Jesus is not regional, exclusive and isolated—He came for all the world.

6. Received up in glory—Jesus finished His work and went back to take His seat on the right hand of God the Father, where He lives to make intercession for us. He is our advocate in heaven, who paved the way to heaven for us through His life, death and resurrection.

. . .

THE LESSON here is to see God's great love for you. The "mystery of Godliness" unfolds the great love of God for man.

> *The mystery is now told,*
> *God's love is clear,*
> *Jesus loves you*
> *and forever holds you near.*

DISCOVERING GOD

JEREMIAH 33:3

"Call to Me, and I will answer you, and show you great and mighty things, which you do not know."

God is full of surprises. I believe a He loves to surprise us just like a parent loves to surprise their children on Christmas Day. Part of the romance in a relationship with God is the surprise discoveries He shows us. Many of those are discoveries about Himself, which are glimpses into all that is good.

Discovering God helps us understand everything else, because God is at the core of all there is. One will never discover the true nature of things without God, as in Him all things consist (Colossians 1:17). Knowing God then is to have wisdom regarding everything else. That's why "the fear of God is the beginning of wisdom" (Proverbs 9:10).

Being rightly related to God will rightly relate us to God's creation. Jeremiah, here in our text, was in a distressful situation, being in prison. You may find yourself bound up in some way, stuck in a dilemma, tied to a circumstance or locked in a tough spot. You may be going through a hard and difficult time. These are often the best times to discover God through His revelation, as distressing times make great listeners and passionate seekers.

. . .

THE LESSON here is to call on God when in need. Learn to go to Him first as an automatic response to trials. Seek Him and you will find "great and mighty things you did not know." Take the opportunity in your unique situation to seek Him for there is a blessing, a gift or a surprise waiting for you. You may be in a bind, but God has great things in store for you.

PLEASURE

1 TIMOTHY 5:6

"But she who lives in pleasure is dead while she lives."

Life is not meant to be lived for pleasure, nor is a life of pleasure good. Not that we can't enjoy ourselves and that we won't have pleasure, it's just that pleasure is a result or byproduct of being close to the creator of pleasure and not something to live in pursuit of. Living in pleasure will never satisfy because it only feeds the flesh, which is never satisfied (Proverbs 27:20).

Pleasure, when detached from God is at odds with God. It indulges the flesh, which is contrary to the Spirit. Satan uses pleasure to trap people in the flesh, which ultimately leads to overindulgence. Imagine if one did whatever they "felt" like doing, every impulse fulfilled without restraint. It's easy to see how pleasure can be a trap. When the flesh is our master, we will be mastered by our flesh.

Pleasure is the world's way of saying "there is no need for God." Pleasure can keep one entertained to death and thinking no further than the next mode of pleasure and ultimately missing the deeper things of life, the spiritual things. Only God can truly satisfy and fulfill. At His right hand are pleasures evermore (Psalms 16:11).

God doesn't want us to be miserable, He wants us to be Godly. The reward for Godliness is goodness, and without the painful side effects of sin. We have no need to indulge our flesh when we have life in the Spirit. Living waters will over-flow us with the love and joy of Christ. Our pleasure will be from the inside out when we live for God and not for pleasure.

· · ·

THE LESSON here is to delight in the Lord. Let Him be your satisfaction and be content in Him. No amount of pleasure can give you what only God can. It will leave you empty and hungering for more. It will leave you dead inside and perpetuate the feeling of need for more pleasure. Feed your Spirit and not your flesh, and pleasure will be yours to enjoy.

Jeremiah 37:1 38:28, 1 Timothy 6:1 21,
Psalm 89:38 52, Proverbs 25:28

GODLINESS WITH CONTENTMENT

1 TIMOTHY 6:6

> *"Now godliness with contentment is great gain."*

The richest condition of the human heart is "godliness and contentment." They are the dollars and cents of spiritual riches. A person who has them has everything and a person that doesn't, has nothing. Godliness with contentment is the greatest attainment of all.

The human heart is made for so much more than any material possession can give. It craves to be satisfied and fulfilled yet it will not be tamed by the earth's offerings. The human heart was made for God, nothing less will do. Until the heart is filled with God, it remains restless.

Find joy in giving thanks for what you have and know that what you don't, you're not supposed to have. Follow your God-given dreams and don't wait to "get somewhere" but embrace where you are. Let love flow from your heart and let your success be Christ. He will direct your paths and fulfill all that He has for you. Don't waste your time and emotional energy trying to be somebody because you already are in Christ.

. . .

THE LESSON here is to find your contentment in God and exercise Godliness. There you will enjoy life to its fullest and be free from the traps of the world that tell you "buy more, get more and have more." In Christ you have it all, so exercise yourself in Him utilizing your spiritual gifts and spiritual activities.

DEALING WITH FEAR

2 TIMOTHY 1:7

> *"For God has not given us a spirit of fear, but of power and of love and of a sound mind."*

Whenever we are afraid we can know that it is not of the Lord. As children of God, we have something different, something supernatural. This is very helpful because when we recognize this we can deal with it appropriately. Fear never has to control a Christian.

Instead of fear, our text tells us three things that we have instead. The first is power. Fear can result from the feeling of helplessness when we think we are up against something that is too strong or big for us to handle. However, the Christian has the power of God, which is never outmatched. When God is in control there is nothing too much for Him to handle.

The second is love. When we feel anger or hatred toward another we know, this is not the Lord. It's the flesh, which has been crucified with Christ (Galatians 2:20). Surrendering to God gives great love for others. The answer then to hatred and anger is to surrender to the Spirit. It starts with obedience. God's love through obedience. Take a step of faith and love those you don't. God will bless your obedience.

The last thing we see is a sound mind. God gives us the power over panic and confusion. He gives us control over our mental battles and stresses. There may be times where medication is appropriate for chemical problems, but faith will always be needed for a sound mind. Learn to take your thoughts captive to the obedience of Christ. Learn to think on true things and meditate on God's Word. God will clear things up and give you peace in your mind.

. . .

THE LESSON here is to recognize that fear is not from the Lord. Whenever you have fear, fight back with faith. Give your fears to God, rest in Him and let Him fight for you. Don't let fear hold you back from God's plan, rather, embrace life with fearless trust in the Almighty Savior.

SOLDIER LIFE

2 TIMOTHY 2:3-4

> *"You therefore must endure hardship as a good soldier of Jesus Christ. No one engaged in warfare entangles himself with the affairs of this life, that he may please him who enlisted him as a soldier."*

Every Christian faces the battle of being "in" the world but not "of" it. When the Bible speaks of the world, it is speaking of the invisible system in which we live that opposes God and pressures people to rebel against Him. The "world" then, is the temporary material place that is tainted with sin and influenced by Satan. It is the place that wants to squeeze us into its mold by conforming us to its ways (Romans 12:2)

There are no two ways about it, the Bible says that when we are friends with the world we are enemies of God, and vise versa (James 4:4). Loving the world is hating God, and loving God is hating the world. The world tries to draw us in like a magnet, using three weapons, "the lust of the flesh, the lust of the yes and the pride of life (1 John 2:16).

With the world being the invisible system against God that tries to pull us in, and Satan and his demons being the invisible forces that come and tempt us away from God, and our own flesh is the invisible part of us that wants to sin and rebel against God. Our three foes must be taken seriously and battled against continually.

In our scripture we see this warning from Paul regarding our life as Christians in this fallen world. We see four points he makes regarding how to win the battle. The first is that we "must endure hardship." Winning the battle against the world means we are going to have to weather some storms. With all that is against us, we need the power of God to overcome.

The second point Paul makes is that we have to understand who we are. We are "good soldiers of Jesus Christ." As "good soldiers" we belong to Jesus, we follow His lead, we obey Him, we know He is our boss and as "good soldiers," we know we are in a battle. As "good soldiers" we know who our enemy is. Finally, as "good soldiers" we know we are in a fight, engaged in warfare.

The third point Paul makes is that because we are in a war against the world, we are not to be involved with the things of life to where we become tangled up like flies in a spider's web. The "affairs of this life" can take our focus off The Lord making us susceptible. Neglecting what's most important, our life with Christ, is to get tangled up so that we are rendered useless for all God wants to do in our lives. If I can't get fired up, then maybe it's because I'm too tangled up.

Finally and fourthly, a "good soldier" looks to "please God" and not man. Seeing this as our aim, and counting on the Holy Spirit to empower us to do so, we can now seek God first and at all times. Nothing should interfere with our relationship with God and when it does we need to get rid of it. Our aim is to be pleasing to Him, and if it is, then we want it, if it's not, we must lose it.

. . .

THE LESSON here is to know you are in a battle and to see yourself as a "soldier" of Jesus Christ. Know there is power in Christ when you choose to live with Him and for Him. Don't get entangled in things that will hurt your walk. Cut out what is bad and put in what is good. As a soldier, fight the good fight of faith every day, God will be with you, He will fight for you and you will be blessed. Be careful of the little traps set up all around you, keep your eyes on Jesus, Soldier.

Jeremiah 44:24 47:7, 2 Timothy 2:22 3:17,
Psalm 94:1 23, Proverbs 26:6 8

THE SAFETY OF TRUTH AND THE DANGER OF COMPROMISE

2 TIMOTHY 2:24-26

> *"And a servant of the Lord must not quarrel but be gentle to all, able to teach, patient, in humility correcting those who are in opposition, if God perhaps will grant them repentance, so that they may know the truth, and that they may come to their senses and escape the snare of the devil, having been taken captive by him to do his will."*

Truth is like a highway, as long as we stay on the road we will be safe. However, when we begin to stray off onto the shoulder, we will find all kinds of potential hazards until eventually we break down or crash. There is nothing good outside of the truth, only hazards.

When our life strays from the truth, we will find ourselves in difficult circumstances. In our text, Paul gives instructions about how to help those who have strayed. We must be gentle, not argumentative, able to teach and patient. They are to be humble knowing it's not about winning the argument but helping someone back to the truth.

Jesus said the truth will set you free (John 8:32). What happens when one strays from the highway of truth, they will find Satan lurking in the darkness of the shoulder of the road. That is where he hangs out. He puts traps there to snare us.

Sin has destructive capabilities most people underestimate greatly. As it has been said, "sin will cost you more than you want to pay, take more than you're willing to give and keep you longer than you want to stay."

The traps are not on the highway of truth, only on the shoulder of compromise and lies. It's no laughing matter that once in Satan's trap, he takes his victim prisoner. The most alarming thing is that he then uses them to do his will. That's right, they will be a tool of Satan.

. . .

THE LESSON here is to never underestimate the danger of compromise. Stay in the truth. Don't harden your heart to conviction. Listen to the Holy Spirit's warnings and if you have fallen or strayed, repent and get back on the highway of truth where you will be safe.

SOUND DOCTRINE

2 TIMOTHY 4:3

"For the time will come when they will not endure sound doctrine, but according to their own desires, because they have itching ears, they will heap up for themselves teachers."

One mark or sign of the end times that points to the rapture of the church, the seven year tribulation, the second coming and the millennial reign of Christ, is the way people respond to God's Word. God's Word will be relegated to man's ways, seen as irrelevant, inaccurate and even false. When this happens, the end is near.

In these days, people won't be able to handle the truth of God's Word, which will confront their sin and way of life. People won't want to hear it and will make up all sorts of lies to appease their consciences.

They will even justify their denial of God's Word with "religious" undertones. While they won't put up with "sound doctrine," they will enjoy listening to so-called teachers who say things they want to hear. Their religion is no more than the worship of self.

No matter how popular, charismatic or skilled their teaching, don't let that be your gauge for truth. Paul said himself that it wasn't in persuasive words or flattering speech that he came, but when he spoke it was a demonstration of the power of the Holy Spirit (1 Corinthians 2:4).

Let God's Word be your guide and don't try to guide God's Word. It's not a matter of "if" a departure from sound doctrine will occur, it's a matter of when. Of course we see this now and will continue to do so at an increasing rate. Pay no attention to these deceivers and their followers, stick to the sound doctrine found in God's Word, and you will be safe and secure in a crazy world.

. . .

THE LESSON here is to stay true to God's Word. You may not like what it says, but it will always say what you need. Avoid any church or teacher who will deny the whole counsel of God in lieu of human philosophy, psychological teachings, intellectualism, secularism, materialism and the like. Sound doctrine is a sound life.

Jeremiah 49:23 50:46, Titus 1:1 16,
Psalm 97:1 98:9, Proverbs 26:13 16

THE LAZY MAN

PROVERBS 26:14

"As a door turns on its hinges, so does the lazy man on his bed."

Work is a biblical principle and good for mankind. It is good for the individual and good for society. Work is not a curse as God worked in creating the world and all that's in it. Before the curse, man was to work in the Garden of Eden. The fall came with a curse that made work a struggle so that we feel the stress of work when not done in the Spirit, unto The Lord. Thus, a battle ensues to be lazy or a worker.

Here are some keys to help you to be a worker that is happy and blessed.

1. Work is good and not bad.

2. Work for God by doing whatever you do for His glory.

3. Have a great attitude toward work knowing it's a blessing by being thankful for it.

4. Pray for strength and enabling.

5. Make a difference.

6. Keep growing and improving in your work.

7. Give God the glory.

8. Be a blessing to others by serving and not just working for yourself.

9. Balance work with rest, fun, family, faith activities.

10. Find your reward in how you work not in accolades or accomplishments. Those will take care of themselves. Every single thing you do for The Lord is rewarded by Him.

11. Put others first.

12. Overcome disappointments, frustrations, conflicts, unfair treatment, favoritism and other issues by surrendering them to the Lord, knowing God

is working out His plan, knowing He is taking care of everything and that whatever you are faced with is an instrument of your growth in The Lord. Ask God to help you and keep going in faith with perseverance.

. . .

THE LESSON here is to work, and do it for the Lord in the Spirit. Laziness is not part of God's plan for you and is an indication something is wrong. God wants you to thrive with purpose and power. Work unleashes that stored up power, glorifies God and edifies you. Don't be the Lazy man, for the lazy man never truly lives.

LESSONS OF GRACE

TITUS 2:11-12

> *"For the grace of God that brings salvation has appeared to all men, teaching us that, denying ungodliness and worldly lusts, we should live soberly, righteously, and godly in the present age."*

What does God's grace teach us? What can we learn from God coming into the world to save sinners? What can we glean from a perfect man being murdered for no cause? What does an innocent man taking our place in judgment tell us?

The actions of Jesus on the cross dying and then rising from the dead not only makes the way of salvation by becoming a sacrifice for our sins, but also tells us how we are to live. Grace, or God's unmerited and unearned favor, is not a license to sin, but freedom not to. So we see the lessons of grace from our text.

First is the importance of "denying ungodliness and worldly lusts." Considering that ungodliness and worldly lust come with the price tag of condemnation, punishment and death, which is why Jesus had to come and ransom us, living in the place where we were slaves is another form of slavery. Jesus died to free us, not so we would be slaves again.

We also see what Jesus had to endure these destructive forces of "ungodliness and worldly lusts" in order to save us. To cherish the very thing that caused Jesus to suffer and die means we have not learned God's grace. God's grace is transformational, transforming us away from "ungodliness and worldly lusts" not toward it. To deny this transformation is to deny the work of the Holy Spirit inside of us to conform us into His image.

Next, God's grace teaches us to live soberly. This means we are to keep our wits about us, understand what the world is all about and wants to extract from us. God's grace teaches us that we must see sin correctly and be aware of Satan's devices to pull us away from God. God's grace tells us that Jesus was tempted and overcame so we will be tempted and can overcome by turning to Him in the battle.

God's grace teaches us to live righteously as we see Jesus live in the way He treated others. He was selfless and concerned about others. He saw people as His priority and would be close to others, even the "undesirables" around Him that others wouldn't touch. He led by example, demonstrating love and fulfilling the commandments by loving His neighbors. Jesus lived it out.

Finally God's grace teaches us to live godly like our example Jesus. We see His commitment to the Father's will and His unshakable focus on Him. He lived "rightly" in other words, right in obedience to the Father's plan with perfect obedience. Jesus lived life before the Father, not before men. He lived to honor and glorify Him not for Himself and His own will. God's grace tells us righteousness is the best way to live and the way God has made for us to be blessed and close to Him.

· · ·

THE LESSON here is that it's all about what God's has done and frees you to do. Growing in His grace as a life long journey as you enjoy and explore God's goodness, seeing the wonder of living on the right side of grace. May you let God's grace pull you toward Him, not the world. May His grace pull you toward people and not against them. May His grace pull you into His love, which He has set upon you.

CLEAN

TITUS 3:4-5

> *"But when the kindness and the love of God our Savior toward man appeared, not by works of righteousness which we have done, but according to His mercy He saved us, through the washing of regeneration and renewing of the Holy Spirit."*

Do we need to get cleaned up before coming to God? Maybe ditch some sinful habits or lose some bad friends. Maybe we should get it all together and then God will accept us? These are typical thoughts and ideas people have regarding religion, Christianity and God.

Nothing could be further from the truth. As sinners, we can't clean ourselves up by removing our own sin, all we can do is come to God, just as we are, and let Him wash and clean us up. This is the glory of the gospel.

When Jesus came, it was due to His kindness or grace. He is kind to us, loves us and wants to help us. When Jesus came He was on a rescue mission to save us. Driven by love, He appeared to do what we couldn't do for ourselves.

Our own "works of righteousness" could not clean and save us, so Jesus did. How did He save us? Through "washing of regeneration." Our sin stained souls needed to be cleaned. This is how we are made right with God, we are made sinless, clean.

There cannot be many roads to salvation, considering what keeps us from it. Who or what else could wash clean our soul of sin and regenerate it or make it new? Nothing but the blood of Jesus, shed on the cross for our sin.

Jesus did the work of cleansing at the cross and making it possible for the Holy Spirit to come reside with us in our hearts. This new relationship gives us new desires for God, righteousness and eternal things. We are transformed from inside out and the Holy Spirit empowers us to do what we could never do.

. . .

THE LESSON here is to see that this incredible account of the work of God toward men is available to all who will come to a Him, surrender their lives to Him and allow Him to restore us to who we were meant to be. Jesus your savior, making all things new, showing love and changing hearts the way only He could do. Rejoice, for the kindness of God has come! You are forever clean!

NO WOOD, NO FIRE

//

PROVERBS 26:20

"Where there is no wood, the fire goes out; And where there is no talebearer, strife ceases."

This is great wisdom for dealing with strife or conflict, especially when it comes to gossip. Gossip is like a fire that is fueled by continual feeding of flammable material. Fire needs something to perpetuate itself. Our involvement in the strife or gossip is like putting wood into the fire.

Christians must fight this temptation of adding to the problem. Involving oneself in issues and matters that don't concern us and investing time and energy into things which lead to nothing but division, hurt and slander. Our flesh loves the fire of gossip and is attracted to it like a moth to a flame.

We must be mature enough to know when we are wood and adding to the problem. Satan loves to pit people against one another knowing that a house divided cannot stand. If you have an issue with someone, talk to THEM about it and contain the strife, don't spread it. If not, there will be a wildfire of destruction coming your way.

· · ·

THE LESSON here is, to just take away the wood when you are put in the position to be the wood. Be aware of this very important issue, be a peacemaker not peace taker; no wood, no fire. It's as simple as that.

GOD'S MERCY

LAMENTATIONS 3:22-23

> *"Through the Lord's mercies we are not consumed, Because His compassions fail not. They are new every morning; Great is Your faithfulness."*

There is a shining jewel that rises above all that is dark. No matter how bad things are, God's mercy is bigger. It stands above, triumphantly conquering all its enemies. His mercy is His character and does not change.

The Prophet Jeremiah is lamenting a terrible time in the history of Israel. Unfaithfulness and disobedience had caused a great fall from grace. God's warnings ignored, they were now captives to the Babylonians. Yet in all the horror, he remembers God's mercy.

Maybe you've gotten yourself in a tough spot? Maybe you are going through a dark time and can't see your way out? Remember God's mercy.

His mercy is never consumed or used up. It's always there and available. He has compassion for you, understanding your pain and sadness. He extends His great mercy today. He loves you. He is faithful.

· · ·

THE LESSON here is to not worry about your circumstances and let God do that. Take care your relationship with Him and all will flow from there. Repent, if needed, and open your heart to God's great mercy pressing forward into His grace. He's not done with you, He's just getting started. It's a new day, and a fresh supply of His mercies have been provided.

FORGIVEN

//

PSALM 103:12

"As far as the east is from the west, So far has He removed our transgressions from us."

What a thought! Our sin, that disease of our soul that is so deeply intertwined with our whole being, has been removed. The tumor of death which has no remedy outside of Jesus Christ our Savior. That cancer of the human life that leaves us broken and lost, has a surgeon that is none other than God Himself.

How far has He removed our sin? As a Christian, the scarlet stain of sin is as white as snow. Jesus became sin so we could be forgiven. Our sin is as far as one person that heads east eternally and another who heads west eternally.

In one fell swoop, God has put our sin completely away as if it never existed and never will. Sin is gone for good, never to be counted against us, no more price to pay, no more sacrifice to make. Sin has met its match at the cross on Calvary.

· · ·

THE LESSON here is that you might rejoice in forgiveness today. There is no condemnation to those who are in Christ Jesus (Romans 8:1). You wear a crown of forgiveness. You are free to be all God has intended you to be. You have full access to the throne of grace (Hebrews 4:16). Go in grace today, forgiven, loved and restored.

REST

//

HEBREWS 3:18-19

> *"And to whom did He swear that they would not enter His rest, but to those who did not obey? So we see that they could not enter in because of unbelief."*

To be at rest inwardly is to have peace where it counts. It's when our heart is without conflict, tranquil and able to enjoy life and fellowship with God. Inward peace can be elusive, if not impossible for those who do not know where to find it or how to have it. Our scripture speaks to this issue of rest.

There is just one singular answer to the issue of true inward peace, or rest, and that is FAITH. This means that unrest comes from the lack of faith. Of course it all starts with saving faith, which gives us peace with God. Then, we walk by faith giving us the peace of God. This means we simply order our way, our steps, by the Word of God.

Walking by faith is when we trust Him, His plan and His way, surrendering to His will, no matter how it looks. Faith tells us that all things work together for good (Romans 8:28). It says that everything happens for a reason and that we can rest knowing God is in control.

This is so important to understand. Instead of fighting what's going on, accept what's going on and look to God for strength and continual guidance. Don't lean on your own understanding but in all your ways acknowledge Him and He will direct your paths (Proverbs 3:5-6). Rest comes from faith, unrest comes from unbelief.

We have an example of this with the Children of Israel. When Moses led them out of Egypt, through the wilderness and up to the promise land, they didn't go in because of their lack of faith, which resulted in disobedience. They rebelled, and like the Children of Israel, when we rebel against God and His will, the result is unrest.

Even though God had miraculously brought them all the way through the wilderness, and said He had delivered the land into their hands, they refused to continued in faith and didn't go in.

They rebelled instead of believed, ending up as wanderers in the wilderness until they died.

A sad picture of missing out on the abundant life and rest that comes from walking in faith. The promise land is a picture of the Christian life lived by faith. It's a life of abundance, adventure, miracles and victory. Sure, there are battles to fight and enemies in the promise land, but faith gives the victory in all situations and circumstances.

· · ·

THE LESSON here is that rest comes from faith. Are you resting in God, His plan, His will, His promises and His character? Are you resting in His love, grace and mercy? Faith is the answer to your anxious, restless heart.

THE LIVING WORD

///

HEBREWS 4:12

"For the word of God is living..."

God's Word is special. Unlike any other writing, it is supernatural, outside of time and space. It declares the end from the beginning (Isaiah 46:10), proving that its origin is from God and not man. One of those characteristics is that it is "living."

God's Word is <u>living</u> as opposed to dead. It has the ability to interact with us because the Author is alive and inside of us. The Author can speak loving things to our living souls, because behind the words is a real Being applying those words to our inner being, precisely how we need them at the moment.

God's Word is <u>relational</u> and <u>personal</u>. It speaks like a person to us but more intimate and deep. Our relationship with God finds the Living Word as the primary source of communication. Unlike books written by mere humans, God's Word is interactive, fostering our desire to be close to Him. God's Living Word is God's real time voice speaking as He unfolds truth and divine revelation.

God's living Word <u>eternal</u> and <u>spiritual</u>. It is able to continue speaking to us once we've read it, or heard it, because it is written on our hearts. Our hearts are like a personal conference room where God deposits His truth. Once there, He can continue to speak through those deposits showing us how to use them and how to apply them. He can encourage us with them and council us. Unlike other books, which we have to remember in our minds, God's Word speaks to our innermost being and actually becomes a part of us, woven into who we are.

God's living Word is <u>refreshing</u>. It breathes fresh life into us. Like mouth to mouth resuscitation for our soul, God is able to breathe the pure air of His divine goodness. His Living Word can clear out the decay that clutters the soul, while it brings new living treasures like a rose garden for the soul.

. . .

THE LESSON here is to live by every word that comes from God's mouth (Matthew 4:4, Deuteronomy 8:3). Don't read The Living Word like a regular book, read it as if God is there whispering in your ear because He is.

MILK AND MEAT

HEBREWS 5:14

> *"But solid food belongs to those who are of full age, that is, those who by reason of use have their senses exercised to discern both good and evil."*

This is a rebuke to those who remain in a state of spiritual immaturity. It speaks to those who stay on the milk of God's Word, when they should be on meat of God's Word. It's not as if they were just young in The Lord, they neglected The Lord, especially His Word. There is a great danger in not growing and maturing in our faith, and we should never feel as if we have "arrived."

These Christians had not developed because they had not progressed in their diet. Like a baby that goes from milk to solid food, we too must progress on to the deeper things of The Lord. God has opened up His storehouse of treasure for us to explore and acquire. We are to keep pressing in.

The positive side of maturity in our faith is the increasing capacity to enjoy God. As we grow we are able to have a deeper and more intimate relationship with God. We can understand Him more and relate to Him more. We also have greater wisdom in how to live our life correctly, which allows us to live a more meaningful and purposeful life.

The negative side of not maturing in the Word is not being able to tell the difference between good and evil. Like a baby who can't tell the difference between something dangerous and something safe, not growing in the Word keeps one immature in their ability to know the difference between good and evil. Those lines are getting increasingly blurry in an increasingly confusing world.

· · ·

THE LESSON here is the importance of growing in the Word of God. Like viewing the ocean from the surface, you will miss so much of when you don't go below the surface. Make God's Word a priority; explore it, pray over it, study to show yourself approved, a workman who need not be ashamed (2 Timothy 2:15). Delight in it, walk in it, may it become part of the fabric of your being. Once you eat steak, milk is hard to go back to.

Ezekiel 10:1 11:25, Hebrews 6:18 28,
Psalm 105:16 36, Proverbs 27:1 2

LIVING FULL

//

PROVERBS 27:1

> *"Do not boast about tomorrow, For you do not know what a day may bring forth."*

Tomorrow is never promised. All we really have is today. Each moment is a gift that we are to live with gratitude to The Lord. What we do with those moments is really what our life becomes, increments of opportunities in the moments we are given.

We have to be careful of the tendency to live in the future and miss the present. Worry can fill our hearts as we ponder the "what if's" of life or we fantasize about better things without living the real things. There is nothing wrong with dreaming, just don't miss the real life dreamy unfolding right in front of you.

• • •

THE LESSON here is to live in the present. Embrace today as a gift from God. Cherish the moments, they are divinely ordered. Remember that the past is history, the future a mystery but the present is a gift (that's why its called the present). Be patient with the future and trust the God of the future. Place all in His hands so you are free to embrace all of today's blessings. Make the moments count and life will be full.

STANDING AGAINST FALSE TEACHERS

///

EZEKIEL 13:16

"That is, the prophets of Israel who prophesy concerning Jerusalem, and who see visions of peace for her when there is no peace,' says the Lord God."

False Prophets come in all shapes and sizes. They appeal to the many different things man likes to hear. They say things that appeal to the fleshly nature of man and they come speaking in the name of God. Perhaps that's how they get their credibility.

The Bible says we are to "test the spirits whether they are of God; because many false prophets have gone out in the world" (1 John 4:1). The thing is, just because someone is speaking as an authority, or as a representative of God, doesn't mean they are. The tricky part is they say what we want to hear.

The text speaks of Prophets in Ezekiel's day that said there would be peace for Israel at that time, when there was no peace. What people needed was the truth, not a lie. These prophets were judged heavily for their actions because they spoke lies in the name of God.

• • •

THE LESSON here is the importance of truth over fables. Truth doesn't change to conform to the world. Be aware of what you want to hear versus what you need to hear. The truth will set you free, while lies take you captive. Let God's Word be your guide and not false teachers, for then you will see clearly what God sees. Adjust your life to God's Word instead of adjusting God's Word to your life. False Prophets come and go, along with their doctrine, but the word of God stands forever.

MARANATHA (OUR LORD COMES)

//

EZEKIEL 14:14

> *"'Even if these three men, Noah, Daniel, and Job, were in it, they would deliver only themselves by their righteousness,' says the Lord God."*

God's judgment is inevitable. The Bible has shown God's judgment in instances like the flood in Noah's day, Sodom and Gomorrah, and the Children of Israel being taken captivity by Assyria and Babylon.

The Bible also points to a future judgment that will come in the "last days", and as sure as the past judgments have occurred, so too will this future judgment come. The Bible refers to this 7-year period on earth as the "tribulation," where God pours out His wrath in judgment of a wicked world (see the book of Revelation and Matthew 24:21, Daniel 12:1, Matthew 24:12, Revelation 3:10).

Many signs are given in the Bible as to what it will be like right before this time. There will be great evil on earth, wars and rumors of war, increased information, famine, pestilence, earthquakes and natural disasters, and the reformation of the Nation of Israel with the return of many Jews from across the world back to the Holy Land.

There are many other signs given as well but the key is that these signs will increase in frequency and intensity. They will pave the way for a One World government, a One World economy, a One World religion and a One World dictator, the "Antichrist." It's obvious from scripture that we are in the last days and judgment is very near.

Our text, which speaks of the Jewish captivity to the Babylonians as judgment for their rejection of Him, shows us that there will come a point where the prayers of the righteous won't change the inevitable judgment to come. Wickedness and the hardness of hearts will create such a bad state of affairs that God will intervene. However, we also see in the text that the "righteous" will be delivered. Christians are declared righteous by their faith in Christ and this text gives us a good principle in regards to our role in the tribulation.

An event called "the rapture" or the "catching away" is described 1 Thessalonians 4:15-17. We find that the rapture is how God rescues, or delivers, His children from His wrath by "catching" them up or "snatching" them away before this terrible time on earth.

In verse 18 of 1 Thessalonians 4 it says to "comfort one another with these words." In the book of Revelation we see the church on earth in chapters 1-3, then the church is in heaven in Chapters 4-5, and then in chapters 6-19 we see the tribulation on earth while the church is in heaven.

The seven year tribulation is when God pours out His wrath on the Christ rejecting earth, then we see the church come back to earth at the end of the tribulation with Christ, as He sets up His thousand year reign on earth with His bride, the Church.

. . .

THE LESSON here is to see that God always delivers the righteous. With the events of our day The Lord could be coming soon. You are to be encouraged and comforted knowing God will deliver you.

Watch the signs, watch Israel, and watch the pieces of the puzzle come together to give birth to a new day. Until that time God has so much for you to do to reach your generation. Keep your focus on His plan, His will and purpose for you in these most important last days leading up to His return. Most importantly, keep your eyes on Jesus, for your redemption draws near. Maranatha (our Lord comes)!

Ezekiel 16:42 17:24, Hebrews 8:1 13,
Psalm 106:13 31, Proverbs 27:7 9

SATISFACTION

PSALM 106:14

> *"But lusted exceedingly in the wilderness,*
> *And tested God in the desert.*
> *And He gave them their request,*
> *But sent leanness into their soul."*

This scripture shows us the importance of contentment and thankfulness in relationship to the satisfaction of our souls. It speaks of the Children of Israel, whom God was teaching dependence, allowed them to be placed in situations to see that all they needed was God and that He would take care of them.

He was teaching them to find contentment in their relationship with Him and not in material things. Instead of taking them immediately into the Promised Land, God took them through the wilderness. There shoes never wore out teaching them to trust God every step. A cloud would appear in the day and a pillar of fire by night to teach them to follow His lead and that they would be lost without a His guidance.

In order for them to do well on the Promise Land they would have to learn to be dependent even when the had more prosperity. A hard thing to do without the strengthening of the inner man through tests and trials. Here we see a breakdown of faith occurring with the food God provided.

Manna (Exodus 16) was provided for them each morning. The bread like substance would appear, giving them the perfect food and nourishment they needed each day. It was to be eaten and not stored so that they would have to trust that God would have their daily provisions ready each morning. If He didn't, they would starve.

Contentment and gratification became lusting and complaining. They begged God for meat and God gave them meat. However, the price tag was leanness for their souls. They traded the temporary pleasure of indulgence for the satisfaction of their souls. That's exactly what sin does. It robs our souls of fulfillment while feeding our flesh. It blinds us to what we really need.

. . .

THE LESSON here is to know that true and lasting satisfaction can only come from God. No earthly or material thing can do what only God can. Never trade the world's pleasures for God's riches. Be content in God, giving thanks to Him and your soul will be full.

THE MERCY SEAT

HEBREWS 9:5

"And above it were the cherubim of glory overshadowing the mercy seat."

The mercy seat was where the High Priest would meet with God, once a year in the Tabernacle and Temple. It was the place of God's presence and where the weight of His glory was experienced. The mercy seat shows us how we can meet with God.

We can never meet with God on our own accord. The drastic difference between His holiness and our sinfulness separates us at an immeasurable distance. In fact, it was only the High Priest, only once a year, only through tedious cleansing rituals and procedures, only in the proper attire, only through the spotless animals sacrificed blood, only on the specific day at the specific time of the year and only with the proper application of the blood of the spotless sacrificed animal, and only at the mercy seat inside the innermost place in the tabernacle or temple separated from the next innermost room by a veil, could there be any type of connection with God.

This is all meant to picture for us the basis upon which we can meet with God now, through Jesus Christ. At the moment Jesus died on the cross, inside of the temple, that veil was torn from top to bottom indicating that it was God who tore the veil. His sacrifice granted entrance to His presence for those who believe.

Now we can meet with Him because He has bridged that divide of our sin and His holiness. It was His own blood, the blood of the Lamb who was slain from the foundation of the world.

It was His mercy, His righteousness, His sacrifice and His purification by which we come. It was the veil of His flesh that was torn that granted us entrance.

Jesus is the Lamb, the Great High Priest, the Tabernacle, and the Scapegoat who made the way for us to experience His glory.

· · ·

THE LESSON here is to see the great privilege of meeting with Jesus completely on the basis of His mercy, by which he acted so radically in order for you to be reconciled to Him. The mercy seat shows you that it's His presence and His glory that He wants to share with. Make it a habit to live in His presence for it is there you will truly be alive.

APPOINTED ONCE TO DIE

HEBREWS 9:27

"And as it is appointed for men to die once, but after this the judgment."

The mystery of "what happens when we die", can only be answered by the one who is outside of time and space, sees all and knows all. The mystery of death opens the door for all sorts of superstitions and myths. One thing is certain, we will all die. Our scripture gives us three important facts about death from the One who knows.

First we see that death is an appointment. We are "appointed" to die. This means that death is not random nor is it without purpose. God being sovereign or in total control, knows exactly when that day is.

In fact it's as if He has a calendar in heaven with each persons "appointment" day. We all have that day and it's set. From our vantage point, death can seem so surprising, painful, pointless and meaningless. Death is very painful and hard to make sense of at times.

We say, "They were taken too early" when those don't have the opportunity to live long lives. The way people die can also be so painful, terrible diseases, sense-less tragedies and shocking accidents.

However, everyone has to die somehow and having an eternal perspective gives one hope that death is really a homecoming for God's children. Death is not the end but the beginning and heaven is the goal not earth.

The second point we see is that we die "once", speaking of physical death. We are not reincarnated and we do not have several chances once we die to "get it right".

The Bible is clear that we die once, and that the life we have on earth before we die is the only time we have to not die "the second death" which is separation from God for all eternity.

God, being a fair, impartial and just God gives each person everything they need to respond to His offer of forgiveness. No one is without excuse and what we do regarding what Jesus did will determine our life after death.

Finally we see that after death comes judgment. Our eternal destiny is determined by what we do now, not what happens after death. There is no more opportunity to change our eternal state once we depart from our temporary state.

There is no intermediate condition where loved ones can make amends for us. Judgment will come, our fate will be sealed and our eternity set by what we chose in this life.

We can see how important this life is now for all eternity. Receiving Jesus Christ as your Lord and Savior is the primary purpose of life on earth. Without salvation there is nothing and no point to anything.

Death looms and eternity waits. All of life then is to bring a person to the point of salvation in Christ because the stakes are so high.

God will work to bring a person to His salvation all the way to the point to where they must exercise their free will to make a decision. Once a person receives Christ and their eternity is set, life is now about serving Him and preparing for eternity. When we understand death we can truly live.

. . .

THE LESSON here is to understand life this side of eternity and live accordingly. This is not heaven, this is not the end, and this is not our final destination. This life is all about the next. Preparing for real life, eternal life is what it's all about. Knowing Him, serving Him and sharing Him. That's what life is all about.

HIDING FROM EVIL

PROVERBS 27:12

> *"A prudent man foresees evil and hides himself;*
> *The simple pass on and are punished."*

Evil looms around every corner looking to encroach upon unsuspecting customers. As God said to Esau, "sin lies at the door, and its desire is for you". Sin comes in all different packages and it's important to be aware.

Taking a vigilante approach to sin is a must. Having a complacent, nonchalant attitude toward sin is to already be defeated. Satan wants us to have our guards down, think it's no big deal and think we won't and can't be affected. These are the "famous last words" of a great many men and women of God who have greatly hurt by sins attacks.

Satan's strategy for many believers is to inoculate them to the reality of sins damaging effects by enticing in small doses. A crumb wets the appetite for a bite and a bit wets the appetite for a meal and a meal wets the appetite to buy the store. We end up as shop owners when all we wanted was taste.

Sin is not static but dynamic. It doesn't just stay the same but grows like leaven. It will keep growing until it is crucified by the power of God through repentance. The Christian has this effective power in their lives and must activate it or else sin will take a hold and get out of control.

Foresight is the key as we see in our scripture. This means that we can tell or discern a bad situation and stay away from it. This means not putting oneself in bad situations and not being involved with those who may put us in bad situations. Foresight sees the cliff and goes the other way.

· · ·

THE LESSON here is simply to stay clear of sin, sinful situations and people that will lead you into sinful situations. No one is strong enough say that they don't have to watch and be wise regarding sin. If David can fall so can you. Be wise, stay clear and never underestimate the power of sin and never overestimate your ability to resist.

DON'T FORSAKE
THE ASSEMBLING

HEBREWS 10:24-25

> *"And let us consider one another in order to stir up love and good works, not forsaking the assembling of ourselves together, as is the manner of some, but exhorting one another, and so much the more as you see the Day approaching."*

One the greatest blessings this side if heaven is the fellowship of the Saints. To gather together with believers, worshiping God in one accord. Throughout the New Testament we see the beauty of the "body of Christ" and the gift it is from God.

Christians need each other and the local assembly provides this opportunity. Here in our text we see the importance of gathering and the exhortation NOT to forsake it.

There were some in those days, like many today, who were missing the blessing and their own need for gathering with the body and not understanding why gathering with the body is so important.

There are those who think they don't "need church" meaning they don't need to be a part of a local assembly and don't need to participate in corporate worship with the Saints. They see it more as "what is the church doing for me" and "what can I get out of it". This thinking is all wrong.

A local church body meeting together and organized to serve the Lord in their communities and beyond is not jut for the individual. It's more for other people. That's right. Have you ever thought "I'm going to go to church because other people and not me"?

As we see on our text, along with the mindset of Christ, as Christians we are to consider others more than ourselves (Philippians 2:3-4). This applies as well to our attendances at church gatherings. The thinking is "let us consider one another" when it comes to our participation.

So it's much more than "what's in it for me" it's more about "what's in it for others" and "how can I bless my fellow Christian in my local assembly". Just showing up in itself is a blessing and encouragement.

As we "consider one another" we show up. Then as we "consider one another" we consider how to "stir up love and good works". There must be INTERACTION and INVOLVEMENT with our brothers and sisters in Christ.

These interactions have the intent of activating love and inspiring good works. We all play a big role in the encouraging the lives of fellow believers and this is one of the great things about the body of Christ.

Finally we see that our participation in the local body, which is about others and stirring them up, it becomes more and more important as we get closer and closer to the end.

This means that there has never been a more important time in the body of Christ to be involved and to be an encouragement. The closer we get to the end the harder it's going to be to live as a Christian.

· · ·

THE LESSON here is to see that we need each other as Christians and that you have a major role and responsibility to participate in your local assembly. It does matter that you are involved, encouraging, serving and using your gifts in order for the whole body to be healthy and strong.

Ezekiel 24:1 26, Hebrews 11:1 16,
Psalm 110:1 7, Proverbs 27:14

FAITH AND PLEASING GOD

HEBREWS 11:6

> *"But without faith it is impossible to please Him, for he who comes to God must believe that He is, and that He is a rewarder of those who diligently seek Him."*

Faith is the key to all that a Christian does. It is the vehicle by which God works in and through a life. Faith connects us with God's activity and is the difference between mans work and His.

God is not pleased with "our work". He is not impressed by what we can do or accomplish. If we saw how He sees, what we can do would look pretty ridiculous compared to what He can do.

Man has no ability to do anything in the realm if the spirit which is the reality of all that exists. That's why Jesus said, "without me you can do nothing" (John 15:5).

Pleasing God is a matter of faith. Faith is "believing that He is" or that we believe in Him correctly as the Bible tells us. We must believe He is the creator of all and that He is without beginning or ending.

We must believe that He is all-powerful, all knowing and all present. We must believe that He is completely separate from creation and that none are like Him. He is God and we are not and never will be.

Faith that pleases God not only "believes that He is" but also then comes to Him on His terms. We come to Him on the basis of His grace and mercy. We come to Him on the basis of His righteousness and not our own.

We come to Him as forgiven sinners because we are saved by grace through faith (Ephesians 2:8). We come to Him body based on what He has done and not on what we have done.

Finally, faith that pleases God will seek Him. It will see the great privilege of the opportunity to be connected to Him. It will see how open He is to the forgiven sinner. Faith says come, come with all you have because you can. Faith says God is our great reward and believes God will continue to bless and give.

. . .

THE LESSON here is the importance of living by faith. Seeing that you can please God with your faith and how powerful it is. You have a whole other way to live, not by what is seen and not by what is known, but by faith that sees and does what can only be done though God. Faith is the key to the supernatural and the key to pleasing God.

Ezekiel 27:1 28:26, Hebrews 11:17 31,
Psalm 111:1 10, Proverbs 27:15 16

A SUBJECT WORTH STUDYING

//

PSALM 111:2

"The works of the Lord are great, studied by all who have pleasure in them."

God is amazing and He does amazing things! The wise Christian takes time to look for the greatness of God in everyday life. All around us we can find miracles of grace on display to marvel in. When we do, we will have a sense of awe and wonder for The Lord.

This is what is so fascinating about God's Word! We see God's great works throughout human history that continue today. We see the end spoken of from the beginning (Isaiah 46:10). We see them in the past, we see them now and we see what He will do in the future. We see the supernatural working of God's plan and find pleasure.

Like the pleasure we get when we see a great pass or catch in football, or a great sprint or jump in track and field, or a great artist or musician at work. They give us great pleasure because of the great work. So the Christian finds great pleasure in God's work. This pleasure encourages us to study His works.

. . .

THE LESSON here is to make it your habit to be a student of God. Study His Word, study His handiwork in creation, study His working in your own life, study His working in the world and study His work in reaching the lost.

GODLY FRIENDS

PROVERBS 27:17

"As iron sharpens iron, so a man sharpens the countenance of his friend."

People need each other. Sometimes relationships can be hard and Satan would love to isolate us with the intention of making us feel alone and disconnected. We are most vulnerable when isolated. Also, God has placed a great value on our relationships, using them as instruments of our growth and development.

This scripture speaks to us about the importance of our Godly relationships. Not only do we need them, but they help us be the best version of what God intends us to be. Our role in others lives is to be those who sharpen or make better.

To do this we must be connected and see the value we have in others lives and the value they have in our lives. Godly friendships, when genuine, will foster Godliness. They will be intentional about encouragement, edification, honesty and help. Ultimately, Godly friendships are necessary for Godly growth.

. . .

THE LESSON here is two things. Do you have Godly friends and are you a Godly friend? Be sure to not be a "lone wolf" Christian for you will be more vulnerable to Spiritual attacks, and be sure you have Godly friends around you that want what God wants for you. Godly friends make for sharp swords in the hands of an awesome God.

FULFILLMENT

///////////////////////////////////////

PROVERBS 27:20

> *"Hell and Destruction are never full; So the eyes of man are never satisfied."*

How does the thought of never being satisfied sound? To live unfulfilled, craving and lusting after anything to fill the emptiness. Such is the condition the eyes of man that look to fill the empty heart. However, a heart without God will never stop looking for fulfillment. If it doesn't find true fulfillment it will look in all the wrong places, to the harm of the soul.

In our text we see that hell and destruction always look for more. They can never reach saturation. No matter how much is put in, hell and destruction stays empty. Their search for more people to add to their appetite never ceases and that is why so many fall to them. They are relentless in the mission to add new members.

With hell and destruction hunting us, and our own appetites driving us to find fulfillment, we are doomed without Christ. He is the answer to our search for fulfillment. He alone can satisfy the human heart and the searching eye.

· · ·

THE LESSON here is that there is no fulfillment outside of Christ. It's our flesh that is never satisfied. Don't be deceived and led by your flesh which will never find fulfillment. True fulfillment is found deeper, in our inner man. With Christ, you are watered from inside out. Look to Him, the source of living water, and you will overflow.

DON'T TOUCH THE GLORY

//

PSALM 115:1

"Not unto us, O Lord, not unto us, but to Your name give glory."

Glory is a dangerous thing. It belongs to God, and Him alone. No glory originates from man and at best we merely reflect God's glory. The moment we appropriate it to ourselves, we have robbed God and others of the true glory. Be careful who gets the glory.

It has been rightly said, "Don't touch the glory." God is very particular about this, not because He is an "egomaniac" but because it right and true. When we are tempted to take the glory, we mislead and misrepresent the truth.

When we want people to think more of us, or that we are better humans than them, or that there is something about us that is deity, we have made ourselves an idol and have distorted the gospel.

Whatever a man has, it is given. Talent, looks, wealth, ambition, ability etc., is all just something received and should point back to the greatness of the Giver not the greatness of the recipient. We must refuse any adoration that doesn't point to Christ.

· · ·

THE LESSON here is the importance of the glory of God. May everything you do be done as simple caretakers of God's gifts. Use all you have to demonstrate God's glory. Be excellent in your effort and let God shine through all you do. To God be the glory forever and ever, amen.

HOW TO HAVE JOY IN TRIALS

JAMES 1:2-4

> *"My brethren, count it all joy when you fall into various trials, knowing that the testing of your faith produces patience. But let patience have its perfect work, that you may be perfect and complete, lacking nothing."*

Trials will come, there is no doubt about it. As we see in our text, they come in "various" ways or in all shapes and sizes. They vary in how they come but the way through is always the same. Here's how to have joy in trials, from our text.

1. KNOWING

When trials hit, and you are a Christian, you know things, and must remember them when tested. A great deal of stress and agony comes because we forget, panic or are unsure about what may be happening. We must always get back to **knowing**.

What are we suppose to know?

a. Trials are always a faith test—what's being challenged ultimately is our belief in God, His character and His plan for our lives. Knowing trials are not about the trial but about our faith, we will be able to get through with faith. No matter what, have faith. Trials will test faith and when faith is exerted, faith is strengthened. So trials actually strengthen that all important weapon of the Christian, our faith. We know trials are a faith test and faith passes the test.

b. Trials produce—we might think a trial takes away, makes less, or subtracts – but trials are actually very productive. They work things in us. They work "God" things in us. They produce, develop and add. Without them, we are weak and undeveloped. With them, when met with faith, they make us into who God wants us to be. Our text specifically says they produce "patience" or the ability to remain under the pressure of the trial. It's the inner strength of character to stay in the place of development and growth. Trials produce this.

2. LETTING

Letting is cooperation. This means that we allow God to work on us instead of fleeing from the flames that forge us into steel. It means we don't look to cope with the trial in ways that are not of faith, ways that make us feel better in the flesh, ways that cover the pain and limit our exposure to exerting faith. We "let" the trial work Godliness and strength in us. We are not afraid of the pain because we know God will never give us more pain than the capacity He has given us to deal with it. We let the trial work God's will. This takes ultimate trust.

3. TRUSTING

Finally, when in trials, we know we have all we need from God to get through it and we know it improving us. We see in our text that God uses trials to make us "perfect, complete and lacking in nothing." This is the end of our faith in the trial. God is bringing us to a place that is the full development of the full experience of God in our lives. He uses trials to make us whole and that is a place of complete dependence on Him, complete trust and complete satisfaction in Him alone. A person like this needs nothing else.

• • •

THE LESSON here is that when trials come—know, let, and trust. Then joy will be had, even when trials are at hand.

RELIGION

///

JAMES 1:27

> *"Pure and undefiled religion before God and the Father is this: to visit orphans and widows in their trouble, and to keep oneself unspotted from the world."*

What does it look like when God has taken residence in a human soul and that soul yields to His wishes? This is what religion is, the working out of the life of God through a person. This is religion at its purest and most undefiled way.

Religion becomes impure and defiled when it is man's workings. Whether it's traditions of men replacing the Holy Spirit, or rules and regulations replacing grace, or external shows replacing inward fellowship, or self-righteousness replacing God's righteousness, it's all defiled when it is man and not God.

Pure and undefiled religion will be seen in its relationships, first being its relationship with God. Simple fellowship and intimacy with God is the height of religion. This personal relationship is the purpose by which God had created man and this very same intimacy and relationship is what Satan came to destroy. At the cross, is where Jesus restored this relationship for those who believe. True religion then, is relationship.

We also see from our text that pure and undefiled religion, "visits orphans and widows in their trouble." In other words, there will be care for, and have compassion upon, the needy and or those in trouble. Just as Jesus had a tender heart for the least, the last and the lost, so true religion is God caring for people through us. Jesus wants to touch the needy.

Finally, pure and undefiled religion has a relationship with the world that is "unspotted". True religion is not worldly and compromising with the things of the world. Jesus came into the world to save the world. He loved those in the world, reached out to them and gave His life for them, but never became part of it nor was tainted by it. He was on a mission to be "in" it but not "of" it.

. . .

THE LESSON here is to see what religion really is. What it all comes down to is, "it's all about Jesus." Having a relationship with Him, having a relationship with those in trouble like Jesus did, and having a relationship with the world that is to save and not to become a part of. This is religion that is pure and undefiled.

FAITH AND WORKS

JAMES 2:18

> *"But someone will say, 'You have faith, and I have works.' Show me your faith without your works, and I will show you my faith by my works."*

What is the connection between "faith" and "works"? Faith is what we believe and works are what we do. What we believe is unseen and what we do is seen. It seems obvious then that our unseen belief would be seen by what we do. However, that's not always the case.

What do our works say about what we believe? Do our works say we believe in a God of love, that we don't have to worry because He is in control? Do our works say we believe in a forgiving God who has a plan for our lives that He is working out all together for good?

Do our works show we believe in a kind God full of compassion and tender mercies? Do our works show that are free from the bondage of sin and no longer have to be slaves to sin? Do our works show we are not citizens of the world any more but now we are citizens of heaven but fulfilling our mission on earth?

Maybe our works say that God leaves the burden to us to carry. Maybe they say God isn't in control and doesn't have a plan. Maybe our works say God can't help us so we must do it on our own. Or our works say God doesn't care about sin or worldliness. Our works may say God is afraid, incapable and powerless. Maybe our works say we really don't believe at all.

· · ·

THE LESSON here is to see that true faith walks the walk. Not that we are perfect and do everything right all the time, but that we want what we believe to be seen in what we do. God hasn't left it up to us but is transforming us from inside out. He has given us Spiritual desires and appetites.

May your works be as your faith, one in the same. To God be the glory.

THE WORLD

JAMES 4:4

> *"Adulterers and adulteresses! Do you not know that friendship with the world is enmity with God? Whoever therefore wants to be a friend of the world makes himself an enemy of God."*

The earth was created by God but "the world" is a system controlled and influenced by Satan. Since the fall in the Garden of Eden, the world has been broken, tainted and fallen. With Satan at the helm, and all of mankind feels the effects of his dominion.

The "world" is not what it is supposed to be, the way God created it. One day God will restore the world and eventually make a "new heaven" and "new earth," but in the meantime we have to deal with its fallen nature. Jesus came to restore us through His sacrifice, but He has not taken us out of it yet. This is where our struggle lies.

Christians are restored as "new creations" (2 Corinthians 5:17) having God's Kingdom inside of them, yet they are not inside God's kingdom. Christians are not at home in the world but are pilgrims and sojourners (1 Peter 2:11). One day we will go home where we will be in God's Kingdom, but until that day we are left here by God to fulfill our calling. That is the only reason God has left us in the world.

With God's Kingdom and the "world" in opposition to one another, it is not possible to be friends with both. The life and death of Jesus is an example of how the world feels about God. The world hates God and influences people to also hate God.

There is no two ways about it. When we are friends with the world, we are hating God. It's comparable to adultery, as our text says. The tricky part is living in a place with a system that hates God. Pressure to compromise is a daily battle as the world wants to conform us into its image (Romans 12:1) using all types of pressure. To compromise is to give up something we have in Christ.

. . .

THE LESSON here is to first decide who and what you will live your life for. Paul said "for me to live is Christ, to die is gain" (Philippians 1:21). Next is to arrange your life around this singular purpose. You must reject all that which opposes your goal and receiving that which contributes to your goal. Watch those areas of your life where the things of the world have become part of you, or part of your lifestyle. You are either a friend of a God or a friend of the world, and it is much better to be a friend of God.

NOVEMBER 21

Ezekiel 42:1 43:27, James 5:1 20,
Psalm 119:1 16, Proverbs 28:6 7

PERSEVERANCE

JAMES 5:10-11

> *"My brethren, take the prophets, who spoke in the name of the Lord, as an example of suffering and patience. Indeed we count them blessed who endure. You have heard of the perseverance of Job and seen the end intended by the Lord—that the Lord is very compassionate and merciful."*

Every Christian has to deal with the fact that the Christian life isn't easy. There will be struggles involving suffering. God has a track for each Christian to run their race on. This track is individualized and specific to each one. No two tracks are alike.

This track will require perseverance. This may be one of the most important characteristics a Christian can have, to just keep going no matter what struggle. Perseverance is forged through trials when faith is applied. We grow stronger in our perseverance muscle, allowing for an increased capacity to stay under the weight of the burden or in the heat of the fire.

The Bible is full of examples of people who persevere like the Prophets and Job. The key is to keep going, in faith, depending on The Lord to carry us through. He will bring us through and He is taking us to "the end intended by The Lord." This is the great encouragement, that He is taking us somewhere.

Not to an arbitrary or random place, but to the place at the end of "our" track. There will be an end and the end is good. The Lord will take care of us and even carry us to ultimately find that The Lord is "very merciful and compassionate".

• • •

THE LESSON here is perseverance. Just keep going. Everything you want is in perseverance. There is nothing good in giving up. Jesus will be with you, and Jesus will be your reward. He is enough, He is all you need.

THE VALUE OF FAITH

1 PETER 1:6-7

"In this you greatly rejoice, though now for a little while, if need be, you have been grieved by various trials, that the genuineness of your faith, being much more precious than gold that perishes, though it is tested by fire, may be found to praise, honor, and glory at the revelation of Jesus Christ."

For a Christian, faith is the currency of God's kingdom. With faith we receive forgiveness of sin, move mountains, defeat the enemies attacks, press forward, see God's plan unfold, invite God's will and many other eternal, supernatural things. Faith is how a Christian lives and how God moves.

Peter knew the value of faith and wanted other Christians to as well. Here in our text we see that faith must be genuine. In other words, it must be pure. There are many false substitutes for faith, some that are easily passed off as true but really aren't. It takes fire to test faith, trials that burn away the false.

God sees faith as so important, so much more than any earthly possession, that He will do whatever is necessary for faith's development. Just as a good parent would make their child complete their homework, even if they complain and don't want to do it, because the parent wants what is best for the child, so God our Father wants the best for us, which is genuine faith.

When we have the right view of faith, one that values it as much as God, we will rejoice when trials come to purify our faith. The trouble comes when we experience trials and fail to see that their purpose is to suffer away all that is not of true faith so that pure faith and enduring faith emerges and remains.

When trials are seen as God's love for us, bringing about great things, we can rejoice because being rich in faith is to be truly rich. To be rich in things that will pass away at the expense of genuine faith that won't is true poverty. A rich soul is better than a rich wallet.

What is true genuine faith? It praises, honors and glorifies God no matter the situation. It is one thing to praise God when we have a lot or things go our way, but to praise, honor and glorify Him when we don't, shows who and what we really trust in. Faith is most genuine when it is all we have.

THE LESSON here is that you would value faith as much as God does, seeing that it is better to be rich in faith than rich in the world. Make faith, and the exercise of it, what you value, then you will be rich in what matters.

THE NECESSITY OF GOD'S WORD

1 PETER 2:2

"As newborn babes, desire the pure milk of the word, that you may grow thereby."

How important is God's Word to our lives? According to our scripture, it's vital. The Word is as important as food for our bodies. Here it's compared to baby's milk and we all know how important that is.

Our attitude towed it should be one of great need and even desperation for it. We are to have an appetite for it which we normally will as Christians unless we are spiritually sick or filled with spiritual "junk food". Sin will quench our appetite for the Word as well.

We are also to desire the "pure milk" meaning we are not to tolerate additives that taint the Word. We must pray for clarity and wisdom and not complicate the Word with our own bias. Just the simple pure Word feeding our Spirits and not just our minds.

Finally we must see that it is by the Word that we grow. Growth does not occur without it because this is how our souls are fed and how we know God in a deeper way. The Word is how we base our life and go through struggles. It's by the Word that we become mature and developed.

. . .

THE LESSON here is the absolute necessity of God's Word in the believer's life. It is not an option but must be the book that you. It only build your life upon, but also feed off for all our spiritual nutrition. God's Word, desire it, consume it, live it.

CALLED TO SUFFER

1 PETER 2:21

"For to this you were called, because Christ also suffered for us, leaving us an example, that you should follow His steps."

Suffering is more characteristic of a Christian life than comfort. Some Christians find it surprising to suffer and most think it's strange when it first hits. Some even deny suffering as part of the Christian life all together or attribute it to a lack of faith. Nothing could be further from the truth, as we see in our text.

We are actually called to suffer. Jesus, being our example, showed us what it's like to live completely for the Father's will and suffered as a result. If a perfect sinless man who only did what was good and right to others suffered, and we can expect too as well. His suffering was due to this dark evil world that hates light and rejects God. The crucifixion shows us how much the world hates Jesus, who lives inside every Christian.

Suffering is viewed as "bad" from a worldly perspective but God uses suffering for "good." What Satan means for evil, God means it for good (Genesis 50:20). Suffering is used to deepen our walks, grow our faith and enhance our closeness to God. Suffering also brings out the impurities in our faith. Suffering is needed and good, indicating God wants to do greater things in the sufferer's life.

. . .

THE LESSON here is to have the right view of suffering. Knowing you are called to it, that it is leading to greater things, and that God will see you through. Suffering is God's instrument of your sanctification (separation from the world and separation from self). Look to God when you suffer, ask what He wants you to learn and know that there is an intended end God has in mind. Let God suffer you to greatness, like Jesus who was highly exalted, your suffering will mold you into God's masterpiece.

AFFLICTIONS ARE GOOD

///

PSALM 119:71

"It is good for me that I have been afflicted, that I may learn Your statutes."

The words "affliction" and "good" are an odd couple to pair together. However, here once again, we find this thread that runs through the Bible of "affliction" related to "good".

It's a great prayer that asks to have the same mind as Christ (Philippians 1:5), to think like Him, to see things like He does and to feel the same about things as He does. When it comes to suffering and affliction, he had a mindset that was deeper than the affliction. The writer of this Psalm also saw affliction as good.

Not that the affliction in and of itself was good, but what it accomplished was. All our afflictions have the potential for great good if we have the right perspective and approach to them. Feeling the emotions of sadness, anger, pain, hurt and grief, to mention a few, are not wrong to feel. What important is coming back to seeing the bigger picture. Having an eternal perspective is the key.

Having an eternal perspective allows one to see that affliction works on the eternal things in my life. Afflictions produce Godly fruit and Spiritual rewards. Sometimes we have a hard time seeing the value of the eternal things, but they are far more important than anything temporary.

Specifically our text tells us that afflictions helped the Psalmist "learn God's statutes." He saw that he was growing in understanding God's ways, which would lead him into a greater closeness with God. He saw that "learning God's statutes" were greater than the absence of afflictions.

The question you must ask yourself is, "Do I desire God's will greater than I desire the absence of affliction?" Do you place such a high premium on your relationship with God that you would be willing to go through whatever is necessary to grow closer to Him? Those are hard questions but they are the only way to Godliness.

· · ·

THE LESSON here is to have an eternal perspective when it comes to your suffering. The way to get through is faith. When you have faith in "who" God is, you can easily submit to what God does. Knowing He is good, that He has a great plan for your life and that He is working that plan out perfectly, will allow you to also see that it is good for you to be afflicted.

Daniel 2:24 3:30, 1 Peter 4:7 5:14,
Psalm 119:81 96, Proverbs 28:15 16

YOU'LL NEVER GET BURNED FOR DOING THE RIGHT THING

DANIEL 3:26-27

"Then Nebuchadnezzar went near the mouth of the burning fiery furnace and spoke, saying, 'Shadrach, Meshach, and Abed-Nego, servants of the Most High God, come out, and come here.' Then Shadrach, Meshach, and Abed-Nego came from the midst of the fire. And the satraps, administrators, governors, and the king's counselors gathered together, and they saw these men on whose bodies the fire had no power; the hair of their head was not singed nor were their garments affected, and the smell of fire was not on them."

The boys from Judah faced a great temptation to compromise. They were highly favored by the King of Babylon, Nebuchadnezzar, and singled out for good positions with the King. Their talent and ability brought opportunity to be specifically trained for special service. The only problem was they were not willing to compromise their beliefs.

It was an offense worthy of death by fiery furnace to not bow down and worship the golden image of the King. The boys couldn't and wouldn't do that. Yet if they compromised they would be spared from such a terrible fate.

We all face temptations to compromise our convictions. We think about the consequences that may come if we don't. It may not be a fate of death by fire but there may be consequences we don't like all the same.

Pressure to conform is a daily battle and our faith may cost us. It is in these moments we must never compromise. It may be easier, but it's not better. Sometimes doing the right thing is costly but in the end you will never get burned for doing the right thing.

As we see in our text, the boys were thrown into the fiery furnace, willing to do what was right no matter the cost. They knew something very important, that the cost of violating their convictions comes with a much greater price tag than the cost of paying for them.

Better to stand on your convictions and sacrifice for what is right than to violate them and suffer for what is wrong.

The boys were thrown in the fire and that's where they saw Jesus, right there in the fire with them. We too will see Jesus in our times of fires. They we not burned and God was glorified in the end.

. . .

THE LESSON here is to see that you will never be burned for doing the right thing. You may suffer loss, it may hurt, but God will see you through and you'll be better in the end.

THE BIBLE

2 PETER 1:20-21

> *"Knowing this first, that no prophecy of Scripture is of any private interpretation, for prophecy never came by the will of man, but holy men of God spoke as they were moved by the Holy Spirit."*

The Bible is no ordinary book. It is a Spiritual book, meaning it is understood when one is connected to the author. It cannot be merely intellectually understood, otherwise it would be understood by the intellectually elite only. Those who look "to" God and "for" God when they read the Bible will have a better understanding.

This is because the Bible is a "God book." Although it does contain history, Science, Philosophy, Poetry and so forth, all those things point to God. More than anything, the things of the Bible are "revealed", not figured out. That does not mean that diligent study is not necessary but that RELYING on diligent study, and not on the Holy Spirit, will prove futile as mere knowledge without revelation puffs up (I Corinthians 8:1).

In our text we see why the Bible is a Spiritual book and must be approached Spiritually. The Bible is written by the Holy Spirit. No human has contrived these sacred writings but they are the very words of a God written by men as the Holy Spirit dictated.

The men were like pens in the hand of God, dictating His words. The Bible has proven over and over again that it is a "God book" not a "man book" through things like prophecy, archeology, manuscript evidence and statistical probability.

The Bible says things that cannot be known and then those things come to be. This doesn't just happen a few times but over and over again throughout all of human history. The Bible is not just right some of the time but 100% of the time and even stakes it's claim to authenticity by being 100% correct.

. . .

THE LESSON here is to see that the Bible is a Spiritual book written by the Holy Spirit and therefore you must read it with Spiritual eyes. Read it prayerfully, read it looking for God and trusting in the Holy Spirit. Meditate on its truths and put into action those truths in practical ways with the empowering of the Holy Spirit. Read it with an open heart and mind to the Holy Spirit allowing for transformation and Spiritual growth. Read it to draw close to God and ultimately to know Him more.

Daniel 5:1 31, 2 Peter 2:1 22,
Psalm 119:113 128, Proverbs 28:19 20

MENE, TEKEL, PERES

DANIEL 5:26-28

> *"This is the interpretation of each word. MENE: God has numbered your kingdom, and finished it; TEKEL: You have been weighed in the balances, and found wanting; PERES: Your kingdom has been divided, and given to the Medes and Persians."*

King Nebuchadnezzar had a dream that needed to be interpreted. Daniel was a man who heard from The Lord in matters like this and The Lord would bless Daniel with the knowledge of the dreams and their meaning.

Daniel always gave glory to God and lived to follow God and not the crowd. He wasn't concerned about the "popular thing", he was concerned about the "right thing".

He saw God as his audience and not man. The result was great closeness with God and even though he was taken captive by the Babylonians, he maintained his faith in God. His faith wasn't oriented toward what was easy, it was rooted in what was true.

On the other hand, Nebuchadnezzar was a man of power, popularity and wealth. He was more into what the world thought than what The Lord thought. As a result he was found without forgiveness and grace. Here are three consequences of rejecting God.

1. MENE MENE – "God has numbered your kingdom, and finished it"- all earthly endeavors will come to and end. They will be finished and dried up with no eternal value. The lesson here is – Don't chase after, and invest in, that which will pass away. Don't live your life for temporary things but a truly meaningful life is one that will never fade away.

2. TEKEL – "You have been weighed in the balances, and found wanting"- God is the ultimate and true judge. Only His words matter, for they are truth. At the end of our life we will stand before Him. Only those who have put their faith in Him will NOT be found wanting. There will be no excuses and no other way but through the blood of Jesus Christ shed on the cross. The lesson here is – Don't be found wanting when you are weighed in the balance. We will all have our day and Jesus will be the only way.

3. PERES – Your kingdom has been divided, and given to the Medes and Persians." – You will lose everything that is not committed to Jesus Christ. Eventually material things become reduced to nothing. You will be less than God has intended for you, until eventually you are completely lost forever.

· · ·

THE LESSON here is only Jesus can make you whole. Don't be a Nebuchadnezzar, with nothing to show for your life. Be a Daniel and live for God's Kingdom, where there is no end and that can never be taken away.

GROW IN GRACE

///

2 PETER 3:18

"But grow in the grace and knowledge of our Lord and Savior Jesus Christ."

Of all things we should be growing in, grace is at the top of the list. True growth in The Lord is growing in the understanding of His righteousness, His forgiveness, His love and His mercy. Growing in grace is growing in the character of God which says that He is good and wants to share all His goodness with us.

Growing in grace is growing in understanding of what God has done and where we stand with Him. As believers we stand in His COMPLETED righteousness. We do not earn but receive but it is a gift that has been delivered and now we are free love Him and serve Him if we have received His grace by faith.

Growing in grace means that He is strong so we don't have to be. It means that He has accomplished so we don't have to. It means that He is rich so we we don't have to be.

It means that we are all He is and all He says we are. It means we know God is faithful to complete what He has started in our lives (Philippians) 1:6). It means we are resting in Him and what He has done so we aren't working and fighting our way up the stairway to heaven.

Growing in grace growing in our love for our brothers and sisters in Christ because our relationship is based on brotherhood not on performance. It's loving the lost and having compassion on others even though they don't share our views. It's growing in desire to share the message of grace, the gospel with those who need it.

• • •

THE LESSON here is to make sure you are growing in the right thing, grace. Make sure you are not growing in legalism, religious performance and outward shows of piety not rooted in a personal relationship with Jesus Christ. Make sure you are not growing in condemnation, guilt and judgment. Make sure you are not growing in isolation from the lost world who needs the light of Jesus. Make sure you are not growing in pride, selfishness of greed. Grow in grace, and you will be growing in the right direction.

Daniel 7:1 28, 1 John 1:1 10,
Psalm 119:153 176, Proverbs 28:23 24

THE TREASURE OF THE WORD

//

PSALM 119:162

> *"I rejoice at Your word, as one who finds great treasure."*

What is your attitude toward God's Word, the Bible? Where does it rank on your scale of importance? What priority do you give to it and how much time do you spend in it? How do you feel when you think about it? What sacrifices do you make in make to read it?

The proper attitude for one who really understands the value of the Bible is to treasure it above all other possessions, knowing it is the truth, containing the answers to life's questions, the details about the future, the insight on the right way to live and the key to wisdom that unlocks the mysteries of the universe. The Bible is how to know and understand God and fellowship with Him.

The Bible is food for our Spirit and strengthens our soul. It is a light unto our path and a lamp unto our feet (Psalm 119:105). It tells us how to go to heaven and what happens if we don't. The Bible has the cure for sin, weakness, anxiety and depression. The Bible tells us how to have love, joy and peace. The Bible is a book from the heart of God revealing the greatest knowledge a person can have. The Bible is the most precious possession containing all one needs for life's journey.

Those who value the Bible, and read it with spiritual eyes, will find great joy in it. There will be rejoicing as one discovers God's love and all that He has done for them. It is a love letter from God, speaking directly to the heart. It is alive, speaking personally to us and to what we may be going through. It is transformational as it changes us from inside out.

. . .

THE LESSON here is to see the value of God's Word and to properly esteem it in your life. As you do, let the Bible be your treasure above all else, treating it with awe and respect, reading it humbly, depending on the Holy Spirit, believing it and living it out practically as the Holy Spirit empowers.

Ultimately, may the Bible become a part of you as it is written on your heart. May it become the fabric of your being and may you see the world through its eyes. May God's Word be your treasure and may you rejoice over it.

OUR HEARTS ARE FOOLISH

PROVERBS 28:26

"He who trusts in his own heart is a fool."

When the Bible speaks about out "hearts" it is speaking of our inner feelings and emotions. It is often said to "follow your heart". But is that good advice? Will our hearts lead us in the right direction?

Not unless our hearts are surrendered to The Lord. When we just do what we "feel" like doing we can be carried away by our emotions in the wrong direction. The Bible says that "our hearts are deceitfully wicked above all things, who can know it". That doesn't sound like a good compass for a good life.

Our heats can pull us one way and the Holy Spirit the other. This conflict is a battle of wills, ours versus God's. This is when we must choose to follow God by faith and not our own desires.

The key is a surrendered heart. When we just want His will, we will want what He wants. He puts His desires in our hearts so our desires are His desires. That's when He gives us the desires of OUR heart.

Sometimes it's hard to tell the difference between our heart and the Holy Spirit. This is when we need to be careful. If it's God's will we won't need to force it. We will be relaxed and have peace. We won't be afraid of losing or not getting because we will be satisfied in God's will and trusting that what He is doing is best.

It will also line up with the Bible. An unsurrendered heart will lead one away from God and the Bible. When we have to lie, hide, compromise or manipulate to get what we want, it is our heart and not God that is directing us and it is down the wrong road.

. . .

THE LESSON here is don't trust your heart. You will be foolish to do so. Better to trust in The Lord and His "better than anything" plan for your life. Let Him lead, you follow. Be sensitive to the Holy Spirit and delight in Him. As you do, God will unfold His plan to you delight and pleasure. Your Heavenly Father knows best. Better to trust God and be wise than to trust your heart and be a fool.

Daniel 9:1 11:1, 1 John 2:18 3:6,
Psalm 121:1 8, Proverbs 28:27 28

MANY ANTICHRISTS

1 JOHN 2:18

> *"Little children, it is the last hour; and as you have heard that the Antichrist is coming, even now many Antichrists have come, by which we know that it is the last hour."*

Coming to this world one day will be "The Antichrist" with a capital "A". He will be an "instead of" Christ that will draw people away from the true and living Christ. He will do it through deception, first offering the world what it really wants and is already looking for, namely, peace.

He will be popular, charismatic, smart, charming, wealthy, dynamic, well spoken, good looking, funny, strong and powerful. He will fill the role everyone wants him to be. He will look the part, act the part and talk the part. He will be the epitome of what "success" in the world's eyes looks like. He will be loved and embraced as the world's hero.

The world is being conditioned to receive this man and even now there are "Antichrists" with a small "a". Many people who are smaller versions of the "Antichrist" who set the stage for him. These Antichrists we are told, are "many". They come in all forms and they will say and do things that minimize the real Christ and magnify humanity and the world.

These Antichrists even come in "religious" clothes speaking small truths wrapped in lies. They will emphasize man over God, self over selflessness and success over submission. They will speak more of riches than of faith, more of success than suffering and more of ego than humility.

They may have a Bible for a prop but rarely use it unless they can find a scripture to take out of context in order to support their cause. They will fleece the flock with incessant pleas for money in order to build their kingdom and not God's. Our scripture says "by this we will know it's the last hour.

· · ·

THE LESSON here is to watch for these Antichrists. Watch your own walk, stay true to the Word, stay clear of pride and greed. Stay clear of selfish ambition and vain conceit.

Stay focused on Jesus, stay humble and loving. Keep yourself in the love of God. Be careful of societies "stars" and the worlds darlings who form opinions and thought without a Biblical view.

Daniel 11:2 35, 1 John 3:7 24,
Psalm 122:1 9, Proverbs 29:1

GOD IS GREATER

1 JOHN 3:20

> *"For if our heart condemns us, God is greater than our heart, and knows all things."*

In everything, God is greater. He is the "greater than" sign and no matter what it is, He is greater. This is good to know for the Christian, for any temptation faced, God is greater. For any affliction encountered, God is greater. For any hardship, heartbreak or disappointment, God greater.

Knowing God is greater when it comes to our heart is very comforting. He is greater than our broken hearts. When it comes to the guilt we feel of condemnation, He is greater than what our heart tells us.

When we sin, our hearts tell us we are lost, failures and rejects who can't get anything right. Our hearts can become so heavy when weighted down with guilt that we are impacted physically, emotionally and spiritually. However, God is greater and has declared us innocent at the cross, once and for all. Faith believes "there is now no more condemnation for those in Christ Jesus" (Romans 8:1).

. . .

THE LESSON here is to always remember that God is greater and believe God and not your heart by faith. When feeling down and hopeless remember that God's work on the cross is greater than all you sin. Simply repent from your sin and begin walking with Him again. Don't believe Satan's lies that hold you in bondage and rob you from God's joy. Whatever it is, God is greater.

THE CURE FOR FEAR

1 JOHN 4:18

> *"There is no fear in love; but perfect love casts out fear, because fear involves torment. But he who fears has not been made perfect in love."*

The Bible gives the answer for fear. Fear is the feeling of something bad happening. Many are actually controlled by fear and their quality of life is greatly impacted. Fear can prevent some from really experiencing all that God has for them because they never do anything that may have an adverse effect.

Fear is broken in a relationship with Jesus Christ. In that relationship we know that "all things work together for good" (Romans 8:28). When we follow God by faith we are in His love, which does no harm. Love replaces fear when love is in control.

When a Christians fears it's really a love problem. In other words, it's a doubting love. We doubt if good is really going to come. We doubt if God really cares. We doubt if everything is going to be okay. We doubt that God is in control. God's love is not perfected in us because of the lack of faith to believe God's love.

. . .

THE LESSON here is to remember that your fear is conquered by love. If you are afraid of something put you faith in God's love. Look to the cross where His love was put on display and know that that same love is working in your life now.

THE LORD IS ON YOUR SIDE

///

PSALM 124:1

> *"If it had not been the LORD who was on our side."*

What a difference The Lord makes. The psalmist expresses this here in the text. He recognizes that if it weren't for The Lord, the whole nation of Israel wouldn't have made it. He knows God had brought them through many very difficult trials as He will us.

For a Christian, The Lord is always on our side. The Bible says, "if God be for you who can be against you?" What a great promise to carry with us each day. It's hard to even imagine all the Lord has brought us through. The seen and unseen things. God is always right there, right on our side.

With God on our side we have the biggest advocate with the means to get us where we need to be. We have a provider to take care of every need. We have an all powerful, all knowing, above all God who takes personal responsibility for the care of our lives.

· · ·

THE LESSON here is to know that everything is going to be okay. Know it because God is on your side. Know it because He promises "all things work together for good". Don't waste time wondering if it's going to be okay, it just is. God is "for" you, who can be against you.

Hosea 4:1 5:15, 2 John 1:1 13,
Psalm 125:1 5, Proverbs 29:9 11

GOD KNOWLEDGE

HOSEA 4:6

"My people are destroyed for lack of knowledge."

The knowledge being referred to here is the Knowledge of God and God's ways. The Children of Israel suffered greatly from not knowing. It's not as if they couldn't know, it's that they wouldn't know.

"God knowledge" is the best and most important knowledge to have. You can know all there is to know about science, art, philosophy, finance, sports, politics, technology, politics or what have you, but if it's not "God knowledge" then it can't help eternally and in walking in the good and safe ways of The Lord.

His way is perfect and is the way of eternal life. He will lead us well and wisely with divine wisdom. Knowing Him and His ways is true knowledge from which all knowledge flows.

We have assurance when we know Him and His ways that it will lead us down the right path. It's easy to observe how the living apart from this knowledge and according to our own ways can be very destructive and ultimately leads to hell.

It's not JUST knowing information, it's putting active faith into the information. Many have read God's Word, heard it preached, grew up around it yet never act upon it.

It's the "doing" or implementation of the knowledge that brings the knowledge to life. Hearing without doing is useless. It takes faith to say that God's way is better. "God knowledge" that leads to God actions will transform our lives.

It's also not just knowing "about" God, but it's knowing Him personally. It's being in a vibrant connection with Him that takes mere information to relationship. Now the knowledge becomes growth in a relationship and not just growth in intelligence.

. . .

THE LESSON here is to pursue "God knowledge" with all your heart in order to know God with all your heart. The result is you won't be destroyed for know knowing. Stop doing things your own way and do them God's way.

DISCIPLESHIP

///

3 JOHN 1:4

"I have no greater joy than to hear that my children walk in truth."

Of all the joys one can have, the greatest, according to John the Apostle, is the joy of a disciple walking in truth. His use of the word "children" shows the love and care he had for them. It shows the investment he made in them. It shows the greatest desire if all Christians for others.

Seeing the "light turn on" in regards to God and the truth is an amazing moment. It's when the working of the Holy Spirit meets a receptive heart. To see a person meet Jesus and then to order their lives around Him. To see the seed of the gospel spring forth and bud. This is great joy.

We don't always have this joy. Christian work can be heartbreaking. Yet all the sacrifices made, heartbreaks experienced, and frustrations felt, we know that all our work for The Lord is worth it, especially when that labor falls on good soil.

. . .

THE LESSON here is to see the importance of discipleship. Work hard in this area, invest in people and give of yourself. You may get hurt, but there will be joy. The greatest joy of seeing lives change for eternity.

WHO'S BUILDING IS IT?

PSALM 127:1

"Unless the Lord builds the house, they labor in vain who build it."

There is a lot of "work" that happens in Christian life. Things we do "for the Lord" in order to bring about the fruits of His kingdom. Then there are our own personal lives that we want to be built for His glory. When it comes to "work" or our efforts, we have to consider whose work it really is. Who's really doing the building.

Is His "work" really ours? Are we trying to bring about our thing and ask God to bless it? Are we the initiators and God the assistant? Are we building God's kingdom or ours, is it His will or our will? These are important questions. Again, who's really building?

It's quite possible that much of what goes on in Christianity could be done without God. Pride and competitiveness between ministries or other believers can bring carnal results.

"Keeping up with the Jones'" doesn't work with God. He's not into that. The god of "success" can creep into the church and when it does no one succeeds. As John the Baptist said, "He must increase, I must decrease"(John 3:30)

Maybe we are glorying in the lords work when The Lord had nothing to do with it. Like Sarah, when she told Abraham to go into her maidservant Hagar to have "the promised child" that she thought she was too old to have, even though God promised she would. Is it possible we could be applauding our "Hagars'" when God has yet to bring about His Isaac (Genesis 16).

Be careful of the "more is better" "bigger is better" mentality. It's not about how much you can produce, it's about what He produces and how faithful you are. Don't waste your efforts on empty work, let God work though you and simply follow His lead.

Work hard at His thing and your efforts will bring Jesus things, which never fade away. It may not look like you think but it will look like what God wants. Better God builds something lasting and eternal than we build something temporary that fades away.

· · ·

THE LESSON here is that The Lord must be the builder. Knowing your role as a distributor and not the manufacture will ensure that your labor is not in vain.

RESTORATION

//

JOEL 2:25

"So I will restore to you the years that the swarming locust has eaten."

One thing is for sure: God is an expert at restoration. No matter how far one has fallen, God is excited for them to come back to His love. We see this in our text as the Children of Israel are in a bad spot due to their rebellion.

With God's restoration, He not only brings one back to where they have fallen, He also gives back what was lost. It may not be the specific thing or things that were lost, but it will be the restoration of the destructive effects of falling away. He will give back the lost and wasted years.

What a great and encouraging promise. What is the way back one may ask? The way back is always the same no matter what the cause, repentance. To repent is to turn. In other words, change the direction of your life of sin to asking for God's forgiveness and then walk in obedience to Him by His power given to do so. Agree with Him about your sin, confess it to Him, and He will be faithful to restore (1 John 1:9).

• • •

THE LESSON here is the importance of restoration through repentance. Don't let Satan keep you down and out. Don't let him keep you spiritually paralyzed. You are not useless and your life is not wasted. Turn to Him and let Him do the work of restoration. Don't let anything hold you back from His grace, which is always bigger than your sin.

WALKING WITH GOD

AMOS 3:3

"Can two walk together, unless they are agreed?"

Once a person is saved, their life receives a track to run on. In other words, God has a plan for their life and unfolds that plan as time goes on. Our "track" is centered around "walking with God" by staying connected with Him as one.

A Christian is one who is "positionally" right with God. Their sins are forgiven by God and a place in heaven is reserved for them. Jesus, our mediator sits at the right hand of the Father making intercession for every believer (Mark 16:19). However, "practically" speaking we fight to walk with Him because of the dual nature of our flesh and the Spirit which are contrary to one another (Galatians 5:7).

Walking with Him is the great joy of the Christian life, as scripture says, "in His presence is fullness of joy" (Psalm 16:11). The key to "walking" with Him, being united in close fellowship, is "agreement". As with any relationship, disagreement causes friction, agreement brings harmony. If God is truth (John 14:6) and His way perfect (Psalm 18:20), we must conform to Him and not Him to us.

When we align our lives with His, we are waking with Him. If we do our own thing, which is not His thing, we are not walking with Him, and thus are not living in accordance to our salvation and our "track" that God has for us.

• • •

THE LESSON here is the aligning of your will to God's will. You aren't going to find the blessings and benefits of your salvation through rebellion to God's will but by agreeing with and walking in God's will. Walking with God then comes down to agreeing and doing the will of God empowered by the Holy Spirit. When you do we find being in fellowship with Jesus is the greatest life there is.

AUTHENTIC CHRISTIANITY

///

REVELATION 3:1

> *"These things says He who has the seven Spirits of God and the seven stars:
> 'I know your works, that you have a name that you are alive, but you are
> dead.'"*

This warning is given to the church at Sardis and has great meaning for us today.
God sees what we don't because God looks at the heart. He sees what's really going on and what really matters. It's easy to judge by what is seen but what really
matters is what is not seen.

The church at Sardis may have looked good from the outside. They may have
gave the impression that they were doing things for God and wanted what He
wanted. Their name even said that, but the reality was, they were dead.

From out text we see that it is possible to be dead spiritually yet have the appearance of not being dead. It's possible to cater to the world's standards and then
apply them to our relationship with God and feel a false sense of spirituality.

• • •

THE LESSON here is to make sure there is a reality inwardly to what people
see outwardly. Make sure there is a real connection with God in your heart and
don't suppose that just because there are some "Christian activities" that those
activities are the proof of God living in you.

Amos 7:1 9:15, Revelation 3:7 22,
Psalm 131:1 3, Proverbs 29:23

THE MATERIAL VS. THE SPIRITUAL

///

REVELATION 3:17

> *"Because you say, 'I am rich, have become wealthy, and have need of nothing'—and do not know that you are wretched, miserable, poor, blind, and naked."*

Material things are no substitute for spiritual things. Sometimes the material things can give a Christian the false sense of spiritual reality because they are imitations of he real thing. When they replace the real thing there will be a great lack.

In our text we see these words to the church at Laodicea, also know as the "lukewarm" church. This is because Jesus said that they were neither hot nor cold so He would spew them out of His mouth. These guys had become so lethargic or apathetic in Spiritual matters that they were not able to do anything. They had become useless.

Jesus describes this condition of spiritual malaise as "wretched, miserable, poor blind and naked". The cause being the substitution of material things for spiritual things. These material things masked their true spiritual need to the extent that they became desensitized to spiritual things.

They danger of this condition is not even knowing you are in it. They continued on without even thinking about their desperate need for God. This condition is being like sick and dying without knowing it.

There is hope. Jesus tells them to turn, seeing they have substituted the material for the spiritual. The lesson here for you, especially if you are doing well materially, is to not ever mistake the material for the spiritual. Open your eyes to see the danger that materialism presents.

· · ·

THE LESSON here is to check your appetites, are they for God or the world. Check your passion, your time, your expenditures and see where your heart is. Then come to God for all your needs, lean on Him for you strength, drink of Him for your thirst and eat of Him for your food. Only Jesus can truly satisfy.

A SCENE FROM HEAVEN

REVELATION 4:8

"The four living creatures, each having six wings, were full of eyes around and within. And they do not rest day or night, saying: 'Holy, holy, holy, Lord God Almighty, Who was and is and is to come!'"

What's going on in Heaven? Sometimes it's hard to imagine what heaven will be like because when we try and understand something we do so by comparing what is known to what is unknown. We hear or say things like "it sounds like" or "it looks like" or "it's kind of like" when we are explaining something. However, heaven is unlike anything we know.

The Apostle Paul said that he was able to get a glimpse of heaven and what he saw so incredible that to try and describe it would be unlawful (2 Corinthians 12:4). Words that compare heaven to earth will only make it less than it is. He also said in another place that "Heaven is better by far" (Philippians 1:23).

Suffice it to say, as we see in our text, that heaven is completely centered around God. These angels surrounding the throne of God were continuously saying "Holy, holy, holy, Lord God Almighty, Who was and is and is to come!". They weren't forced to say this, they just couldn't help themselves. God was so amazing this was their reaction and they couldn't stop.

That being so we know that heaven will be good, it will be infinitely greater than the best we can even fathom now. It will not be dull and boring but full and exciting. We don't have to worry about being disappointed when we get there for if God is there, all will be there, minus the bad.

· · ·

THE LESSON here is to know that everything will be worth it one day. Life on earth is not heaven and will never be. You cannot ever be satisfied here outside of Christ. However, until you meet Him face to face, heaven is in your heart where Christ is. If heaven is centered around Christ then the best way to live now is to center your life around Christ. Live heaven now and when you get there it will be familiar.

STUCK IN THE BELLY
OF REBELLION

JONAH 2:17

> *"Now the LORD had prepared a great fish to swallow Jonah. And Jonah
> was in the belly of the fish three days and three nights."*

Running from God may seem better at first, but in the end it will swallow you
up. There is nothing good outside of God's will and running only prolongs the
agony and keeps one confined to their own prison of self will.

As we see with Jonah in our text, he was running from God's command to
preach to those on Nineveh. They were very barbaric people who hated Jonah's
God. Jonah also had a deep hatred for them and wasn't about change. Or was he?

Many come to God when they are in the dark belly of their own bad choices. Suffering the consequences can cause a person to have a better perspective,
looking outside themselves for answers. One thing is for sure, running from
God is never the answer. Like Jonah, you will find yourself in a bad place.

· · ·

THE LESSON here is to listen and obey God. This is the way of peace and joy.
Not that there won't be storms to whether, but that paradise is living right where
God's will is. Don't look at what you want, look at what God wants. When you
are put in the place of decision, ask "what do YOU want God".

BIG GOD

//

PROVERBS 30:4

> *"Who has ascended into heaven, or descended? Who has gathered the wind in His fists? Who has bound the waters in a garment? Who has established all the ends of the earth? What is His name, and what is His Son's name."*

We are not like God. He has no equal and there is no one that can compare to Him. He is separate and distinct from us and is completely self-sufficient in and of Himself. God does not need us, yet chooses to include us and share His love with us.

In our text we see this description of God that distinguishes Him from us. We see He is completely supernatural as He "gathers the wind in His fists". We see He is all-powerful as He "bounds the water in a garment. We see He is all wise as He "establishes all the ends of the earth". There is nothing God can't do.

He has no limits, no weakness, no lack or supply. God is all and in all. Yet, He has made Himself low so we can know Him. This infinite, all knowing, Almighty creator of the universe and everything that is in it, has come as a vulnerable infant baby, born in a filthy manger (Luke 2:7) and had no place to lay His head (Matthew 8:20). He did this for us. So we can know God and have a relationship with Him.

. . .

THE LESSON here is to grasp the "big-ness" of God and the humility of God. He is not to big for you. He knows all about you, His thoughts are so numerous toward you they can't be counted. He is near you, and even in you. He hears you and cares about you. He became one of us, so you could become part of Him. Turn to Him in your time of need. He's a Big God, big enough to become small enough, for you.

FORGIVEN

///

MICAH 7:19

"You will cast all our sins in the depths of the sea."

To understand the gospel is to understand the extent of a believer's forgiveness. This verse tells us that we are so forgiven that God casts all our sin in the depths of the sea, everyone of them.

ALL our sin means all our sins past, present and future have been taken away. How far away is our sin? So far it's as if we never have sinned. God had completely removed our sin from us judicially, so that we never have to stand trial for them. We are so forgiven that our sins can't be held against us. No matter how bad it is,

God's grace is bigger. No more guilt or shame. No more atonement to be made because Jesus has already completely atoned for them once and for, all at the cross.

As forgiven people we now have the power of God to live as forgiven people. That means that although a Christian is forgiven from their sin and the penalty of sin, they must still strive against the sin that still remains in our flesh. This practical aspect of our forgiveness means that we are now free not to sin, as we have been delivered from the power of sin in order to live in the power of the Holy Spirit.

• • •

THE LESSON here is the importance of applying the gospel to your life. You are forgiven and counted Holy before, the Almighty God. Use your freedom to worship and serve Him.

MONEY

///

PROVERBS 30:8-9

"Give me neither poverty nor riches—Feed me with the food allotted to me; Lest I be full and deny You, and say, 'Who is the LORD?' Or lest I be poor and steal, and profane the name of my God."

What is the right perspective regarding money? Sometimes it's hard to know how much is enough and how we should direct our prayers regarding money. Does God want us to be rich, as some would say? Is being poor more holy? What should a Christian's attitude be?

Here in our text we get the answer and it has to do with balance. First he prays that his food would be provided and he recognizes that God has an "allotment of food" for him. This means that God is in control of our food supply and our resources in general. So we see that we are to pray for this necessity of food and that God will take care of it.

Next he says that when he exceeds the allotment of food, he would deny God. This is interesting because it tells us of the danger of over abundance. We have a tendency to deny God when we have surplus.

This may not always be the case but In general, when we have more than what we need we feel a false sense of security and put our trust in the surplus and not in the reality of our daily desperate need for God. Our entire surplus can come and go in a moment, but God is the same yesterday, today, and forever.

Then he says that there is another extreme is that there would not be enough provision, which would lead to theft. The poor are tempted to take what is not their allotment, ultimately bringing dishonor to God. The Christian is to keep God's name above all temptations and can trust God to provide exactly what's needed.

. . .

THE LESSON here is to have the proper attitude toward money by trusting God. He knows the best allotment for you. If it's a lot, then use it for His glory and not your own. Do good with it.

If you're poor, don't take matters into your own hands. Do your best and let God take responsibility for your life. He knows exactly what's best for your pocketbook.

When it comes to money, balance is the best way to pray.

THE JUST SHALL LIVE BY HIS FAITH

HABAKKUK 2:4B

"But the just shall live by his faith."

The most important question one could have is how to be made right with God. How can one be made clean, washed and righteous before a holy God? Maybe some don't even quite know they have this question but inside they wonder about good and bad and what they might be. Many think they are "good" but are they?

The question is important because the requirement for heaven is holiness. Not just "some" holiness but prefect holiness. Paul calls this God's righteous requirements in the book of Romans (Romans 8:4), which is moral perfection in thought, word and deed. In other words, the requirement for heaven is sinlessness, which nobody is.

The problem with many is that they think "some" holiness will do or "some" goodness will be sufficient. Or, if the good outweighs the bad then that's what God is looking for. This is not what the Bible says at all. To be right with God we must be "just" or righteous 100%.

Here in this all-important text, which is quoted three times in the New Testament (Romans 1:17, Hebrews 10:38, Galatians 3:11), we have this definitive statement about life's most important question "the just shall live by faith".

So what we couldn't do, be sinless, we put our faith in the One Whom did, Jesus Christ. He was sinless, and was therefore, able to take our place in judgment, rise from the dead, conquering death and making it possible for anyone to meet God's righteous requirements by simple faith.

. . .

THE LESSON here to know that if you have put our faith in Jesus Christ and trust in His work for salvation then you are totally and completely forgiven and righteous before God. You couldn't be more saved, more forgiven and more loved.

YOU ARE PRICELESS

Zephaniah 3:17b

"He will rejoice over you with gladness, He will quiet you with His love, He will rejoice over you with singing."

Sometimes we wonder what God thinks about us. Especially when we fail or fall. However, scripture is clear, if you are a Christian, God is not mad at you! His mercy endures forever and His feelings toward us don't change. He will never stop loving us.

Here we see God's love toward the Children of Israel who had blown it! Yet God was still at work restoring His children. First we see that "He will rejoice over you with gladness". God is blessed by us. He is celebrating us as a proud parent. Not because of what we do, but because of who we are in Christ. He is glad about us, we make Him happy.

Next we see that "He will quiet you with His love". God's love will silence all our fears and doubts. His love will satisfy our restless hearts. His love will calm our anxiety and complaints. When our hearts and minds are loud, we need His love.

Finally, "He will rejoice over you with singing". We are the song in God's heart. When gladness turns to expression it's often in the form of singing. God is singing about us as His pride and joy.

This is how God feels about you.

• • •

THE LESSON here is to know how priceless you are. Your value led to His sacrifice for you. The value that cared enough to come and save you. The value that wants to spend eternity with you. You mean the world to God.

FINDING YOUR PURPOSE IN LIFE

HAGGAI 1:6

> *"You have sown much, and bring in little; You eat, but do not have enough; You drink, but you are not filled with drink; You clothe yourselves, but no one is warm; And he who earns wages, Earns wages to put into a bag with holes."*

Ever feel like you are just spinning your wheels in life, like a hamster on a wheel, going nowhere, yet working hard. It seems like you aren't going anywhere and can never get a head. It seems like you're always going against the wind and uphill never able to get momentum. Maybe you are having a hard time trying to figure out what to do with your life, being uncertain about your future and confused about where to go and what to do.

If you do you're not alone. Here in our text the Children of Israel were in exactly the same place. The reason why maybe the same reason we go through times like this, because our priorities are all wrong. When we don't put God first and our service to Him as our priority, we will be on an endless search to find direction when we are without a compass.

In this all-important passage we find that as we put God first, everything else comes into focus. If our priorities are something other than God we will never find meaning and purpose in life, even though we may have found some success in the world. Without being in God's plan all is empty and meaningless.

. . .

THE LESSON here is to put God first and all else will fall into place. In doing so, make serving Him and knowing Him your purpose in life. Without God as a priority nothing will ever satisfy, but seeking Him and His plan first will bring everything else in perspective and is how you will find true purpose in your life.

DECEMBER 21

Zechariah 1:1 21, Revelation 12:1 17,
Psalm 140:1 13, Proverbs 30:17

OVERCOMERS

REVELATION 12:11

"And they overcame him by the blood of the Lamb and by the word of their testimony, and they did not love their lives to the death."

To overcome we will need to know what/what the obstacle is and what weapons are at our disposal. To overcome we have to know how to use the weapons and the strategies involved. The ultimate battle that we all must overcome is the battle with Satan for our souls.

His strategy used here in Revelation 12 is to accuse us day and night before God. He accuses us of sin continuously. He has so much ammunition that he can keep going on and on about all we do wrong. The worst part about it is that he is right. Our sins are his fuel to bring before God and appeal to God's justice. So he has an airtight case against us.

We have nothing in our arsenal that can fight these accusations. We are guilty as charged. However, as we see in the text, we CAN overcome "by the blood of the Lamb, and the word of our testimony and not loving our lives to death. We can stand in the courtroom before God with confidence and assurance.

Overcoming Satan and his accusations which are true is due to what Jesus did and not what we do. All accusations brought against us have been paid by the blood of Jesus Christ. When we are accused we can point to Jesus and say, "He already paid for it". His blood given once and for all at the cross is sufficient to wash away our sin and to declare us innocent before God the Father.

It's also "the word of our testimony" that conquers Satan's lies against us. The testimony of putting our faith in Christ, the testimony of His grace that took our place in judgment. The testimony of His forgiveness. The testimony of our Savior conquering death and raising from the dead on our behalf.

Finally we overcome be "not loving our lives to death". When we put our faith in Christ we are surrendering the rights to ourselves over to Jesus. We don't hold on to ourselves but Christ holds on to us. We don't put barriers up to how far we will go and we don't put up conditions. This ends us looking like "obedience" to God's will no matter what the situating. This is how we walk with God and stay strong.

. . .

THE LESSON here is remembering that Christ has overcome for you so now you can rest in His finished work. All that needs to be done has been done, you are going to heaven, your sins are forgiven and now God has a plan for your life that will take root through obedience. No weapon formed against you shall prosper because you are an overcomer!

Zechariah 2:1 3:10, Revelation 13:1 18,
Psalm 141:1 10, Proverbs 30:18 20

THE POWER OF THE GOSPEL

REVELATION 13:8

> *"All who dwell on the earth will worship him, whose names have not been written in the Book of Life of the Lamb slain from the foundation of the world."*

There will come a day, spoken of here in Revelation 13, when the Antichrist will rise to power over the whole earth. He will use great deception with "signs and wonders to gain his following. The time spoken of is called the "Great Tribulation" which is a seven year period on earth where God's judgment will be poured out.

During this time the church will be in heaven through an event called the rapture (1 Thessalonians 4:17, 1 Corinthians15:52) while turmoil will hit the earth like never seem before. This will be the Antichrist's time to shine.

He will be effective, as our scripture tells us "all who dwell on the earth will worship him". No one will be able to escape his ways, except for one category of people.

Those "whose names have been written in the Book of Life of the Lamb slain from the foundation of the world". Here is the only power which can overcome the power of Satan and the Antichrist. This power is the power of God who laid down His life in order for all those who believe to overcome. He was as a lamb, slain for our salvation.

• • •

THE LESSON here is to see the power of the gospel. The power of a death that brings life. The power that saves us from the clutches of Satan. The power that is no match for evil. The power that forgives, makes new and protects. The power that conquered death and lives forever more. May the power of the gospel not only save you, but transform you to shine brightly for Jesus Christ and to shine that light for all the world to see.

EVERY GOOD ENDEAVOR

ZECHARIAH 4:6

"So he answered and said to me: This is the word of the LORD to Zerubba-bel: 'Not by might nor by power, but by My Spirit,' says the LORD of hosts."

Every good endeavor the Christian is involved in can only be done by the work-ing of the Holy Spirit in and through their life. In fact, there will come a day when all our works will be judged, not for salvation but for reward. The works done in the Spirit will be rewarded, the works on the flesh will not.

The Christian needs to be aware, in regards to if the endeavor is their own thing or God's thing. Is it God working in the heart to will and to do or is it really ones own desires to will and to do. Then, when determined it's The Lord, is it His strength, which empowers or ones own strength. These are the important questions.

In our text this is pointed out as the word came to Zerubbabel, who had the task of rebuilding the dilapidated temple. It was God's will to rebuild, yet it was not possible without His strength. God often calls us to do things we cannot do, to show us that He can. God can and will do the impossible if we simply let Him work.

The way this is accomplished is simple obedience to the Spirit. He will put de-sires on our heart, then lead the willing vessel to the supernatural working. This is the great thrill of the Christian life. God gives us the privilege to experience Him through the work that He calls us to. The results are always perfect because they are a His works.

The Christian then is free from the "results oriented" mentality that says the re-sults dictate success. When God is working, the results are up to Him and we can take pleasure in the process, enjoying Him personally and experiencing Him deeply. When we leave the results up to Him we are free to let Him work His way.

· · ·

THE LESSON here is to learn to let the Holy Spirit work. Be open, pray and seek Him and when you do you will find that there are things you will get excited about. Perhaps unexpected opportunities will cross your path and maybe even things you were praying about.

REFUSING GOD

//

ZECHARIAH 7:11

> *"But they refused to heed, shrugged their shoulders, and stopped their ears so that they could not hear."*

Not much good can happen when we get to the point of refusing God. This destructive condition has the double impact of hardening the heart toward God while being led down a destructive road away for Him. All while the refuser is blinded to what is really happening as they become desensitized to sin and evil that belies them.

The Children of Israel reached this point and were suffering greatly. Sin has a way of denying the obvious, that we are in trouble without God. Pride refuses Him when needed the most, with a posture that's "shrugs it's shoulders" in apathetic denial as if to say "I don't care God". The ears stop listening to the solution as if not listening will make the problem go away.

The thing is, when we are the problem, the problem never goes away. The problem always follows. We can't outrun ourselves. Relief is not found in more refusal, but in acknowledgment. This is where healing takes place.

It takes humility to say "I am wrong" "I messed up" and "you are right God". It's the place of being "poor in Spirit" that ushers in "the kingdom of heaven" (Matthew 5:3). The place of brokenness is the place of healing. Repentance is the only cure for the refuser, if they will just see their need.

. . .

THE LESSON here is to be sensitive to the Holy Spirit. His conviction is to help not hurt. Heed Him, heed His voice. Don't venture from His direction, don't ignore His alarms. Keep close watch on your life and never ever violate your conscience. The condition of refusal is road that leads to nowhere good. However, repentance is just a prayer away.

MIND YOUR MIND

//

ZECHARIAH 8:17

"Let none of you think evil in your heart against your neighbor."

Our thoughts must be watched over as much as our actions. It's easy to have a sinful thought life and not think much about it because the actions aren't following. However Jesus said "if we look at a woman in lust we've already committed adultery with her in our hearts"(Matthew 5:28).

We are also to love The Lord God, not only with our heart, soul but also our minds (Matthew 22:37). We are to take every thought into captivity to the obedience of Christ (2 Corinthians 10:5) and to meditate on things that are just, pure, lovely, of good report, virtuous and praiseworthy (Philippians 4:8).

The question for us is "does our thought life glorify God? Are our minds an instrument of praise and glory to the Lord. Does He have our minds? Have we submitted them to The Lord as well? Are we being transformed by the renewing of our minds (Romans 12:2).

Satan's knows the power of our thought life and therefore attacks our minds relentlessly. He knows that we can only resist the action for so long if our minds are entertaining the sinful thoughts.

We see in our text that part of the instructions to the Children of Israel for their restoration was not even "thinking evil in their hearts against their neighbors". An evil thought is an evil deed too.

. . .

THE LESSON here is to watch your thought life. Feed your thoughts with the Word of God, meditate on them day and night. Guard your thoughts, casting out evil ones. Direct your thoughts to The Lord. Think of yourself less and God more. May your mind be a beautiful instrument of praise, glory and honor to The Lord as you mind your mind.

STOP IT

PROVERBS 30:32

> *"If you have been foolish in exalting yourself, or if you have devised evil,
> put your hand on your mouth."*

We can sure be foolish at times. It's good to know God loves us despite of us and
yet instructs us in our foolish ways. His instructions are simple but difficult and
that is why He not only instructs us but also empowers us.

It's good to keep in mind that God's enables where He leads. In other words, He
doesn't leave us to ourselves but if we will submit our will to Him, He will enable
us to do His will. Here in our text we have this simple exhortation to a couple of
our biggest struggles.

When it comes to "exalting ourselves" or "devising evil", we are told to simply
"put your hand on your mouth" or to out it another way, STOP IT. Just don't do
it anymore.

You may feel left hanging because in our "modern sophisticated society" where
we need to know steps on how to stop, a program or a book about it so we can
understand all about it. We want to talk about it and discuss the life out of it.

I'm not downing those things in and of themselves, but there is no substitutes
for the power of Jesus Christ. Never underestimate the power of God, that raised
Jesus from the dead, to raise you above the sins of the flesh.

It may come down to the fact that we may not really want to let go of a particular
thing. Maybe it's more of a won't instead of a can't. More of a surrender issue
than a capability issue.

Maybe if we look at what God can do more than we can't do. Maybe if we
saw that the gospel makes us new and the power of the Holy Spirit is real and
available in our lives now and can be depended on in all aspects of our lives,
then the gospel will reach down into our souls not just for salvation but also
for transformation.

. . .

THE LESSON here is to see that the power of God is actively working to free you from the everyday sins that encroach upon your life. That you may look to God's power to work in your obedience to bring about total and complete practical wholeness and health.

Zechariah 10:1 11:17, Revelation 18:1 24,
Psalm 146:1 10, Proverbs 30:33

COME OUT

///

REVELATION 18:4

> *"And I heard another voice from heaven saying, 'Come out of her, my people, lest you share in her sins, and lest you receive of her plagues.'"*

Throughout the Bible we see a contrast between the Kingdom of God and the world system. We are to see that the world system is against God and Godliness and a Christians involvement with it should be "in it, but not of it".

We see the struggle the Children of Israel had with it and how they're choosing to be "like" the other nations around them when God called them to be separate from those other nations. We see compromising with the world is comparable to spiritual adultery.

As we come to the end of the Bible, here in the book of Revelation chapter 18, we see the end of the world system called Babylon, the world system finally meets its end. Total collapse will make way to God's thousand-year reign on earth called the Millennial Kingdom.

A glorious time where Satan and his demons will be locked up as they await their final judgment. This will be a time where God will set things in order, with God in control, the way it was always suppose to be before sin entered in and Satan was given control.

The final exhortation in our passage is the final cry to those "world lovers", but is also an urgent cry today. The warning is "come out, lest you share her sins and receive her plagues".

This gives us an idea what the world system is all about and why we are to be "in the world but not of the world". We are to stay away from the temptations that will suck us into sin resulting in harm.

. . .

THE LESSON here is to "come out" of any "sharing" of the evil in the world. The world is not a place to invest your life in because if you do you are investing in sin. Come out and come in to God's throne room of grace. Come out of darkness and into the light. Come out of plague and into life.

THE END

///

REVELATION 19:1

> *"After these things I heard a loud voice of a great multitude in heaven, saying, 'Alleluia! Salvation and glory and honor and power belong to the Lord our God!'"*

We have heard the phrase "hindsight is 20/20". Things do become more clear when we are able to look back and see the whole picture, when in the present it's hard to see how things will turn out. One day, in the end, as we see in our text, everything will become clear.

The end will be as God has always said. The atheist, the skeptic, the false religion practitioner, the humanist, the mocker or whatever person there is who rejects God will face Him as He is one day.

How is He? In the end He will be worshiped by "a great multitude in heaven". He will be exalted above every name. He will be worthy of all honor, praise and glory. Those who know Him say, "Alleluia" meaning "Praise ye The Lord" or "God be praised". No other creature will be praised for no other is worthy.

In the end, salvation belongs to Him. There is no other name by which men will be saved other than Jesus. He is our Savior and in the end He will be acknowledged and celebrated as such. No matter what one may say now about many and different ways to heaven, in the end it will only be through Jesus.

In the end, glory will be ascribed to Him. He will be seen in all His glory and the weight of His glory will resonate throughout all of heaven for all eternity. His glory will be so attractive that angles will continually worship Him, night and day as if they just started. His glory will shine for all to see.

In the end He will receive honor. Many today scramble for respect and honor from the world, yet the creation has no honor but to give honor to the creator who deserves it.

In the end, we will see that the power that has been holding the universe together has been the power of Jesus. We will see that He is all-powerful and that nothing is too hard for Him. We will see how He has used His power in the world and in our lives when we may not have ascribed that power to Him. His power will be completely revealed.

• • •

THE LESSON here, is that in the end, it's all about Jesus. Knowing this we can treat Him the way He deserves right now. Center your life around Jesus and you will experience a little taste of heaven on earth, until that day when you will stand face to face with Jesus Himself. Alleluia!!

LOVE REQUIRES A CHOICE

REVELATION 20:1-2

> *"Then I saw an angel coming down from heaven, having the key to the bottomless pit and a great chain in his hand. He laid hold of the dragon, that serpent of old, who is the Devil and Satan, and bound him for a thousand years."*

Here we see that Satan is "bound" and not destroyed. God has a plan to use him one more time after Christ's one thousand-year reign on the earth. The good news is that during this "Millennial" reign of Christ, Satan won't have any impact. It will be a wonderful time of habitation with The Lord on the earth.

Why is Satan not destroyed? What is God's purpose for him? Well, there will be people born during the thousand years that never had a choice to chose God because there will be no alternative during that time. With Satan bound there will only be good, and love requires a choice.

God hasn't made us robots that are programmed to choose Him. He has made us as "free will" people who have an option not to choose Him as well. Throughout the Bible we see that one is required to exercise the grace God gives to every person to chose Him while also having the option not to chose Him. This is because our relationship with God is a relationship of love, and love requires a choice.

At the end to the thousand years, Satan will be released in order to give that choice to those who never had it. Astonishingly, some will chose to go with Satan and rebel against God. Once there choice is made, they, along with Satan and his fallen angels will be cast into the lake of fire for all eternity.

· · ·

THE LESSON here is to choose to love God. Like in the Garden of Eden, choices are merely opportunities to exercise your free will to love God. It's not so much about what the opposing choice is, a tree as in the Garden or an Arc as in the flood with Noah or the turning of stones into bread with Jesus, but about opportunities to choose God instead. Make it a practice to love God by choosing Him above that, which opposes Him.

Malachi 1:1 2:17, Revelation 21:1 27,
Psalm 149:1 9, Proverbs 31:10 24

ALL THINGS NEW

//

REVELATION 21:5

> *"Then He who sat on the throne said, 'Behold, I make all things new.' And He said to me, 'Write, for these words are true and faithful.'"*

The not so careful observer will notice that things are not what they should or could be. All of mans efforts seem to have little lasting effect of turning things in a better direction. Things are not getting better.

Man at his best seems to make a mess of things. Man cannot get along with his neighbor more less his own family members. Advancement in technology seems to have opened Pandora's box of more complex issues in which there is no precedent on where it all may lead. One must ask if "advancement" has really improved quality of life.

The way things are is not the way God made them. Sin has tainted His creation and Satan now has dominion. All creation even groans for God to make things right and many people also groan, with the ache of disharmony and discord. Man in his heart craves for more that can't be had in the realm of the material world. One must conclude that we were made for more than this.

Our scripture breaks in as light pierces the morning darkness. "Behold, I will make all things new". It won't be like this forever. This is not all there is and all there will ever be. God is working toward something. He has a plan to make things right and it is unfolding.

He will make things new. There will be an untainted creation where His glory illuminates His new Heaven and new earth. There will be no more tear, no more sorrow. There will be no more struggle, no more pain. There will be eternal joy. There will be perfect satisfaction and glorious pleasure. There will be relational peace without relational conflict. Peace will reign, as love will rule the day.

. . .

THE LESSON here is to know that no matter how bad it gets, God will make all things new. Focusing on the eternal will give you a proper and necessary perspective to go through life.

IT COMES DOWN TO GRACE

REVELATION 22:21

"The grace of our Lord Jesus Christ be with you all. Amen."

Here we read the very last words of the entire Bible. It's no wonder these final words are the bestowal of God's grace upon mankind. Isn't it fitting that all God's words in His Holy writ end in grace. Grace is the message of God's Word.

Starting in Genesis and running through each book is the story of what God does and has done for man. It's the story of Him giving what man could not get and doing what man could not do. It's the story of love that pursues man even when man runs and hides. Grace, could be said, is the story of the Bible.

God's grace is displayed through His Son Jesus. As we see on our text, it's the grace of Jesus. In Him we see grace and understand what grace does. In Him we find grace. Jesus is the Man of Grace leaving no doubt about God's love for mankind. Jesus is grace in action, willing to suffer and die as an innocent man for guilty sinners.

Perhaps we should read the Bible with eyes toward grace. The Bible takes on life as we see grace in the words and feel the love behind the words. As we see in the last line, it's God's desire that His grace be with us.

· · ·

THE LESSON here is that it all comes down to grace. It's all about what God has done, and not what you do that is the message of the Bible. Learn to see yourself as the greatest benefactor or the greatest gift there could ever be. God's word and work toward man is Grace. Take it in, drink it up, bask in it and walk in it. He has done it all for you, the end!

Made in the USA
Middletown, DE
30 December 2016